SOCIAL AND COMMUNITY DEVELO

SOCIAL AND COMMUNITY DEVELOPMENT

AN INTRODUCTION

JOHN EVERSLEY

macmillan international
HIGHER EDUCATION

RED GLOBE PRESS

© John Eversley, under exclusive licence to Springer Nature Limited 2019

All rights reserved. No reproduction, copy or transmission of this publication may be made without written permission.

No portion of this publication may be reproduced, copied or transmitted save with written permission or in accordance with the provisions of the Copyright, Designs and Patents Act 1988, or under the terms of any licence permitting limited copying issued by the Copyright Licensing Agency, Saffron House, 6–10 Kirby Street, London EC1N 8TS.

Any person who does any unauthorized act in relation to this publication may be liable to criminal prosecution and civil claims for damages.

The author has asserted his right to be identified as the author of this work in accordance with the Copyright, Designs and Patents Act 1988.

First published 2019 by
RED GLOBE PRESS

Red Globe Press in the UK is an imprint of Springer Nature Limited, registered in England, company number 785998, of 4 Crinan Street, London, N1 9XW.

Red Globe Press® is a registered trademark in the United States, the United Kingdom, Europe and other countries.

ISBN 978–1–137–50211–7 paperback

This book is printed on paper suitable for recycling and made from fully managed and sustained forest sources. Logging, pulping and manufacturing processes are expected to conform to the environmental regulations of the country of origin.

A catalogue record for this book is available from the British Library.

A catalog record for this book is available from the Library of Congress.

To Josephine Klein

CONTENTS

List of Figures ix
List of Tables x
List of Boxes xi

1 Introduction **1**
History 3
Intellectual: Theory, theorists and practice 5
Geography and culture 9
The themes of the book 9
The style of the book 10
The structure and argument of the book 11

2 Beyond Society and Community **13**
Introduction 13
Is there a difference between society and community? 13
Language 14
The study of societies 15
The study of communities 16
Dimensions of community 17
Interests and condition 21
The nature of social groups 36
Summary and a proposed analytical framework 40
Implications for practice 45

3 Development **46**
Introduction 46
Historical overview of 'development' 46
Development for? And how? 47
Metaphors of development 66
Conclusions 82

4 Collective Action **84**
Of cabbages and kings 84
Multi-disciplinary perspectives on action 85
Why individuals act 86
Why do people act together? 88
Summary and conclusion 125

5 Equality and Emancipation — 128
Introduction — 128
Human rights — 129
Rights as individual aspirations — 132
Needs as a way of reconciling individual aspirations — 132
Institutions — 135
Rights as ideology — 136
Justice — 138
Equality — 142
Power and emancipation — 152
Overcoming oppression — 155
Ideological level — 157
Conclusions and implications for practice — 163

6 Learning Together: What and Why — 166
Introduction — 166
Why people learn — 167
What people learn — 172

7 Conclusions and Getting Started ... — 203
Personal reflection — 203
Theory — 203
History — 204
Society and community — 205
Development — 206
Collective action — 207
Equality and emancipation — 209
Learning together — 209
Doing it right — 211

Notes — 215
Index — 269

LIST OF FIGURES

2.1	Overlapping domains of ethical communities	41
2.2	Interacting levels and domains	44
2.3	How issues are seen on different levels	44
3.1	Domains and levels of development	48
4.1	Duncan's model of the relationship between individuals, group consciousness and collective action	102
4.2	Gaventa's power cube	112
4.3	Kersting's model of invited and claimed participation in the online world	112
5.1	Linking domains of development to aspirations, human rights, justice and equality on four levels	163
6.1	A synthesis of reasons for learning	172

LIST OF TABLES

3.1	CDPs' strategies for social change and levels	78
5.1	Rights, justice, equality and emancipation on four levels	137
5.2	Strategies for emancipation on four levels	165
6.1	The characteristics of different motivations for learning	171

LIST OF BOXES

1.1	Activities	12
2.1	Suggested activities	45
3.1	Implications for practice and activities	83
4.1	Activities	127
5.1	Activities	165
6.1	Activities	201

1
Introduction

We have experienced directly, witnessed or heard of many situations which we want to change:

- Not being treated fairly or being able to fulfil our hopes or potential.
- Other people unable to fulfil their potential because of the direct or indirect actions of others, or self-destructive behaviour.
- Seeing a child or adult who is abused, bullied or harmed.
- Groups of people being blamed, victimised or not getting a fair chance.
- Exploitation, harming or letting down the users, customers or workers of institutions such as companies, government agencies and charities through their goods and services or working practices.
- Countries and regions at war internally or with other countries, or where lives are lost because of human actions or lack of protection from, or preparation for, natural disasters.
- Ideas or slogans that belittle us or other people and which seek to justify brutal or discriminatory treatment.

Beyond asking 'What can I do?', we may ask 'Why do these things happen?', 'What works to change these situations?' This book is not an analysis of all these 'ills' or a guide to the campaigns or organisations that seek to 'cure' them. It is not a celebration or an evaluation of interventions. I have spent 40 years directly involved in trying to change some of these situations and teaching and researching with many more people who have been activists and practitioners. The book is a reflection on what should be the underlying principles of community or social development, and how they can be turned into practice.

The book is intended as an introduction for students and practitioners to an activity which they may see as part of a profession, as a paid job or as something they will do as a volunteer or an activist.

My central argument is that social change starts inside individuals and individual change often begins with social change. They are both achieved by people learning from each other, not a one-way process. Writing a book for people to absorb a single author's knowledge and ideas might seem to contradict this. Two very different commentators perhaps help to explain the paradox. Lilla Watson, an aboriginal artist said, speaking on behalf of a group Australian activists:

> If you have come here to help me, you are wasting your time. But if you have come because your liberation is bound up with mine, then let us work together.[1]

An Oxford philosopher said in the introduction to one of his books:

> Primarily I am trying to get some disorders out of my own system. Only secondarily do I hope to help other theorists to recognise our malady and to benefit from my medicine.[2]

The book didn't start off as therapy. I thought that the years of practice, thinking about the issues and teaching had challenged and taught me enough theory and enough about what works and doesn't work in practice to know pretty much what I wanted to say. In fact, as the book argues, the process of reflection makes one question whether the theory-in-use is the espoused theory (the theory we say we are using). We often need to ask ourselves, are we really doing what we say we are, and is there another way of doing things?[3]

I hope that trying to sort out my 'disorders' will help other people in a number of ways:

- To appreciate the things that they do know and understand, perhaps contributing a vocabulary and theory for some people and ideas about putting theory into practice for others.
- To explore issues that people may not have thought about or may not have resolved.
- By challenging more often than providing answers. As Paulo Freire says, the role of the educator is to 're-present the world, not as lecture but as a problem'.[4]

Two threads run through the book: roots and routes. By *roots*, I mean the origins of social and community development. This includes the history and the intellectual roots. The intellectual roots are the explanations and theories underlying the practices and some of the people and activities that have inspired or sustained practitioners. Exploring the roots may help answer questions about *why* things do or don't happen: understanding the origins of inequality and oppression, for example. The linguistic roots of the word *route* lie in the indentation a wheel makes as it breaks the ground it covers – a 'rut'. It has the same roots as *rupture* and *rout* (a crowd of people). In the following section, the implications of this are discussed.[5] *Routes* in this book refer to both strategies and goals (where are you going and why). Roots and routes can be historical, intellectual and geographical or cultural.

The book argues that accounts of the roots and routes of social and community development have often been twisted to suit particular agendas. At the very least, activists and practitioners should know that this has happened.

Originally, I intended that one volume would cover both the theory, the principles and detail about the method. It would have made the book too long. This book therefore restricts itself to the general directions ('compass points') rather than a detailed guide (a 'walking map').

History

Throughout the book, the historical contexts of social and community development are explored. Often social and community development are presented as relatively new and/or Western concepts. They are also frequently presented as top-down planned strategies. Although the language currently used may have these specific origins and Western concepts inform much of what is promoted, it will be argued here that the substance has its roots in many places and over a long period of history.

Typical accounts of the development of community work start with its origins in nineteenth-century European social welfare and twentieth-century European (especially British) measures to rule its empire. In this account three responses to poverty and social unrest in England emerged. The first was a shift from a kind of compassionate or idealistic charity, philanthropy or almsgiving to a more 'scientific' assessment of individual cases which in turn led to the development or a model of social work as casework. The second development was social investigation or social research, particularly into the causes of poverty and what could be done to relieve it. The third strand was a more collectivist response which might be expressed in initiatives with, for or by groups or movements of poor people. The colonial tradition of community work is usually expressed as an evolution of 'indirect' rule, co-opting local elites and engaging local populations in activities in the interests of the empire (e.g. cash crops or raw materials extraction for export) through mass education facilitated by expatriate Colonial Development Officers and local assistants.[6] It will be argued they are distorted and incomplete accounts.

The Party in George Orwell's *1984* says:

> Who controls the past controls the future: who controls the present controls the past.[7]

Even if the typical accounts are not the whole story they have become influential in how community development is perceived. They are 'memes' – 'facts', ideas or beliefs which are repeated or imitated and develop a life of their own.[8] Thus the perception that social and community development are recent and Western or imperialistic in origin is widely held and is sometimes a barrier to adoption. A related idea is that 'traditions' can be and are invented. There are many well-established traditions which were the invention of an individual or group at a particular time and perhaps for a particular purpose.[9] Culture and identity are very important to people, but they are not 'set in stone' or 'sacred'.

Memes developed as an idea in relation to evolution. In public policy there are two similar concepts which are important: *Path Dependency* and *Historical Institutionalism*. Path dependency refers to the fact that because things have happened we make decisions today – they are '*ruts*'. The most frequently quoted example of this is that the latest English language smartphones still have keypads which begin with the letters QWERTY. Originally it was to avoid mechanical arms sticking on the frequently used letters on typewriters. There are many instances of it in public policy: debates about whether to ban harmful drugs are based on beliefs about whether alcohol prohibition in the USA in the 1930s worked or not; the failure of appeasement of Hitler in the 1930s was used to justify the invasion of Suez in 1956 and Iraq in 2003.

Path dependency analysis often leads to a view that things only ever change incrementally. When the debate is specifically about the behaviour or capability of a particular institution, the assumption that past patterns will repeat themselves is called historical institutionalism.[10] Against this view is the argument that sometimes people or circumstances can change the course of history – the rupture which is also partly the root of 'route'. In 1915 the sociologist Max Weber wrote that:

> material and ideal interests, directly govern men's conduct. Yet very frequently the 'world images' that have been created by 'ideas' have, like switchmen [Railway signal switchers], determined the tracks along which action has been pushed by the dynamic of interest.[11]

More recently, Ashis Nandy has written about how the experience of colonialism has been internalised into the Indian Self. He also highlights that although Gandhi (a key thinker in community development) may have been an example of an 'uncolonized mind' he also valued Western education and ideas highly.[12] People, institutions, communities and societies can follow more than one path at once or switch tracks. History is neither servitude nor freedom.[13]

Intellectual: Theory, theorists and practice

We all use theory (and evidence), whether we are conscious of it or not. If a light in the home is not working, we use our theoretical knowledge of electricity (however elementary!) to guess the cause. Consistent with the approach of this book, the change required may be an individual one of checking it is switched on or replacing the bulb (with a long-life, low-energy bulb?). It may require resetting, or repairing, a fuse or a generator for several lights or paying for fuel. It may be a power cut outside the home, which may be more or less difficult to influence. The word 'theory' comes from a Greek word which was concerned with looking or observing, with the same root as 'theatre'. It is concerned with seeing what might not be immediately obvious: patterns, explanations or ideas which underpin what we see or do.[14] This book uses theory as a way of systematically interpreting experience and as a guide to how to act. We interpret what we 'see' whether or not we explicitly use theory, but it is better to be open and clear about theory to make explicit how we are interpreting what we see and to show what we have identified as important or discarded.

Exploring the intellectual origins and patterns of society relevant to this book involves a wide range of academic disciplines and professional practices. The social sciences, arts and humanities and theology are often referred to in books about community development. (Natural) scientists, architects, planners, engineers, clinicians, statisticians and mathematicians are less often drawn on or seen as both a resource and the audience. However, no one person can hope to have an in-depth understanding of all the practices and disciplines. Where my knowledge is most limited, I hope that I have used reliable guides to introduce the subjects. Readers with more in-depth knowledge may find errors and misunderstandings for which I am solely responsible, but hopefully even those errors will encourage readers to explore these subjects in greater depth.

Unfortunately knowing what you don't know is not always easy. T. S Eliot thought we knew what we don't know.[15] At least in theory, Donald Rumsfeld, the former US Secretary of Defense knew it is more complicated:

> There are things we know that we know. There are known unknowns. That is to say there are things that we now know we don't know. But there are also unknown unknowns. There are things we don't know we don't know.[16]

In social and community development, there is a very important additional area of knowledge – 'unknown knowns' – things that we know but don't know that we know. This book tries to explore the 'known unknowns' whether they are areas of scholarship or experience and to encourage people to become aware of their unknown knowns. I can only apologise for the omission of the unknown unknowns.

There are dangers in how theory is presented and used:

- It can very easily turn into 'One Dead Guy after another':[17] often the preoccupations of Western intellectuals frequently expressed in terms of their disagreements with each other.
- The *'trapeze method'* – swinging from one theory to another.[18]
- 'Polishing the tainted [sic] mirror of theoretical heroes':[19] trying to explain some flaw or mistake of a long-dead author, for example Freire and Gramsci's lack of attention to gender.
- Not relating the theory to practice.

The book tries to address these problems in several ways:

Drawing on a diverse range of theorists

Even though the sources are limited to generally works written or translated into English, it draws on a range of disciplines and contexts.

Highlighting that knowledge is a collective effort

On the side of the British £2 coin, it says 'On the Shoulders of Giants'. It is a reference to Isaac Newton, the late seventeenth/early eighteenth-century, scientist who said: 'If I have seen further, it is by standing on the shoulders of giants', simultaneously acknowledging his debt to others and claiming authority because greater men [sic] than he had said similar things (as well as putting down a rival).[a]

Broadly, the book addresses theory through the concepts and their application rather than who said what: the point is to learn from the theorist rather than about them.[20] It will be clear, for example, that this book owes much to the ideas of the Brazilian writer and activist Paulo Freire. However, it is important to acknowledge that similar ideas were developed independently by others such as John Dewey; that Freire worked with many other people, some of whom wrote but others

---

[a] In fact, he was altering a statement made centuries before which he felt showed too much respect for the 'old' authorities.

who drew, sang, wrote and directed plays, practised psychiatry or took photographs – developing and practising many of the ideas they worked on together.[21] Flaws and blind spots in his writing and practice are acknowledged.[22] If readers want introductions to the theorists rather than the theory, there are many books and websites available.[23]

Re-presenting knowledge in a different way

Valuing what previous writers have said runs the risk that readers will say that I have said nothing new. That may be true, but – like many other writers – I take comfort in what the seventeenth-century mathematician Blaise Pascal said:

> Let no one say that I have said nothing new; the arrangement of the subject is new. When we play tennis, we both play with the same ball, but one of us places it better.[24]

Specifically, the book rearranges knowledge using a framework of four different levels of action – individual, interpersonal, institutional and ideological.

From circuses to street markets

Walter Laqueur described the field of Terrorism Studies as a circus.[25] Treating theories as a trapeze act is only one aspect of a circus. Particularly, in relation to theories and models of learning, it is necessary to outline many different theories. They are presented as stalls in a vibrant street market. You can get not only the ingredients to cook a dish of your choice but the means to cook and eat it. There is more than you need on offer but not everything you might want is there: you will need to be creative.

Exploring the relationship between theory and action

Better theory is a tool for better practice. Kurt Lewin's often-quoted comment is valid:

> There is nothing as practical as good theory.[26]

Action without theory will often fail, but that theory without action is of little value. Paulo Freire argued that reflection (which he saw as a form of theorising) without action is *'verbalism'* – idle chatter – and action without reflection is 'activism' making the process of cooperation for social change ('dialogue') impossible.[27] Policy-makers, universities and others may expect theoretical rigour if they are to support the practice and study of social and community development. The book will, however, argue that social and community development have not always been well served by academic disciplines.

Theory needs to be rooted in, and reflect, everyday experiences. Athletes, parents, cooks or development practitioners may not be aware of the theories they are using but they are still using them. Donald Schön noted the distinction between *Espoused Theory* – the theory we say or think we use – and *Theory-in-use*. He argued that we need critical reflection to identify the theory in use.[28]

The poet Adrienne Rich, in an essay on the 'politics of location', highlights that ideas do not have a life of their own floating above the heads of ordinary people:

> Theory – the seeing of patterns, showing the forest as well as the trees – theory can be a dew that rises from the earth and collects in the rain cloud and returns to earth over and over. But if it doesn't smell of the earth, it isn't good for the earth.[29]

bell hooks[b] highlights the value of theory even more personally:

> I came to theory because I was hurting ... I wanted to make the hurt go away. I saw in theory [then] a location for healing.[30]

Theory does not, however, always keep pace with the complexity and dynamism of events. As R. H. Tawney said:

> Life is a swallow, theory is snail.[31]

If theory moves slowly, as the metaphor suggests, practice moves fast. The metaphor may not be completely apposite: often theory migrates further than practice. Originally, I planned to use many examples from practice in this book. As I undertook research for the book, I became increasingly frustrated with the examples in other books. For the sake of brevity, case studies are often not set in the context of the time and place they occurred and often the examples seemed very dated, specific to a situation and frequently lacked a perspective of key actors – the voice of funders, academics and onlookers are amplified. The voices of participants muted. Too often, different authors use the same examples and they are often from the Global North. Rather than repeat that distortion, only a few examples have been used, usually with signposts to where more about them can be read and hopefully the principles and practice discussed will make the reader think of examples from their own experience. Theories are the lenses through which practice can be examined.

---

[b] bell hooks is a pen name and is always written in lower case.

Geography and culture

The voices which are most often heard are the people (often men) who have had the opportunities to write, to share their knowledge and ideas through education. Ideas are expressed as though they are simply the product of individuals. Here I will try to discuss the ideas in the context of the times and places in which they were developed, to explore whether similar or different ideas have been developed in other contexts.

One of the challenges in writing (and probably reading) this book is that the theory of social and community development is often implicitly or explicitly presented as a product of the Global North.[32] The analysis here rejects the view that they are separate worlds: many of the 'opposites' such as North and South, East and West or Judeo-Christian and Muslim, Good and Evil are not as different ('Binary' or 'Manichean') as is often asserted. Neither North nor South are homogeneous or exclusive. Nevertheless, it is important that social and community development redresses the imbalance in the voices which are heard.[33]

The themes of the book

The key concepts underlying social and community development are outlined in documents such as the (English) National Occupational Standards (NOS) for Community Development[34] and the strategic plan of the International Association for Community Development.[35]

The text explores:

> **The key values and principles of social and community development** – these include collective action and participation; social justice through emancipation or empowerment; learning together through experience; accountability and good governance in groups, movements and organisation; and critical engagement with the state.[36] This book advocates these values but also argues that what they mean is open to interpretation and how they are put into practice must reflect the specific context in which they are to be applied.

> **The concept of multi-level interventions** – this tries to demonstrate that interventions have to operate on levels from the personal or individual (developing self-esteem, a sense of 'agency', critical consciousness and so on) through the interpersonal (dealing with conflict, developing collaboration); the institutional level (often dealing with different levels of government); and social and cultural change

(ideologies, deep-seated practices and attitudes which may challenge fundamental social, economic and political arrangements).

- **Different strategies for bottom-up or inside-out social change** – Three broad strategies are analysed: Consensus, Pluralist and Conflict models.[37] The analysis recognises 'fused discourses'[38] and 'cross dressing' where people use the same words to describe different things (e.g. self-determination, capacity or social capital), or when different words are used to describe the same thing.

Specific methods and techniques of community development are beyond the scope of this volume.

The style of the book

It will be evident from this first chapter that both academic and non-academic sources and terminology have been used. A lot of academic writing is verbose and hard to follow. Sometimes the unfamiliarity of the language is helpful because the reader is made aware that they are learning something new. However, often it is off-putting and a barrier to understanding.

To try to make the academic writing more accessible, memorable, but 'on tap not on top',[39] this book has used two devices.

Firstly, metaphors have been used to categorise ideas. Writers have used metaphors, more or less consciously, for millennia. There is a growing literature which uses them to compare and contrast ideas and explain theories. They can be illuminating but they can also be misleading. Applying the wrong metaphor can be fatal: *'removing the cancer'* can turn out to be destroying healthy tissue.[40] The central argument of the book is a critique of an organic metaphor. Development is not simply the edible part of a plant but is the roots of the plant, the nutrients which feed or poison it, the other plants and animals that interact with it, the weather and climate (short-term and long-term environments) in which it exists.

Secondly, the style of referencing – endnotes for each chapter – is designed to minimise the interruption to reading from citing the sources while acknowledging the very considerable debt to other writers. The sources cited are intended to be a balance between sources which can be accessed at little or low cost on the internet, not only those that need library subscriptions, and hard-copy texts which might be in university libraries that don't have specialist social and community development collections.

It would have used other devices – poetry, music lyrics and visual images – but issues about copyright and production costs made such content unfeasible. The importance of drawing on 'expressive knowledge' is discussed in Chapter 6, 'Learning Together'.

The structure and argument of the book

Chapter 2 explores the terms 'Society' and 'Community'. It argues that they do not have essential and differentiated characteristics: they are not separate, opposites and static. They are overlapping, may – but don't necessarily – have many different characteristics, and change. Development practitioners need to be able to analyse the context in which they operate to identify who to work with, and whether change, or stability, is necessary and feasible.

Chapter 3 considers 'Development'. At its crudest, 'development' is simply change. The chapter argues for a rigorous analysis of what development is, who it is for, how it is done and what it achieves. It is not automatically good or bad. The rest of the book focuses on two strategies for change: collective action and learning together.

Chapter 4 analyses collective action. What makes people act or not act is a mixture of personal psychology, the nature of relationships with other individuals and groups, structural constraints and enablers and constraints and ideas. The chapter only touches on different strategies and forms of collective action. It is argued that collective action which is only based on coalitions of people willing and able to work with each other is likely to reflect and increase only inequalities. We need to engage people unwilling and unable to collaborate with each other.

Chapter 5 discusses equality, human rights, justice and power. It explores what the relationships between the terms are but argues that there is no right or singular answer to what they mean. It suggests that the twin goals of enabling people to achieve capabilities and emancipation are compass 'coordinates' to aim for.

Chapter 6 looks at why and what people learn. The conception of learning is much broader than the kinds of knowledge and skills usually associated with schools and colleges. Building on the analysis of the previous chapter, it is argued that why and what are learned are centrally concerned with emancipation or liberation and that has implications for how people learn. How people learn is discussed in general terms.

The final chapter reprises the arguments but also introduces some of the most challenging issues which are not fully addressed here:

➢ The circumstances in which it is legitimate and possible to challenge other people's beliefs and behaviour and how to do so.

➢ Social and community development in violent to post-violence situations.

Box 1.1 Activities

1. Thinking about:

- Where you live
- Where you work (paid or unpaid)
- How you learn
- Other people
- Yourself

Is there any theory that you have found useful to explain the way you think, feel or act?

Discuss it with other people and try to explain why you think it is important.

2. What ways do you think the past, personally or more generally, influences the present?

What difference does it make to how you think, feel or act?

Discuss this with other people.

2
Beyond Society and Community

Introduction

There is a widely used distinction between 'society' and 'community' in English and in many, but not all, other languages. This chapter argues that this is an inaccurate and unhelpful way of describing structures and relationships.

The chapter begins with the origins and development of the binary distinction, noting how it has served political and economic agendas and has been reinforced, even magnified, by academic subject disciplines. At one extreme, there are determinist explanations of what makes a society or community. The nineteenth-century, Nazi and neo-Nazi idea of 'Blood and Soil' (*Blut und Boden*) is that ancestry and long-term presence in a place are essential to belonging.[1] At the other extreme, people argue that being part of a society or community is either a completely personal choice or it depends on whether other people accept you as part of a community. I reject both positions.

The chapter explores the characteristics which members of communities, observers and analysts have argued hold communities together. Any or all of these may be signs of a community, but none are essential, and none are unconditionally desirable. Choices are constrained and structured. The characteristics of communities and societies need to be analysed in terms of what holds them together and who they are keeping out.

The chapter finishes with an alternative way of thinking about social structures and processes and how this can be used to support practice. It is argued that social organisation operates on multiple interconnected levels.

Is there a difference between society and community?

In English, the everyday meanings of 'community' and 'society' seem straightforward. Community is usually used for personal or face-to-face relationships, often between people who live in the same neighbourhood or have a common activity – be it work, leisure or worship. Society is more often used to refer to a unit of social organisation in which people do not necessarily know each other or see each other face-to-face but they may be aware of each other or have transactions with each other. This 'common-sense' understanding has a long heritage. It follows a distinction made by the German writer Ferdinand Tönnies in the 1880s. Tönnies' distinction is in a tradition of political philosophy derived from the much earlier work of Thomas Hobbes. Tönnies is explicitly concerned with the distinction between communism and socialism. As Raymond Plant points out, he was writing in the German tradition which saw the idea of community as a political entity – the Greek *polis*. Community and society were contrasted by Tönnies and his followers as traditional versus modern; rural versus urban; stable and immobile versus ever-changing and mobile; integrated versus fragmented; one based on personal relationships and collectivists, the other anonymous, transactional or contractual and individualistic. Although Tönnies was an opponent of the Nazis and sacked from his job by them, his enthusiasm for community and regrets about society replacing community were shared and reinforced by the Nazis; they even used a slogan *Community instead of Society*.[2] Often the contrast has been between communities being religious and society being secular. Often, implicitly, communities are described in terms of who does not belong.[3]

The literature on development (discussed in the next chapter) treats 'social development' and 'community development' differently, broadly following the society/community division.

Language

The words society and community in English are not always translatable into other languages. Either the same word is used or the words convey additional or different meanings. For example, the word *Ummah* in Arabic is widely used to refer to the global Muslim community. It conveys the unity and equality of people to whom a prophet has been sent, whatever their background. However, it may be used to refer to 'the People of the Book', that is, including Christians and Jews or followers of particular Muslim traditions.[4] It is also used to refer to nations and the Arabic translation of the United Nations. In German *Gesellschaft* is used to refer to businesses – 'company' – and *Gemeinschaft* is used in relation to the European Community (*sic*) – an association of states. Just as community is used in relation to European states, society is used in English to refer to institutions, which may be very small. A group of people who rent plots of land to grow flowers and vegetables may be an Allotment Society; a business association is called the Society of Motor Manufacturers and

Traders; or a trade union, the Associated Society of Locomotive Engineers and Firemen. Also, in the context of the extensive use of community to mean a locality, it is worth noting that German has another word for neighbourhood which is *Gemeinde*. As Plant reminds us, the study of Linguistics has taught us not to assume that all uses of a word share a meaning.[5] It is possible to identify words in many languages which convey different aspects of the English words 'society' and 'community' but arguing they are 'equivalent' requires assumptions which are often not justified, particularly because they ignore the context in which words developed or are now used.

The study of societies

The term society is generally seen as positive, apart from the former British Prime Minister Margaret Thatcher and like-minded people.[6]

The Latin roots of the word society are in bonds between people for a common purpose and also companionship, fellowship or affinity. Its earliest use in English was in the sixteenth century. Later uses of the word put more emphasis on society as a forum for transactions and this has both economic and political dimensions. These are discussed further in Chapter 4 on Collective Action. For now, it is enough to say that the idea is that collaboration confers advantages. It also has a specific use to describe privileged people – as in 'High Society'. Many of the uses of the word historically are indistinguishable from forms and activities which also apply to communities.[7]

Social scientists have been trying to categorise societies for centuries. Perhaps the first important attempt to categorise and characterise societies was Ibn Khaldun (1332–1406). His life highlights that distinctions of geographies (East and West) and disciplines are often blurred rather than binary opposites. Khaldun was born in Tunis to a family that had lived in Spain for generations but probably originated in (modern-day) Yemen. He was most likely of Arab origin though he has also been claimed as Berber. He lived in Cairo and Fez among other places. He was an adviser to various rulers and a judge. He is the inspiration for important ideas in the history of Anthropology, Sociology and Economics. He contrasted static and nomadic societies and the relationship between them. He suggested that history moves in cycles. He used the term *Asaybiyyah* to mean social cohesion or solidarity. He analysed how solidarity is achieved in different kinds of society and the impact of living in towns or cities. He was clearly thinking about how vertical relationships between rulers and the ruled are created and maintained but also those between people who were more equal. Some of his ideas have a strong contemporary feel, such as whether urban and rural communities cohere differently or how static or migrant or traveller communities operate. Other ideas such as how temperaments[a] varied according to the distance from the equator might be viewed more critically.[8] There is some evidence of Khaldun's direct and indirect influence on later writers in Europe such as Arnold Toynbee and Auguste Comte in Europe,[9] and Ali Wardi in the Middle East.[10]

The preoccupations of contemporary Sociology only partly reflect the agenda set by Khaldun. A standard introductory text has a lot to say about social stratification, conflict, cohesion and urbanism and rather less to say about culture, community, rural societies and horizontal relationships and no mention of Khaldun.[11] Some of the latter issues are more often the domain of Anthropology.

The study of communities

> Genocide, After All, is an Exercise in Community Building.[12]

The quotation above should alert us to the possibility that there is another side to 'society' and 'community' which we should be concerned about. The Latin roots of community are in

> Joint possession or use, participation, sharing, social relationship, fellowship, organized society, shared nature or quality, kinship, obligingness.

From the fifteenth century onwards it meant both a group having equal status – 'the commonality' – distinguished from the privileged class and

> A body of people who live in the same place, usually sharing a common cultural or ethnic identity.

It is to some extent true that society is used for more instrumental behaviour and thought, and community is more expressive. Although the stress of the early uses is on equality, commonality and reciprocation, from the first uses in English to later uses there is increased emphasis on a community having characteristics which distinguish it from other parts of society such as in 'religious community' or a 'community of wives' (both from the sixteenth century) or a 'scientific community' (eighteenth century).[13]

---

[a] Though a phrase like 'Latin temperament' suggests not everyone agrees.

The Italian philosopher Roberto Esposito has identified the roots of community (and immunity and municipality) in the Latin word *munus* – encompassing the idea of a unilateral gift rather than commonality. Immunity is not being obliged to make a gift or perform a duty – as in 'diplomatic immunity'. Esposito's argument, that community and immunity are not opposites but that immunity is a consequence of seeing community as commonality, is discussed later in this chapter.[14]

Although sociologists have studied communities, some of the work has been criticised on methodological grounds or has used methods that are more familiar or more developed by anthropologists.[15] Historically many anthropologists in the colonies of Europe combined their academic studies with advising or training colonial administrators.[16] More recently, anthropologists have played an active role in advising the US military on counter-insurgency in Iraq and Afghanistan.[17]

Etymologists and philologists have studied the origins of words and generally argued that they have original meanings and their proper use involves common meanings. Linguistics scholars are more inclined to say that words don't necessarily have an essential meaning. Society and community, as analysed here, reflects the Linguistics approach.

Society and community are overlapping concepts. Their meanings are contested and contextual in place and time. That doesn't make them meaningless or useless, but they need to be handled with care. When using them, it is important to see whether different people have a shared understanding. Often they won't but that is a starting point for positive change, as well as a warning signal about potential conflict.

In the next section the characteristics which have been used to identify community are analysed. The overlap with characterisations of society is noted.

Dimensions of community

Tönnies identified three types of association leading to community – blood, place and mind – though he suggested that shared locality may lead to or sustain the other kinds of community.[18] Blood and place have endured as ideas. 'Mind' is generally not a single construct now but underlies ideas such as identity, values and culture.

Ancestry

'Blood' refers to common ancestry. It is today most often used in two contexts:

➤ Nationality or citizenship: the right to be a citizen of many countries is automatic if you are born in the country or have a parent or grandparent born in the country. For people who are forced to emigrate, not being born in the destination country is a barrier. The host country may even argue that they must return to where they 'belong'. On the other hand, refugees and their descendants may have the right of return.[19]

➤ 'Ethnic, Religious or Racial Group': people are identified as belonging to groups according to who their ancestors were. This can be internal, when, for example, a religious group says you can only be one of us by descent as opposed to conversion. It is also used externally by governments and hostile groups to say someone is one of 'them' not 'us', notably by the Nazis and Apartheid South Africa. Both internal and external ascription based on descent invoke 'purity' to explain or defend their position.[20]

Place or territory

The very frequent association of community with neighbourhood has many possible roots.[21]

Some evolutionary biologists have argued that humans share with animals a need for territory and aggressively defend it if threatened. This view has also been contested as an exaggerated assertion, not based on evidence either about humans or about animals. People have also questioned whether animal behaviour is relevant to human behaviour and whether territoriality is innate or learned behaviour. John O'Keefe won the Nobel Prize in 2014 for identifying a part of the brain which acts as a 'Global Positioning System' that helps animals and humans locate themselves, although this does not necessarily make territory more important to well-being than other factors.[22] The anthropologist Ashley Montagu makes interesting distinctions in the ways that animals relate to territory:

> A territory is a defended area; the home range is the whole area in which the animal lives – usually shared with other animals. 'Core area' refers to an intensively and exclusively occupied area within a home range or territory. 'Area of

dominance' refers to a dominion from which submissive individuals are not excluded. 'Personal space' refers to the 'on sight' defensive reaction to another animal.[23]

The idea of community as territory is a very physical idea of 'place'. Social geographers and others highlight that place and space are not the same thing. It has been argued that people increasingly think of space without place when they think of belonging and ownership.[24] However, defence or invasion of place is central to many violent conflicts between communities.

Community is certainly connected to the assertion of individual property rights. Many social systems have rules or laws, in which land and buildings are owned by individuals and can be passed on to descendants. However, it is important to emphasise that not only are there social systems which do not recognise individual ownership, such as Aboriginal Australians and Native Americans, but there is also a long tradition of common land, even in societies where individual property rights are well established. There are conflicts, often violent, between peripatetic or nomadic groups and static groups. Sometimes these can be seen very clearly as conflicts over resources, but they can also be differences about whether identity is expressed individually or collectively, or a conflict between the right to property or the right to roam. Elinor Ostrom, who won the Nobel Prize for Economics, argued that people voluntarily cooperate to hold resources – such as land or fishing stocks – in common because it is in their interests. This is considered further in Chapter 4.[25]

A specific aspect of the notion of community as territory is the association of community with rural environments. Villages are seen as natural communities. Cities are perceived as difficult places to establish and maintain community. The urban/rural contrast has implications for social and community development. As the World Health Organization highlights, in 2014 urban populations accounted for 54% of the total global population, up from 34% in 1960.[26] There are variations across the world but even where the changing balance is slower it is still dramatic. In Bangladesh less than one-third of the population lives in cities but in Iraq it is believed to be more than two-thirds.[27] We certainly must address how cities and mega cities are going to function, but we also need to understand how (or possibly whether) rural communities will survive and that they will be different from the communities of the past and from urban areas. Although this may partly reflect the way in which income is measured (see Chapter 3), the fact that four-fifths of people who live in extreme poverty live in rural areas is of serious concern.[28] On the other hand, 'urban' and rural may not be binary opposites – with both having shared characteristics and differences within each category.

Territory is important in several academic and social contexts. In Philosophy and Theology (specifically the Abrahamic religions: Christianity, Judaism, Islam) the questions of whether space has an independent reality or is simply perceived, whether the universe was created by God, and whether a particular space belongs to people of the faith are very long-established debates but with acute historical and contemporary implications.[29]

There are significant examples of where religion and claims of territory are tied up. There was certainly a religious dimension to the expulsion of Jews from England in 1290 but earlier in that century the expulsion of Irish people did not have a religious connotation.[30] Elsewhere in Europe the first ghetto was created in Venice in the sixteenth century where it served as both a place of confinement and one of refuge for Jews persecuted and expelled from other places, including the expulsion of Jews (and Muslims) from Spain and Portugal after 1492.[31] The readmission of Jews to England in 1656 was not enacted into law because of an argument about whether Jews should go to Palestine – the so-called Restorationist belief or heresy.[32] It is significant that the idea emerged at the same time as English and Scottish Protestants were settled in Ireland.[33]

In the 1920s, German Conservative nationalists (precursors of the Nazis) associated community with 'blood and soil', with racialist connotations of which people were entitled to territory. The claim to territory is often linked to identity of ethnic or national or religious groups and has been a dimension of violent conflict, including in Northern Ireland, the former Yugoslavia, the Horn of Africa and Iraq. There are many examples of 'demographic engineering': deliberate or spontaneous population movements to increase or reduce specific populations in particular areas. Saddam Hussein's policy of Arabisation in Iraq provided incentives to (mainly Sunni Muslim) Arabs to move to predominantly Shia or Kurdish areas. It was coupled with brutal treatment of those who were living there recently. More recently, there have been moves to reverse some of those trends.[34]

Many of these examples associate society and territory. They are closely tied up with the idea of the nation-state. In Chapter 4, we consider the state as a form of organisation but, for now, we simply note that not all societies are states – there may be countries within states (as Scotland is, within the UK, at the time of writing) which are certainly distinct territories and can be argued to be distinct societies too. Equally there can be populations that are concentrated in a specific location but not limited to a state, yet which have characteristics of a society. Arguably Kurds in Turkey, Syria, Iraq and Iran fit this description.

The fact that territory has an influence on health and well-being at the social level is not surprising. This might be the influence of the organisation of the state or the social system.[35] However, there is an extensive literature on more local, neighbourhood, effects on health and well-being. This includes education achievement, experience and fear of crime, (healthy) life expectancy, the quality of housing, access to services and amenities, and similarities and differences in socio-economic and ethnic characteristics. Some studies strongly suggest that the place itself has an impact on people's well-being and that neighbourhood characteristics are not simply the result of the type of people who live there.[36] There is a lot of interest in the idea that being near people who are richer or poorer or from similar or different ethnic background (*ethnic density*) can affect health.[37] There is also a literature on neighbourhoods as a vehicle for allowing different behaviour and values – 'liberated zones', or controlling or imposing norms – which may be argued to be positive – controlling anti-social behaviour – or negative – a prison punishing or stigmatising people who are in some way different. An enclave or fortress may be a good or bad thing.[38]

In summary, the association between community and neighbourhood is a powerful one. It is one which has been applied in some cases in a very oppressive way, but it also has the potential to be emancipatory or enhance health and well-being.

Interests and condition

The idea that people join together to serve their interests (but at a price) goes back a long way. John Locke, in the seventeenth century, said:

> The only way by which anyone divests himself of his natural liberty and puts on the bonds of civil society is by agreeing with other men to join and unite into a community.[39]

Many communities are based on shared interests in the sense of having a stake in something or a common status. Sometimes this overlaps with geographical communities, for example if an area:

➢ Has a large employer (a company or an industry such as mining or agriculture).

➢ Is affected by something which will have a major impact on its environment: flood or drought; the building of roads, railways, airports or dams.

➢ Has tenants with the same landowner.

Communities based on interest but not necessarily on locality would include communities based on socio-economic group or class. For many analysts, it is not enough simply to share a characteristic: 'no class without class consciousness'.[40] The idea that for interests to form a community a shared consciousness is essential was highlighted by Karl Marx:

> The great mass of the French population is much [like] potatoes in a sack form a sack of potatoes ... These small peasant proprietors are merely connected on a local basis and the identity of their interests fails to produce a feeling of community, national links or a political organization among them, they do not form a class. They are therefore incapable of asserting their class interest in their own name, whether through a parliament or a convention. They cannot represent themselves, they must be represented.[41]

Even if unconscious, to be a community there must be some element of collective behaviour, thought or treatment which is distinctive. The idea of communities based on interest has been taken by some writers to suggest that there cannot be inequalities or conflicts of interest within communities.[42] We question whether such homogeneity is a characteristic of communities.

The legitimacy of self-interest is often a challenge for social and community development. When it is combined with locality it may be called Nimbyism (Not In My Back Yard). The word has been used since at least the 1980s. Originally it was a self-description of people opposed to the dumping of toxic waste in their area but now it is often used negatively, for example about owner occupiers not wanting social housing in their areas.[43] The argument for it being illegitimate is usually a basic utilitarian one that it is in the interests of wider society that something should happen and the benefits to the winners outweigh the costs to the losers. The argument for self-interest is usually either that there are certain rights which can never be taken away or that the self-interest coincides with justice based on another principle such as needs or overcoming barriers to the achievement of capabilities.[44] The argument about what justice is, is explored further in Chapter 5. Dams provide an example of the complexity of arguments based on community self-interest. Opponents of dams argue that Indigenous and tribal peoples have been disproportionately negatively affected by large dams but also that the benefits to both those communities and wider societies have been exaggerated and that there are better alternatives.[45]

Self-interest of communities may also be argued to be justified based on past wrongs as well as present need. The Indian-American feminist philosopher[b] Gayatri Chakravorty Spivak argues that a human rights narrative based simply on what is in the interests of one group (for example, women

---

[b] Note the multiple identities.

and formerly colonised peoples in the past and present) will not lead to a just world: it may simply rearrange injustice. She describes the scapegoating and fetishising of past wrongs as *the Mugabe Complex* which is not sustainable.[46] A further issue about identification of communities through their needs is that they are frequently only expressed in terms of deficits – the absence of something. It is frequently stigmatising. It does not consider people's need to be recognised for what they have got, their positive attributes and assets.[47] How needs can be identified and contribute to social and community development is explored further in Chapter 6.

Identity

As the examples of formerly colonised people and women highlight there may be overlap between communities based on interest and those based on identity. A community of interest might be based on a characteristic shared by members of a community which they and others are not necessarily aware of. The difference is one of degree rather than absolute. However, the differences between them are that the fulfilment of a need, desire or right may be sufficient as a goal for a community based on interest. A community based on identity is potentially based on not only achieving a goal – for example, 'equal rights' – but the recognition of who they are including being different or of the right to be either separate or included.

Social identity (Social Psychology) theorists would distinguish between personal and social identities. Personal identities are generally derived from close interpersonal relationships and personality characteristics. Social identity comes from the groups which we belong to (class, ethnicity, gender, etc.) but also the social context. How, and how much, personal and social identity are connected is contested within psychology.[48]

Some theorists of communities based on identity suggest that communities have three elements to them: an identity, an adversary and a goal.[49] The importance of identity being based on an adversary or an external enemy is picked up again in explorations of other dimensions later in the chapter. In relation to identity it is important to note that as well as being a source of security and well-being for people it can also be a source of insecurity and destructive conflict. As John Paul Lederach has said:

> Identity is at the root of most conflicts and best understood as relational ... if we had no other colour than blue, blue would be colourless.[50]

Communities (and social movements) based on identity are based on either self-identification or identification by others. Self-identification requires a group of people who recognise each other as sharing something and that they are different from others. The perception of others that a group of people are different and have something in common may be positive, negative or neutral but is generally an imposed identity: categorising other people. Identity is generally associated with a wide range of impacts or consequences. Manuel Castells suggests that there is a growth of communities based on exclusion or resistance – for example, indigenous communities where 'settler' communities have come to dominate societies and migrant or minority communities are marginalised or excluded, and communities which are based on the perceived failure of a society or an ideology (including religion) and which are perceived as failing or corrupt institutions. Although some communities of identity may come from resistance, others arise from a desire to legitimate domination or control (nationalist movements, for example) or a project to transform or conserve the social structure (a movement to conserve a way of life or a physical environment, for example).[51]

Individual and group identity may be linked. Psychology and Psychotherapy study how individual identities are formed. Put very simply, the general view is that people's identities are a mixture of exposure to experiences, predispositions or 'drives' and choices, not all conscious. A distinction is often made between primary and secondary identities. A primary identity might be derived from impairment which is turned into 'disability' by society (the imposed experience of discrimination including stigma).[52] Many primary identities of individuals are formed in infancy. The relationship between individual and group identity is evident in the influence that families and peers have on the formation of identity. Secondary identities are often formed as people grow up through roles they take and status that they achieve. The social influences on roles as a 'young person', 'worker' or 'mother' are even more evident as we learn what 'people like us' do. The study of the characteristics and process of achieving social identities are often associated with Social Psychology and Anthropology with the same themes as individual identity. Sometimes identity is argued to be fulfilling universal and positive functions or needs (a sense of 'we', or rules to live by). Some theorists (such as Sigmund Freud and Herbert Marcuse) have argued that many of these collective identities can be negative and imposed on people to control or exploit them. Others have argued that either there are no universal patterns or that people make choices about whom they identify with and how or that identity is more symbolic than functional. Anthropologists and sociologists have argued for a long time about whether there is any historical course or evolution in identities taken – for example, a rise and fall of national identities. It has been argued that the twenty-first century has seen a move towards, simultaneously, more global, cosmopolitan identities and more local ones.[53] Jacques Derrida identifies another characteristic of communities based on identity – *the narcissism of minorities* – meaning only seeing identity in terms of the status of the group and not in a wider social context.[54]

Whether nationalism is an expression of self-determination or a form of hostility to other groups has been much debated. George Orwell distinguished between different kinds of nationalism and argued that there is a difference between 'Nationalism' and 'Patriotism'. Although they both involve pride, the latter does not seek to impose it on others.[55] In practice, patriotism and nationalism are often used interchangeably. Their legitimacy is questioned by those who associate them with hostility to the 'alien' or minorities (undermining equality and universal human rights) or those who see them as limited campaigns, which replace one elite with another. Others argue that these criticisms of nationalism are based on a version of nationalism that sees it as a political project to create sovereign nation-states with discrete territories. Other forms of nationalism have existed historically and may be growing more important based on 'nations of nations', popular movements (particularly of subordinated groups) and cultural expression.[56] There are gender issues in the construction of national identity. On the one hand, the struggle for national identity may be in substance and presentation a very masculine one (though women are often involved in campaigns), while the image of the country (captured or free) is often embodied in an image of a woman and women play a central role in biological, social and ideological construction and reproduction of 'the nation'.[57]

Recent writers have taken the view that identity has become more fluid and provisional and that communities are imagined rather than physical in place or according to the appearance of people. This is often associated with the idea that identity is not binary – Black or White; Masculine or Feminine; Straight or Gay – but a continuum, dynamic or fluctuating.[58] Frantz Fanon observed that people can have multiple and contradictory identities: *the zebra-striping of the mind*.[59] The idea that there are primary and secondary identities is also challenged by the concepts of Solitarism and Intersectionality. These are discussed further in Chapter 6. *Solitarism* is only seeing identity in terms of one dimension and usually as an opposite of something else – for example, Christian versus Muslim. *Intersectionality* is the recognition that inequality or oppression cannot be understood in terms of one characteristic of a person – for example, just race or just gender in the experience of Black women.[60]

Another way of thinking about identity is Andrew Solomon's concepts of Vertical and Horizontal identities. Religion, race, language and nationality, he suggests, are passed down from parent to child, vertically; 'horizontal' identity refers to traits or characteristics not shared with parents which include disability or sexuality, for example. He suggests that vertical traits are generally seen positively by families and the individuals themselves but horizontal ones are seen initially as flaws though people may change their view and become proud of horizontal identities.[61] It may be that some of Solomon's examples of vertical identities are actually horizontal ones too as people identify with religious, ethnic or linguistic groups in new ways, but the idea of vertical and horizontal identities fits with the idea of multiple and intersectional identities.

This discussion of identity, superficially, reflects the contrasting approaches of community as determined and community as constructed by choice. However, much of the evidence from Psychology and Anthropology is that what looks on the surface like personal choice is in fact structured. The more identity is seen as both individually and socially constructed and a dynamic, multifaceted and temporary phenomenon, the more difficult it is to pigeonhole people as 'belonging' to (just) one community. This is even more evident in relation to the idea that communities are formed of exclusive values or shared cultures.

Values

There is a close association between the idea that people are held together by identity (or culture, as discussed later in the chapter) and that they share values which make them distinct from other groups. Tönnies argued that communities were often morally and culturally homogeneous (but also that there were conflicts within them). In the UK there has been a lot of discussion about whether there are 'British Values', what they are and whether everybody living in the UK or who wishes to become a British citizen should subscribe to them, or at least be familiar with them. To become a British citizen it is a requirement to take a *Life in the UK* test which contains *True* or *False* questions of the following kind:[c]

> There is no place in British society for extremism or intolerance. You must treat everyone equally, regardless of sex, race, age, religion, disability, class or sexual orientation.[62]

Trying to differentiate people and, more particularly, to exclude them from a community or a society based on values is ethically dubious and impractical. It is ethically dubious to say that someone must hold a particular view to become a citizen of a state, but an existing citizen need not. Survey evidence shows that there is not an overwhelming

---

[c] These are not actual questions and the answer given by a private company offering preparation for the Tests to the second question is 'True' which is not correct in law in relation to class discrimination.

consensus on values among people who consider themselves British or that there are values which are peculiar to British people in comparison either with other European countries or globally.[63] Why are certain values more important, relevant or superior to others? For example, in the UK Citizenship Test, *treating others with fairness* is listed as a British value. When the test was first introduced, buying a round of drinks and offering to replace a spilled drink in a pub was the 'British' thing to do ... but avoiding getting drunk was not suggested as a way of treating others with respect! At the time of writing, knowing that pub quizzes are popular is seen as important, but the guide to *Life in the UK* does not say whether it is okay to cheat in a quiz. Similar questions to the UK tests exist in the German and Dutch equivalents.[64] These examples show how difficult it is to express values that are important, enduring and particular to a society or a community. It is also important to recognise that beliefs don't always correspond to behaviour. We often do things which we think are 'bad'. We don't always do things which are 'good'. This is explored further in Chapter 6.

Social capital

The concept of social capital, put forward by the twentieth-century Communitarians, suggests that societies and communities are held together by both identity and interests. Crucially, different people are held together in different ways. 'Bonding' social capital is the tie that binds people who see themselves as like one another and who share interests, values or experience or exchange resources on a peer-to-peer basis. 'Bridging' social capital is a relationship between unalike people. It could be an alliance or expression of solidarity, but it could also be using a person with high status or contacts to get a job, for example. It has been argued that individuals, communities and societies with more social capital are more successful economically. Whether social capital creates success or success creates social capital for individuals can be debated, but when social capital is measured it is clearly unevenly distributed. Some surveys suggest social capital is declining in many countries. Studies of different kinds of social capital such as 'Most people can be trusted', 'I get support from other people' or 'I take part in a local activity or neighbourhood group' don't necessarily correspond with each other or change in the same direction. It is also argued that bonding social capital may reinforce exclusive identities and homogeneity. Supporters of the value of social capital argue that it is desirable and possible to increase the capital of those who lack it.[65]

Networks and meshworks

Social capital theorists and practitioners focus on who you know, trust and can draw on. Others focus on networks. Chapter 4 will consider networks as a form of collective action. They are also an analytical tool or description of groups. Another way of looking at the difference between bridging and bonding social capital is to see them as vertical and horizontal networks. Not all networks are informal, though many are, which opens the possibility that people can be part of many networks and can associate or not according to circumstances or wishes. Networks can be highly localised and personal but also global and impersonal, physically close or virtual, for example through social media. *Meshworks* are also communities. They may be localised, but they are also global with the organising principle of being non-hierarchical with decentralised decision-making. They have been used to describe anti-(Global North) globalization movements.[66] The absence of networks is a barrier to creating communities, but the existence of networks can also be a barrier: they can be elites or 'old boys' clubs' (a reference to males who go to school or university or play sport together). They may also prevent other kinds of bonding. It has been argued that in Northern Ireland, Israel and South Africa ethno-religious networks have been a substitute for, or have undermined, class-based organisations such as trade unions.[67]

Culture

The earliest uses of the word culture are associated with the same kind of meaning as agriculture; later it meant refinement or training the body or mind. It was not until the nineteenth century that it began to be used for a society or group with shared customs or behaviour.[68] Much of the systematic study of culture has been within the discipline of Anthropology. It therefore reflects some of the historical issues discussed above: social scientists from the Global North observing the Global South, often with an attitude of superiority and a mission to control or change. It is possible to identify two major traditions: the first is a Positivist or Materialist one which basically sees culture as a reflection of social structures. It has often been associated with an evolutionary approach to Anthropology (and Development) in which societies move from 'Traditional' and 'simple' to 'Modern' and complex. In other words, culture is generally instrumental. The other tradition starts from the Idealists who are more inclined to see culture as expressive of meaning; some of its proponents have emphasised its symbolic nature. The Idealists often stress that culture was diffused – spread – rather than evolved.

Although both traditions found arguments for saying that there are cultural aspects that are 'universal', the materialists were more likely to suggest that the forms were context-specific, that there are practices and beliefs which perform similar functions everywhere. Although the two traditions put different emphasis on the importance of structure and agency, they do both start from the idea that culture is a social construction. The Positivists, however, came out of a tradition of evolutionary biology.[69] The implications for understanding how useful or not the idea of shared culture is for understanding what a community is are many and varied:

➣ If culture is only about meaning and interpretation, then it means whatever people say it is. People can simply assert that some thing or someone is or is not part of their culture. One can discuss whether it is a sincerely held belief or a justified belief. One could also ask whether it is a view that others share. Ultimately, on this view of culture you have to say either that every person's view is equally legitimate or beyond criticism – this is sometimes called 'Culturalism'.[70] – An alternative view, which is argued here, is that there must be some way of deciding whether one view carries more weight than another. There are many examples of people asserting that their nationality, ethnicity, religion or tradition is to behave or believe things which disadvantage, devalue or discriminate against others. Other assertions are harmless but not necessarily as deeply founded as people believe. Sometimes it can be shown that a particular tradition is more recent, less widely held or more artificial – 'invented' – than people realise. Famously the wearing by some Scots of tartan kilts has been shown to be an invented tradition, as well as not practised by many Scots kilts are worn by many people who are not Scots.[71]

➣ If culture is defined by adherence to specific beliefs or behaviour, it becomes a form of essentialism: you can only be a true Scotsman (*sic*) if you wear a kilt. At the social or national and global levels there are many attempts to identify shared and distinctive cultures. The World Values Survey, for example, divides the world into eight clusters of values.[72] On the other hand, bell hooks points out that critiques of essentialism can seem very threatening to marginalised groups, and a *chocolate box* [pick and choose] approach to shared identity can be used to exclude less powerful groups and individuals.[73]

➣ Eric Wolf also makes the point that treating cultures as internally homogeneous and externally heterogeneous is a 'billiard ball' approach:

a model of the world as a global pool hall in which the entities spin off each other like so many hard and round billiard balls. Thus it becomes easy to sort the world into differently colored balls, to declare that 'East is East, and West is West, and never the twain shall meet'.[74]

- If culture is more a reflection of structure and self-interest, then many of the issues discussed in the section above on community as shared interest apply: When does one group's self-interest 'trump' another?
- As suggested above in relation to identity, culture can become restrictive. Individuals or groups within a community can be prevented from or made to do things against their will, in effect, to disguise differences: homogenising.
- Culture can also be used to polarise or accentuate differences – 'othering' people. There has been much criticism of anthropology historically for exoticising and belittling other cultures while being self-congratulatory about their own – for example, with descriptions such as 'modern' or 'traditional'.[75]

Culture is often put forward uncritically as a good thing to affirm. It is clearly something that individuals value and which can be a magnet that brings people together or a glue that holds people together. However, it can, like magnets, be repulsive and, like glue, can prevent necessary movement. The broader implications of these metaphors for cohesion and solidarity are discussed later in the chapter.

Language

Intertwined with identity, culture and place is the question of whether shared or differentiated languages bond or divide groups of people. For instance, having a shared and distinctive language is a possible defining characteristic of an ethnic group in British Law but what a 'language' as opposed to a 'dialect' is, is often contested. The right or requirement to speak a language is often a major issue in reinforcing the identity of a community. Like many of the other issues discussed in this book, simple binaries, such as monolingual and bilingual and national or minority language, do not adequately express the role language plays in identity or culture. People use different languages in different contexts and for different purposes ('*Plurilingualism*') and there are hierarchies in the way languages are viewed – 'Pidgins', 'Creoles'/'Kweyols', 'Community', 'Modern' and 'International'.[76] Languages' ability to divide has been commented on for thousands of years – a legend in Hinduism, the Tower of Babel and *shibboleth* in the Old Testament, for example.[77]

Monolingualism has often been used to promote domination by one group of another or others. Linguistic diversity has been mistakenly (often deliberately) blamed for social divisions or social costs. More often it is a consequence of social divisions and the costs to societies lie in not recognising it.[78]

Hospitality and exchange

All the dimensions of society and, more particularly community, have been widely discussed in the social sciences over a long time. More recently, however, the French philosopher Jacques Derrida suggested that 'hospitality' is the defining characteristic of community. His starting point was that it is a historical fantasy to believe that understanding, consensus and harmony can be achieved in communities of small size, physical proximity and homogeneity, and that it is impossible in large impersonal and diverse communities, even with modern technology. He thinks that non- or miscommunication is inevitable. He suggests that pure hospitality is an unconditional openness to newcomers or 'the other'. Individuals are not independent of each other but nor are they the same as each other. He thinks a conditional hospitality is possible in which we are receptive to (some) newcomers. His analysis of how or why hospitality is possible is influenced by his ideas on friendship derived from Aristotle. Aristotle says that there are three types of friendship. First, there is higher friendship based on virtue; second, the friendship grounded on utility and usefulness, and this is political friendship; and third, friendship grounded on pleasure.[79] So, to abstract from Derrida, we might argue that though communities are often defined or identified by difference from others, what makes them ethical, useful and pleasurable is their openness to others. The relationship between communities and difference is explored later in the chapter. However, Derrida's three kinds of friendship can be seen as three different motivations for hospitality: *Obligation* (in effect rights and duties); *Need* (the need of someone for sanctuary or the need of a host for, say, labour) and *Pleasure* (wanting friendship or to please others).[80] It is obvious that these different motivations will lead to different forms of hospitality being offered to different people.

Derrida also said:

No Community is possible that would not cultivate its own auto-immunity.[81]

Derrida saw community becoming defensive, aggressive and ultimately self-destructive through protecting itself. The idea is taken further by Roberto Esposito. He argues that rather than community and immunity being opposites, it is the nature of communities to reject outside bodies. He and others argue that the sanctuary element of community has become both a xenophobic fortress, excluding outsiders, and also a cage, trapping insiders. He points to the many examples of where it is argued that to save a society or community, it is necessary either to kill or imprison its members (Eugenics, the treatment of terrorists or dissidents) or to expel or refuse admission to outsiders (immigration policies of many states). He is specifically criticising the notion of community put forward by Tönnies and the twentieth-century (neo-)communitarians (discussed above in the section on Social Capital). Esposito suggests that a fundamental problem is that we have privatised many of the common spaces. He argues that the physical environment, intellectual property and communication tools have become the property of individuals and more importantly organisations, rather than public property. He argues that we need to make systems that exclude all people ('immune systems') more porous (to become 'relational filters').[82] Essentially, this means individual and corporate property rights would not be absolute. This is a point which is discussed further in Chapter 5 in relation to different conceptions of justice.

Other authors also highlight that societies tend to see themselves as under siege (from within or without) and to suspend 'normal' rules of democracy or human rights in a 'state of exception'. However, some of them are more optimistic that it is possible to respond to emergencies by anticipating them with mitigating or preventative measures, deliberative and participative responses rather than authoritarian ones.[83]

In this context, Michael Ignatieff's analysis is significant. He was a Liberal politician in Canada and, at the time of writing, is Rector of the Central European University in Budapest, Hungary. He argues that the 'hospitality' discourse has worked much better for refugees than the European 'Rights' discourse. He argues that people in Canada have been willing to welcome refugees on a case-by-case basis – a gift – and *'in return the citizen expects the newcomer to acknowledge that gift and be grateful for it'*. Ignatieff's sceptical view of Human Rights is discussed further in Chapter 5. It is interesting too that he sees the giving as one-way: he does not see refugees as giving to the society they join.[84] Other writers, such as Mireille Rosello, argue that hospitality requires:

> in some ways, both the host and the guest accept, in different ways, the uncomfortable and sometimes painful possibility of being changed by the other.[85]

What all these writers have in common is that they provide a basis for analysing competing claims for legitimacy, between and within communities. At its simplest, a community which mistreats either people within it or 'outsiders' is not an ethical community. Chapter 5 considers in more detail what mistreatment might mean but treating people as different or differently is the starting point. Whether the community perceives itself or is perceived by other people as different, including superior or inferior to others, is the next dimension that we turn to.

Difference

There is a very long history of using difference not simply to distinguish but to discriminate against others and define them as outsiders. Everyday behaviour – language (discussed above), clothing, eating, what people watch, read or listen to, are all used to say, 'this person is "other"'.

Iris Marion Young's ideas follow on from Derrida. She says community privileges unity over difference or heterogeneity. Her starting point is that much of the writing on community is based on a rural model of community. It implies a vision of dismantling the city which is 'hopelessly Utopian'. She argues that community is idealised as overcoming opacity and the perception of 'otherness'. She warns that if community is an idea of shared subjectivity or identification, it may be both impossible and dangerous on two grounds: a lack of respect for people with whom they do not identify (which may or may not go with a kind of chauvinism) or excessive loyalty to those with whom they do. She also suggests that community privileges face-to-face relations over other kinds of relationship. This contrasts with other theorists who assume that face-to-face relationships are more immediate, pure and authentic than relationships over time and space.[86]

Young points out that even when it is just two people together, when and how they communicate is mediated – assumptions are made, there are conventions which may or may not be shared; power relationships are involved, there is the possibility of violence; my good time may be a bad time for you. Young also points out that a degree of anonymity is often preferable for people, if a close face-to-face community treats them as 'deviant', for example because they are 'independent' women, Lesbian or Gay or socialist and so on. She proposes a different kind of social relationship in which people can, together, accept each other as different – 'open to unassimilated otherness' – while still being strangers. What she describes is perhaps like the shared feeling with strangers that you get at a festival or a demonstration where you know you have something in common with other people as well as knowing that you may be different.

Although Young's starting point is rather different from that of Sigmund Freud, they both end up saying that differences need to be accepted. In a book first published in 1930 Freud wrote about the peculiar fact that peoples whose territories are adjacent, and are otherwise closely related, are always engaged in constant feuds and ridiculing each other, as, for instance, the Spaniards and the Portuguese, the North and South Germans, the English and the Scotch, and so on. I gave it the name of narcissism in respect of minor differences.[87]

Freud argued that extreme intolerance by Christians of outsiders was an inevitable consequence of St Paul's assertion that (only) Christianity is based on love. He suggests that identifying outsiders (not even necessarily an enemy) is a way of building up solidarity within a community. He suggests that the people most like you are the people who disappoint you most when you find they are different. This accounts for the pain of splits among family, friends, co-religionists or political fellow travellers. Support for sports teams by people all passionate about that sport can be harmless outlets for energy or limited aggression but they can turn into life-threatening scapegoating. Religious, national or ethnic identification can become genocidal hatred.

Harmful communities or unethical communities

Freud, Derrida and Young's approaches offer ways of addressing fundamental problems in simply saying a category or a group is a group because people say or feel it is. People have argued that street gangs are communities and potentially good for society.[88] However, the evidence that gangs are exploitative and harmful to their members as well as outsiders is very strong. A report on Child Sexual Exploitation in Gangs and Groups defines gangs as:

> relatively durable, predominantly street-based, social groups of children, young people and, not infrequently, young adults who see themselves, and are seen by others, as affiliates of a discrete, named group who (1) engage in a range of criminal activity and violence; (2) identify or lay claim to territory; (3) have some form of identifying structural feature; and (4) are in conflict with similar groups.[89]

Furthermore, sexual violence is treated as normal within the 'community'. In a qualitative study of sexual violence in gangs more than half of the incidents which were characterised as accepted behaviour, initiation into the gang and other activities, involved young women being *'passed round'* as *'sharing'*. One young woman said:

> I'm used to it ... It's normal ... It's wrong, but you get used to it ... Welcome to our generation.[90]

Jay Belsky has argued that the causes ('aetiology') of child abuse within families have to be understood as a four-level ecosystem that includes a level of individual behaviour which they are responsible for but may be predisposed to (*ontogenic development*); a *microsystem* of dynamics within the family; an *exosystem* which is the economic and social system of the family; and a *macrosystem* of the values and child-rearing practices that characterise the society or subculture in which the individual, family and community are embedded.[91]

Networks of child abusers clearly have many characteristics of communities. A police agency in the UK highlights the fact that many local grooming networks are based on pre-existing social networks; they operate through peer reinforcement and through practical mutual aid such as sharing mobile phone numbers.[92]

There are many examples of where crime, including violence and corruption, within 'institutions' is covered up or condoned because people feel a loyalty to each other and a hostility to outsiders or people who threaten the image or interests of the institution. Just some of the examples are faith groups, sports organisations, workplaces, schools and colleges, political parties and movements, police services and the military. Many such institutions are essential vehicles for social and community development. In these situations, they have all the positive and negative features of communities.

It can be dangerous not to recognise that people are part of communities. Media, government agencies and organisations identify individuals convicted of extreme violence as 'lone wolves', ignoring the networks from which the individuals drew inspiration and resources. Their motivation is portrayed as having individual grievances and psychological problems rather than an ideological agenda and institutional affiliations.[93]

These examples highlight that communities are not always a 'good thing'. Combining Derrida and Young's concepts, we might recognise that the immunity that communities grant themselves is inhospitable and unethical. We can then take a normative position that such communities do not deserve respect. However, it may be useful to recognise them as a basis for change. Organisations working with perpetrators of child sexual abuse may, for example, promote work with men who are '*troubled by their sexual thoughts*' to help them change while recognising that others are '*not motivated to change and present an on-going risk to children and young people*'.[94]

This analytical framework requires identifying the different groups correctly and understanding what works to change behaviour.

Diversity

Based on what Young and Freud have argued, community based on homogeneity or separating people who are different is both impossible and undesirable. Durkheim's concept of solidarity is discussed later in the chapter, but one of his key ideas is that diversity is beneficial. The division of labour means that:

> Each can attain his end without preventing the others from attaining theirs.[95]

That is, wanting different goods, services and lifestyles makes it easier to share spaces and enjoy different things. It also relates back to the idea of community being based on pursuing (self-)interest.

This review of the different characterisations of community highlights four points:

- People mean different things by community: there is no agreed definition with essential characteristics.
- Mental and physical constructions of community may overlap and not be consistently applied. They are fluid and messy.
- They all have negative as well as positive aspects.
- Society and community are not easily distinguishable.

The nature of social groups

There are several questions which run through each of the dimensions discussed above. They include:

- What holds social groups together and what makes them separate?
- Do groups have to be defined in terms of just one of these dimensions?
- Do social groups have to be defined as one or the other 'community' or 'society'?
- Who decides what a group is?

We now try to answer these questions.

Solidarity and cohesion

Running through all the dimensions of society and community discussed above are explicit and implicit ideas about what keeps social groups together. Right from the earliest uses of the word *cohesion* in English, for example by Thomas Hobbes and John Locke, there have been different ideas about what bonds people, reflected in contrasting metaphors: 'bound' together (as with a piece of rope) or organically attached (as with the fibres in a piece of wood, parts of a plant or the organs of a human body). In the nineteenth century Durkheim talked about *Mechanical Solidarity* and *Organic Solidarity*. Analytical thinking about the sources of solidarity can be traced back much earlier to Ibn Khaldun and his concept of solidarity – *Asabiyyah*.[96]

These and other metaphors remain important. The mechanical analogy is often used when commentators talk about the importance of members of society accepting the legitimacy of control by the state, often expressed as respect for the ruler(s) – for example, monarchy or for the forces of law and order (the police or the army). When shared values bond people together, chemical 'glue' metaphors are used. More accurately, in physics and biology cohesion is the joining together of like substances and the joining together of different substances called *adhesion*.[97] Also from physics are examples of how opposites attract: magnets. Hooks and loops are used in the fabric Velcro for adhesion. Opposites attracting or cooperating for their mutual benefit are established concepts in sociology (including in Durkheim's philosophy) and psychology. In biology 'hybridity' has been much studied: hybridity can lead to either enhanced vigour (grafting fruit trees) or sterility (female horses and male donkeys mating to produce mules which are sterile). In ecosystems different organisms can have either positive (*symbiotic*) or negative (*parasitic*) relationships. Organic metaphors often reflect value judgements about whether uniformity or diversity are preferable. What might or might not be harmless in how vegetables or flowers look, can be life-threatening when it comes to humans. Other analyses are more negative, asserting that mixing leads to violence or a weakening – as the Nazi eugenicists argued.

All of these are ways of bonding. They may imply different ideas about what a good society or community is. A society held together by mechanical solidarity may only work when its borders are not porous, and its population is homogeneous. That may not be realistic, desirable or sustainable. A situation in which a population has little or nothing in common or which is in constant flux may also not be feasible or desirable. States, regions and settlements where boundaries have been created by laws, international treaties or conquest, rather than voluntary consent, can be fatal for their inhabitants or the people who are deemed to be outside. Bonds that work in one generation or economic situation may become intolerable in changed circumstances.

Conflict

The opposite of what keeps people together is often suggested to be 'conflict'. Paradoxically, conflict may actually bring or keep people together. Different schools of sociology have approached conflict in various ways – some seeing it as functional or positive, as a way of addressing injustice or a way of individuals and groups establishing identity; others as a destructive source. They have also disagreed about how fundamental it is as an organising principle of society. For some, organising around interests is fundamental but with different perspectives on whether these interests are primarily economic, expressed in terms of class, or are about authority or power, often expressed in terms of elite rule.[98] As we shall see in Chapter 4, conflict is seen as an important tool of social and community development by many theorists and practitioners. It should not be equated with violence. Ending violence often involves repressing difference ('conquest') or separating the parties, sometimes physically ('cartography').[99] Furthermore, the absence of conflict is not a necessary condition for a social group to be a community. However, many accounts of community play down or ignore conflicts – and violence – within community. The difficulties surrounding conflict with 'outsiders' have been discussed above.

Self-definition or not

An identity may be both imposed and self-identified. Frantz Fanon's analysis of identity at the individual, group and social level deals with the way that identify can be imposed as a negative category and simultaneously a chosen, emancipatory consciousness.[100]

Anthropologists, biologists and colonial administrators have often imposed designations on people as members of communities, societies or belonging to states, based on dubious science or clear self-interest. Classification of people into 'races', tribes or nationalities has frequently had catastrophic consequences including genocide. The devastating consequences are not only the result of categorising 'superior' and 'inferior' but even simply as different or 'other'.[101]

There are many examples of people who are categorised by others as outsiders, deviants or inferior based on gender, ethnicity, religion, disability or sexuality. Sometimes negative terminology is adopted by members of the group as an identity – for example, 'Queer' used to describe homosexuals was originally (in the 1890s) derogatory but since the 1980s has been used by at least some gay people as a positive identity.[102] The difference between how members of a community identify themselves and how others do is clearly illustrated by the word 'Nigger' or 'Nigga'. Used by a White person to refer to a person of African, Aboriginal or Maori descent, it is likely, and rightly so, to be seen as offensive. Used by an African American (and increasingly younger Black people in the UK), it may be positive or self-deprecating but not negative.[103] Historically, many marginalised or oppressed individuals and groups have had their voices silenced or not heard.

It will be argued in later chapters that self-identification is a necessary condition of any process of community development, but it may not be a sufficient condition for defining a group of people as a community.

Combinations, change and location

From this account, it is obvious that conceptions of society and, more particularly, community differ widely and are contested. Only to describe or analyse social groups in terms of one or two dimensions misses their subtlety. It will lead to overlooking important dynamics. Where social structures are constituted in terms of quotas or targets for what are considered to be salient identities of religion or ethnicity, for example, it can perpetuate the 'otherness' while ignoring other dimensions such as gender or class which may be very important. This is returned to in Chapter 4 in relation to organising political representation and government around social segments (*Consociationalism*). It can also be an issue in relation to civil society organisations or targets for workforce composition or public services delivery and in Chapter 5 it is addressed through the concept of *intersectionality*.

Another significant aspect of the multifaceted nature of social groups is that perceptions, and what is important, change. Descriptions of identity illustrate this. Self-description and imposed descriptions have changed from Negro to Black to African American for people of African heritage living in the USA. The term Black is also used as description of Aboriginal Australians. The term 'politically Black' has been used in the past to describe people who have a common experience of race-based oppression without a close shared ancestry or ethnic identity but is less used now. In the USA, 'people of color' is used more. Individuals' identification with these labels change over time and place. People may move from a national identification to a religious one or vice versa or have a dual identity. This has been described for Bangladeshi Muslims living in the UK, for example. There are people alive today in the UK who came to the country as pre-independence 'Indians', then became East Pakistani Bengalis, often described and self-described as Asians (or pejoratively as Pakis), later they became Bangladeshis who now identify or are identified as Muslims (and who may have significant differences about what it means to be Muslim) and who may have British citizenship and identify as British and/or, say, Londoners.[104] An identity where people feel solidarity can help overcome conflicts based on other identities. Identification based on gender has played a significant role in changing inter- and intra-community relations – in Northern Ireland, Cyprus and Somalia, for example.[105]

Where you are, at a particular moment, also influences how you describe yourself. The musician Phil Lynott was born in England to a

White Irish mother and a Black Guyanese father. He was brought up in Dublin by his maternal grandmother:

> When I'm in Ireland, I say I'm from Dublin. When I'm in Dublin, I say I'm from Crumlin. When I'm in Crumlin, I say I'm from Leighlin Road and when I'm in Leighlin Road, I say I'm a Lynott.[106]

People may be more or less immersed at different times and different contexts and what they get from or give to a group may change. A framework for involvement in gangs, for example, suggests that for individuals within gangs there are moments when people are looking for something (*Gotta be, Wanna be, Going to be*) and times when individuals are completely identifying with the values and activities of the group and are dependent on it for self-esteem as well as for meeting material needs and contributing to it materially.[107]

Summary and a proposed analytical framework

This chapter has analysed the history and meanings of the terms society and community. It has found that there is no overarching definition or differentiation which works in all contexts.

Issues

There are several oversimplifications which beset analysis of social groups:

1. Seeing everything as binary opposites
   This takes many forms: society or community; rural, urban; traditional, modern; insider, outsider; Christian, Muslim; as 'us versus them'; and vertical relationships. Such classifications do not recognise the many levels on which individuals and groups operate and the possibility or necessity of being many things at once.

   One of the most damaging binaries is that either you are part of a society or community or you are not. People may feel or be identified by others as on the edge or central, at different times and in different contexts.

2. Essentialism and homogenising communities
   There is tendency for definitions of community to stress what its members have in common and even to go one stage further and say or imply that members are all the same. There is more diversity within communities and there is more commonality between communities

than this approach allows. Gender is an issue in both neglecting differences within communities and commonalities between communities.

The idea of overlapping elements of communities can be represented by a Venn diagram (Figure 2.1).

However, in mathematical theory, there is a theorem which says that there are always more sets than there are members of a set ('*Cantor's Theorem*').[108] In relation to people, that means there are always more ways of grouping people than the number of people and there are more ways of constructing communities than the criteria for identifying them.

3. Focus on territory
   There is often a default position that communities and societies have physical boundaries. All or most people within the boundaries are or should be part of it. Outsiders are outsiders! In fact, many societies and communities are not defined in this way, probably increasingly so.

4. Conflict is seen as external
   Conflict within societies is either ignored or seen as avoidable through exclusion and expulsion. The legitimacy of this is questionable. Gender,

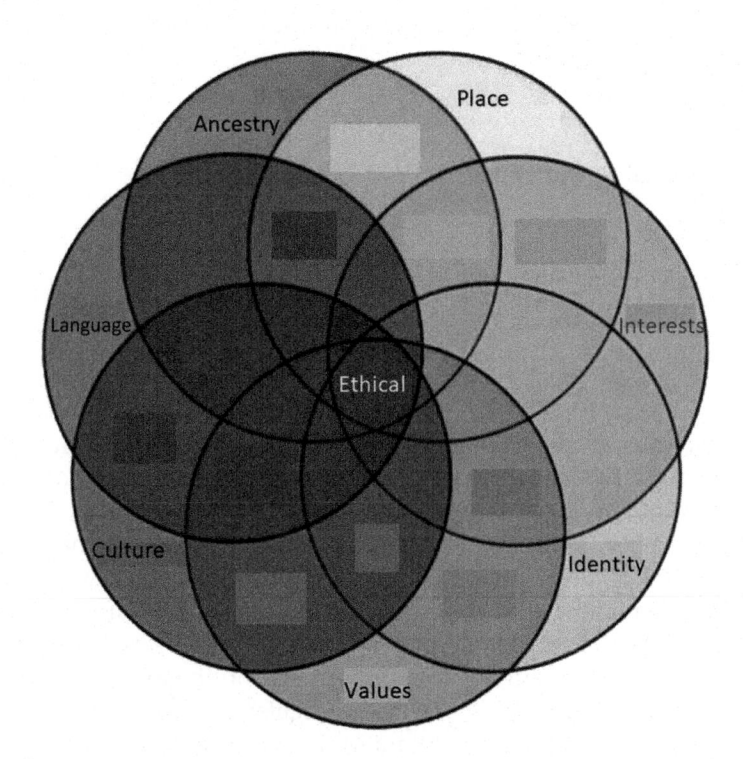

Figure 2.1 Overlapping domains of ethical communities

race and religion are often significant in identifying who is perceived a threat.

5. There is an ambiguity or indifference about whether social groups define themselves or may be defined by others
Social and community development must be aware of both, and practitioners must be willing to challenge such classifications when they are oppressive. This is discussed further in Chapter 5.

A multi-level approach

Many different disciplines have adopted a multi-level approach to observing phenomena such as decision-making or social change.

Many of them use combinations of Greek words such as Nano, Micro, Meso, Mezzo, Macro, Exo and Meta. Widespread though their use is, it is not immediately obvious what they mean.[109] Other writers use Personal, Cultural and Social, or Personal, Relational, Structural and Cultural which is clearer but is a more restricted view of 'community' than we have explored here.[110]

Pawson and colleagues use a four-level model which is clearer and seems to avoid some of the problems that a simple community/social distinction does. The four levels are:

- Individual
- Interpersonal relationships
- Institutions
- Ideology or infrastructure.[111]

The individual level

This corresponds to the *nano* or personal level of other authors. It incorporates people's individual identities, interests and aspirations, and relationships. Many of the insights into how people develop, behave and think at this level come from psychology. One of the recurrent themes in community and social development is that issues move between levels. 'Private troubles' can become 'public issues' – unemployment, for example. Societies can decide that public issues are private matters or vice versa – sexuality or how people dress, for example. Responses can be on the interpersonal, institutional or ideological levels.[112] The neurolinguist George Lakoff reminds us that aggregates of individuals – 'pluralities' – are not necessarily anything more than that. The tendency to call people using public transport a 'group' or a 'community' can be misleading. They do not necessarily have common characteristics or goals or even see each other as sharing anything.[113]

The interpersonal level

The *micro* or interpersonal level of personal relationships incorporates the ideas of social capital and the informal and personal networks people feel part of: who we see as our peers, our enemies or our superiors or inferiors. The disciplines of microsociology and social psychology and behavioural economics and microeconomics can be used to understand processes at this level.

The institutional level

The *macro*, *meso* or structural level frequently relates to formal institutions including the state and civil society organisations to which people belong. Many of the movements which are discussed in Chapter 4 operate at this level. However, it also incorporates the social structures and the social order in which such movements operate. It includes the demographic and economic context of people's lives. It leaves open the question of how much it is intentional action, planned behaviour and so on that influences what people do – *Agency* – or social (including cultural) and economic determinants – *Structure*. Micro- and macroeconomics, political science, management studies and anthropology are tools to analyse institutions. Again, Lakoff highlights that we often treat institutions as though they are people – 'the school thinks ...'. Institutions do exist independently of the people in them and vice versa. By treating institutions as though they were people, which the law does in many countries, they acquire rights to free speech or privacy, which can, for instance, interfere with the ideas of one person, one vote, transparency or corporate accountability.[114]

The infrastructural or ideological level

The infrastructural, *meta* or cultural level incorporates the ideological context of social groups – which could be as broad as individualist or collectivist ideologies, religion or secularism in general or major belief systems; the social and economic systems (such as kinship systems or market, subsistence or planned economies). Anthropology, Theology, History, Cultural Studies and Philosophy all contribute to analysis at this level. What is meant by *ideology* is discussed further in Chapter 6.

A multi-level approach to multi-dimensional communities looks like this (Figure 2.2).

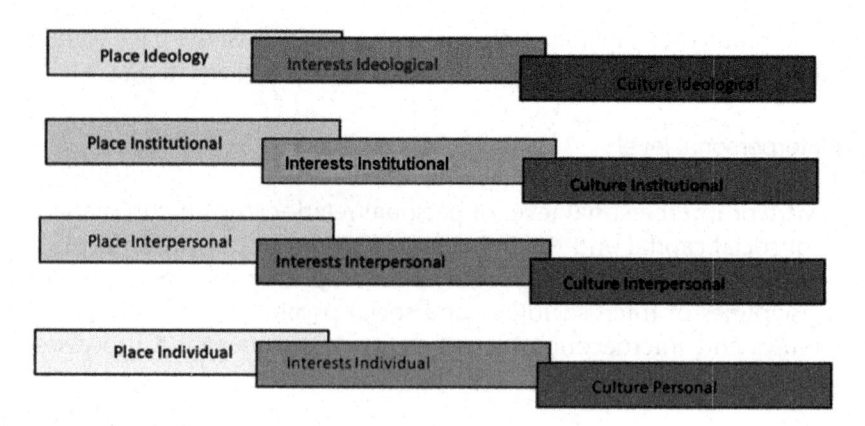

Figure 2.2 Interacting levels and domains

Disability and Domestic Violence are issues which reflect the importance of seeking to understand how societies and communities operate at all four levels:

➢ A state of consciousness and experiences
➢ How other people treat us, and how we treat other people
➢ The way that institutions behave
➢ How behaviour and experience are justified, rationalised or challenged (Figure 2.3).

Social issue	Disability	Domestic Violence
Level		
Individual	Consciousness of impairment	Experience of physical, emotional violence
Interpersonal	Family, peers treat individual as equal, different or inferior	Aware or not of other people in the same situation; support or not from peers, family
Institutional	Segregation or inclusion; networks or organisations of other disabled people; services for disabled people; impact of disability discrimination on economy	Availability of refuges; legal protection; support for leaving abuser; legislators and criminal justice system condoning or punishing abuse; cost of abuse
Ideological	Religious teaching on taking part in religious life, e.g. Leviticus 21:16–23 or used to justify equal treatment; medical model of disability	Religious teaching used to justify abuse or suffering; political support or hostility to seeing Domestic Violence as human rights issue

Figure 2.3 How issues are seen on different levels

The way in which the different levels interact with each other is explored in Chapter 4.

Implications for practice

A practitioner or activist needs to:

1. Work with other people to see what they think makes them a community and what the boundaries of the society or community are
2. Be prepared to challenge them about issues such as homogenising or essentialising 'us' and othering and excluding 'them'
3. Identify the forces which bind people together and divide them
4. Be clear at which level(s) s/he is trying to act. There is not a single right level, and action is likely to be more effective if it is on several levels.

Box 2.1 Suggested activities

1. By yourself: Referring to the dimensions identified in this chapter, which are important to you? Do they reinforce each other? Are there tensions between any of them? Have they changed over time and according to where you are?
2. With other people: What are the commonalities and differences in what (place, culture, language, etc.) is important to you?
3. With other people: What do you feel about people who are not part of your community? What do you feel about being outside other people's community?

3
Development

Introduction

The previous chapter argued that societies and communities get legitimacy from ethical relationships – specifically, being hospitable. In this chapter I argue that development, both as a process and as an outcome, also needs to be ethical – specifically, being inclusive and sustainable.

The term development invites much more immediate reaction – negative and positive – than society and community do. It has multiple and sometimes contradictory meanings which people may react to like the smell of roses or the stench of a skunk.[1]

This chapter explores how the term development has been used over time and in different places. It highlights that the term reflects values and ideologies. Metaphors are used to explore this while noting that there are dangers in this approach.

The implications of development being an unclear and contested concept are strategic and operational. There are important unresolved questions about:

➤ Who and what is development for?
➤ What levels does it operate on?
➤ What methods does it use; how is it measured?

Historical overview of 'development'

As a word, development's origins are in twelfth- to fourteenth-century French and Italian: relating to (un)wrapping or (un)folding as you would a flag or banner. By the eighteenth century in English it meant the process of bringing out a fuller version or a latent version.[2]

Development for? And how?

Pursuit of freedom, autonomy or happiness

Amartya Sen at one time argued that the pursuit of economic development was simply part of trying to achieve freedom. Subsequently, with Martha Nussbaum, he has argued that it is about achieving capabilities. This is discussed further in Chapter 5. Others have argued that the goal is autonomy, happiness or well-being.[3] In all these cases, there is an interaction between economic, social, civic and political development both in what is measured and in theories about causality, for example that some, but not all, economic development increases happiness or that democracy and happiness are correlated or even that democracy increases happiness. There have been large-scale studies which have sought to show such relationships.[4] The problems with this approach are discussed further in the section on Cultural and Sustainable Development later in the chapter.

Development of humans?

The intended beneficiaries of development policies and practice are almost invariably (only) humans. However, they are frequently presented as objects, consumers or recipients of interventions rather than as actors or subjects. Sometimes this is deliberate – to highlight the right or responsibility of states or international agencies such as the United Nations (UN) to undertake development. Sometimes it just seems to be a default position to look at issues from the perspective of institutions and professions which analyse, plan or implement policies and practice – something that is done to people, not that we do for ourselves. Here an approach is proposed that looks at a range of domains of intervention in which the lives of the subject are central and which can incorporate interventions from the individual level through to the infrastructural, starting from the idea of human rights. Rights are discussed further in Chapter 5, including questions of intergenerational and non-human rights.

The 1948 UN Declaration of Human Rights did not spell out groups of rights, though different categories were widely discussed; but by 1966, in the International Covenant on Economic, Social and Cultural Rights (which came into force in 1976), the UN recognised that:

> in accordance with the Universal Declaration of Human Rights, the ideal of free human beings enjoying freedom from fear and want can only be achieved if conditions are created whereby everyone may enjoy his economic, social and cultural rights, as well as his civil and political rights.[5]

Levels Rights	Community and Social	Economic	Political	Civic	Cultural and Sustainable
Ideological					
Institutional					
Interpersonal					
Individual					

Figure 3.1 Domains and levels of development

The covenant goes on to say:

> All peoples have the right to self-determination. By virtue of that right they freely determine their political status and freely pursue their economic, social and cultural development.[6]

Each of the domains of development – social, community, economic, political and civil, cultural and sustainable – have specific histories. Following on from the analytical framework of Chapter 2, development is explored by looking at both domains and levels (Figure 3.1).[7]

Community development

Many writers on community development trace its origins back to social policy either or both in the nineteenth century in Britain or in the British and other European empires. In the British context, the general line of argument is that the mid-nineteenth century saw major rethinking of social policy by different social elites, often because of a fear of political unrest or revolution. Anglican, Catholic and Jewish religious organisations and individuals saw a need to do something about the material welfare of the population as well as their spiritual or moral well-being. The degree that this was motivated by faith or self-interest is debateable and discussed further in Chapter 4. Politicians, notably Benjamin Disraeli with his *One Nation* concept, also promoted new ways of tackling social issues. Several distinct approaches can be identified. Sometimes they have gone hand-in-hand, sometimes they have been vigorously contested alternatives:[8]

➢ *Assessment of individual needs*: The Charity Organisation Society emphasised the importance of identifying individual needs, and not giving alms (charity) indiscriminately, as they saw it. This gave rise to the practice of casework, with social workers assessing who deserved support. Although casework focused on individuals from the earliest days, many of the people and organisations involved in social work also engaged in responses on a collective or institutional level, including initiatives in housing, education, employment and public open spaces. In the 1950s the Younghusband report said social work comprised casework, group work and community work and the Seebohm Committee report in 1968 also included community work in social work.[9]

➢ A *social investigation* tradition – Most associated in England with Charles Booth and Seebohm Rowntree as assessing population needs rather than individual needs with a lot of effort put into categorising people and places.[10]

➢ *The interaction of different social groups* – A Christian Socialist or Practicable Socialism tradition associated with the historian Arnold Toynbee and Samuel and Henrietta Barnett stressed the interaction of more affluent and poorer people as essential to understanding one another. It was expressed through the settlement movement which started with the founding of Toynbee Hall in East London where (male) students and graduates from Oxford and Cambridge universities went to live or work. Christian Socialism or Practicable Socialism were explicitly an alternative to revolutionary socialism.[11]

➢ *Solidarity* – For example, a social catholic tradition, led by the Catholic (convert) Archbishop Henry Manning, who argued that the church needed to be on the side of the common people and supported the development of trade unions to fight for better conditions. He thought the church needed to offer leadership and guidance to counter communist influence.[12]

➢ *Encouraging self-help* – The Jewish Board of Guardians was established in 1859. It had some characteristics in common with the Charity Organisation Society, but it particularly stressed the importance of avoiding dependency and so stressed giving applicants for relief (literally) the tools to maintain themselves.[13] Samuel Smiles, for example, praised the 'vigorous efforts which the seventeenth century Huguenot refugees made to help themselves'.[14]

➢ *Mutual aid* – For example, Peter Kropotkin, the anarchist writer; the Utopian Socialists; and the actions of the trade unions and the cooperative movement.[15]

These traditions have indeed contributed to some degree to theories and practices in community and social development. However, focusing on development as a top-down process and only on events and ideas in

England provides only a partial picture of the UK, Europe and the world more generally. In the UK context community workers are not usually called social workers though internationally 'social worker' may refer to applied social researchers, workers with groups and campaigners.

The imperial or colonial period contributed to theory and practice in various ways. Frederick Lugard was a key figure in the development of British colonialism. He provided the rationale for Colonial (later Community) Development. In 1926 he said the trustee (the colonial power) had a Dual Mandate:

> on the one hand, for the advancement of the subject races, and on the other hand, for the development of its material resources for the benefit of mankind.[16]

Lugard, however, did not regard economic and community development as of equal importance. He would probably have endorsed the approach of J. Albert Thorne, the Barbados Pan-Africanist doctor. He proposed resettling people from the Caribbean in Africa in the 1890s:

> the first aim should be to make the colony itself a practical success, in which case its influence on surrounding tribes will be for good. To initiate it primarily as a missionary exercise for the betterment of indigenous races is ... 'to put the cart before the horse'.[17]

In the mid-1930s Lord Hailey modified Lugard's approach: Britain should take responsibility for the economic development of the colonies, including ensuring adequate social services for their peoples; and encouragement should be given to the development of local government institutions and to the admission of Africans into government service.[18]

The concept of community development (and social development) in the British colonies emerged out of the Colonial Office's perceived need for social work in the 1930s. 'Mass Education' during World War II had had the broad aims of developing health and living conditions, economic well-being, and *'the development of political institutions and political power until the day arrives when the people can become effectively self-governing'*.[19] However, activities on the ground focused on the war effort, in terms of both soldiers and economic development. A Mobile Propaganda Unit in East Africa was trying to increase civilian support for African soldiers in the war.[20] In the Gold Coast (now Ghana), Mass Education was used to increase cocoa production before and after independence but the same programme was used by the by Kwame Nkrumah's party to promote independence.[21] At the Cambridge conference of colonial administrators in 1948 it was declared that: *self-government is not an aim in itself – there is need for wider and higher loyalties.*[22] The same conference resulted in the first courses designated as Community Development led by Margaret Read and T. R. (Reg) Batten at the London Institute of Education from 1949.[23] In the 1940s and 1950s the Colonial Office and different African countries, used, often interchangeably, the terms Mass Education, Social Development and Community Development, though the 1948 conference had announced *'Community Development as the official term'*.[24]

It is a mistake to look in isolation at the British approach to social and community development in the colonial and decolonising eras. Ideas came to and from other European powers and the USA and the colonised countries themselves, of course, were influential. Examples of the diverse origins include:

➢ North American influences – The colonial authorities in Kenya set up a training centre in 1925 to train teachers in a wide range of development activities, including agriculture and health. It was influenced by Booker T. Washington's work in the USA and modelled on and funded by the Jeanes Fund which had developed such schools to train *'Negro teachers to work in the Negro States [sic]'*. The education practice in the Philippines of the American missionary Frank Laubach was taken up by the Nationalist leader Norman Manley in Jamaica and later copied in Africa, though it was not initially successful in Jamaica.[25] Later, the US involvement in wars in Korea and Vietnam led to the use of international aid and counter-insurgency techniques in community development activities.[26]

➢ The French Empire – Decolonisation of the French Empire impacted on social and community development, albeit with a slightly different vocabulary. The dominant model of decolonisation was one of 'Assimilation' in which the colonies would continue to be part of France following the same path to development as Metropolitan France. A second model of 'Association' was proposed, not dissimilar to Lugard's Indirect Rule. A French Minister for the Colonies said:

> A colonial system cannot survive unless it is operated from within by the natives who are supposed to benefit from it.[27]

➢ *'Animation Rurale'* was promoted in some French colonies. It took several different forms from a technical diffusion model, through a structural reform agenda to being a tool for liberation.[28]

➢ The Indian subcontinent – The ideas that came out of the Indian subcontinent illustrate the limitations of trying to put the history of community development into 'colonial', 'indigenous', 'anti-colonial' or 'post-colonial' boxes. At the same time as colonial administrators and educators were promoting models derived from Europe or transferred from other continents, long-established development practices were refined, and new ideas were developed from within the subcontinent. On the one hand, the British Commissioner F. L. Brayne (in the Punjab) had little lasting impact. On the other hand, the rural development project of the American Spencer Hatch (at Marthandam in Kerala) has lasted. Rabindranath Tagore developed Shanti Niketan[a] in West Bengal, working with Leonard Elmhirst, a British agricultural economist. Tagore and Elmhirst's methods have had an enduring impact in India and in the UK. The independence movement in India was critically concerned with development. Gandhi was apparently influenced by Tolstoy's analysis of the submissiveness and cooperation which made British rule in India possible.[29] Gandhi's idea of *Swaraj* (loosely, autonomy and self-rule) was that Indians would:

> Cease to play the part of the ruled ... we shall not help you.[30]

> *Swaraj* and *Swadeshi* (self-sufficiency or self-reliance) have had a significant influence on ideas about political, economic and community development, both as a process and as an outcome. His ideas about non-violence (*Satyagraha* or Truth Force) and education (e.g. teachers learn from their pupils) have influenced processes which are discussed further in Chapters 4 and 6. Jawaharlal Nehru shared some of Gandhi's ideas, arguing for development from below (discussed later in this chapter) but supported industrialisation and a central role for the state with which Gandhi would have disagreed.[31]

Social development

The term 'social development' was popularised before and just after World War I by Leonard Hobhouse to refer to a deliberate process of development as opposed to the inevitability of evolution or revolution. Consciously or not, it was picked up by British colonial administrators in the 1950s and later by the UN and used extensively in international development. It has come to be associated with the idea that social and economic development need to be integrated, led by state intervention in welfare and have mechanisms for income redistribution. It has focused on the product of interventions, with the process simply being designated 'planning'. It has been

---

[a] Shanti Niketan is a town started by Rabindranath Tagore which has become an educational and spiritual centre.

challenged from many quarters. Critics from the left and the right have seen the state as part of the problem rather than the solution. Free market proponents see the state as inefficient, interfering with market mechanisms. Left-wing, feminist and post-colonial critics see the state as representing imperial, capitalist and patriarchal interests. The idea that social development reflects a consensus on ends and means is widely challenged.[32]

Today, in the UK the term Social Development is not so widely used. However, the New and Expanded Towns built after World War II often employed Social Development Officers. In Northern Ireland, between 1965 and 1972, there was a Ministry of Development. Between 1999 and 2016 it was called the Department for Social Development. In 2016 it became the Department for Communities.[33]

James Midgley suggests as a definition:

> A process of planned social change designed to promote the well-being of the population as a whole within the context of a dynamic multifaceted development process.[34]

With an outcome of greater well-being and a process of planned social change it looks like a catch-all definition. However, the inclusion of the word 'planned' is in fact restrictive. Not only does it reflect Hobhouse's legacy described above that change results from agency or intention rather than structural economic or social forces, but it also leans towards a top-down, state or international multilateral agency-led process, though some of its advocates argue that participation of the affected populations is essential.[35] Also, in practice what is included in 'well-being' is often quite narrow and the pattern of social development pursued has been limited – often replicating patterns in different parts of Europe or North America. This has frequently been portrayed as natural progression, for example towards 'welfare states', rather than a pattern imposed by the richer and more powerful nations and agencies associated with them.[36]

Measuring social development

In 1987 the UN Brundtland Commission proposed its vision (introducing *Sustainability* to the UN's development lexicon). It led to the South Commission in 1990, which in turn led to the development of the Human Development Index (HDI) and Human Development Reports. The HDI aims to measure three dimensions of human development – a long and healthy life, knowledge and a decent standard of living – in practice by measuring life expectancy at birth, years of schooling and gross national income per capita.[37] The first UN Human Development Report quoted Aristotle (384–322 BCE):

Wealth is evidently not the good we are seeking, for it is merely useful and for the sake of something else.[38]

The goals of social development

Aristotle's point suggests a much broader range of goals than income, schooling and life expectancy such as Sen's concept of development as freedom or Sen and Nussbaum's goals of achievement of capabilities.[39] Proponents of social development say it 'harmonises' economic and social goals and that social development promotes economic development.[40] Even if the focus of development is on health and education, there are more sophisticated measures than years of schooling and length of life. For example, UNESCO's *Education for All* programme has six goals, included education of girls, adult literacy and quality of education.[41] The World Health Organization identifies seven health-related targets of the Millennium Development Goals including access to safe water and sanitation, reduction in maternal mortality and reduction in tuberculosis.[42]

With the adoption of the Millennium Development Goals the range of social development goals expanded the HDI somewhat to include gender equality and environmental sustainability. The Sustainable Development Goals for 2030, agreed in September 2015, further widen the agenda.[43]

Social development is still promoted as a distinct approach though, for example in the World Bank's Social Development Strategy written in 2005.[44] It is within the tradition that development is a technical process led by governments and international institutions at the national level, with the aim or necessity of achieving change through planning (implicitly by consensus).[45]

Rather than a binary distinction between social and community development, the history of the terms suggests the levels at which they operate are mixed (or muddled) up. The four-fold distinction introduced in the previous chapter goes some way to clarifying the different levels on which development takes place.

Economic development

The idea of international development goes back at least as far as the nineteenth century. However, many writers give it a more recent and precise start date: 20 January 1949. This was when the US president Harry Truman announced a programme (*'Point Four'*) to aid the development of the economically underdeveloped areas by making available technical resources and capital investment in them.[46]

Truman's *Point Four* clearly regarded development as material well-being, specifically economic growth. Even if the motivation for it was political (supporting the free peoples of the world as described above), the measurement of success was in increases in gross domestic product (GDP) or income per head. Development was about catching up. Within countries, national policies might be targeted on particular populations – young people, 'backward regions' and so on; growth of specific sectors – agriculture, information technology; or individuals – for example, long-term unemployed people.

The International Covenant on Economic, Social and Cultural Rights identifies many specific rights – for example, to freely dispose of their natural wealth and resources, the right to work – and states are given responsibility for:

> technical and vocational guidance and training programmes, policies and techniques to achieve steady economic, social and cultural development and full and productive employment.[47]

The extracts highlight that economic development may be measured according to whether an individual has a job or training course or a level of income through to infrastructural questions about whether a country is self-determining in its use of natural wealth and resources.

Measurement

The measurement of material well-being raises not just technical challenges but also what were the goals of development and what value judgements are involved. There is an age-old question about 'What is money for?' The economist Amartya Sen argued that economic development/income is not necessarily valued for itself but because it increases freedom of choice[48] (see the section on Social Development below). Many analysts of poverty would argue that there is a need to address not just material deprivation, but exclusion and lack of power. The relationship between economic growth and more general well-being is not straightforward. For example, while suicide rates have been shown to go up in recessions, life expectancy, where there is a degree of social protection, may actually increase – so-called *'healthy degrowth'*.[49]

The problem is that measurement is not 'neutral'. It reflects the goals of development and can also change the pattern of development. International Food Aid illustrates this. Christopher Barrett has conceptualised a model of the consequences of food aid on the micro, meso and macro levels, very similar to the four-level model proposed above.[50] The rationale of American food aid is not only to feed hungry people. It is also designed to stimulate the creation of local markets in food and demand for American grain. By monetising food consumption it can increase GDP thereby appearing to make a country richer while not necessarily improving living standards. Indeed, it can lower the living standards of local food producers unable to sell their produce. It can also shift food consumption patterns in the long term – away from coarse grains, tubers and rice towards wheat bread. For example, sub-Saharan Africa has seen a massive increase in wheat consumption which may be partly due to rising incomes in some countries but is also due to food aid.[51]

Besides food, there are many other economically valuable activities that are not exchanged for money (*monetised*): gifts and labour exchanged within households and families, and volunteering which are generally not counted in economic development measures.[52] On the other hand, there are activities which might be illegal or undesirable but are nonetheless economic activity such as illegal drugs sales, people or arms smuggling, or prostitution.[53] There is now much more awareness that present consumption may have a cost to future generations in terms of degradation of environments (e.g. deforestation) or using up finite resources.

Right from the beginning, there were questions about whether measuring the gross income of a country (or even averages per head) was useful. Also, averages did not consider income inequalities within countries. In 1990 extreme poverty was defined as people who were living on less than a dollar a day, in 2008 it was revised to be $1.25; in 2015 it was increased to $1.90. Even a relatively narrow concept is challenging to measure because what money will buy depends on costs in different countries, so the concept of Purchasing Power Parity is used. This concept has brought forward such indexes as the Big Mac Index which highlights, unintentionally, the problem with one-dimensional economic measures: that not everyone in the world, or within a country, has access to a Big Mac and that there may be many people who don't and would like to and many who do but don't specifically want one or whose well-being is not served by their availability.[54]

Economic models

What is counted is part of a wider question about what models of economic development are used.

The two dominant models of economic development have been the so-called '*Standard*' model and '*Neoliberalism*'. The standard model associated with writers such as Arthur Lewis and Walter Rostow saw development mainly in terms of industrialisation, urbanisation and (agricultural) modernisation.[55] Although its leading proponents assumed it meant a market-based economy, clearly many state-led systems, notably China, have also followed this pattern. The origins of neoliberalism lie in the 1930s, although it can be argued that its meaning had changed by the 1980s. It was widely understood to mean promotion of markets not only as the mechanism to create material well-being but also for the efficient delivery of public services, frequently by creation of markets in public goods, by the privatisation of services and co-payments or charges for public services. It was specifically a rejection of the idea of John Maynard Keynes and William Beveridge that the state had a central role in creating the conditions for economic (and social) development by regulation and stimulus and in protecting and nurturing vulnerable populations. The supporters of the standard model and neoliberalism have argued that economic inequality is good for the poorest because it creates incentives and opportunities for people to work in order to pay for their own welfare and, where necessary, to pay taxes to support others who cannot pay for their own welfare.[56] The neoliberal model anticipated that this strategy would reduce or eliminate absolute poverty, but relative poverty or inequality is essential to the model to create incentives. An earlier version of the approach is the 'trickle down' or 'rising tide' strategy. John Kenneth Galbraith pointed out that in the nineteenth century trickle down was called the horse and sparrow theory:

> If you feed the horse enough oats, some will pass through to the road for the sparrows.[57]

John F. Kennedy used the rising tide metaphor which Jesse Jackson then criticised saying:

> Rising tides don't lift all boats, particularly those stuck at the bottom. For the boats stuck at the bottom there's a misery index.[58]

The criticism that the standard and neoliberal models simply don't work for the poorest is complemented by critiques of its negative impact on women and the environment and a more general critique that it reinforces dependency and underdevelopment.[59]

Conventionally, the two main alternatives to market-based economies are (state-)planned economies and subsistence.[60] In fact, not all state-planned economies are the same – state planning may be centralised (nationalised) or diffused (municipalisation). Collective control may be through elected politicians or state-appointed managers, or it may be a more syndicalist or mutualist approach in which the state enables worker- or consumer-managed cooperatives, for example. The non-monetised transactions referred to above are traditionally closely associated with subsistence but there is much evidence that they play a significant, possibly growing roles (even) in societies. Open source software or information sharing (*Wikipedia*, Citizen Journalism or open science) or using the web for 'freecycling' are just a few examples of new forms of a very old way of people sharing 'the commons', co-production or gift relationships (both discussed further in Chapter 4).[61] The *Degrowth* movement seeks to reduce consumption, enhancing well-being while societies 'live within their ecological means'.[62] Kate Raworth has proposed 'Doughnut Economics' in which economic development includes a floor of a (widely defined) standard of living but with a ceiling which is ecologically sustainable.[63]

Related, but not the same, are forms of economic cooperation or mutuality. Examples include:

- Worker and consumer cooperatives; social enterprises
- Local Exchange Trading Systems (LETS)
- Crowdfunding
- Collaborative consumption or the Sharing Economy
- Time banks.[64]

They may operate within the capitalist or planned economic systems. Worker co-ops still trade within the market or are licensed by state planning systems. Crowdfunding is being used to raise capital for market traded goods in a similar way to shareholding; collaborative consumption can just be used to gain a discount in the market by increasing the power from individual to group consumer – not all of these are that different for capitalism. However, some of these forms are exchanging something other than money such as time or are not-for-profit.

Over centuries, theorists have argued that economic development is a necessary condition for political development – specifically democracy and some have claimed evidence for it.[65] Even if there are obvious relationships between social and political structures, the idea that economic conditions are necessary and sufficient prerequisites for political conditions is not borne out by evidence. Wealth and economic (in)equality are not simply correlated with specific political systems and the causality can work both ways. Political development, if it is desired, has to be a goal in itself. It will not be a by-product of economic development and vice versa.

Political and civic development

Even before the era of colonial development, powerful states justified their 'dominion' over weaker states on the grounds that they were incapable of defending themselves externally and self-governing internally. A variety of arrangements were established during the colonial period: 'Protectorates' (formalised in Africa by the Treaty of Berlin in 1885), Dominions (mainly from the mid-nineteenth century), Mandates and Trusteeships (established after World War I) and subsequently Occupations. Since the period of decolonisation and the end of the Cold War there have been a variety of formulations of justifications for interventions or development programmes in the name of:

- *Strengthening Civil Society* – with organisations such as the Open Society Foundations working to *'build vibrant and tolerant societies whose governments are accountable and open to the participation of all people'* and the UN Development Programme running programmes to develop Civil Society Organisations.[66] Some versions of strengthening civil society put less emphasis on the state and more on the role of social capital but some analysts have expressed scepticism about its potential.[67]

- *Good Governance* – agencies such as the International Monetary Fund, the World Bank and the UN make funding conditional on specific structures and processes of governance including transparency, accountability and respect for human rights. Several indexes seek to measure the state of countries in relation to these concerns.[68]

- *Humanitarian Interventions* – under the 'Duty to Protect'. These are generally about the treatment of groups of people (often defined by ethnic or religious identity) within countries.[69]

They have in common that they include some things that are ends in themselves, but many are means to other ends. A common, but not universal, thread is that people must be involved in development processes. The wide variety of goals and practices which are implied by 'participation' are discussed in Chapter 4. However, there are still interventions to impose political systems, including 'democracy', in which participation is minimal. Much of the measurement of political and civic development is at a state or country level. It is about institutions such as parliaments and courts. However, community development is often, in name or in practice, a strategy to create or sustain activities reflecting individual and group aspirations and identities.

Cultural and sustainable development

In the colonial era, the British and other imperial powers saw development as conformity with the metropolitan culture: imposing English or French on education; missionaries introducing Christianity; Western medicine; and clothing and so on. A lot of international aid and foreign investment today is being carried out in the same tradition. However, there were colonial administrators and advisers (often anthropologists by training) who took a more positive view of 'indigenous culture', and the idea of cultural rights and development predates the creation of the UN and the Declaration of Human Rights. The United Nations Education, Scientific and Cultural Organization (UNESCO) was created in 1946. Although education was central to its original creation its current mission is to:

> contribute to the building of peace, the eradication of poverty, sustainable development and intercultural dialogue through education, the sciences, culture, communication and information.

With the objective of:

- Attaining quality education for all and lifelong learning.
- Mobilizing science knowledge and policy for sustainable development.
- Addressing emerging social and ethical challenges.
- Fostering cultural diversity, intercultural dialogue and a culture of peace.
- Building inclusive knowledge societies through information and communication.[70]

Many of UNESCO's concerns are with collective (interpersonal and institutional) rights and development: the education of women and girls, maintaining languages and cultural artefacts, fostering science in the interests of humanity. These have implications at the infrastructural and individual level, so historical buildings and landscapes are 'World Heritage sites' creating rights and obligations for both states and individuals. There have been some attempts to measure the state of culture.[71]

It has been argued by some scholars that cultural development as a goal is not specific to individual states and societies – that it is about the development of values and is connected to levels of economic development.[72] Although this approach may focus on developing emancipation, discussed below and in Chapter 5, it is different in important respects. It implies, both as description and as a desirable end, the goal that societies progress economically, socially and politically, in broadly linear and convergent patterns. I argue that social change is more complex and diverse.

Many states or groups within them have misgivings about cultural rights of minorities or where the interests of 'traditional culture' are seen as impeding goals such as modernisation, economic growth or cohesion. On the other hand, the right to speak a mother-tongue, worship in a particular way or preserve historical sites is frequently asserted as fundamental to identity or self-determination.

Cultural and sustainable rights and development are often closely related. Cultural diversity is seen by UNESCO as both a goal and a means of sustainable development.[73] In 1987 the UN's Brundtland Commission defined the aim of sustainability as *'meeting today's needs without compromising those of future generations'*. This definition was used at the UN Earth Summit in Rio in 1992 but it is not one of the principles agreed at the summit. The first principle of the Summit declaration was that:

> Human beings are at the centre of concerns for sustainable development.

And it says, for example:

> Indigenous people and their communities and other local communities have a vital role in environmental management and development because of their knowledge and traditional practices.

Although it goes on to declare the principle:

> to conserve, protect and restore the health and integrity of the Earth's ecosystem.[74]

It is literally human-centred ('anthropocentric') and implies that humans are either the most or only valuable beings on the planet and that the environment does not necessarily have an intrinsic value but is only valuable insofar as it serves the interests of humans.[75] The idea that humans are superior to all other animals is generally seen as characteristic of the Abrahamic faiths. This view is not shared by all faiths and by some people without religious faith – for example Hinduism, Buddhism and the deep ecology movement – and it is challenged within the Christian, Jewish and Muslim traditions.[76] Although the Declaration mentions the need to protect the poorest people in the world and a number of specific vulnerable groups, it has been criticised for preventing the poorest of the world getting richer in the name of the environment,[77] while not seeking to reduce the standard of living of the richest people in the world. Attempts to overcome this possibility by strategies to promote improving the quality of life of populations without conventional economic growth building on specific cultural traditions include *buen vivir* or *Deep Growth*. Buen vivir emerged in South America. As one of the people who has promoted it, Eduardo Gudynas, has argued it comes out of the tradition of alternatives *to* development rather than alternative developments or post-development and as a post-colonial challenge. It is a cluster of ideas including:

> An ethical principle for development about the harmony or co-habitation of humanity and nature: *'rejecting Western dualism'*.
> A rejection of instrumental or utilitarian ideas of development in favour of something more expressive.
> Highlighting human rights associated with culture and nature.
> Emphasising spiritual as well as or more than material well-being: *'resizing the value of capital'* or *'dematerialization of economies'*. It has an ambivalent relationship to degrowth which Gudynas describes as *'not an objective, but a consequence'*.[78]

There are several potential criticisms (and responses to them) to the buen vivir concept. The concept is vague or abstract. Arguably this is inevitable and not necessarily a fault in any bottom-up movement. It has been pointed out that where it has been used it has been small scale so that in Bolivia and Ecuador it has not made much difference to economies still based on extractive industries which are inconsistent with its principles. Its supporters say it can be scaled up. Part of the point is that it is not meant to be replicated (mass-produced copies) but reproduced (a process in which change occurs). It has been argued that where it has not reduced inequalities or improved the material conditions of the worst off, it is no different from the conventional models of development which it rejects.[79] One response to this is to say: 'Not everything can be done at once.' This may be more than pragmatism in that it is inevitable that programmes or actions will focus on specific issues. It may reflect a goal of tailoring development to the goals of the people most affected. The discussion of different domains is a cue to ask why an initiative has or has not been prioritised. Does it reflect the voices of the most or the least powerful in the situation?

Overarching issues

There are several issues which are relevant to several or all the domains of development discussed above.

The organisation of development

Programmes of development are organised in many ways. They reflect different conceptions of what development is:

- Many are territorial, whether it is whole continents or large numbers of countries – such as within the old British Empire or the World Bank Africa Strategy. It may also be specific to regions within countries or groups of countries such as the European Regional Development Funds or rural areas.
- Initiatives focused on domains (economic, cultural, etc.) or sectors (such as agriculture) or those which are rights- or needs-based (such as housing or education).
- Institutional – designed to change institutions such as strengthening Civil Society Organisations or channelled through particular kinds of institutions, for example schools and colleges or local government.
- Population-focused – targeting, for example, women and girls or specific ethnic, linguistic or religious groups.
- Issue-based – for example, promoting national identity, countering insurgency or terrorism.
- Target/goal-based – such as reducing poverty or illiteracy. It may be couched in terms of 'needs' or 'human rights'.
- Intervention-based – which could be a process such as participation or engagement or a mechanism, for example micro-credit.

All these approaches have been criticised because they generally assume that *all* and *only* the people in a target group need an intervention and can benefit from it, and that the area of intervention is more significant than any other intervention. For example, if you live in the 'wrong' place or your priorities are not the same as those of the promoter of an intervention, you miss out. It is also important to see the connections and disconnections between the different domains and issues. Even without the crude determinism that economic development is necessary for political development and vice versa, change in one without the other may be harder to achieve. Social development, say in the form of education, will often have huge implications for economic and political development.

Hybrid and new measures

There are many measures of development in use. *Gapminder World* uses over 500 measures.[80] The Organisation for Economic Cooperation and Development (OECD) is developing new measures.[81]

Having many and more sophisticated measures does not necessarily address the criticism that the measures fragment or compartmentalise people's lives and frequently express people's lives in terms of the services they receive or that are available – health care rather than health for example.[82]

Focus on specific population groups or areas

There are many attempts to focus development of many kinds on specific population groups that are considered to be particularly vulnerable or a priority, for example women, young people and older people, with indexes to measure the status of the groups.[83]

Most of the measurements use countries as the unit of analysis. However, many countries have specific zones on which they want to focus resources. Historically, in the UK, for instance, this has included Congested Districts in Ireland and Scotland[b] at the end of the nineteenth and start of the twentieth centuries; the Special Areas in England, Scotland and Wales in the 1930s; and Deprived Urban or Inner Urban Areas and Community Development Projects in England in the 1960s and 1970s. The European Economic Community also designated regions within countries in need of Regional Development. In some cases, the interventions have been closely linked to a perceived political threat and data to support such interventions has often (but not always) been collected.[84] Currently, for example, England, Scotland, Wales and Northern Ireland all have Deprivation Indexes which are used for allocation of resources and for measuring the state of areas.[85]

Population and area-based interventions have often been linked to a perceived threat of insurrection or unrest both in the UK and globally. The *Congested Districts* policy in Ireland was described as '*Killing Home Rule with kindness*'[86] and the British Army recommends short- and long-term job creation as a means of pulling away community support from insurgents.[87]

Equality

The argument that population groups or areas get left behind by development can also be analysed in terms of an argument that too much emphasis in development has been on vertical notions of development (states, regions). This approach ignores divisions within societies which means that development may benefit some groups and make no

---

[b] At the end of the nineteenth century. Based on the idea that overpopulation in rural areas was the cause of poverty.

difference to or harm others, often the poorer and less powerful groups. This is discussed further in Chapter 5.[88]

Objectivity and subjectivity

Running through many of the statements of goals and measurement of development are different approaches to what is important.

A starting point is different perceptions of 'truth'. One view is that there is an objective truth about people's well-being measured as what they have or what they need. Another view is that what is important is people's lived experience or subjective hopes or fears. At first this looks like the classic distinction between positivism and interpretivism. However, on closer scrutiny, it is more complicated. We have already seen the value judgements which go into measuring GDP. There are many value judgements in identifying and measuring needs – norms, expressed, comparative as well as felt needs and whose needs?[89] Many of those who think that serious attention should be given to felt needs would question whether they are always justified – being prone to manipulation or the possibility that people mistake what they need. This is discussed further in relation to consciousness in Chapter 5.

The words which are used to describe states of desirable or undesirable outcomes are revealing: *Heaven, Hell, Paradise, Utopia* and *dystopia* are used not only to describe desirable or undesirable environments and conditions but also processes which are the result of human activities. It is important to note that within and between religions there are important differences in belief about whether there is an afterlife and if there is, how an individual 'gets there' (e.g. whether it is preordained, through faith or through works) and what it is like. So, while religious and (broadly) humanist or political prescriptions are often intimately related to, and play a significant role in notions of development, the implications may be very different. If some psychologists and social psychologists discussed in Chapter 4 are right, for example, fear of death may be an important part in motivation to take collective action.[90]

Infrastructural and institutional focus

Perhaps inevitably, descriptions of development goals focus on infrastructural or ideological aims such as *Local and Community Driven Development* which the World Bank is currently promoting. Analysis of interventions concentrates on institutional arrangements: organisations created, money spent. Individuals' and groups' presence is generally evidenced, superficially, with photographs of smiling faces or stories of how programmes have helped individuals. The wider context of lives and aspirations of programme participants in their own voices are less often reported.[91]

The overarching issues need to be borne in mind when considering any type of programme. The chapter now turns to how metaphors can be used to explore the ideologies underpinning different programmes.

Metaphors of development

The development literature is drowned (*sic*) in jargon and acronyms. The same names are used to describe different things and different names are used to describe the same things. It is not possible to provide a static and comprehensive set of descriptions or definitions of different approaches to development. Fortunately, they all use metaphors to describe what they are and what they are trying to do. Critical analysis of these can help us understand the strengths and weaknesses of the approaches. Gareth Morgan, a writer on organisational theory, has identified eight metaphors into which ideas about organisations can be fitted.[92] Metaphors can aid insight. However, it is important to remember that metaphors can close our eyes to alternative perspectives as well as open them. Using a metaphor can lead us to lethal destruction of ourselves or others.[93]

Development as an organism

People have known for millennia that individual animals and plants have changed their size, appearance and abilities, interacting with the environment in which they lived (e.g. sun, water) and what they ate or drank. The idea that societies might develop because of their location, political and economic circumstances was articulated by Ibn Khaldun in the fourteenth century. He saw it in terms of cycles of rising and falling, as political dynasties became more 'sterile'.[94] Medieval Christians saw a process of progress towards a more perfect form. Specifically, they saw the wisdom of earlier religious leaders as providing guidance to succeeding generations: *dwarves perched on the shoulders of others*.[95] The mid-nineteenth century saw the use of the term development applied to both individual organisms and populations: *'the butterfly is the development ... of the grub'* was written in 1845.[96] Charles Darwin saw development in terms of biological evolution. His followers and other writers saw it in terms of social evolution: societies became more advanced. They tended to focus on 'natural selection' – adaptation to environments – the explanation Darwin gave rather than the possibility of 'drift' – chance mutations – or that organisms might shape or choose their environments.

DEVELOPMENT

When Karl Marx died his friend and collaborator Friedrich Engels said:

> Just as Darwin discovered the law of development or organic nature, so Marx discovered the law of development of human history.[97]

Marx had prejudices about 'backward' or 'primitive' people. Many of the contemporary and later European writers, religious leaders and colonial administrators had even more pronounced views. They argued that Western, Christian society was the most developed and that other societies needed to develop along the same lines, thereby justifying colonial rule as a route to 'civilisation'. Although many of the key analysts of development saw the changes as structural rather than simply the result of human action (agency), many interventions were designed to promote development.

One of the leading theorists of Truman's vision of international development described it as *'Evolution not revolution'*.[98] The comparison with biological evolution almost certainly implied the idea of 'survival of the fittest', although biologists, botanists and zoologists have argued that evolution in nature is often about 'survival of the fitting' – a process of adaptation rather than resilience. Many writers on community development have expressed the process and outcome in terms of realising communities' potentialities, nurturing their growth or detoxifying their environments.

The word 'regeneration' has been often used since the late 1980s instead of 'redevelopment' of localities. The word's origins are in the idea of either spiritual rebirth (in Christianity) or the repair of a lost or damaged organ (long before tissue or cells were discovered).[99] It may carry implications of a return to an earlier, better state.

Revolution

The image of revolution in development reflects several metaphors. The original meanings of revolution were the idea of circular movement, particularly associated with the movement of the planets and the sun. Later uses contain the idea of an event with a beginning (though not always an end) and a turning over of an existing order or arrangement. In some contexts, but by no means all, it is associated with conflict or violence.[100] At the infrastructural and institutional levels, the most famous 'development' revolution is probably the Industrial Revolution in Western Europe, starting in the seventeenth century. There are many explanations for it, including specific inventions (effectively a machine metaphor), attributed to individuals through to political and religious movements changing mindsets (overcoming psychological prisons or a power struggle). More recent revolutions such as the Green Revolution, likewise have, often competing, technological, social and political explanations, for example about the motivation, mechanism and impact of introducing high-yielding seed varieties in various countries.[101] At the interpersonal and individual level many events, changes in behaviour or attitudes are described as revolutions. The 'sexual revolution', supposedly starting in the late 1950s in the Global North, is another example of competing explanations: technological (the invention of the contraceptive pill); economic (increased participation of women in the paid workforce); intellectual and social (changing consciousness). The sexual revolution is significant for thinking about development both as a process (was it driven top-down or bottom-up?) and as an outcome (is its significance material, psychological or about health and well-being and education participation?) Is it part of an even wider social change towards identity-based social organisation that also includes age, ethnicity, religion or national identity? This example also highlights that social changes, whether revolution or evolution, do not only happen on one level between rigidly definable dates or places.

All metaphors carry the danger that we are sucked into believing that the human interactions that we are observing really behave as the metaphorical thing does. The complexities of what difference our lived experience, belief systems or intentions make, for example, may not be accounted for. In the case of the organic metaphor a danger may be that it stresses structure over agency: change or inertia is 'inevitable'; the efforts made by individuals or groups are of marginal importance. The organic metaphors which are based on the idea that change is always progress carry specific risks of hiding value judgements behind a pretence or presumption that they are dealing in objective facts or the values they reflect are universal. The poet T. S. Eliot warned that a superficial understanding of evolution can mislead us into thinking that development is a sequence (linear progress) rather than a pattern.[102]

Machine

Writers with diametrically opposed views have used similar machine metaphors. Marx saw societies developing through stages of feudalism, capitalism and socialism. The explicitly anti-Marxist Walter Rostow talked about the Stages of (Economic) Growth with the crucial stage being 'Take Off' – generally understood to be an image of an aircraft taking off.

Several different community development approaches draw on machine metaphors. *Community Planning* and *Asset-Based Community Development* both start from the idea that successful development is about identifying the right resources and using them optimally, implying parts, purpose and a controlling mechanism – the essential elements of a machine. The opposite of asset-based community development – seeing communities in terms of their deficits or failures – sees development as repairing, replacing or adding damaged or missing parts. The idea that a developed society or community is one in which all the parts fit together to produce the most efficient outputs fits into the consensus model of community development.[103]

The machine metaphor implies that there are right and wrong ways of doing things – a technical problem rather than a political one, for example – and that they must happen in a particular order, under specific conditions. This kind of Newtonian Iron Law approach to development does not reflect what happens in the real human world. Social policy analysts are very aware that context is critically important. What works or doesn't work in one place at one time does not necessarily have the same results in another place or at another time.

Culture

Many of the explanations of underdevelopment are rooted (sic) in the political and social environment in which they grow. The image of development as an infectious disease may be seen in this context. Gandhi said:

> Railways, lawyers and doctors have impoverished the country so much so that, if we do not wake up in time we shall be ruined ... They are the carriers of plague germs. Formerly we had natural segregation. Railways have also increased the frequency of famines because, owing to facility of means of locomotion people sell out their grain and it is sent to the dearest markets.[104]

Cultures have often been analysed in terms of superiority and inferiority – labelled as primitive or traditional as opposed to modern; collective versus individualist cultures; materialist-oriented or not.

Superiority and inferiority have often had a religious dimension, that is, whether cultures express or encourage religious values and lifestyles – for example, the idea that the Protestant Ethic encouraged hard work and accumulation of wealth so facilitating capitalism. The language of development interventions is often quite religious – international development programmes are often called Missions and may have an aim of inspiring the copying of other countries or systems.[105] The values need not be religious, as when the basis of development is, for instance, asserted to be human rights.[106] National programmes of development may locate the mechanism of development in values which are said to represent a country's established or desired values: a culture of self-reliance (*Ujamaa*) in Tanzania or Gandhi's concepts of *Swaraj* and *Swadeshi* in India.[107]

The idea that beliefs and behaviour may be more or less useful to certain kinds of development is also central to the functionalist Sociologists and Anthropologists. This also reflects the 'survival of the fittest' version of evolution. Beliefs and behaviour not fit for purpose will be discarded. The idea that population groups are interdependent, part of an (ecological) system needing each other to thrive, underpins pluralist models of community development discussed later in the chapter.

If the machine metaphor puts too little emphasis on context, the danger of the culture metaphor is that it puts too much emphasis on it. As we saw in Chapter 2, if culture is seen as static, homogeneous and constraining, the need and potential for change and diversity may be missed.

Oppression or psychological prison

The idea that culture can be a trap or prison in which people are not free to do or be who they want to be was referred to in the previous chapter. When the image is one of being enslaved by external forces it is often referred to as repression or oppression; when it is an internal or internalised mindset, it is a psychological prison. In relation to international development, the argument is that first the European empires exploited the colonies, denying them economic development and self-determination but also education and self-esteem. Later, the external exploitation was by new forms of imperialism, exercised by the USA (and, in some versions, the Soviet Union and China) or by multilateral institutions such as the World Bank or the International Monetary Fund.

Underdevelopment or dependency is seen by writers such as Andre Gunder Frank not simply as a state but as a deliberate act which is caused by their being a part of a global system rather than an 'other' system, and the solution lies in being independent of the global system rather than more integrated in it.[108] In 1990 the South Commission (chaired by Julius Nyerere of Tanzania) argued that the Global South had been oppressed and the way forward was *'effort of, by, for the people'* and in South–South collaboration.[109]

Antonio Gramsci argued that the state wasn't simply the political and bureaucratic institutions of the state which controlled the way people think and act, but the employers, the religious and educational institutions and many civil society organisations which exercised hegemony.[110]

Writers such as Michel Foucault and Frantz Fanon argued that it is not just at the level of the political, social and economic system that oppression operates, but at the level of group and individual consciousness, particularly in Fanon's case through the concept of internalised oppression.[111] Gramsci and Paulo Freire, with his concept of the oppressed needing to overcome naïve consciousness to develop a critical consciousness, have been influential in developing a theory of community development. In both cases this is probably because they set out methods for escaping from the psychological prisons – ideas that are discussed in Chapter 6. Oppression based on race or ethnicity was central to the analysis of Fanon and Freire. These writers have been criticised for their neglect of gender as a source of oppression, but their ideas have been taken up and extended by feminists.[112]

The problems with the internal or external prison metaphors lie in the perception people have of their situation. People may see themselves as free or in solitary confinement or enduring a life sentence, but an observer may see their situation differently. To decide when and what sort of intervention is legitimate to free people there must be some principles and mechanisms. These are discussed in Chapters 5 and 6.

Political system

The political system metaphor applies to any conception of 'them' and 'us' in competition or contest. In relation to international development there have been many such divisions. They include East (Oriental) and West, North and South, Believer and Infidel (or *Kofer* or *Kafir*), Communist or Capitalist, or Free World and so on. When Truman launched the Point Four programme he talked about a programme for the 'free peoples' of the world, as opposed to the 'Peace loving Peoples' – which included the communist countries as Allies in World War II. The subtitle of Rostow's book on the stages of growth was: '*A non-Communist Manifesto*'.[113]

'Third World' was widely used between 1952 (when the term was coined) and 1989 (when the Berlin Wall came down). The First World was used to mean the capitalist, industrialised West; the Second World, the Communist bloc; and the Third World, everywhere else.[114] After 1989 some influential Western theorists in particular argued that the West had won, history was over.[115] Others argued that there would be a clash of civilisations – 'the West versus the Rest'.[116] Although the idea of a multipolar world predates the fall of the Wall, it took on new significance then.[117] The concepts of the Global North and South have their origins in the Brundtland Commission of 1980.[118]

Within countries, it is common to see communities polarised into parties or tribes, with the less powerful or well-regarded 'other' being labelled 'backward', 'traditional', deficient in skills and resources, in need of development. The more powerful group is characterised, by its opponents, as only self-interested and callous, usually in need of abolition or replacement rather than development. There are many examples of a 'conflict' model of community development. The most well known of these are probably Saul Alinsky's *Community Organising* and *Community Action* models. Alinsky divided people into 'Haves' and 'Have-Nots' and proposed broad-based alliances or coalitions to challenge powerful interests. The Community Action model has frequently been used to describe the struggle of the working class, but it is also applied to Black or White people or men and women, landlords and tenants or consumers and producers.[119]

In the next chapter we consider social and community development as collective action used both to strengthen and to challenge or resist the state. When it is used to challenge the state the question arises of what methods are legitimate (e.g. violence, coercion, non-violent direct action)? Here we highlight one specific form of development on a *Them* and *Us* model: counter-insurgency. States (domestic or foreign interventions) use social and community development to win control over or isolate people they regard as illegitimate. The British Army has used community development in various places, including Northern Ireland.[120] The current US Government Counter Insurgency manuals say:

> A wedge may ... be created through the use of carrot (political, economic & development benefits) and stick (detention & disruption) operations.[121]

The operational manual talks about the importance for engagement by Education, Empowerment and Participation, and goes on to say:

> Some of the Best Weapons for Counterinsurgents Do Not Shoot ... dollars and ballots may have more important effects than bombs and bullets.[122]

The British Army counter-insurgency manual misquotes the American manual to make it even blunter:

> The Best Weapons for Counterinsurgency Do Not Shoot.[123]

There are several dangers in a binary approach. It homogenises both 'us' and 'them'. It may assume that social or community values, needs and behaviour are all the same which can be seriously misleading in any kind of development programme. It can also lead to a simplistic blame/

blame avoidance game. In 1985, the organisation *Médecins Sans Frontières* and its sister organisation *Liberté Sans Frontières*, criticised *Third Worldism,* an attitude which blamed the West for looting the Third World and defended despotic regimes in the Third World but itself promoted the (Manichean) idea that doctors are always good, and they can legitimately challenge or bypass anyone they think is doing something wrong or not doing the right thing. Edward Said questioned their position, pointing out that whereas many people (in the Global South) had denounced despots and dictators, the North was complicit in supporting many of them.[124] Northern leaders still blame southern leaders for corruption while protecting businesses which pay bribes, and overlooking abuses by allies.[125]

Brain, flux and transformation

Gareth Morgan uses 'Brain' as shorthand for metaphors which refer to the collective action of many autonomous elements such as brain cells or digits in a computer program, drops in an ocean or snowflakes in an avalanche. They are of course all examples of other metaphors – organs, machines and cultures – which is a little confusing. However, the idea that human development comes about because a lot of individual decisions are made, and they lead to big social changes, is an important insight. Decisions to move from a village to a city, to send a child to school or out to work, to vote or not vote in an election may all be personal ones but when aggregated they may have more impact than institutional or macro-level decisions on aid or investment.

In relation to development, it is often closely connected to '*Flux and Transformation*'. This refers to a metaphor, usually attributed to Heraclitus about 500 BCE. It was the idea that 'you can never step into the same river twice' – the water is always changing, that is what makes it a river rather than a lake or a dried-up riverbed. It is the nature of rivers or fires that they are ever-changing and capable of transformation and it is similar with individual humans who can be asleep or awake, young or old, alive or dead. Apparent opposites are actually part of a whole, and the whole is more than the sum of its parts. However, the whole may have opposite consequences for different organisms for example:

> Sea is the purest and most polluted water: for fish drinkable and healthy, for men undrinkable and harmful.[126]

The conception highlights the idea that living systems have emergent properties – the possibility of change. The idea is taken up in relation to development, suggesting that all societies and communities have potential (or immanent properties) for transformation. Development may not be deliberate; it may emerge unexpectedly. 'Emergence' and 'emergency' have the same root. Also, what is a good for some people may be bad for others.

It is probably no accident that the community development programme of work called *Training for Transformation* is described, in terms recalling Heraclitus, by one of its founders as:

> a great river originating in a number of different springs.[127]

Critical to both the brain and flux and transformation conceptions is that there is no single element which controls or directs the others: it is self-organising. In the section below on development strategies, we consider some of the bottom-up or inside-out strategies which have been proposed or used. Here the point is a more general one that people combine voluntarily, often spontaneously and informally. The impact may be on any of the levels described in Chapter 2.

In recent years a lot of attention has been given to the idea that (electronic) social media can be used not only to organise collective action but also as a process of development, such as e-petitions to government or crowdfunding initiatives and also to define the goals of development, such as deciding on a community's or society's priorities outside elections of representatives or referenda or even older methods such as Opinion Polls or Focus Groups. Networks and *Meshworks* are seen as forms of organisation which facilitate this way of working.[128] This is further explored in Chapter 4.

This metaphor appeals particularly to libertarians of both the left and right who see problems with the state or with the concentration of decision-making in the hands of big corporations. Critics highlight the difficulties in challenging the state or capitalism, or argue for the legitimacy of either representative democracy or property rights. There are concerns that the people able to organise through electronic media, or able to collect and analyse massive numbers of individual decisions (algorithms based on Big Data and Artificial Intelligence), are the most privileged and powerful.

Each of the metaphors gives an insight into what development might be for and how it 'works'. Use of the metaphors draws out ideas of how advocates of the different approaches think the world should change. It helps cut through some of the jargon and covering up of what is really intended. Being aware of the paradigm a development programme is in helps identify what questions to ask, what it might be emphasising or neglecting. However, to repeat the earlier health warnings: metaphors should not be taken literally – otherwise you can drown in them, get run over by them or be defeated by them, and so on!

Development strategies

Before concluding this chapter, I offer an overview of some of the terms which different institutions and writers have used to describe different strategies of development.

Vertical and horizontal strategies

Development strategies have been variously described as top-down or trickle-down, bottom-up, centre-periphery or peer-to-peer. The original logic of 'top-down' development in the 1950s was that urban, industrialised and modernised agriculture would create greater returns or surpluses which could be redistributed to poorer communities. Although economic in rationale, the political and social implications of prioritising an urban elite were clear. The phrase *'Development from Below'* was certainly used as early as 1961 by Ursula Hicks and adopted by Jawaharlal Nehru, Prime Minister of India. It included agricultural development, a prominent role for local government and village development albeit in a state-led centrally planned economy. Nehru explicitly talked about community development and about the importance of India's diverse tribes not losing their distinct identity. In the mid-1970s there was a fresh critique of top-down and state-led development from the right (favouring market-led changes) and the left (noting that states were the captives of a global capitalist system dominated by the rich of the rich countries). A dissociation of the poor from dominant institutions who extracted value from the poor was seen as necessary by critics of underdevelopment and skewed development. The chain of causation was generally that economic autonomy would lead to political autonomy. Frequently the mechanism for such bottom-up interventions has been non-governmental organisations (NGOs) promoting small farmers and microbusinesses using microcredit or rotating small loans. The *Grameen Bank* and *Proshika* initiatives in Bangladesh (and arguably BRAC, the largest NGO in the world) and the Self-Employed Women's Association (SEWA) in India represent these traditions.[129]

Perhaps counter-intuitively, simply because a programme is described as 'community development' it does not mean that it is as bottom-up or peer-to-peer as one might expect. We have seen how colonial officials directed international and national programmes of community development.

The notion of peer-to-peer development was also given impetus, as was suggested earlier, by the South Commission, in 1990, chaired by Julius Nyerere. It is often said that the pattern of development assistance has shifted from the Global North to countries such as the BRICS (Brazil, Russia, India, China and South Africa) or the oil-producing countries. Patterns of bilateral and multi-lateral aid, remittances and foreign direct investment (FDI) all need to be included on the donor side. On the recipient side, which countries and what sort of projects or sectors are funded need to be considered. Also, the money raised from national taxation and government revenues needs to be taken account.

Taking Africa as an example, the picture is complicated. Official remittances (unofficial remittances are extremely important too) account for one-third of international flows, more than FDI and Official Development Aid. Nigeria and Egypt are the destinations of the bulk of official remittances. In relation to FDI, in the financial year 2013/14, the leading investors were the United Arab Emirates (USD 45.6 billion), France (USD 21 billion), the USA (USD 10.7 billion), Greece (USD 10 billion, concentrated in Egypt), the UK (USD 6.9 billion) and Belgium (USD 5.2 billion). European countries accounted for 41% of FDI to Africa. The majority of FDI goes to 'resource-rich' countries – to oil, gas, metals and agribusiness.[130]

Community-driven development

The World Bank argues that poor men and women can effectively organise to identify community priorities and that this is an important element of an effective poverty reduction and sustainable development strategy. They call this *Community Driven Development* (CDD). It is couched in terms of demand-responsiveness, greater downward accountability, and enhanced local capacity. In other words, the poor are consumers who lack information, capacity and resources to whom governments and other institutions are accountable. Its advocates claim that it 'empowers' communities in a way that 'community-based' strategies do not.[131]

Community-led local development

Within the European Union there is a similar concept – *Community Led Local Development* – which makes funds available through Local Action Groups which are defined as groups of representatives of:

> local public and private socio-economic interests, such as entrepreneurs and their associations, local authorities, neighbourhood or rural associations, groups of citizens (such as minorities, senior citizens, women/men, youth, entrepreneurs, etc.), community and voluntary organisations, etc. At least 50% of the votes in selection decisions should be cast by partners which are not public authorities and no single interest group should have more than 49% of the votes.

Assets-Based Community Development (ABCD) or meeting needs

The concept of *Assets-Based Community Development* was briefly discussed in relation to the machine metaphor above. It is also in a tradition of individual and social psychology which argues that strong self-esteem and a sense of efficacy or agency are necessary for people to want to act. It contrasts with strategies that are based on outside resources filling an empty 'basket' with necessities. Critics note that the ability to act through ABCD may be constrained by economic and social circumstances.

Capacity building

When development strategies talk about 'capacity building' the model is frequently one of a knowledge or skills deficit which is to be reduced or eliminated by the knowledge and wisdom of the teacher. In some places what is called Community Development is in other places called Informal or Community Education. An alternative model of stimulating independent thought or critical consciousness is discussed further in Chapter 6.

Sticks, carrots and 'throffers'

Many academic writers would resist the notion that development is to be imposed by force but there is clearly a tradition, in practice, of precisely that. Examples would include the Highland Clearances in Scotland, the collectivisation of Soviet Agriculture and the *Great Leap Forward* in China.[132] The use of incentives to promote development is common to most development strategies. Often it is money but food-for-work or education, subsidised land, premises or materials are also used. The term *Throffer* was coined in the 1970s (inspired on the *Godfather* film: 'I'm gonna make him an offer he can't refuse') in which an offer contains both a benefit from compliance and a penalty for non-compliance. Many development strategies contain throffers.[133]

Theories of change

In an article written in 1969, Harry Specht identified four tactics for achieving planned social change.[134]

Specht identified four perceptions of what change is Rearrangements of resources which could be achieved by collaborative consensus. This has come to be called the Consensus model Redistribution of resources by campaigning to do so – this has come to be called the Pluralist model Relationship change: a redistribution of power which involves disruption and contest – the Conflict model Reconstruction of, or overthrowing, the whole system which may involve violence-Insurrection.

He rightly pointed out that one person or party's rearrangement may be someone else's redistribution, or someone's campaign is another person's insurrection. Specht's categorisation was taken up by the British Community Development Projects (CDPs) but without the Reconstruction/Insurrection/Violence option and adding the idea of different levels (Table 3.1).[135]

These levels are similar to three out of the four levels identified in Chapter 2. The fourth level is reflected in the work of Peter Westoby, John Paul Lederach and others who recognise the importance of personal consciousness and relationships as starting points for both conflict and collective action.[136] This is discussed further in Chapter 4.

The four models remain very influential.

Consensus

The consensus model is based on the idea that different groups and individuals, globally, nationally and locally are not fundamentally at odds with each other. There are no fundamental divisions of ideology or interests which divide them. It may be reflected in slogans such as

Table 3.1 CDPs' strategies for social change and levels

Basic Assumptions Level	Consensus	Pluralism	Structural Conflict
National	Social Planning	National Lobby	National Pressure
Local	Organisational and Service Development	Local Lobby	Local Pressure
Grass-roots	'Traditional' Community Community Development	Community Organisation	Community Action

Source: CDP Inter-Project Report (1974)

'*One World*', '*One Nation*', '*One Race, the Human Race*' or '*We are all in this Together*'. Clearly the critique implied by the other models is that this is not the case. However, in terms of understanding consensus as a strategy for development, there is another critique of it which is that it is based on the idea of a technical model of transferring ideas, institutions, technology from one context to another – one size fits all. Lederach argues that knowledge or technology transfer undermines knowledge that is rooted in societies and communities – indigenous development.[137] The consensus model is most associated with the Planning and Partnership approaches to social and community development. The appeal and ambiguity of the model is demonstrated by the fact that, for instance, 'One Nation' is both the name of an international humanitarian organisation inspired by Muslim ethics and an Australian Nationalist political party which is anti-Islam.[138]

Pluralist/difference

The pluralist model in political theory, is often only associated with the idea that people organise in interest groups which bargain or negotiate with each other.[139] However, the idea of plural societies has its origins particularly in colonial societies which were not only heterogeneous but unequal.[140] Some scholars have focused on the diversity element and argued that federal or consociational structures can hold societies or associations of countries together and enable development.[141] However, others have said that the issue is either that many plural societies are segmented or stratified. They argue that either differences need to be dissolved, or, in the case of the 'holism' theories of Jan Smuts, the South African general and politician, segregation of unequal groups, legitimised as 'differential development'.[142] This underlines the problems with an approach which assumes that though there are differences between individuals and groups, they are not caused by conflicts of power or resources and do not need to be resolved through structural change. Harold DeRienzo says it is a 'static enhancement model.' It 'reinforces current power relationships, seeking only to enhance the capacity of individuals to deal more effectively with prevailing circumstances'.[143]

Conflict/dissensus

The conflict model sees that the social, economic and political structural circumstances play an important part in relationships. Many proponents would argue that the relationships are often violent but that they can be transformed without violence. This reflects a widely used distinction between conflict and violence. Conflict refers to incompatible goals or behaviour. The conflict may be open or latent and it may be at the surface (when goals are compatible but behaviour is not) or more deep-seated (when goals and behaviour are incompatible). Behaviour and goals are not limited to people: institutions including states, systems (such as markets) and ideas (e.g. freedom of expression versus freedom from fear) can be in conflict. Conflict can be creative, positive, desirable and necessary. The field of *Conflict Transformation* (or less commonly *Conflict Management* or *Conflict Resolution*) is concerned with the transformation of violence into conflict.[144]

Conflicts (and violence) can be both vertical (dominant and subordinate states or social groups) or horizontal/lateral (relations within social groups and between individuals). The political theory most widely associated with conflict as a basis of organising social and community development is probably that of Antonio Gramsci.[145]

Violence/insurrection

While mainstream advocates of social and community development have ruled out violence as strategy or tactic, it has been in the background in both theory and practice. In practice, social and community development interact with violence in very significant ways:

- Social and community development has been used as a tool of fighting forces by both established regimes and their opponents in order either to win support for themselves or to undermine support for their opponents. Examples were given earlier in this chapter in relation to counter-insurgency.
- Governments have used the giving and withholding of social and community development funds to isolate groups using (or perceived to be using) violence.

Social and community workers working in violent situations cannot ignore violence. They may be directly trying to address the causes or consequences of violence or simply trying to do everyday things, taking into account and trying to mitigate the risks of violence.

This model sees violence as inherent in social relations and that violence plays a part in changing those relations. There are a number of authors who are associated with the idea that violent overthrow of existing structures is necessary and legitimate, but perhaps the authors most associated with it as a strategy of community and social development through identity-based groups or 'new social movements' are Frantz Fanon, Herbert Marcuse and, more recently, Arundhati Roy.[146] Fanon argued that non-violent intervention simply maintains – and, even worse, perpetuates – violence. He suggested that the independence struggle in India, the civil rights movement in the USA, and the anti-apartheid movement in South Africa are considered 'non-violent' because only very small numbers of the oppressors were killed but they were violent because of the large numbers of oppressed people killed in those conflicts.[147] Marcuse later revised his views to promote *'the long march through the institutions'* and the development of *'counter-institutions'*. His basic argument was that democracy was an illusion for most people and that they had no voice. While he opposed the violence of the established society, he supported violence to overthrow it.[148] Clearly, 'established society' and states which see themselves as legitimately governing, for example because they were elected, generally disagree with Marcuse's position but so do critics of violence who see it as an ineffective tactic or simply morally wrong.

A detailed discussion of violence as a strategy for change is beyond the scope of this book but the key points are:

➢ There are many different kinds of violence. It is not only individual and collective acts, but it can be a pattern of behaviour or a system (institutional behaviour) which predictably, but often not intentionally, inflicts harm or injury.[149]

➢ There are at least three potential kinds of argument for and against using violence in social and community development:

  ➢ Whether it is morally justified or not

  ➢ Whether it is an effective means to the desired ends

  ➢ Whether it is a productive or counter-productive part of being an activist or paid development worker. Supporting a political party or declaring the superiority of one religious belief over another may be harmful or beneficial to development. Similar arguments could be made in relation to violence.

That being said, I would argue that it is not advocates of non-violent social change who are naïve, relying on the optimism of the will, but rather that those who see violence as a solution are ignoring the evidence of the intellect:

➢ *The effectiveness of violence is exaggerated, if not invented.* Violent conflicts more often end in stalemate than one side winning.[150] If one side does win...

- *Violence does not end violence.* The 'Win-Lose' dynamic of violence is the source of problems rather than a solution. Even if there is 'victory', the grievances arising from the violence or desire for revenge for defeat may mean a resumption of violence but also conflict is rarely binary with right and winners all on one side, wrong and losers all on the other. For both victims and veterans, the scars often outlast the wounds. Ironically, this is abundantly clear from Fanon's own writings as a psychiatrist.[151]

- *The people who lose most are often the least powerful.*[152] This is reflected in the African proverb: '*When elephants fight/mate, it is the grass that is crushed.*'[153] This also reflects the fact that…

- *Violence is not limited to those who have chosen it.* Whether we are talking about gang violence, civil or international wars, distinctions between civilians and combatants are unclear with conscripts, including child soldiers, human shields, 'collateral damage' from deliberate aggression and also the catastrophic effects of violence on physical and mental health.[154]

Conclusions

It is tempting to say that the meanings of development are so diverse and contradictory that the word should either be ignored or not used. Certainly, attempts to come with inclusive definitions or descriptions all risk either being bland or excluding significant ideas.

Gilbert Rist says development is characterised by:

- Direction
- Continuity
- Cumulativeness
- Irreversibility.[155]

Although the idea that it is a deliberate, planned and linear activity has some appeal, an important part of the process of development is often that it is spontaneous or at least not centrally planned. It may be cyclical, or going forward in one area may be accompanied by going backwards or standing still in another.

As well as being both a process or a method and a goal or outcome, it is other things too. It is an ideology. It is a programme or a mechanism.

The example of counter-insurgency highlights that it is problematic to simply look at development as a process independent of context and outcomes or look at means without looking at ends: one person's development is another person's destruction.

> **Box 3.1 Implications for practice and activities**
>
> A process for arriving at what development means in any specific context might include:
>
> 1. Identify the range of ideas people have about what development is or might be – using metaphors, for instance. This involves listening to people in groups. It is important to segment into different groups, the people with an interest in a situation ('the stakeholders'). This is necessary for the differences to become clear between funders and planners, operators or intended or would-be participants (reflecting their diversity too).
>
> 2. Look at the historical context of what development has meant. For example, are there colonial, anti-colonial and post-colonial traditions which are relevant? This might be done through collecting oral histories or a transect walk.[a]
>
> 3. Identify whether the programmes being considered are international, national or local?
>
> 4. Analyse how people's aspirations or needs are related to broad ideas of human rights (Social, Economic, Political, Civic, Cultural, Sustainable). The kinds of groups identified under step 1 above might be used but using the kinds of 'expressive learning' methods to be discussed in Chapter 6.
>
> 5. Identify whether there is an overall strategy such as 'top-down' or 'bottom-up'?
>
> 6. Identify what level(s) of social relations development is addressing (Ideological, Institutional, Interpersonal or Individual). See the comments about groups in step 4 above.
>
> 7. Consider what theory of change is involved (Consensus, Pluralist, Conflict, Violence). See the comments about groups in step 4 above.
>
> 8. Identify whether there is any choice or prescription of a vehicle or organisation for a programme?
>
> This last question is the starting point for the next chapter on collective action. Later chapters highlight the place of equality and justice in development and how learning plays a central part as a goal and as part of the process.
>
> ---
>
> [a] For example Keller, S. (2018) 'Transect Walk' Toolbox Sustainable Sanitation and Water Management https://www.sswm.info/humanitarian-crises/urban-settings/planning-process-tools/exploring-tools/transect-walk Accessed 28 July 2018

4
Collective Action

Of cabbages and kings

Theorists and practitioners of social and community development say that collective action is very important.[1] However, they are clearly not always talking about the same thing. People act together in all sorts of ways. A family might collaborate to grow vegetables in a garden, smallholding or farm. In World War II the British royal family dug up some of their ornamental gardens to grow vegetables: 'Digging for Victory'. In the early years of the twentieth century and between the wars, allotments were promoted as a measure to help unemployed men and as a form of socialism. In the twenty-first century they have been encouraged to improve mental health and community cohesion. People might club together to buy fruit and vegetables or go to a food bank and receive free food. Even in what might seem to be the direst of situations – such as in a refugee camp – people cooperate to grow flowers and vegetables.[2] These activities are called self-interest, self-help, mutual aid, volunteering, philanthropy, altruism or just living. The terminology may not be important but there are significant questions about:

- Whether all forms of collective action are equally legitimate and valuable?
- Whether they are all effective in the same ways?
- What facilitates or impairs collective action?

This chapter argues that we need to use many perspectives rather than any single one to foster desirable action or stop undesirable action. The perspectives come from different academic disciplines and by looking at actions on the four levels introduced in the previous chapters.

Multi-disciplinary perspectives on action

Many of the differences in views about why people act or not reflect different units of analysis and intellectual approaches. As with the discussion about development in the previous chapter, the differences could have been explored using metaphors. For example, people talk about collective action as a journey in a vehicle, snowflakes causing an avalanche or fruit ripe for picking. Some of these will be mentioned, but for a systematic analysis Gareth Morgan's work provides an introduction.[3]

Philosophers talk about Free Will and Determinism[4] – whether people have the freedom to act at the individual level. Theologians in the Abrahamic traditions talk about Theism, predestination or *qadar* in Arabic – the idea that God created the world and continues to be responsible for everything which happens in it – or Deism in which God is responsible for Creation but not subsequent events.[5] Those are both explanations at the ideological (theological) level though theologians may also use similar language to philosophers. Different interpretations of the concepts are not esoteric debates but raise vital (or fatal) questions about rights, responsibilities and duties among Muslims, Jews and Christians.[6]

Different schools within History focus on the influence on events of materialism (social and economic conditions), intentional action by people (ideas playing an important part) or accidents and blunders (contingency, the unforeseen and unknown being important). The sociologist and historian Philip Abrams argued that action is influenced by institutions (rules, expectations) but institutions are changed by action.[7]

The sociologist Max Weber differentiated between action which was instrumental or goal-oriented (interests) and actions which were based on values (ideas). He argued that the interaction between interests and ideas was that ideas were like the railway signal operator (the 'Switchman') who switches the track on which the train runs (the train being the interests with an energy of its own).[8]

Other sociologists have explained choices in terms of their usefulness to the decision-taker (conscious or not) or society – *Functionalism*. Yet more sociologists talk about *Agency* when action reflects deliberate choices that people make. The alternative approach is that our behaviour is determined by forces that we do not control: *Structure*. The middle way is that our intentions or beliefs have some influence but there is an underlying determinism which may come from economic, social forces or biological (including physiological and biological) drivers. This is called *Structuration* or ways in which decisions are shaped by the context, including other people's behaviour – *Habitus*.[9]

Psychologists have several different perspectives on action:[10]

- Motivation based on needs (biological), drives (such as a state of arousal) or incentives (a negative or positive push).
- Whether people believe their actions influence outcomes ('locus of control'; 'self-efficacy').
- How people learn behaviour (e.g. observational learning).
- How decisions are made: a mixture of rational, non-rational and 'short-cut' methods. There is increasing convergence between Psychology and Economics in the field of Behavioural Economics.[11]

Jim Orford, a Community Psychologist, is critical of Psychology for being too individualistic and (following Willem Doise) has proposed a four-level model of theory and interventions very similar to that introduced in Chapter 2.[12]

In the following sections we will explore what different disciplines, including Economics, Biology and Social Psychology, have to say about the science behind collective action specifically.

Why individuals act

There are two main contrasting approaches to analysis of why individuals do or don't act: they must or they choose to. A 'third way' combines these.

Action, agency and actors

The sociologist Margaret Archer (and the philosopher Roy Bhaskar) do not think people have innate human natures, nor that they are passive victims programmed by social structures – constraints and *'enablements'* (enablers). Archer suggests they respond and act according to certain patterns. They argue that structure and agency can both be 'causal' factors in change but on different timescales and that culture needs to be considered as a separate variable. Archer suggests that the relationship between structure, culture and agency is a process of conditioning, interaction, reflexivity and elaboration. Archer's concept of the *internal conversation* is a very important starting point for agency challenging and transforming constraining structure. She suggests that the internal conversation is not a psychological faculty but a property which we all have through our relationship with the exterior world. We all have the potential to see ourselves differently through internal conversation, so it is an *'emergent property'*. Archer says that everybody has Agency but not everyone can be an Actor – some people may not have the opportunity. Martha Nussbaum and Amartya Sen use *'capability'* to refer to the opportunities and the constraints which enable or prevent or penalise individuals exercising choice (discussed further in Chapter 5). Archer distinguishes between primary agents which are collectivities sharing the same life chances and corporate agents which have articulated their aim and developed some form of organisation to pursue them. Primary agents have the internal conversations just with themselves; corporate agents pool their deliberations.[13] So, in Archer's conceptualisation, some people are more collective than others in deciding whether to act or not. They decide more or less self-consciously.

The question of how much control individuals have is often expressed in analogies of forced and restricted choice: a fork in a path or road, one of which must be taken; or making a choice to play a card in a game, based on the hand of playing cards that you have been dealt. The metaphor for freedom of choice is the apparently unlimited choice fish in the sea have. However, they are undoubtedly constrained by food sources, water temperature and predators, for example. Anthony Giddens' idea of structuration, rejected by Archer, merges structure and agency. It can be explained through another organic metaphor: the environment is critical to action – plants need roots, nutrients, sunshine and rain to grow. Napoleon described the relationship between background conditions and the right time to stage events as when *'the pear was ripe'*.[14] Che Guevara, on the other hand, said:

> The revolution is not an apple that falls when it is ripe. You have to make it drop.[15]

These analogies and metaphors are a little simplistic but give the general idea. Karl Marx expressed the relationship between intentional action and context thus:

> Men make their own history, but they do not make it as they please; they do not make it under self-selected circumstances, but under circumstances existing already, given and transmitted from the past. The tradition of all dead generations weighs like a nightmare on the brains of the living.[16]

These analyses highlight that the distinction between individual action and collective action is not a rigid one – action takes place in the context of relationships.

Why do people act together?

Just as at the individual level there are two major competing explanations of why people act at the interpersonal and institutional level: self-interest and altruism. Within each of those explanations theorists argue that they lead to cooperation or conflict. Collective action out of self-interest especially, but also altruism, has been seen as rational behaviour. Viewing behaviour as rational has been questioned by psychologists and, more recently, by behavioural economists.

Explanations from nature

The natural world provides inspiration for many ideas about the value of cooperation. However, the natural environment is not necessarily a guide to how humans behave. Drops in the ocean, snowflakes and avalanches are all cited as examples of how there is strength in numbers, even if they do not have minds to reason. Even a casual observation of a flock of birds or a herd of animals stimulates thoughts about whether, why or how they are cooperating or competing and what part reason or instinct plays.

Charles Darwin is often remembered for something that he didn't originally say, and when he did use the concept, he didn't necessarily mean it in the way that it is often interpreted! This is the idea of the *Survival of the Fittest*. The phrase was originally used by Herbert Spencer to describe Darwin's theory of Natural Selection. It is often interpreted as meaning that competition is necessary for survival. Some of Darwin's successors have argued that, in biology, pursuit of individual self-interest by organisms is essential to surviving and thriving. Whether change happens at an individual organism level, at a group level or at a sub-individual level has been debated over a long time. There have been arguments about whether behaviour is innate or learned and the relative importance of 'nature' and 'nurture'. Understanding the behaviour of groups of animals was studied initially as Ethology and later as Behavioural Ecology.[17] Sociobiologists have argued that human societies functioned and evolved in similar ways to individual organisms and groups of animals. These ideas have also been taken down a level from organisms to genes in the idea of the *Selfish Gene*.[18] However, the idea that competition has been the organising principle in biological evolution has been challenged since the earliest development of the theory (including by Darwin himself, who gave a more balanced account). Peter Kropotkin argued that *Mutual Aid* was the organising principle of evolution.[19] Edward O. Wilson originally argued that apparently altruistic acts in nature were for individual self-interest. Later, he came to the view that they developed for the good of the population or community and that cooperation confers evolutionary advantage.[20] Two interesting refinements of the biological model are those of Robin Dunbar and Yuval Noah Harari. Dunbar's work suggests there is an optimal maximum number of people we can cooperate with. Based partly on studies of primates, he argues that the maximum number of people with whom we can feel affinity or trust is 150.[21] Harari has argued that *how* we cooperate is to invent 'stories'. For example, by believing that paper, metal or plastic 'money' is valuable, exchange can be made easier and that conveys advantages to the cooperators.[22]

Economics

Just as Biology and Zoology are divided between scientists who believe that the natural state is cooperation and those who think it is competition, so too is Economics. Fundamentally Economics is the study of mechanisms for producing, distributing and consuming scarce resources. Much attention is given to markets and how value is created and measured. However, markets are not the only means of exchange (barter is another form of exchange) but other economic systems exist too: self-sufficiency (producing what you use); gifts; or an agency which organises production and collects and distributes resources (today, typically the state, but faith organisations, trade unions and groups based on ethnicity, clans, tribes and kin have also organised resource allocation) and still do in many parts of the world.[23] Even apparently individualist systems such as the market may be underpinned by concepts of collective action. Although the thesis is challenged, Max Weber argued that the roots of capitalism lie in Protestant (Calvinist, specifically) religious belief.[24] Other religious traditions also impact on economic organisation, including the idea that all resources are divinely created. Recent work in Economics has explored the revival or extension of economies not based on markets or state planning.[25]

Markets

The underpinning idea of markets is that we are (primarily or exclusively) motivated by the desire for wealth and that we behave rationally to maximise our material benefits – *Homo economicus*. On sellers, back in the eighteenth century, Adam Smith famously said:

> It is not from the benevolence of the butcher, the brewer, or the baker that we expect our dinner, but from their regard to their own interest.[26]

This has been taken by many, but not all, of his successors to mean that the pursuit of individual self-interest is in the common interest. In its crudest form, it is the idea that 'greed is good'.[27]

Markets are not homogeneous. They embrace global and impersonal institutions – some not even operated by humans, for example computer algorithms buying or selling stocks and shares. Other markets involve much more personal interactions between makers and users of goods and services. New forms of market are emerging. Proponents use terms such as *crowdfunding*, *peer-to-peer lending* or the *Shared Economy*. Other analysts use terms such as the *gig economy* or the *platform economy*, but whatever they are called, they are now a substantial part of some economies used, for instance, to offer or find taxis, accommodation, trades people or life partners.[28]

The common assumptions are that the world is divided into buyers and sellers. Consumers want more for less. Producers want to sell as much as possible for the best price. Platforms may match producers to consumers (ride hailing) or consumers to consumers (ride sharing or dating). Political philosophers have taken it further to argue that markets are a means to political democracy. Voting is buying a policy or point of view.

It has been argued that markets are the only, or most effective, means of improving the condition of poorest and promoting equality (selling goods and services to all; opportunity based on ability not arbitrary discrimination).[29] Gérald Berthoud argues that the market itself is a form of collective action:

> An aggregate of strangers willing to exchange with each other for their mutual advantage ... a form of exchange in which personal relationships are minimised.[30]

Gary Becker claims that:

> the economic approach is a comprehensive one that is applicable to all human behaviour.[31]

Becker won the Nobel Prize for Economics for extending economic analysis to a very wide range of human behaviour. He proposed market mechanisms for areas such as tackling discrimination, crime, family relationships and organ donation. He believed that people make rational decisions about the costs and benefits in all these areas, and that by altering the costs and benefits behaviour can be changed.[32]

Becker's ideas have been taken up as part of the neoliberal project since the 1980s. Neoliberalism has been both an economic and political programme. The economic programme has been one of *structural adjustment* – reducing state intervention; introducing market mechanisms to areas where they had previously (or not recently) existed in health, education, welfare, justice, the environment; and growth without redistribution. The political programme is one where self-help rather than state support is both necessary and desirable to overcome a perceived risk of 'dependency'. Social and community development has been seen by many of its promoters as creating conditions for the development of markets.[33] Other people and movements have proposed changes to the way in which markets can work to promote social goods such as *'philanthropy at 5%', Social Impact* and *Development Bonds* and sustainability through the *Circular Economy*.[34]

The arguments for markets have been challenged from several points of view. Back in the nineteenth century John Stuart Mill argued that, as buyers, we also want leisure and to consume *'costly indulgences'*. There is much evidence that markets do not help the poorest and reinforce inequalities.[35] Analysis of discrimination shows that it is generally non-rational but also that rewards and punishment are ineffective and inappropriate (see Chapter 5). Behavioural Economics suggests many decisions are not strictly rational, but the choices people make reflect the way they make decisions.[36] Among the insights from behavioural economics are that:

- People often prioritise short-term gains over long-term losses or rewards – So people don't save for when they are older or think about the long-term consequences of health-harming behaviour. There is some evidence that more disadvantaged groups prioritise the present more. The process is called *Hyperbolic Discounting*.
- How a choice is framed is critical – For example, people dislike losses even more than they like gains. This is *Framing*.
- *Inertia* – People often choose the default or easy option.[37]

Qualified reasoning

A refinement of theories which suggest that economics determines cooperation or competition identifies conditions in which one or the other happens but that interests are not 'objective facts' but social constructions.

Resource mobilisation theory predicts that collective action only takes place when structures and relationships make it possible and advantageous to do so. Critics have argued that interests are a social construction. How are priorities or preferences formed? The critics' answer is – often – through identity. It is also possible to have action without organisation or strategy and organisation and strategy without action. The contrast between resource mobilisation theory and identity-based theory is a classic example of the debate about whether action is instrumental or expressive. One way of integrating the two is to see them as macro and micro processes, both of which are necessary for effective action.[38] This insight is built on later in this chapter. The debate about resource mobilisation also highlights the fact that organisation often favours the privileged.

Cooperation and self-interest

Two hundred and fifty years ago, Adam Smith argued that cooperation favoured the privileged:

> The masters, being fewer in number, can combine much more easily; and the law, besides, authorises, or at least does not prohibit their combinations, while it prohibits those of the workmen. ... In all such disputes the masters can hold out much longer. A landlord, a farmer, a master manufacturer, or merchant, though they did not employ a single workman, could generally live a year or two upon the stocks which they have already acquired. Many workmen could not subsist a week, few could subsist a month, and scarce any a year without employment. In the long-run the workman may be as necessary to his master as his master is to him, but the necessity is not so immediate.[39]

A different perspective in economic theory is that cooperation does not pay. Mancur Olson argued that, for most groups, particularly larger ones, the economic costs to individual participants outweigh the benefits they will receive. One reason for this was that, unless there are sanctions against non-participants, there will always be 'free riders' enjoying the benefits without paying the costs, thus reducing the benefits available to those who do contribute if the benefits are finite and beneficiaries are competing for their consumption. Furthermore, he argued that it was easier for small groups with concentrated interests to organise in the collective interest than larger groups with more diffuse interests, which could mean that minority interests can overwhelm majority interests. He acknowledged that if free riding could be prevented (by exclusivity or sanctions) or one participant's benefits were not at the expense of another's, the problems would not arise. Olsen was well aware that he was making a statement about politics and public policy in this argument and he was explicitly thinking about trade unions.[40] On the one hand, it is easy to think of examples where groups do operate as Olson predicts – a few people contribute time or money to a cause and others benefit without having contributed;[41] a small group of people with a strong common interest resist or insist on a course of action when a larger group take a different view – Not In My Back Yard (Nimby) is an interesting example of both. Nimbies may either be small group of activists with little economic power but a powerful concentrated voice or a well-resourced group protecting its privileges. In both cases a larger group may benefit or suffer from their activity.

Commons

An alternative view to Becker and Olson was put forward by Elinor Ostrom, a political scientist who also won the Nobel Prize for Economics. Her work analysed how groups of people manage resources collectively. She identified that some goods and services have low *subtractability of use* (one person's use doesn't deprive another person) and it is relatively difficult to exclude potential beneficiaries – such as irrigation systems, fisheries and forests. Other goods and services have low subtractability but it is easier to exclude people: community peace and security or weather forecasts. She demonstrated that if certain conditions are met and principles are followed, resources can be sustained for the benefit of the community. She demonstrated that multiple providers of public goods (*polycentric systems*) were not necessarily less efficient than centralised monopolies. She also coined the term *co-production* to refer to the engagement of communities in the design, delivery and evaluation of public services. By articulating an alternative to both the market and the state, Ostrom has attracted interest on both the ideological right and the left.[42] New forms of commons are emerging – for instance, open source technology (for example, Mozilla Firefox or Linux); the World Wide Web and much of the knowledge available through it (not just Wikipedia but open journals such as the Public Library of Science, or PLoS); and social networks or publishing under Creative Commons licensing.

Game theory

Game theory is the study of conflict and cooperation behaviour using mathematical models. Its origins are in the nineteenth century but it wasn't until the 1940s that it really took off, introducing the key concepts: the benefits and costs (*'payoffs'*) of different behaviours (*'strategies'*) of decision-makers (*'players'*) in a situation (a *'game'*). It was not until the 1950s that John Nash developed the most influential models of cooperative and non-cooperative behaviour. Cooperative game theory analyses the conditions that are necessary for a coalition of players to achieve a successful outcome. Central to his approach is that the solution will depend on the relative bargaining strength of the players. In non-cooperative games, paradoxically cooperation may still result, but the individual players pursue self-interest and the solution(s) depend on the procedures (the '*game tree*') for decision-making that are followed. The most famous illustration of game theory is probably the *Prisoners' Dilemma*. Two prisoners are accused of a serious crime for which there is no independent evidence that they did it. If one gives evidence against the other, the accuser will go free and the accused will get a long sentence. If both admit guilt they will get a lighter sentence but not as light as if neither admit guilt. Cooperation leads to the most desirable outcome for the prisoners (though not necessarily society) but if both behave individually selfishly ('*defecting*') the outcome may be less bad than if only one does. Two of the key factors in whether players will defect or cooperate are trust and whether they communicate. The same principles can be applied to situations of violence (de-escalation of conflict such as making and breaking ceasefires; disarmament), the dumping of waste, pricing the buying or selling of goods and services, or victims' compensation for loss of life or property. Among other key ideas in game theory are that:

- Repeated situations work differently from those which are one-offs (strategies may evolve).
- Some games are 'zero-sum' where there must be a winner and a loser, but others are 'plus' games in which all parties can win.
- There are equilibria – there are rules where, if everybody follows them, no one can improve their position individually. What the actual rule is may not matter but that everybody follows it is – for example, which side of the road drivers use.[43]

The wisdom of crowds

Statisticians have also argued for the benefits of collective action, or the *wisdom of crowds*. In 1906 Francis Galton witnessed a competition to guess the weight of an ox at an agricultural fair. Although no one person guessed the exact weight, the average of nearly 800 people was almost exactly right. Analysis of the TV programme *Who Wants To Be A Millionaire* has found that asking the audience more often gets the right answer than phoning a friend.[44]

Economies without money

Much Economics is written about economies in which there are clearly distinct buyers and sellers and money is the medium of exchange. As we saw in Chapter 3, on development, a lot of the theory or ideology underlying international development has been that societies will move towards economies based on buying and selling goods and services. However, economies not based on buying and selling are surprisingly important and resilient, and some economists and other social scientists think that we should be encouraging more non-monetised exchanges. What they often have in mind is cooperative action. It is not coincidence that some of the most powerful work on non-monetary and non-market economics has been done by women such as Eleanor Ostrom, J. K. Gibson-Graham and Gerda Roelvink. David Mitchell puts it starkly:

Men invented money. Women invented mutual aid.[45]

Gibson-Graham and Roelvink identify a very wide range of transactions globally that are not conventional or market- and money-based. Some of their examples are:[46]

- Inter-household flows such as food sharing, childcare sharing and care of house and animals.
- Gifts in connection with big life events such as birth, marriage and death.
- Gifts in connection with religious or spiritual beliefs.
- Charity in money or in kind.
- Remittance funds from family members overseas.
- Gleaning – collecting wild food or cultivated food after it has been harvested by the official owners or cultivators.
- Poaching or theft – including fishing, hunting or logging.

Work on food and housing highlights an even bigger non-money economy. In the first decade of the twenty-first century it was estimated that 70% of world food is produced by smallholders of one kind or another:[47]

- Urban agriculture   15–20%
- Hunting and gathering   10–15%
- Fishing   5–10%
- Farms   35–50%

It is exceedingly difficult to come by robust figures for this kind of activity and it will clearly include products which are sold, though often quite locally. However, it also highlights the fact that many people produce at least part of the food they eat, and that urbanisation is not necessarily a barrier to that. In the UK there is a long tradition of growing food on urban allotments which is continuing and in some places expanding.[48] Cooperation to look after livestock or to harvest crops is an important tradition in many agricultural communities. One of the (intended or unintended) consequences of international food aid is that it discourages non-monetised and locally exchanged production of food.[49]

It is even more difficult to quantify how much of the world's affordable housing is self-built or whether the building process is managed by the occupier or augmented by them ('build as you go'). Much of the housing in informal, irregular or emergency settlements ('slums', 'shanty towns', refugee or internally displaced people's camps) is of poor quality. It is estimated that 40% of the world's population will need access to proper housing by 2030.[50] However, not all informal housing is inadequate. Some policy-makers think self-build is an important part of the solution to insufficient and inadequate housing.[51] Historically mutual aid in building homes has been an important part of social and community life and, in some cases, has become the model for wider cooperation. This is discussed further in the section on ideology at the end of this chapter.

The idea that a rigid division between producers and consumers is not inevitable or desirable has been touched on in relation to the work of Elinor Ostrom on co-production, referred to earlier in the chapter. It has been taken further by thinkers such as Edgar Cahn. He links it to the value of housework and caring (often undertaken by women and not counted as economic activity in official statistics).[52] This is a form of a collective action, even if the terms of exchange may be unfair or oppressive. Ivan Illich criticised the industrial model of production and consumption embodied in institutions of education and medicine, including that they were creating the very problems they were intended to solve. He proposed *conviviality* as an alternative based on autonomous and creative intercourse (or cooperation) between people.[53] Other writers highlight volunteering and giving, which have huge economic value but, again, are frequently not measured as such.[54] Philanthropy and giving are discussed later in this chapter.

In summary, Economics potentially has a big part to play in social and community development, but it needs to be recognised that Economics is:

➤ Not all about individual self-interest

➤ Not just about markets and monetisation

➤ A science of managing scarcity, and a mechanism of exchange and creating value

➤ Not the only explanation of collective action.

Psychology and Social Psychology

Psychology

Not surprisingly, psychology research suggests that states of mind and emotions play a large part in behaviour:[55]

➢ Optimism and hope

Historians and activists are perhaps not generally very particular about the difference between hope and optimism. Psychologists are more concerned.[56] It is suggested that optimism is a belief that things will get better, but that hope is a belief that an individual has some control over whether they achieve goals (agency) and that they identify pathways to change things. There is some argument about whether hope is a rational belief or an emotional state. There are further refinements about whether the goal makes a difference (repairing, maintaining or enhancing situations, for example). Conditions or rules which give rise to hope have been identified:

➢ The chances of achieving the goal must be seen as reasonable (the *prudential* rule). There seems to be some evidence that this is a reasoned or optimistic element of hope – the weather forecast makes you optimistic, for example. However, some people have high hopes even when the outcome is highly improbable.
➢ The goal is seen as personally or socially acceptable (the *moralistic* rule).
➢ The outcomes and events hoped for are assessed as important (the *priority* rule).
➢ People are willing to take appropriate action to achieve their goals, if action is possible (the *action* rule).

The section on Social Psychology later in the chapter suggests that hope and fear may both play an important part in whether people act with others. There is some emphasis on fear and loss playing a bigger role than hope. Psychologists have given attention to how hope plays a part in action. Recent research suggests there may be a genetic predisposition to optimism or pessimism.[57]

➢ Aspirations and passion

A phrase often attributed to Adam Smith is:

> The real tragedy of the poor is the poverty of their aspirations.[58]

This is part of a wider pattern of seeing oppressed people as passive or apathetic. There are several problems with this perception. First, it may simply not be true that poor or oppressed people have low aspirations. For example, a large study of job aspirations of children from poorer backgrounds in England found that in general they did not lack ambition but that class, race and gender all played a part in career routes, particularly putting them off science subjects; that they were unable to access the opportunities available to middle-class children; or that they did not have the cultural capital which would encourage them to make such 'choices'.[59] More broadly, beliefs and behaviours are structured by a variety of institutions, including schools, religion, families and identification with social groups – 'people like us'. This is discussed further in Chapter 5.

Activists identify the power of both negative and positive feelings:

➤ Discontent

Gandhi said:

> discontent is a very useful thing. As long as a man is contented with his present lot, so long is it difficult to persuade him to come out of it. Therefore it is that every reform must be preceded by discontent. We throw away things we have, only then we cease to like them.[60]

Saul Alinsky (who was scathing about Gandhi) argued that Community Organisers had to fan discontent:

> Rub[bing] raw the resentments of the people.

Building their confidence by:

> Picking a cinch fight.[61]

➤ Taking sides

A host of politicians have (mis)quoted Dante's *Inferno* to say that the hottest part of hell was reserved for the indifferent. In fact, he talks about people so defeated by their pain that neither God nor Satan wanted them, and who were neither in heaven or hell.[62]

Gramsci suggested that indifference leads to inertia:

> The indifference is the deadweight of history. The indifference operates with great power on history. The indifference operates passively, but it operates. It is fate, that which cannot be counted on. It twists programs and ruins the best-conceived plans. It is the raw material that ruins intelligence.[63]

Elie Wiesel also saw indifference as destructive and anger as potentially constructive:

> to be indifferent to that suffering is what makes the human being inhuman. Indifference, after all, is more dangerous than anger and hatred. Anger can at times be creative. ... indifference is never creative. Even hatred at times may elicit a response. You fight it. You denounce it. You disarm it. Indifference elicits no response. Indifference is not a response.[64]

➤ Non-conformity and positive deviance

The social psychological evidence referred to above that identifying with other people is an important motivation to protest or to seek change, even if it means being in a minority.[65] Activists are keen to highlight that much social change comes from people willing not to go along with the majority:

> All reforms owe their origin to the initiation of minorities in opposition to majorities ... it is an idle excuse to say that we shall do a thing when the others also do it.[66]

There is considerable evidence of social influence on conformity. Though there are cultural and gender differences and social status matters a lot, there are very strong pressures to conform.[67] On the other hand, there is psychological evidence to suggest that some people are more willing than others not to go along with the crowd – to be different even if they are in minority or isolated.[68]

The Green activist Sara Parkin defines a positive deviant as a person:

> who does the right thing [for sustainability] despite being surrounded by the wrong structures, the wrong processes and stubbornly uncooperative people.[69]

An early use of the concept was with households in Pakistan (both in an established community and in a refugee camp), identifying households whose care of newborn children was different and healthier for the infants ('model care'), and using this local good practice to promote positive practice among their peers who face the same challenges and have access to (only) the same resources.[70]

➤ Reflective, self-conscious and autonomous action

Literally or metaphorically shouting at the TV may make you feel better (or not) but it is unlikely to change anything. It is thought without action. On the other hand, action without thought may or may not be effective. There is a long tradition of political theorists and activists, often on the political left (notably, Lenin), who criticise spontaneity in action, arguing that it is ineffective or counter-productive. They have generally argued that action should follow authority, whether political leaders or divine authority.[71] Paulo Freire did not argue for downward instruction but for inward reflection:

> Without critical reflection ... action is pure activism.[72]

Rennie Johnston argued that the key question for community educators is:

> How to bridge the gap between, on the one hand, 'actionless thought' and on the other, 'thoughtless action'.[73]

Others have argued that spontaneity does have a place. Murray Bookchin argues that it reflects autonomy or self-consciousness.[74] Herbert Marcuse also argued for *seriously organised spontaneity* in which small local groups carry out a variety of activities to escape bureaucratic co-option.[75] The gap between thought and action might be argued to be narrowing through the ease with which a thought can be shared on social media or a signature added to an electronic petition. However, what is increasingly clear is that social media initiatives can be manipulated (and monitored) and can reinforce or reflect social structures as well as transform them.[76] The use of electronic media to promote 'fake news' or suppressed information or to attack or support individuals or institutions means that we are seeing the rise of the 'armed [sic] chair' activist.[77]

In summary, we can say that Psychology makes a strong case for emotions being important in whether action takes place, but it doesn't provide a recipe with a list of necessary and sufficient ingredients and processes.

Social psychology

The starting point for social psychology is that collective action may happen because individuals identify with other people or because they make a rational calculation that action will be worthwhile or that inaction will be costly. However, a lot of social psychology qualifies this simple picture.

In the 1940s Erich Fromm suggested that the fear of aloneness and the development of an awareness of being an individual act as drivers of cooperation. In the 1970s Henri Tajfel suggested that members of low-status groups can maintain or enhance their group self-esteem by collective action. Subsequent research suggested that identifying with other marginalised people was insufficient by itself as a predictor and other research has explored the challenges of hidden groups with 'concealable stigmas'. The Social Identity Model of Collective Action (SIMCA) suggests that two other factors are also important:

- The perception of group injustice rather than simply personal experience of injustice; and

- Confidence that groups can change things (*efficacy*).

Research has suggested that feelings generally (*affective* measures), and anger in particular, are better predictors of collective action than *cognitive* measures of, say, unfairness or discrimination. Some writers would describe this in terms of feelings of solidarity. More recently this has been looked at in relation to people who identify with a low-status group but are not directly discriminated against: allies.

Other research suggests there must be sense of a wider group whose attitude or behaviour must be changed. If that group is perceived as more powerful or has higher status which is considered by the low-status group as illegitimate, this is called *stratum consciousness*. The processes by which people develop group consciousness are discussed further in Chapter 6.

While research and statistics might not be important motivators to take part in collective action, the potential effectiveness of action is important to people. This may not be in terms of achieving long-term external goals. It may be about transforming personal relationships. Although there is some evidence that a belief in personal efficacy is important to whether people take part in collective action, there is another variable which is whether people internalise their anger or direct it outwardly. Some writers have suggested where people have a strong sense of system injustice but a weak sense of control, they are more likely to express their anger through violence.

Lauren Duncan analyses factors in collective action in relation to groups fighting against discrimination on the grounds of race, gender and sexuality or anti-war but also groups that are pro-war, racialist or seek to limit women's rights (though there is less research on these groups). She suggests that different theories of why people become involved in collective action complement each other and together recognise the importance of:

- Personality variables including anti-authoritarian/authoritarian and optimistic/anxious outlooks.

- Life experiences including family background; experiences of discrimination and material circumstances.

- Negative emotions: a sense of deprivation.

- A sense of common fate to experience emotion at a group level.

- An idea of efficacy that converts feelings into action.

- A process whereby they develop a politicised group identity.[78]

102 SOCIAL AND COMMUNITY DEVELOPMENT

William Gamson summarises the requirements as identity, solidarity, consciousness and micro mobilisation.[79]

Another approach has been that there are two pathways to activism: one is an *instrumental* one based on costs, benefits and interests and the other an *identification* pathway, which may include grievances, efficacy, identity and emotions. More recent theorising has been that activism may result from a combination of interests and identification.[80] This provides a basis for synthesis of insights from Economics and Social Psychology.

Duncan argues that the relationship between collective action, group consciousness, personality and life experiences is potentially two-way or reciprocal. Collective action may occur because of personal characteristics, but it can also change personalities: Duncan cites research on the personality changes of women involved in the American Women's movement. Duncan's overall model is set out in Figure 4.1.

Group Consciousness

- Injustice
- Identity
- Efficacy

Path A (Explains different dispositions to act)

Path B (Indirect)

Personality and Life Experiences ← Path C (Direct) → Collective Action

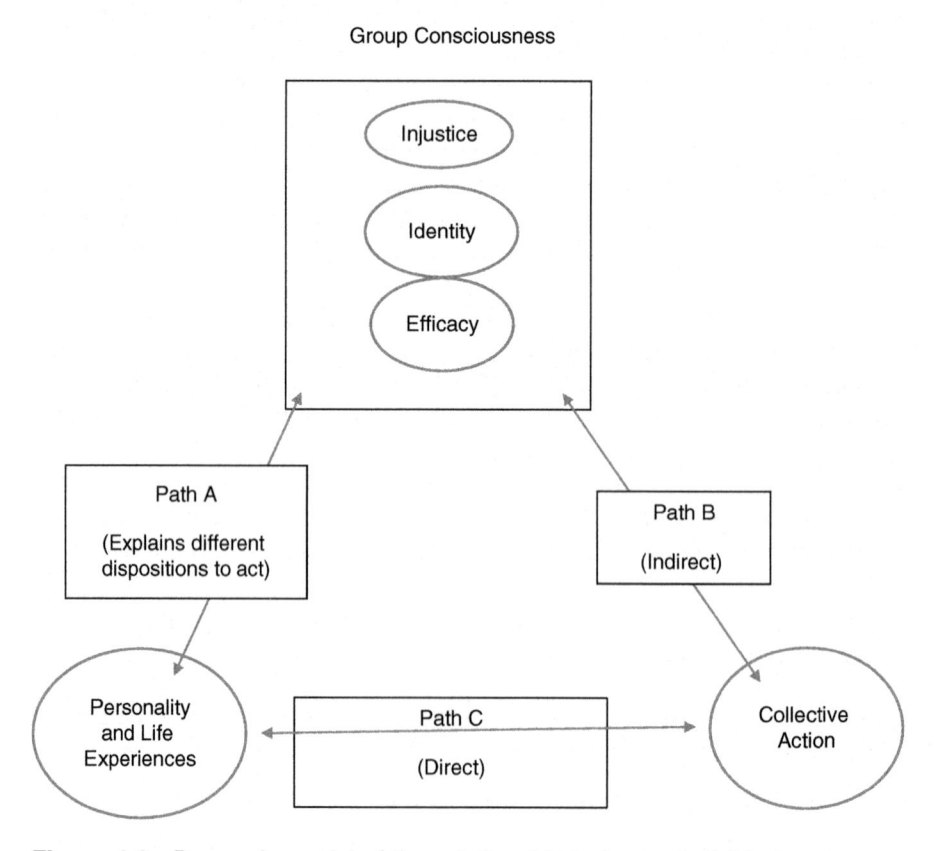

Figure 4.1 Duncan's model of the relationship between Individuals, group consciousness and collective action

Source: Duncan (2012)

Duncan suggests that the indirect paths A and B are most likely to occur when basic needs are met and there is no immediate crisis. The direct route (C) is most likely in situations of crisis.

A different perspective is provided by Hogg and colleagues.[81] They suggest three theories of why people join groups:

- *Sociometer theory* – To increase pleasure (of which self-esteem is a part) and reduce pain. Self-esteem acts as a meter of our inclusion or exclusion by others. This may not explain membership or identification with large-scale social categories such as national, religious or ethnic groups, and the kind of deprivation-based theories discussed above may do so more effectively.

- *Terror management theory* – Seeking out others to overcome our fear of death, confirm our worldview and affirm our existence. The fear of death (or for some what will happen to them in an afterlife) might motivate people to join groups which promise a kind of salvation. It might be an explanation for some of the more conservative groups that Duncan refers to. However, it doesn't seem to fit with the evidence about more liberal or emancipatory groups. It also doesn't seem to explain why we might join leisure or sports groups, for example.

- *Uncertainty–identity theory* – Addressing the need to have certain knowledge about the world: to have confidence in our knowledge about the world and our place within it; and validation for our perceptions, feelings, attitudes and behaviours. This theory is derived from Tajfel's social identity theory discussed above. The uncertainty–identity theory suggests that people will prefer to join groups with clear boundaries and a strong sense of identity to reduce uncertainty. This may explain why people join groups with very strong belief systems. It has been applied to situations of intergroup conflict, such as the conflict in Northern Ireland.[82]

As well as the literature on the psychology of people joining groups, there is also a great deal of knowledge about the processes of taking decisions to support a cause with time and money. A key finding is that the decision is often related to what other people do or will think. Copying and/or trying to impress others are critical.[83]

It does not seem as though there is one social psychology theory which explains why all people join all kinds of social movements. It may be more useful to think of different social psychology theories as potentially complementary or as tools to choose from. Very crudely, in some situations people come together for conscious, positive reasons but frequently a group will not be aware of the reasons and an observer may struggle to discern them. A group may see itself as emancipatory – fighting for justice – when actually it is motivated by fears of aloneness or mortality.

Theology, ethics and political philosophy[84]

One factor which may influence whether people take collective action is whether they feel they have a right or duty to act together, either as an end in itself or as a means to something else.

Theology

Theology operates at the level of individual beliefs and behaviour, groups and institutions, and provides a rationale or ideology at all levels.

Religion and collective action

At the ideological level, religions have argued for and against a right to, or duty of, collective action. Governance arrangements are often sanctioned or endorsed by religious authorities – officially in *theocracies* – or simply in practice; religious belief or affiliation is central to political structures and processes. In Chapter 5 we consider the concept of hegemony – how dominance in society is maintained not only by the political, bureaucratic and military institutions of the state but by the values transmitted by religious and educational institutions and so on. Religious institutions and beliefs play a variety of roles in supporting, shaping or preventing social and community development. It has been argued that in the eighteenth and nineteenth centuries UK, Christian theology (specifically Nonconformist beliefs) contributed to the rise of collective action – in weavers' revolts; in movements like the Chartists and the Luddites; later by trade unions; and then, at the very end of the nineteenth century, the Labour Party. However, there were also many activists not inspired by religious beliefs and many Nonconformists who did not support such actions.[85] The same contest of arguments arises in relation to other religions, ideologies and movements. Activism also occurred in societies which were not Christian.

Theology and control

At the beginning of this chapter we explored whether the decision to act (individually or collectively) is one in which people can act autonomously.

Theologians debate whether power is spiritual and or temporal and whether it is internal (e.g. faith) or external (divine omnipotence).

Theologians have different perspectives on how what rights and responsibilities individuals have. There are also differences about how much power collectivities (e.g. congregations) have: whether there is a 'priesthood of all believers' or whether only clergy or even the head of an institution has legitimate ('divinely ordained') power. Some of the major world religions' approaches to collective action are now considered. It highlights that for religious believers the distinction between self-interest and altruism may not be useful. If someone does something for someone else because they see it as a religious duty and/or they think they will get a spiritual reward in this or an afterlife, which is it?

Theology and forms of collective action

- Buddhism has the concept of 'all being one' which is also the basis of mutuality in human relationships. The Abrahamic religions, Judaism, Christianity and Islam, all have a starting point that human beings are made in the image of God. This has often been interpreted as the basis of treating each other with respect (and latterly as a foundation of Human Rights) and that we have duties towards each other in areas of charity.
- Judaism, Christianity and Islam have several concepts which contain the idea of a responsibility (either an obligation or voluntary) to give to the community – sometimes specifically for religious purposes, sometimes for more general well-being:[86]
  - *Mitzvah* (a gift and commandment), *gemilut hasadim* (righteous acts, acts of loving kindness) *tzedaka* or *tsedaqah* (almsgiving) are broadened out to Justice *or* Charity in many contemporary Jewish communities
  - *Charity* in Christianity meaning love of God and neighbours[87]
  - *Tithes* in Christianity and Judaism
  - *Zakat/zakah/sadaqah* in Islam.

These are examples of a religious justification for giving. In Judaism (J) and Islam (I) there are also religious justifications for actions to promote:

- Justice – such as *Tikkun Olam* or *Tiqqun Olam* (J): healing, repairing the world.

- Sharing – *Shuttafut* (J) and *Sharakah* (I): originally material partnerships established by acquisition or inheritance, now sometimes used to refer to civil partnerships between individuals or interfaith partnerships.

- Partnership (which may include reciprocity) – *Musharakah/Shirkah* (I).

- Consultation – *Sura* (I): mutual consent, collaboration.

- Service/social action – *Khidmah* (I).[88]

- Encouraging self-help or mutual aid – the Koran put it thus: *Allah will not change the condition of a people until they change what is in themselves.* [89]

- Collective action as a way of finding oneself.

The Jewish theologian, philosopher and political activist Martin Buber argued that people only find meaning in their relationships with other people. It was a view formulated in World War I which he saw as an opportunity for the Jewish community in Germany to be part of national community; it led him to argue against mainstream Zionism and for a binational (Jewish-Arab) state. The priority he gave to dialogue also led him to believe that he should talk with 'moderate' National Socialists (Nazis) in the 1930s and for reconciliation after World War II. This commitment to dialogue and inclusion, specifically as a method of education (discussed further in Chapter 6), makes him, along with Paulo Freire, an important influence on community development.[90]

Maimonides (known to Muslims as Musa Ibn Maimun) talked of eight levels of charity of which the highest level is:

> A gift, a loan, form with him a partnership, or find work for him, until he is strong enough so that he does not need to ask other.[91]

In all three Abrahamic traditions there have been arguments about whether obligations are only to believers of the same faith or more widely.

- The Gandhian idea of *Swaraj*, with connotations of independence, autonomy, home- or self-rule, draws on Hinduism with Buddhist and Jainist influences. Gandhi's concept of *Swadeshi* usually translated as self-sufficiency or self-reliance also explicitly meant interdependence.[92]

- The philosopher Peter Singer argues from a secular, utilitarian perspective that we have a duty to give (in cash or in kind):

if it is in our power to prevent something bad from happening, without thereby sacrificing anything of comparable moral importance, we ought, morally, to do it.[93]

He rejects the application of the traditional distinction between a duty and an act of charity: a *'supererogatory'* – an act which it would be good to do, but not wrong not to do. He says it is an act which we ought to do and it is wrong not to do. Furthermore, he argues that the obligation is not diminished by distance or by the number of people in the same position.[94] The implications of this position for collective action are, among other things, that our duties to our 'neighbours' are no greater than our global responsibilities and that you are just as responsible whether you are the only person who can make a difference or one of many. Singer has subsequently gone on to argue that there is a duty to give effectively; this is discussed below in relation to altruism.

Political philosophy and collective action

Collective action is at the heart of political philosophy. There are several different threads to it.

Representation

The argument for extending representation from a single ruler or dynasty can be traced back to ancient Greece and Rome. The English Magna Carta of 1215 said:

> No 'scutage' or 'aid' may be levied in our kingdom without [the] general consent [of] the archbishops, bishops, abbots, earls, and greater barons.[95]

Even though this was only prescribing participation of a male, Christian elite, it is often taken as the origin of a universal 'No Taxation without Representation'.

The Polish Constitution of 1505 said:

> Nihil novi nisi commune consensus [Nothing new without common consent].[96]

This extended influence to members of the council and district deputies (essentially male aristocrats). This is probably the origin of *'Nothing about us, without us'*, a slogan taken up by the disability movement in the twentieth century.[97]

In both the Magna Carta and the Polish constitution not only was the franchise restricted but the range of issues covered was also restricted. In both cases, for example, the representation of Jews was excluded. Representation is also not the same as participation.

Participation in political philosophy

Political philosophers have argued for millennia whether and why participation is important.

David Held argues that the idea of democracy in Athens in Greece over 2,500 years ago was based on government by the governed. It meant 'rule of all by all in turn' as Aristotle put it. Crucially, it was restricted to free men of Athenian origin and only possible because of the work of slaves and women.

It was seen as a duty to oneself – to extend autonomy and live a good life. According to Held, the idea of an active citizen rather than a loyal subject went out of fashion after the ancient Greeks until the Renaissance. Held, following John Pocock, argues that for centuries Christianity focused on the responsibilities of believers to submit to God's will rather than to be active citizens.[98]

Subsequent political philosophers have argued for variations on the idea, including Rousseau, Marx and Engels, libertarian socialists, syndicalists (mainly, but not only, concerned with workplace control) and anarchists. There have been many different forms at different times, including the Diggers during the seventeenth-century English Civil War; through Peter Kropotkin and Tolstoy in the nineteenth century; Gandhi[99] and Murray Bookchin in the twentieth century;[100] and squatters, anti-globalisation protestors and the *Occupy* movement in the twenty-first century.[101]

Raymond Plant says that arguments for participation are broadly of two kinds: efficiency and the realisation of the nature of man.[102] The efficiency or managerialist argument is essentially that the people who are most affected by many decisions are also the people who know best what their needs or aspirations are. Top-down management or outsiders unfamiliar with a situation are likely to waste resources. This echoes *the wisdom of crowds*, collective consumption and production, discussed above.

The realisation argument goes back to the ancient Greek idea: people are not free or complete unless they feel agency, or they are more creative and pro-social in democratic, as opposed to autocratic, groups. The realisation argument often moves away from political philosophy into psychology and psychotherapy, with a specifically therapeutic element. People may be damaged by a lack of participation in decisions, but may improve their physical, mental and emotional health by taking decisions about their well-being and improve their relationships with others.[103]

Held summarises the arguments of writers such as Carole Pateman and C. B Macpherson for participation as:

- Fostering human development (i.e. instrumental)
- A sense of political efficacy
- A reduced sense of estrangement
- Nurturing a concern for collective problems.[104]

On the other hand, there have been arguments put forward against participation:

1. Held and others argue that it is not feasible as an exclusive model, on a large scale in modern complex societies, in the context of global influences and impacts. They do, however, recognise that it can be part of a wider political system such as through Citizens' Juries. The last 20 years has seen a massive expansion of the possibility of people communicating over any distances on a huge range of issues. This takes many forms: electronic media including social media, e-petitions, citizen journalism; travel, including voluntary and involuntary migration. On the other hand, the new technologies can undermine mass participation – for example, algorithms and artificial intelligence, computer hackers, military drones and terrorist attacks are examples of small numbers of people able to take hugely consequential actions.

2. There are advantages in not having participation: the idea that some people have specialist skills and knowledge in taking decisions or have time – arguments for elites, organisations and bureaucracy.[105]

3. Not everyone wants to take part in decisions. The British Labour politician Anthony Crosland claimed:

   the bulk of the population would rightly 'prefer to lead a full family life and cultivate their gardens.'[106]

4. Crosland also argued that participation was a threat to privacy and freedom:

   we do not necessarily want a busy bustling society in which everyone is politically active, and fussing around in an interfering and responsible manner, and herding us all into participating groups. The threat to privacy and freedom would be intolerable.[107]

5. It has also been argued that too much participation can lead to totalitarianism.[108]

6. French students in May 1968 drew attention to the way that participation can favour the privileged:

> Je participe, tu participes, il participe, nous participons, vous participez, ils profitent [I, you, we participate; they profit].[109]

Prefigurative politics

Closely allied to ideas about participation is the idea that the way that change is brought about is part of the change itself and this requires 'popular participation' or 'Popular Planning'.[110] This is reflected in the term *prefigurative* politics, a term coined by the political scientist Carl Boggs and taken up by feminist writers. In one version of prefigurative politics it is simply that the means should reflect the ends. In other versions it is that acting out the change instead of imagining it or campaigning for it *is* the change.[111]

Participation in social and community development

In recent years there has been a great deal of debate among analysts and practitioners of social and community development about the nature of participation – summed up in the titles of two books as the question of whether it a new form of tyranny or a method of transformation.[112] Several theoretical and practical problems with participation have been identified:

1. Confusion about what is meant by participation. Different writers and practitioners describe and prescribe different levels of participation from broad ideological conceptions such as 'citizenship' or 'rights' through to institutional relationships, between international governmental organisations (the UN, World Bank, etc.), states, private sector companies, international NGOs, foundations and Civil Society Organisations.

2. Participation interventions, at all levels, often either don't consider power relations or are not designed to change them. They often do not have any conception of structure or agency. They are often designed to legitimise existing structures and processes. The power structures are usually invisible or naturalised in the bias of the rules of the game or agendas.[113] Many participation initiatives begin with

assumptions that the target population has a deficit or problem of some kind. It has therefore been suggested that effective participation is one which enables oppressed people to recognise and exercise their agency.[114]

3. At the individual and interpersonal levels there are costs for marginalised people to participate in decision-making. It may require time or other resources needed for survival but also suppression of specific needs or identity in the interests of alliances. Ruth Lister has drawn attention particularly to gender issues and bell hooks to issues for Black women, specifically.[115] At the interpersonal level there are problems in creating spaces for participation between groups which perceive each other as unequal. This could be gender, religious, racial or ethnic inequality or technocrats or professionals and laypeople. There is a danger that instead of simply creating 'safe spaces', places are created which reinforce existing relationships by 'playing it safe' but there are ways of supporting people to share intra-group differences and deal with challenges between groups.[116]

4. Participation initiatives often focus on the institutional. 'Space' is defined bureaucratically (often only as 'local' or limited to specific programmes). They miss the importance of space as a social construction which is dynamic and malleable by both the powerful and the marginalised. Feminists have highlighted how 'invited' spaces favour the powerful. Andrea Cornwall has identified different kinds of spaces: those *'invited'* or provided by the powerful; others *invented*, created or claimed. Invited spaces are often constructed by states, with a very instrumental or managerial agenda. They often 'disempower' people but can have emancipatory potential. Invented spaces may also not empower people. Invited spaces are often imported from outside and override indigenous structures of decision-making which even if imperfect or even oppressive could be built on. Even *'deliberative'* spaces, in which population although individuals can learn and discuss, they may only appear to decide because these spaces may only allow particular voices and 'realities' and needs can sometimes be 'ventriloquised'. Cornwall suggests that power is most unequal when fixed spatial locations intersect with closed spaces and (hidden) bias in the rules of engagement. Creating public spaces outside the structures and influences of the state is necessary to avoid simply legitimating the existing political system. However, poor or 'weak' people are very inventive in subverting the strategies of the powerful.[117] The idea of invented or created spaces expresses the potential to open more spaces which can be claimed.[118] Gaventa's power cube expresses clearly where claimed spaces fit into wider power relationships (Figure 4.2).[119]

Figure 4.2 Gaventa's power cube
Source: Gaventa (2006)[120]

Norbert Kersting takes invited and invented participation in democracy into the online world but also shows how it can operate offline (Figure 4.3).[121]

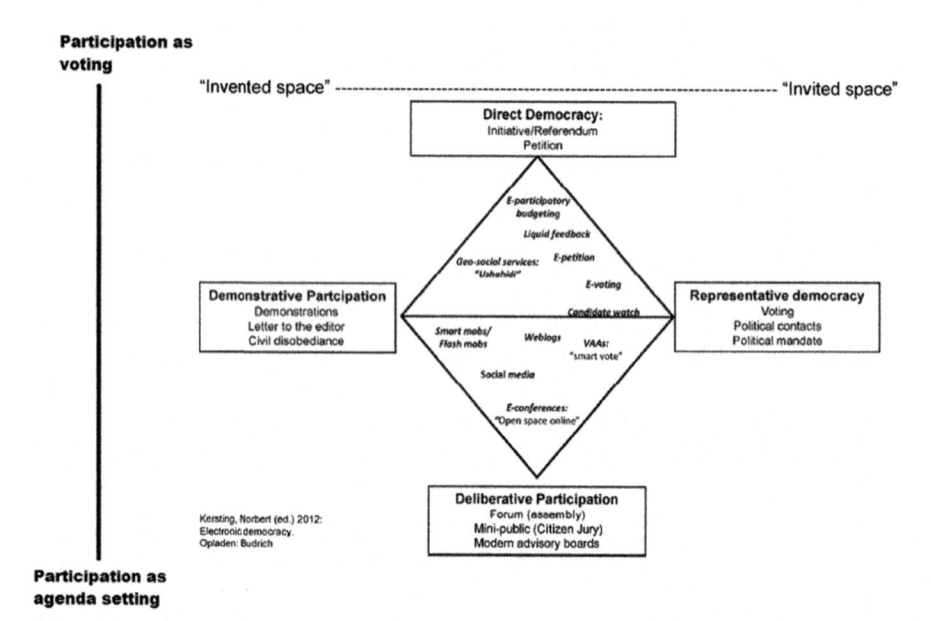

Figure 4.3 Kersting's model of invited and claimed participation in the online world
Source: Kersting (2013)[122] Inderscience retains copyright of the article this figure originally appears in.'

5. Social mobilisation does not in itself lead to social change. The Non-Violent Direct Action activist Howard Clark has argued that militancy can increase the social marginalisation that activists experience, and in turn is likely to narrow the social base for the actions. It can reduce the prospect for change in relation to both the specific issue or more generally to how power is constructed. Clark argues that militancy needs to be accompanied by clear mechanisms for change and commends Gene Sharp's analysis of mechanisms of conversion, coercion, accommodation or disintegration.[123]

Jim Ife suggests that the conditions necessary for meaningful participation are:

- It is about something which the participants feel is important.
- They feel participation will make a difference (agency).
- Different forms of participation must be acknowledged (claimed or invited).
- People must be enabled and supported to take part.
- Structures must not be alienating (which also addresses the issues of invited and claimed spaces and power relations among the participants).[124]

Participation and professionals

The argument that professionals such as planners, architects, doctors and nurses should involve the public or clients in decisions about them is often traced back to the 1960s in relation to urban planning. In fact, such ideas had been put forward earlier, and the idea did not always come from 'enlightened' professionals.[125] Often it was in the face of professional resistance, as in the case of disabled people who adopted the slogan of *Nothing about us without us*.[126]

The state and civil society

In the West, the distinction between the state and the people only emerged in the sixteenth and seventeenth centuries. However, back in the fourteenth century Ibn Khaldun, writing in the context of North Africa, also argued that the state was necessary to limit human aggression in the context of preserving the community, or *'Asabiyyah'* (see Chapter 2) – often translated as nation subsequently. Thomas Hobbes, writing in the context of the seventeenth-century English Civil War, famously said that without it life would be *'solitary, poor nasty, brutish and short'*.[127] Hobbes' willingness to accept the obligation to an absolute ruler is much stronger than Khaldun's who was acutely aware of the failings of rulers.[128] Neither are advocates of an inclusive, active kind of collective action. Not until John Locke and later Jean-Jacques Rousseau do ideas of a social contract between people emerge in Western philosophy. John Locke (1632–1704) said:

> The only way by which anyone divests himself of his natural liberty and puts on the bonds of civil society is by agreeing with other men to join and unite into a community.[129]

Some political philosophers have argued that the state is neutral, and/or an expression of the collective will (Hegel, for example). Others have argued that it is a threat to voluntary association or individual rights (Hayek or Nozick, for example). A third group (including Marx and Gramsci, Feminists and anti-imperialists) have seen the state as representing dominant interests and oppressing other interests.

The early nineteenth-century philosopher Georg Hegel argued that people must meet their needs, their self-interest, through interaction. Critically, he suggested that interactions are not between individuals but between groups: to gain status and recognition they must identify with a class of people with similar interests to themselves. Hegel saw the state as a place where the conflicts of civil society could be resolved because it embodied the highest ethical standards of society. Subsequent writers such as Marx and Gramsci have seen the state as, respectively, the site of the conflicts, the struggles between interests and an instrument of coercion of civil society. Gramsci said:

> Between the economic structure and the state with its legislation and coercion stands civil society.[130]

Gramsci distinguished between political society and civil society. He saw a need to change the nature of civil society. His theorising about *'counter-hegemonic movements'* laid the foundations for a lot of subsequent thought and action in relation to new forms of civil society – *New Social Movements* (discussed further in Chapter 5).

Particularly since the fall of the Berlin Wall in 1989 and the subsequent collapse of many Communist regimes, Civil Society has come to be used to refer to organisations that are neither statutory nor private (private in the sense of profit-seeking and families), and includes what are known as voluntary organisations (or NGOs, Not-for-Profit organisations, the Third Sector), faith organisations, independent trade unions, movements based on identity (e.g. gender, sexuality or ethnicity) or 'causes' (e.g. environmental sustainability or animal rights/well-being). Civil society as a protection against the state follows on from the work of writers such as Friedrich von Hayek and Robert Nozick. Communitarian writers have often been wary of the state and have seen civil society as protecting individuals through civic engagement. Robert Putnam has linked the idea of civil society to social capital.

The International Association for Community Development's *Guiding Principles* talk about the government's supporting role and a collaborative approach between governments, communities and the private sector. While this is plausible where the state is seen as neutral, or the site for negotiation, where it is seen as oppressive, it may not be seen as a credible or desirable strategy. However, social and community activists may not see all states in the same light. A group of people in the UK, mostly working for state organisations, while being critical and trying to oppose or change the nature of the state, expressed their ambivalence at being *In and Against the State* as:

resources we need involve us in relationships we don't.[131]

Opposition to the state has been even more clear-cut in Nationalist areas (and to an extent in Loyalist areas) in Northern Ireland during and since the Troubles.[132] In other countries, the state is clearly opposed to social and community development (e.g. Darfur in Sudan) or so weakened that it may be unable to provide support (in many parts of Somalia, for example).

Sovereignty: the right to self-determination

Sovereignty is a concept which is applied on several levels. State sovereignty has been applied to absolute rulers on the basis, for example, of a divine right to rule. Thomas Hobbes argued for the absolute sovereignty of the state but established by consent. It has also been applied to more democratic forms of government, with legitimacy claimed because it is the will of the people. The rise and fall of state sovereignty has been a long process. A permanent state bureaucracy was not part of the political system in ancient Greece but by the fourteenth or fifteenth century CE, the state was clearly established in many countries. After the seventeenth century (the Treaty of Westphalia in 1648, specifically), the principle of nation-state sovereignty was established for Europe but not for colonies and 'enemies' outside Europe. Perhaps starting with Mary Wollstonecraft in the eighteenth century and certainly in the writing of Marx and Engels in the nineteenth century, the idea of the state as a neutral umpire, judge or instrument of the people, was challenged. In the mid-twentieth century the idea that nation-states had absolute sovereignty was significantly challenged by the rise of international law (especially after the Nuremberg trials of Nazi war criminals) and international institutions (the UN but also regional alliances such as NATO or, more recently, the African Union).

The sovereignty of individuals is associated with Western individualism – the view that individuals have certain rights or liberties which must not be taken away from them by others, including by the state, the so-called 'protective' argument for democracy. It does not preclude individuals voluntarily exercising sovereignty together – through political parties and civil society organisations, for example.

Group or community sovereignty which is not as formal as the state or as specific as an organisation relates to the idea of group rights. Historically, groups have been granted self-government or autonomy within imperial or colonial structures from the Greek and Roman empires through to the Ottoman *millet* system to twentieth- and twenty-first-century consociational structures.[133] As discussed in Chapter 2, it is the basis for much collective action. However, many would argue that it is not absolute. Group sovereignty can challenge, and be challenged by, arguments based on specific universal human rights, state or individual sovereignty. The tensions between self-determination and other human rights are discussed further in Chapter 5.

In the twenty-first century new forms of sovereignty have been identified. In 2008 an intergovernmental conference established by the UN and World Bank defined *Food sovereignty* as:

> the right of peoples and sovereign states to democratically determine their own agricultural and food policies.

The fact it mentions both peoples and states, and several states led by the USA, Canada and Australia expressed reservations about the policy document of which it was part, highlights that different kinds of sovereignty can clash with each other.[134]

Different conceptions and levels of sovereignty often underlie disagreements about '*self-determination*' or '*autonomy*' in social and community development. There are tensions about what level of self-determination takes priority – for example, a state, a social group or an individual.

The relationship between political and social processes

Held makes a distinction in arguments for democracy ('Republicanism') between its intrinsic or developmental value on the one hand, and its instrumental or protective value on the other. The developmental value includes its emancipatory potential. It is this aspect which is picked up from ancient Greece in the Renaissance, later by Jean-Jacques Rousseau (including the idea of the Social Contract), by Mary Wollstonecraft (specifically the emancipation of women) and by Marx and Engels (the emancipation of the working classes). Others have highlighted that simple majoritarian democracy can be fatal for minorities. A saying often attributed to Benjamin Franklin (but very unlikely to have been said by him) is:

Democracy is two wolves and a lamb voting on what to have for lunch.[135]

At least in Europe, there appears to be a trend to increasing numbers of referenda. The USA has increasing numbers of citizen-initiated Propositions. Supporters argue that it promotes the engagement of citizens and holds elected representatives to account. Critics point out that turnout is often poor, that different referenda often contradict each other, and majorities may oppress minorities through referenda (the Irish referendum in favour of gay marriage is an exception).[136]

Max Weber argued that direct democracy was impractical unless people had similar views, skills and social positions and were facing relatively simple and stable administrative functions.[137] The argument that homogeneity is necessary for collective action or that collective action is necessary to preserve homogeneity has been taken to extremes of genocide, expulsions and removal of citizenship rights.

Political systems or collective action built on majority ethnic groups have been called *ethnocracies*.[138] Concern about the rights of minorities leads to *consociational* political structures such as those in Iraqi Kurdistan or Northern Ireland where political representation is guaranteed for specific social groups. Criticisms of the consociational arrangements include that it freezes and prioritises particular divisions, preventing transformation of social relationships or addressing other divisions.[139]

An agenda for emancipatory participation

The lengthy and admittedly dense discussion of participation above is necessary because participatory collective action is so often presented as the cornerstone of community development (less often social development) but scrutiny of the concept suggests that why and whether it is desirable is not always clear. However, this should not be an argument against participation as such. It is an argument for doing it right.

The sociologist Patrick Heller has outlined a helpful model of what emancipatory participation and deepening democracy should look like. He sees civil society organisations as playing a central role:

- Creating new associational spaces.
- Ensuring that there is an ecology of agents by mobilising new actors.
- Formulating and raising issues neglected or repressed by conventional channels of political representation.
- Addressing not only vertical (state–society) relations but horizontal relations (inequality).
- Holding political actors, corporations, state institutions and other civil society actors to account: cultivating an ethical dimension to democracy.
- Direct influence on state institutions.
- Through co-production (echoing Ostrom).
- Capability enhancing development (echoing Sen).
- Through a horizontal model of horizontal learning of seeing and hearing rather than of teaching and learning; of sharing experiences and knowledge.
- Promoting deliberation and negotiation.
- Innovation in the tension between representation and participation, including by direct involvement in governance.
- Bridging knowledge and authority gaps between technocratic expertise and local involvement.[140]

History

The previous sections have considered why people should act collectively, largely on the assumption that they have some choice in whether to do so: 'agency'. In this section, we explore why people act or don't act, using tools from theories about explaining events in history – historicism.

Triggers, catalysts, inertia

A debate about the role of 'spontaneity' in social change has caused major political schisms in political movements. Historians and Political Philosophers have expended much energy on it.[141] Changes in technology and communication may have blurred the distinction between planned or premeditated social change and spontaneous action but how it starts remains an important issue.

Beliefs don't necessarily precipitate acts and it is probably futile to look for predictions from what might have been or didn't happen – what Alan Bennett called *'subjunctive history'*.[142]

The historian A. J. P. Taylor said: 'things happen because they happen' – by chance or contingency, accidents and blunders. The historian John Tosh thinks there are patterns, but events always have multiple and many-layered causes. Revolutions can be examined to explore what historians and political scientists have had to say about what role deliberate social action plays in social change.[143]

Revolutions

There is inevitably not a consensus about what 'revolution' is. The nineteenth-century politician and novelist Edward Bulwer-Lytton said:

> a reform is a correction of abuses, a revolution is a transfer of power.[144]

The idea that elites can and will correct abuses while holding on to power was questioned in the nineteenth century by revolutionary socialists and anarchists. In the twentieth century anti-imperial activists questioned it too. Gandhi had a slightly different perspective, arguing that:

> A non-violent revolution is not a programme of seizure of power. It is a programme of transformation of relationships, ending in a peaceful transfer of power.[145]

Jack Goldstone distinguishes between revolutions and other kinds of social, political or economic movements such as revolts, riots, reform movements, strikes and coups d'état. Revolutions have the elements of an ideology, mass mobilisation and structural change. They involve coercion but not necessarily violence; they may be concluded by negotiation rather than simple overthrow. He also distinguishes between revolutions that are primarily economic or social in their demands; ones that are ideological, for example anti-colonial or Nationalist; and ones that are political, for example democratisation movements.[146]

Populist movements

There is a danger that 'populist' is a label applied to any movement you disagree with. Some authors adopt a 'thin' idea of what populism is, which adherents of populist movements might willingly identify with. One such conception says that populism is an ideology which is based on a distinction between 'pure people' and 'corrupt elites' in which populist movements are vehicles for the pure people to take decisions – 'the general will'. In this view, populist movements include, for example, the Solidarity movement in Poland, the 'Occupy' movement, and opposition parties and governments in many parts of the world.[147] It could also include popular uprisings against authoritarian regimes, and campaigns against environmental threats such as large dams, extractive industries, deforestation and so on.

Superficially, it might seem that populist movements could be an important strategy for social and community development. Closer scrutiny of even the thin version shows that they may not be compatible with some of the core values of social community development advocated here. First, the idea of the pure people implies the opposite too: there are 'bad' people who don't have a legitimate stake in society. This is inconsistent with the idea of ethical, hospitable communities and societies. The criticism of corrupt elites can easily turn into racist and sectarian conspiracy theories about who controls the world. It also implies that there are 'good' elites who are acceptable leaders, vanguard activists and trusted media sources who have special privileges or rights which others don't have. Such elites are likely to be inconsistent with inclusive and emancipatory participation. Lastly, there are problems with the idea of the general will. The ideas of thoughtless action and actionless thought have already been introduced. Chapter 5 considers the ways in which people may mistakenly blame minorities or people who are different for their discontents or bad circumstances. Chapter 6 explores consciousness and the relationships between beliefs and behaviour in greater depth. The analysis suggests that mechanisms for expressing the general will such as referenda and plebiscites may highlight discontents but are not addressing the root causes or providing solutions. Furthermore, paradoxically, populist leaders may also argue that apathy or indifference are expressions of the general will – the 'silent majority' – and that they are saying what others are thinking.[148]

Analysts who use a 'thicker' conception of populism identify even more problems with the concept.[149]

Goldstone sees populist movements as a variety of revolutionary movements. He adopts a 'thicker' view of what Populist movements are. He says, they are typically:

➢ Nationalist – blaming immigrants and international institutions for losses of status and opportunities which critics would describe as Nativist, Xenophobic and Sectarian.

➢ Assimilationist – believing that homogeneity is essential to cohesion and security.

- Coalitions of people who feel victimised – blaming outsiders but crucially blaming people worse off than themselves for trying to improve their relative position and feeling devalued by this.
- Anti government health, education and welfare provision and anti regulation and spending based on taxation as corrupt, inefficient or interfering in private matters but pro spending on defence and domestic security and immigration control.
- Against what they see as elites which may include Big Business, the media, experts and the judiciary though they may be supported by, or even led by, people from 'dissident elites'.
- In favour of strong leadership. Insiders might say leaders are charismatic figures with a direct and accessible style of communication and disciplined structure. Outsiders might see a description of such leaders as authoritarian demagogues as a criticism; insiders might not see that as a problem.[150]

Although one or more of these characteristics can be identified as present in all the examples of populist movements which fit the 'thin' definition, they are not always there and there are other characteristics which are often but not always there. Sometimes the political system is seen as having failed because it is weak or unstable. Sometimes, the political system is seen as failing because it does not offer real alternatives (a cartel of parties) or opportunities for representation or participation in a one-party state or authoritarian regime. There are important differences in the behaviour of populist movements in opposition and office – though even in office they may see themselves as insurgent.[151]

In summary, whether a thin or thick conception of populism is used, it is highly doubtful whether populist movements generally are consistent with the approach to social and community development taken here. That doesn't mean that individual movements are not, but they need to be analysed critically.

The circumstances of revolutions

Tosh quotes Laurence Stone in the *Causes of the English Revolution*, saying that revolutions happen because of:

- Preconditions
- Precipitants; and
- Triggers.[152]

In a book originally written in 1938 the historian Crane Brinton analysed revolutions (in England, France, America and Russia) and identified three strands which contributed to events:

- The actions and reactions of the actors in events broadly based on their intentions or beliefs.
- The social psychology of the situation – highlighting the influence of disappointed or frustrated expectations.
- Social and economic conditions.[153]

Although more than 80 years have passed, historians, policy analysts and various social science disciplines are still working with similar models.[154] Goldstone suggests that there are a range of conditions which give rise to the unstable equilibria that lead to revolutions (social and economic conditions are discussed further below).[155] They can be either an underlying structural cause (such as demographic change) or a transient, contingent cause (such as a rapid increase in fuel or food prices or taxation). The key political conditions, Goldstone argues, are:

- A regime which is characterised by one person (a 'Personalist regime') who can be blamed for events and circumstances.
- Alienation – opposition leading to divisions within elites (for instance, the military or judges either not supporting the regime or joining the opposition).
- Popular anger against injustice which results in both action and coalitions of people with diverse grievances (which may or may not be violent).
- A persuasive and shared narrative or ideology among the protestors (which may be religious or political and may appeal to historical precedents or traditions).
- A favourable international environment – either not interfering or taking actions in support of the opposition.

On the other hand, there are regimes which may be better protected because:

- They have exceptional resources to resist the opposition (for example, revenues to support patronage or security services and military power).
- Political structures allow them to shift the blame (for example, a head of state who can sack a prime minister or advisers).

➢ A potential group of activists or opposition are weakened by events or circumstances such as civil war (though as James C Scott has highlighted, even 'the weak' have ways of challenging oppression).[156]

➢ They have international support.

While after the event it is often possible to see the relevance of these factors, before or during periods of social change it is much more difficult to identify the factors. Predictions of success and failure are often mistaken. As with populist movements there is nothing which makes revolutions automatically conducive or inimical to social and community development.

Economic and social conditions

Chapter 3 was concerned primarily with the deliberate or intentional changing of society. The most purist 'materialist' historians would say that economic and social conditions are the sole drivers or determinants of social change and people and ideas play no role. Most historians would now accept that economic and social conditions play a critical part in social change, but ideas and people not only play a part in social change but influence material conditions as well as being influenced by them in various ways:[157]

➢ A Functionalist mechanism – social movements are agents or products of social change; ones that serve a purpose thrive in the circumstances. Conditions give rise to movements.

➢ Change happens on different levels and what motivates individuals is not the same as, for example, institutional change. They are not 'paired opposites' – individual versus mass or material versus cultural. Marx talked about substructures and superstructures but (even) he recognised reciprocal influences. Understanding the relationship between the different levels may draw on psychology and social psychology but also anthropology looking at how specific beliefs or rituals relate to social structures and systems. Modern anthropology is often wary of the more simplistic functionalist explanations of beliefs and behaviour.

➢ Movements and individuals provide an ideology or justification for economic and social interests. More recently, historians have paid more attention to the kind of language or discourse which justifies or explains beliefs and behaviour and shared and contested meanings.

➤ Many historians would be sceptical about claims to meta or grand narratives in which there are 'Ages' and 'Eras' such as Humanism or Revolution though this does not stop commentators grouping events implying more homogeneity than may be justified – such as the 'Arab Spring' in 2011.

➤ Change does not follow mechanical rules or laws of 'stages', 'progress', cycles of rise and fall or causation. Causation is complex: A does not always cause B. Sometimes it will, sometimes it won't. Sometimes something else will lead to B. Sometimes B will influence A ... and so on.

The implications of the analysis of how political, social and economic conditions give rise to revolutionary and populist movements are, at minimum, that change is neither completely random nor completely determined. Cas Mudde and Cristobal Rovira Kaltwasser, in their analysis of populism suggest that there are three measures of how successful populist movements are, not all equally desired by supporters. The first is electoral success – ultimately getting into government. The second is setting the policy agenda – getting the issues they think are important discussed.[158] The third is shaping public policies – policy impact. Policymaking – the discussion, design, implementation and evaluation of the principles which underlie action – is about change at the institutional and ideological levels. We now turn to analysing how public policy is made.

Policy studies

Policy studies sit somewhere between Political Science and History as a social science.

There is a school of policy analysis which helps explain social change through the ways in which social actors interact with each other.[159]

The essential elements of the model are:

1. Society is an open system which does not have one single overall controller.

2. Any issue or event has multiple stakeholders (individuals, groups and organisations) that have an interest in whether or how the issue is addressed.

3. Stakeholders have multiple perspectives. As well as differences between stakeholders, whether they are individuals or institutions, there

may be significant internal tensions or paradoxes for individual stakeholders.

4. How an issue is framed makes a big difference to how it is perceived. Framing may need to appeal on several levels: for example, individual motivation (self-interest or feelings such as dignity or self-esteem) and also on an ideological level ('equality' or 'self-determination').

5. Stakeholders assemble coalitions to achieve their goals.

6. Settlement of issues takes place through a process of negotiation and bargaining, sometimes with an element of coercion.

This model is very different from ones that suggest policy is made by eggheads ('Policy Wonks') sitting in darkened rooms thinking clever thoughts or only by politicians (possibly in formerly smoke-filled rooms). It is consistent with any of the strategies for social and community development (Consensus, Pluralist, Conflict and Violence). However, emancipatory, inclusive policy-making requires the kinds of analysis of society in Chapter 2, the principles of inclusion in Chapter 5 and the approaches to learning together in Chapter 6.

Summary and conclusion

Collective action for social and community change takes many forms. Just as Chapter 2 on society suggested, a focus on physical geography ignores the opportunities and challenges of many other kinds of grouping, so there is often a kind of short-sightedness about motivations for and forms of collective action:

➢ Motivations may be 'rational' and/or 'emotional' – calculations of cost and benefit, hope or fear. Many academic disciplines offer insight including individual and social Psychology, Economics (not just market-oriented economics), Political Science and Philosophy, Biology, Medical Sciences and Social Anthropology.

➢ Individual or interpersonal choice or agency about whether or how to act needs to be set in the contexts of structures and ideology; *but.*

➢ Structural and ideological changes are made up of many individual and interpersonal changes, which they have influenced.

➢ The opportunities for collective action are both growing and under threat from changes in technologies and organisation.

Implications for practice

1. We need to seek to understand what the forces and drivers are to promote or prevent collective action including at the individual level (psychological and self-interest) and interpersonal (material costs and benefits of collaboration); what the implications are of and for relationships with other people of competing or collaborating; the institutional barriers and springboards; and the ideological context.

2. This chapter offers a range of different explanations of what 'makes people tick' (a clock metaphor!). It questions some of the crude and simplistic accounts of behaviour. The explanations in a particular situation will reflect individual and social circumstances, individual and group psychology.

3. What strategies for collective action are adopted will depend partly on the situation, partly on the values of the activist or practitioner and the level(s) at which they are seeking to make changes or intervene. Among the key decisions which must be made are:

   ➤ At what level are you going to start? In Peter Westoby and Gerard Dowling's language, the possibilities are *Bonding, Banding, Building* and *Bridging* thought and action through creating ideologies.[160]

   ➤ How do you think social change comes about – Consensus, Pluralist, Conflict or Violence? This book has argued that neither Consensus nor Violence are plausible, effective, legitimate strategies.

   ➤ What are the roles of the state, private sector, philanthropic and mutual aid organisations?

   ➤ What models of organisation are necessary and desirable?

   ➤ How can participation be made emancipatory?

   ➤ How is an understanding of individual and group behaviour going to be built into practice?

   The detail of how these questions can be addressed is beyond the scope of this book.

4. Political, economic and social conditions influence the potential for social change and the forms it takes.

Box 4.1 Activities

1. In groups, think of metaphors used to describe collective action. What are the implications for how action comes about?
2. Listen to other people about how much control they feel they have over their circumstances and what their feelings (emotions) are about their situation. Listening may be one-to-one, in small groups, monitoring expressions (e.g. social media) or through social surveys.
3. If people think someone or something has significant control over the situation and their freedom to act, individually or together, who or what is it? What might explain their perception?
4. Think about all the advantages of action or inaction for individuals and groups. Don't assume that people will behave 'rationally' but it may help explain or motivate some behaviour.
5. Analyse the social, political and economic context in which you are operating. One tool for doing this is the STEEPLE analysis – analysing Social, Technological, Economic, Ethical, Legal, Politcal and Environmental factors.

Steeple Analysis.[161]

5
Equality and Emancipation

Introduction

Previous chapters have highlighted many issues about who social and community development is for and what it is trying to achieve. Underlying these questions is a concern about whether the goals and processes systematically exclude some people:

- Societies and communities have considerable potential to exclude people who are within and outside their boundaries. People may reject or devalue people unlike themselves living or working among them. At its most extreme this may lead to genocide. When, if ever, is it okay to exclude people?
- Development can benefit the better-off materially or the most powerful more than the worst-off and least powerful. Is there a basis for deciding what is good and bad development?
- Collective action is action by one group of people often 'against' another group of people. Members of both groups may suffer as a result. When is that justified?

Many theorists have argued that self-determination, autonomy and empowerment are the ultimate goals of societies and communities with collective action for development as the means. This chapter argues that these goals are not enough.

The International Association for Community Development includes the principle of:

> *Diversity, Equality & Social Inclusion:* All community members, regardless of gender, age, ability, race, culture, language, sexual orientation, or social and economic status are empowered and engaged in the community development process and are able to access its social and economic benefits.[1]

The National Occupational Standards for community development for England (similar standards exist for other countries in the UK) include in the key values:

➢ *Social justice and equality*

➢ *Anti-discrimination*

➢ *Community empowerment.*

They say that the process enables communities to work together to (among other things):

➢ *Challenge unequal power relationships*

➢ *Promote social justice, equality and inclusion.*[2]

This chapter explores some of the ideas that lie behind these kinds of statement and the implications for practice.

This chapter analyses the relationship between aspirations, needs and rights. It argues that none of these concepts, individually, can settle claims for resources (both material and non-material). Looking at them together and bringing in concepts of justice, equality and emancipation helps. However, it does not fully resolve these issues. Value judgements are important.

Human rights

It is significant that neither of the formulations above explicitly use the term Human Rights (in capitals because it is being used in a specific way but hereafter used in lower case). If it was deliberate, the most likely explanation is that human rights are seen as being in a Western individualist tradition.[3]

In fact, while the history of human rights can be traced back to debates in Europe in the seventeenth and eighteenth centuries, there have been many critics within Europe, and the roots of the concept are to be found outside Europe and in earlier times.[4]

A starting point for much of the thinking about human rights is that they are a necessary tool of governance: there must be a basis for the relationship between rulers and ruled. Setting out their respective rights and responsibilities provides a basis. Some theorists of human rights like to divide human rights into generations. First-generation human rights are seen as the defence of liberty and civil or civic rights. Second-generation rights are associated with political, economic and social equity or equality. Third-generation rights are associated with group or collective rights – for example, national self-determination, education or the expression of group solidarity. Some theorists add a fourth generation of rights – for example, to live in particular environments (e.g. the right to shape cities) or environmental sustainability. These rights may not be rights for humans only, for humans currently living (future generations must be considered) or rights to live in a particular place (e.g. keeping Antarctica free of human settlement).[5]

First- and second-generation rights are generally interpreted as the rights of individuals with the state responsible for upholding them. In the seventeenth century John Locke connected liberty, equality and the commons when he said:

> the fruits [the world] naturally produces, and beasts it feeds, belong to mankind in common.

Before going on to say that private property was essential and that:

> every man has a property in his own person: this nobody has any right to but himself. The labour of his body, and the work of his hands, we may say, are properly his.[6]

There is a phrase about human rights being 'nonsense on stilts' which is often misquoted, misattributed and misunderstood. The Utilitarian philosopher Jeremy Bentham (and later quoted by John Stuart Mill) said talk of *natural* rights was nonsense on stilts. He thought that rights are derived from the practice of government and, usually, a corollary of duties under the law.[7] As Jim Ife says, human rights are not 'objective facts' to be discovered, but a social construction.[8]

Other arguments have been put forward for the basis of human rights:

- *They have a biological basis* – For example, that they favour survival or that humans have a consciousness which animals and plants don't have or that all actions are derived from actions of the brain. Others argue that even if animals have consciousness, they don't have duties to one another but that humans do.[9]

- *They are divinely prescribed* – Though they have also drawn on secular traditions and prescriptions, it is easy to identify principles of human rights in the major world religions. The Hammurabi Code, named after its compiler, a ruler of ancient Mesopotamia, is seen as the foundation for many of the principles of equality, how to live socially and what to do if someone breaks the rules. It influenced

Jewish, Christian and Muslim formulations of rights and responsibilities. Both Hinduism and Buddhism promoted freedom from fear, from want, from ill-health, and freedom of conscience, the right to knowledge and responsibilities to live selflessly, for example. They also highlighted responsibilities to the natural world. Confucian teaching stressed what humans have in common.

It is a cornerstone of the idea of 'universal' human rights that they apply to all humans. This idea can be found in Jewish, Hindu, Christian, Buddhist and Muslim teachings and in the writings of philosophers in ancient Mesopotamia, Greece and Rome. For example, Judaism, Christianity and Islam all teach that people are created 'in the image of God'. Within each faith some traditions interpret this to mean that all humans must be respected equally. However, in all these faiths some traditions make implicit or explicit exceptions in practice if not in principle. In some traditions rules and rights only applied to believers, or people of the same rank, but even then tolerance might be obligatory. In other traditions rights are applied to all. Contemporary advocates of universal human rights still argue that humans have different capacities and responsibilities to exercise rights and responsibilities: generally, children are seen as having more need of 'protective' rights than adults but fewer rights to make choices.

Michael Ignatieff argues strongly against the dominant conceptions of human rights as 'universal' and trumping other arguments. He argues they are often used (only) to advance particularist causes: people (individuals, groups, states) use them to support specific interests but don't necessarily support the same rights in relation to other interests. States, groups and individuals (notably the USA and its people, he says) also argue that the duties associated with rights do not apply to them. He says supporters of human rights treat them as idols.[10]

The argument about whether human rights 'trump' national sovereignty or vice versa is ongoing, but the idea that human rights take precedence has been incorporated into international law since the end of World War II, with various war crimes trials and then legal instruments to enact the Universal Declaration of Human Rights in 1948. However, governments routinely advance arguments for why a particular right or interpretation does not apply or why another takes precedence.

If human rights are seen as a way of organising social relationships, it is at least possible to imagine that there are different routes and vehicles for achieving common destinations. Bentham identified the goal as human happiness. Martha Nussbaum and Amartya Sen have suggested the ultimate goal is the realisation of human capabilities and that rights are about removing barriers to their achievement.[11] Although he comes to a different conclusion about the value of human rights, Ignatieff says human rights are necessary to protect human agency.[12] By having different layers of means to achieve ends, a framework emerges in which different institutional arrangements or ideologies can coexist but be tested against how much they contribute to and/or undermine human rights. This might include different forms of economic, political or social organisation – such as capitalism and socialism; representative democracy; family life; and religious observance. Thus rules on privacy or free speech are not ends in themselves but are means to an end. Universal human rights does not necessarily mean uniformity. This approach also helps judge between the rights of individuals and groups and between different individual rights. Individual rights need to be balanced with each other.

Rights as individual aspirations

Using the levels presented in previous chapters, we could say that capabilities are individual aspirations. To understand and advance them, individuals need to be conscious of them and believe they have a right to them. If someone believes they are less than equal to others or they do not have the right to freedoms others enjoy, they will not 'claim' them. As we shall explore in Chapter 6, people may be made to believe that they do not have rights that other people do. Some prisoners may believe that they have forfeited all rights. Some lesbian, Gay and Bisexual people may not feel they have a right to same-sex relationships; Some disabled people may feel that their impairments justify restrictions on rights. Survivors of gender-based violence may feel they deserved it or that it is their duty to endure it. How to address limited aspirations, low expectations and internalised blame or a perception of low-self-worth is addressed in the next chapter.

Needs as a way of reconciling individual aspirations

Aspirations are often expressed in terms of the merit of legitimacy of competing needs. In the 1940s Abraham Maslow identified a hierarchy of needs from physiological to self-actualisation.[13] David Harvey argued that there were nine areas of needs:

- Food
- Housing
- Medical care
- Education
- Social and environmental services

- Consumer goods
- Recreation
- Neighbourhood amenities
- Transport facilities.[14]

Later, Len Doyal and Ian Gough argued that there were some basic absolute needs which are universal satisfiers which enhance physical health and human autonomy in all cultures.[15] Their approach was incorporated into British equality legislation as 'central and valuable freedoms' and later these were replaced by a measurement framework based on the capabilities approach of Sen and Nussbaum introduced above. The core capabilities, for adults, were identified as:

1. Be alive
2. Be healthy
3. Be knowledgeable, to understand and reason, and to have the skills to participate in society
4. Enjoy a comfortable standard of living, with independence and security
5. Engage in productive and valued activities
6. Enjoy individual, family and social life
7. Participate in decision-making, have a voice and influence
8. Be and express yourself, having self-respect
9. Know you will be protected and treated fairly by the law.[16]

There are several fundamental criticisms of the focus on needs as rights:

- Very often needs are seen simply as deficits, reinforcing that people are victims, dependent and without agency. Reformulating needs as the ability to use the resources or assets they have, brings the idea more in line with the capabilities approach, as the British equalities measurement framework does.
- Ivan Illich criticised development as creating a habit of *'the organized satisfaction of needs'* rather than the pursuit of peace and justice.[17]
- Needs are frequently conflated with interests: what is good for an individual becomes their right. That is difficult to reconcile with finite resources and it is not relational: it does not provide a mechanism for deciding between competing interests. In fact, as Napoleon observed,

it may generate more conflict: *A man will fight harder for his interests than for his rights.*[18]

- As the example of British equalities framework shows, there is no definitive list of what needs are, even within one state the British list does not cover Northern Ireland). It is not accepted globally.

- There is a problem if needs are seen simply as either only absolute or relative. If we only focus on absolute poverty, we ignore the real injustices of relative poverty in prosperous parts of the world. On the other hand, some needs may seem trivial 'First World' problems. Waiting to be seen for more than four hours in an Accident and Emergency Department in London is generally less life-threatening than the absence of services for people with Ebola at the height of the epidemic in Sierra Leone.[19] Nevertheless, it can be a matter of life and death and, whether it is or not, the sense of injustice can be an important spur to social and political action. Whether something is called a need does not take away the politics of calls on resources. Jonathan Bradshaw suggested a *'Taxonomy of Need'* which identified that needs can be *Normative* (usually defined by experts – for example, nutritional standards); *Felt* (the feeling of hunger); *Expressed* (feelings turned into action – asking for food) and *Comparative* (consumption relative to other people).[20]

- In relation to the hierarchy idea specifically, there is a problem with the idea that food, for example, is independent of self-actualisation because it is an expression of love and identity or that shelter comes before play as a need in children's development – they 'need' satisfying simultaneously.

- In the 1990s Michael Cahill noted that social policy was usually presented from the perspective of the provider or the institutions – for example, Housing, Education or Healthcare. This marginalises the experience of the population: they are treated as consumers – not producers, let alone, agents of their well-being, or even co-producers of home life, learning or health. It also reinforces the silos between providers of dwellings and, say, providers of health and social care in the home.[21]

Nevertheless, 'needs' provide a currency for adjudicating claims for resources. The idea that we have interpersonal duties and rights is expressed in the idea of horizontal human rights,[22] as discussed later in the chapter.

Institutions

The institutional level involves two very different ways of looking at rights.

- *Satisficers*
  Needs must generally be met though institutions. 'Shelter' is a universal need. We cannot say that every individual has a right to a particular form of housing. We might say they have a right to particular accommodation to suit their circumstances. We might also say that if they have the resources they can choose different kind of housing. Doyal and Gough have made a distinction between *Needs* and *Satisficers* which are means of meeting needs. A dwelling or a type of dwelling is a satisficer. If a society decides that there are minimum standards housing, which should be available to all or should be appropriate to specific circumstances, we can call it a denial of rights.[23]

  Satisficers are highly contextual: sleeping in a tent in the mud for a few days might be fun for music festival goers; it might be seen as a necessary sacrifice by volunteer soldiers in a battle; it might be seen as a less bad alternative to death or injuries by refugees or internally displaced people in a camp; but it may also be a denial of rights to 'adequate shelter'.

- *Rights and responsibilities of institutions*
  The discussion about different religious and political approaches to human rights highlights a fundamental question about what the rights and responsibilities of institutions are. Specifically, there is a question about whether states have unique rights and responsibilities. States which have been accused of genocide have generally argued that they have sovereignty over their subjects, so they can do what they like. Individuals accused of genocide have argued that they are not individually responsible because they were obeying orders. The acts of perpetrators and the experiences of victims happen because of their identification with groups. In this context, they are institutions. Killing people because they are a member of a group, is seen, by many, as a particularly reprehensible crime.[24] The debate about institutional rights extends to whether religious institutions and states have the right to prescribe or proscribe a wide range of behaviours: contraception, terminations, polygamy (usually polygyny), same-sex marriage, specific ways of killing animals and so on. These raise questions about whether universal rights and responsibilities take precedence over specific ones, and whether collective rights are more or less important than individual rights. Equality considerations are frequently cited as a way of deciding.

Rights as ideology

The highest level, in terms of abstraction from everyday life, are the rights incorporated in national and international declarations such as the UN Declaration of Human Rights (UNDHR), the African National Congress Freedom Charter and national constitutions.[25] It is argued here that such statements are ideological and infrastructures – 'roads' to a destination. They are both prescriptions of ends and means, needs and satisficers.

They may be specific to a time or place. The view that people in the UK have a right to free health care is not an international right. However, even if it seems under threat to some people, or not always a reality, it is deeply embedded in British social and political life. Even if rights are declared to be eternal and universal, they reflect the times and context in which they are formulated. For example, the UN Declaration says nothing explicitly about sexual orientation. However, increasing numbers of countries interpret the opening statement that *'All human beings are born free and equal in dignity and rights'* to mean that if some people have the right to marry, or have civil partnerships, then all people should. Likewise, the UNDHR does not mention rights to a good and sustainable environment. There is, however, clearly a concern for future generations which has led to the idea of sustainability. A concern with both the environment and the well-being of animals has led some people to question whether human rights are a form of *Speciesism* and others have noted that many religious and cultural traditions see humans as having duties to animals and the environment.[26]

Many national constitutions say nothing or only negative things about equality – for example, rights are 'irrespective' of gender, sexuality, disability, race, religion, ethnicity. They are often amended or reinterpreted to reflect changing attitudes. For example, in 2015, Ireland changed its constitution and became the first country in the world to legalise same-sex marriage after a popular vote. In the next section, equality is explored in depth.

Table 5.1 draws together the concepts of rights, satisficers, needs and aspirations using the four-level framework presented in previous chapters. It also introduces the themes of justice, oppression, equality and emancipation which the chapter will now go on to discuss.

Analysing human rights at these different levels makes clearer the ways in which different actors have different duties and responsibilities. Institutions such as states or associations of states, businesses or service providers have responsibilities to protect, prevent and eliminate abuse and enhance human rights – what are sometimes called vertical human rights. Individuals interacting with each other have a right not to be discriminated against as well as a responsibility not to discriminate against each other – horizontal human rights. It has proved hard in practice to agree what the relationship between horizontal and vertical rights and responsibilities is,

Table 5.1 Rights, justice, equality and emancipation on four levels

	Human Rights	Justice	Oppression	Equality	Emancipation
Infrastructural (Ideological)	Universal Human Rights	Justice as utilitarian, based on property rights or egalitarian Justice as retribution or reparation	Counter-hegemony Liberation ideologies e.g. post-colonial, Feminist	Equality as outcomes, opportunities Cultural Addressing ideologies such as patriarchy and racialism	Overcoming ideologies of unequal worth Understanding different kinds of power relationship: Power within and with as well as over or to....
Institutional (Instruments)	Satisficers Groups have rights and responsibilities	Justice as process; Transitional justice	Overcoming exploitation and repression	Structural Elimination of institutional discrimination Positive action	Making alliances Negotiating conflict Including highlighting how patterns of domination and subordination constrain both Creating structures that foster autonomy
Interpersonal	Needs	Restorative	Challenging marginalisation, e.g. being made invisible or being 'othered' Overcoming violence	Elimination of prejudice, stereotyping and expressions of hate and Solitarism Alliances across difference	Developing alternative ways of exercising power to dominating form Seeing hidden forms of power Developing sense of group agency
Individual	Aspirations	Justice as recognition	Seeing internalised oppression	Identity Intersectionality	Development of self-confidence and self-esteem

with many institutions not wanting duties imposed on them but wanting individuals to owe duties to institutions – specifically states. Theorists talk about *converse rights* which are the responsibilities that individuals owe society (usually the state) and essentially vertical duties owed upwards, and *correlative duties* which all actors (including non-state actors and individuals) owe each other: every right implies a duty by someone.[27]

The idea of correlative rights and responsibilities makes it easier to understand how to address issues of where group rights or individual rights appear to conflict. This could be conflicts within groups or between groups. The implied principle is that non-state actors, as well as state actors, have a responsibility to uphold the rights of other actors.

Whether rights are seen as a universal 'truth' which all institutions and individuals have a duty to uphold or whether they are seen as expressions of potential or aspirations, there are still questions of how they are achieved. One of the characteristics which Table 5.1 highlights is that these concepts fit together as both ends and means. Shelter, achieved through a house, is a goal but it is also a means of achieving capability. Back in the seventeenth century Thomas Hobbes said: '*Covenants, without the Sword, are but Words.*'[28] Instruments include:

- Law
- Economic sanctions
- Other sanctions such as restrictions on travel
- Education
- Force.

There are significant problems with such top-down approaches: imposing self-determination, freedom or autonomy is a contradiction; it can take away agency from the people it is supposed to be supporting. It may reinforce the very abuse of rights it aims to reduce or eliminate. However, doing nothing is also a denial of human rights.

Justice

If the human rights discourse does not, alone, clarify all the issues raised at the beginning of the chapter neither does 'Justice'. This is for several fundamental reasons:

1. In English, *Justice* refers to both the process of justice – the institutions, the rules by which decisions are taken – and the results of decisions. In Sanskrit and other languages different words are used. Some

philosophers are only concerned with whether a process is fair. For example, what would an independent, impartial observer decide or what would parties to an argument about justice decide if they did not know if they would be 'winners' or 'losers'. Others are only, or much more, concerned with outcomes.[29]

2. If we are concerned with outcomes, then there is not just one single principle for the allocation of resources on which everybody would agree, in all circumstances. Take Aristotle's memorable question, *who should get the flute?* – the person who made it (an idea of justice based on property rights); the person who plays it best (a Utilitarian argument); or the person who needs it most (an egalitarian argument)?[30]

3. There can be different views on who or what justice is for: Is it relevant to consider ability to pay, the ability to benefit or benefit others, or the prevention of harm? This may depend on the specific issue being considered – health, education, employment or housing, for example. It also depends on whether it is one or both of *justice as equality of distribution* – often the right to abolish (socio-economic) difference – or *justice as recognition* of (cultural) identity – the right to be different and valued positively. Nancy Fraser argues that many important injustices are both economic and cultural and require remedies that are both redistributive and involve recognition and revaluing identities. As she says, justice in relation to gender may involve abolition of some differences (e.g. pay differences), revaluing others (everyday interactions) and deconstructing others (notions of masculinity and femininity). Fraser highlights that the degree and nature of distributive and recognition injustice may differ between groups. This is considered further in the discussions of oppression and inequality later in the chapter.[31]

4. Justice has an association with the idea of crime and law, as defined by state (or interstate) top-down relationships. Legal systems are often narrower than justice, or specific to a particular notion of justice – property rights, for example. They can also apply to non-humans – corporations can protect property rights; flora and fauna may be protected – though the motivation may be to benefit humans. Legal systems can, however, be a starting point for thinking about how justice relates to social justice. There are many different kinds of process that are potentially tools of development.

Theories of justice in relation to crime mainly start from one of two aims. Justice is either or both for:

➢ *Retribution* – the perpetrator gets the punishment they deserve. That may include an element of reparation or restitution: paying the victim or the state or repairing the damage.

- *Reductivism* – preventing further crime by incapacitation (locking up the perpetrator); deterrence; rehabilitation; or mitigating or remedying the damage by showing remorse or regret to the victims.

Reconciliation or *rapprochement* can be part of either goal.

In war situations, particularly, retributive justice may extend to people responsible for planning or organising acts committed by others – crimes against humanity or genocide, for instance. War crimes tribunals or trials may lead to punishment, but they are also events at which truth may be discovered or evidence uncovered and a kind of rapprochement.[32]

Correcting injustice may be seen to require compensation or reparations for victims or survivors. Many activist campaigns have tried, and some have succeeded, in getting payments for injury or loss of property or dignity for whole communities as well as individuals. In terms of payments to communities, rather than individuals, possibly the biggest payments so far are those of the US government to Native Americans.[33]

Transitional Justice is a kind of justice that can, in theory, be both retributive and reductivist. It is often proposed or implemented at the end of violent conflict or repression. The UN defines it as:

> the full range of processes and mechanisms associated with a society's attempt to come to terms with a legacy of large-scale past abuses, in order to ensure accountability, serve justice and achieve reconciliation.[34]

Restorative justice,[35] as a term, is relatively new though many would argue that it has deep roots in many cultures, faith traditions and political arrangements in which perpetrators and victims face each other, or the wider community or society is involved in dealing with an offence (not just as juries hearing evidence). It seems to offer a radically different model from the idea of crime as a relationship between the state and the perpetrator: it focuses on the idea of the relationship between the perpetrator and the victim – which may be a community not (just) an individual. Restorative justice is increasingly part of criminal justice systems, particularly youth offending and social work.[36]

Theorists and practitioners argue about whether it is an alternative punishment or an alternative *to* punishment. Based on what is known about its results it can be both retributive and reductivist. What evidence there is suggests that it may reduce reoffending; has produced high rates of negotiated agreements for restitution and high compliance rates; and reduced victims' fear of crime. The evidence of how effective it is and how it is effective is relatively limited. There are other issues with restorative justice too. It has been suggested that it is more likely to work in contexts where the bonds between the perpetrators and victims are strong or 'thick'. Where relationships are loose or 'thin' it may not work. It has an unclear relationship with the major theories of what 'causes' crime, let alone social injustice.

Vigilante action. There may be people in the community who claim to be representing the community's values by enforcing behaviour norms through vigilante patrols, threats of punishment and so on. This is particularly evident when the state is not seen as legitimate or effective. Punishment squads in Northern Ireland are a case in point. They do not reflect any of the principles of justice generally, or restorative justice specifically.[37]

Theories about causes of crime

Theories about what causes crime that are relevant to what responses are 'just' include:

- It is a deliberate choice based on rational pursuit of self-interest, even if it is sometimes a bad choice, that is, the actor has agency. In this context punishment might be a deterrent. Restorative justice might work to alter the balance of interests or it might not change anything.
- Structures: it is the result of internal or external factors beyond the control or awareness of the perpetrators. Although in this situation punishment might seem inappropriate, restorative justice might be ineffective.
- Injustice is simply breaking the rules. It is a transgression of, or deviance from, (socially constructed) norms of behaviour or 'order'. However, the rules may be skewed in such a way to privilege some people or behaviour and to punish disproportionately others. Punishment might encourage conformity or further reinforce nonconformity. Restorative justice could reinforce or challenge privilege.

Asking for justice, demanding fair and effective laws, and tackling crime and its causes are often part of the rhetoric of social and community development but they do not resolve all the conflicts within and between communities and societies.

Justice is clearly not the same as equality but is closely related. Wolfgang Sachs suggests that human rights discourse is animated by a concern with absolute justice, and concerns about inequality animated by idea of relative justice. He notes that the conceptions collide when, for example, the middle classes of the Global South want to catch up with the North at the expense of the poorest in the South.[38]

It is to equality we now turn.

Equality [39]

The National Occupational Standards referred to at the start of this chapter relate to equality and inequality, but different conceptions of what this means lie at the heart of many arguments about social and community development. Although Rudyard Kipling may not be the first author one thinks of in relation to equality (an apologist for imperialism, for example), he provides a framework for exploring the key questions about equality: What and Where and When, How, Why and Who? [40]

What?

Like many other concepts, it is easier to define equality by what it is not than what it is. It is not:

- *Uniformity*: being the same or treating people identically. 'We treat everybody the same' can be unequal treatment, a paradox known at least since Aesop's fable of the fox who offers the stork soup to eat from a shallow plate.[41] Different circumstances or beliefs may mean that different treatment is necessary to treat people equally.
- *Treating everybody differently*. Treating people in similar circumstances the same can be equal. It is arbitrary, unfair or unjust differences which are the problem. The question is: What are the relevant criteria?
- *One-dimensional*. Making health care free may address economic inequality but may not address barriers of gender or race discrimination.
- *Always necessary or desirable to achieve*. Some economists and politicians argue that (even growing) inequality is vital to create incentives to generate wealth, with or without redistribution, though many would disagree. This is discussed further later in the chapter. More widespread is a view that access to scarce resources such as a job, or access to a university place, should be based on merit. However, 'merit' is not an objective measure and there is a risk that allocating resources on merit will create enduring elites.[42]
- *An individual status*: it is a relationship. Equality is usually a comparison with other people and always defined in relation to a standard. The harm that inequality does to people better off in some sense as well as to those worse off is an increasingly discussed topic, and considered below.

R. H. Tawney popularised the concept of *equality of opportunity* in lectures given in 1929. He suggested that it was a formula for the removal of barriers based on social institutions (such as class or inheritance) with the possibility of:

> Equal chances of using to the full [people's] natural endowments of physique, of character and intelligence.[43]

The vocabulary of equality of opportunity was taken up in North America and Europe, particularly in relation to race and sex equality from the 1960s onwards. It has often been expressed in terms of access or getting everyone to the same starting line in a race in which there will be winners and losers.

Tawney warned that equality of opportunity could not become a reality if:

> The capacities of some are sterilized or stunted by their social environment, while those of others are favoured or pampered by it.[44]

The recognition that environments shape capacities was addressed both by ideas of positive or affirmative action and by the distinction made by Amartya Sen and others between *capacities* and *capabilities*. Capability is the potential that individuals have which may not be realised or used because of the barriers or penalties they endure as a result of the social group with which they are identified (as women, for example) or disadvantages they may have (the impairments of a disabled person compounded by the environment in which they live).[45] As Napoleon is supposed to have said:

> Ability is of little account without opportunity.[46]

A society simply based on the availability of opportunities might be fairer in allocating those opportunities, but it would still result in substantive *inequality of outcome*. The argument that this matters is considered further in the section on '*Why?*'. Equality of outcome is often measured in terms of whether different social groups have the same shares in the good and bad aspects of society. Groups may be over- or under-represented in terms of good health, for example. This works as a concept when it is a good that everybody wants or wants to avoid. It is not so useful when people have different aspirations. If women are 'under-represented' in the army by choice that is not necessarily a problem. If it is the result of discrimination or (conscious or unconscious) structuring of their ambitions it might be.

The idea that equality of outcome and equality of opportunity are neither necessary nor sufficient conditions is reflected in the idea that it is how people are treated that matters. Tawney talked about *equality of consideration* and other people emphasise equality before the law or *equality of process*. The argument that only process matters is a limited version of equality. It doesn't consider different starting points and is not concerned with outcomes.

The implications of the different conceptions of equality are frequently evident in social and community development. Patterns of segregation and stratification by age, gender, faith or ethnicity are evidence of inequality of outcomes. They may well reflect inequality of opportunity, but they may also reflect inequality of consideration or disparity of esteem. Even if they reflect different values or aspirations, those attitudes may also reflect the experience, for example, that if you are a woman or from a minority ethnic group or religion, you may have to be twice as good to get a job.

Why?

There are several strong arguments for equality, but it is important to address the fact that many of them are used in a (distorted) mirrored way as arguments for inequality.

The *biological* argument that we are all part of the same species is an argument for equality. Acknowledging biological difference such as that women bear children does not change this proposition, but it is frequently used to try to justify discrimination. Likewise, physical, sensory or mental impairments of people are used to restrict access to places and roles. The different treatment that disabled people, women or specific ethnic groups often experience are social constructions, not an inevitable result of biological difference. Biological differences are often exaggerated or distorted.

Likewise, *religious teaching* is used to justify equality (e.g. humans are made in the image of God), but some adherents of specific faiths will argue that this only applies to 'true believers', does not apply to non-believers or heretics or only applies to men. This can often be challenged as a misreading of religious texts. Interpretations of what 'true belief' is usually postdate the texts and there are many examples of inconsistencies of interpretations. *Moral* arguments for equality do not refer to religious authority but draw on a similar principle, that we are all human and nobody is superior or inferior.

The *civic* argument for equality reflects many of the arguments put forward in the chapter on collective action and on human rights. On the traditional view of citizenship, it is a status through which people have rights and obligations but are equally entitled to the protection of the state. A variation on this argument is that unless the *law* guarantees equal treatment, citizens will not respect it. While the status of citizenship covers many people in a country, it does not cover everybody – citizens of other states and people who are deemed to have forfeited their citizenship – and it is quite clear that even among people who are citizens, not everyone enjoys equal rights. There are wider views of the concept of 'citizen' which see it as both a status and a practice of participation, in which everyone has a right to exercise their agency or autonomy. Institutions, especially the state, have a responsibility to remove the structural barriers to exercising agency.[47]

The *economic or managerial* argument is that inequality – specifically, arbitrary discrimination – is inefficient and costly. Not selecting the best person for the job or refusing to provide goods and services to people willing to pay for them or who need them is poor business practice or inefficient. Having a diverse population, workforce, customer or client base brings benefits to societies, communities and organisations.[48]

For individuals, there is also a *self-interest* argument for equality. There is evidence that societies which are unequal, measured in terms of incomes and other ways, are bad for the more affluent people, as well as poorer people, particularly in terms of health and life expectancy. There has been extensive debate since the publication of *The Spirit Level: Why More Equal Societies Almost Always Do Better* by Richard Wilkinson and Kate Pickett about whether its central contention that income inequality is the cause of many other kinds of inequality, including health, education and crime (victims and perpetrators), is proven. Critics have argued that the evidence has been 'cherry-picked'; that they have only demonstrated correlation not causation; that they have been arbitrary and inconsistent in how inequality is measured; and that the statistical methods they have used are inappropriate. The authors have responded to some of these criticisms.[49] The argument that economic inequality is good for people because it increases the size of the cake and/or wealth creation requires inequality, but the benefits then trickle down to poorer people through either redistribution or through the rich spending on goods and services, has been refuted many times, including by the International Monetary Fund.[50]

Where and when?

Not much attention is usually paid to the role of place and time in relation to inequality. However, the forms and targets of (in)equality do vary according to place and time. Literacy is a need, or satisficer, in the framework used above: it is a means to several ends. 'Being literate' both in the narrow functional sense of 'understanding the word' and also in the Freirean idea of critical literacy – 'understanding the world' – means different things in different contexts.[51] It might mean access to 'official' languages like Spanish or Portuguese or languages of elites, like English, in South America or being able to continue to speak 'indigenous' languages such as Quechua and Aymara, or, increasingly, it might be digital literacy. The increasing awareness of communities based on identity with or without shared economic interests changes the nature of inequality. In the 1920s and 1930s Tawney thought race was not as important as it had been during the period of slavery and imperial expansion and that class was the most important form of stratification. However, race clearly remains an important aspect of inequality.[52]

Who?

Human rights statements generally start off saying they apply to 'everyone' but often go on to identify specific groups which are treated unequally. The 1948 UNDHR talks about distinctions of:

> race, colour, sex, language, religion, political or other opinion, national or social origin, property, birth or other status. Furthermore, no distinction shall be made on the basis of the political, jurisdictional or international status of the country or territory to which a person belongs.[53]

The Equality section of the 1996 South African Constitution says:

> The state may not unfairly discriminate directly or indirectly against anyone on one or more grounds, including race, gender, sex, pregnancy, marital status, ethnic or social origin, colour, sexual orientation, age, disability, religion, conscience, belief, culture, language and birth.[54]

The 2010 Equality Act (which applies in Great Britain but not in Northern Ireland) refers to Protected Characteristics of:

> Age, disability, gender reassignment, marriage and civil partnership, pregnancy and maternity, Race, religion or belief, sex, sexual orientation.[55]

Whereas in Northern Ireland it is:

> generally unlawful for service providers to discriminate on five key grounds – sex (including gender reassignment and pregnancy/maternity), disability, race, religious belief or political opinion, and sexual orientation ...

discrimination on grounds of age in the provision of goods, facilities and services is not unlawful. Age discrimination law covers employment and vocational training only.[56]

Although there are clearly differences within and between countries and over time, they all have in common that a risk of discrimination is highlighted because an individual identifies, or is identified, with a group. It is important to note that the individual may or may not identify with the group they are said by others to belong to. From a community development perspective, it is generally important that the individual both identifies and is identified as belonging to a group, otherwise the principle that individuals should exercise agency is not met and also collective action is unlikely to occur.

A general assertion of equality for all would start from the assumption that the default position is that discrimination is not justified unless there are specific, relevant grounds. Thus it links to the idea of justice. It is possible to identify a trend in justifications for discrimination and anti-discrimination. The UN Declaration was challenging discrimination based on perceived 'biological' differences: race, colour, sex, and institutional affiliations (religion, political opinion). Subsequently, there has been a move to recognise more explicitly socially constructed circumstances. There has been a shift from 'race' to 'ethnicity'; from 'sex' to 'gender'. There is increasing recognition of events and circumstances that trigger discrimination, but which also change: pregnancy, maternity or age. Anti-discrimination policy and practice are often about separating the event or the stage in people's lives from assumptions about what those circumstances mean – for example, giving birth does not automatically entail traditional patterns of 'motherhood'. Ideologies of superiority and inferiority play a major part in discriminatory behaviour and beliefs. Arguments based on views of morality are still used to justify inequality – for example, on sexuality. They are increasingly challenged on grounds of inconsistencies in, or reinterpretations of, traditional or orthodox authorities, and evidence that the supposed virtues of one position and vices of another are stereotypical or inaccurate – for example, 'marriage is for procreation'.

Conceptions of inequality as applied to groups have moved more quickly than the idea of 'group' human rights. Sometimes the discrimination or prejudice takes the form of an assertion that (members of) groups can't or don't want a role or a resource – for example, 'disabled people can't ...' or 'women don't want ...'. This is often a form of essentialism too: *'Men are from Mars; Women are from Venus.'*[57] These arguments are generally answered by evidence that some 'disabled people can ...', 'women *do* want ...'. Such arguments are complicated, but not invalidated, by examples of when members of a group can't or don't want to be, or to become, a particular thing. Different aptitudes and aspirations can be both/either a reflection of diversity and/or a reflection of different opportunities in the past or internalised oppression. This links to the idea of capabilities discussed above: that what people want to, and can, be or do depends not only on personal resources but on the context in which they exist. The equality principle is that people should have choice and agency. Group equality is the right to make a choice without penalty. It is also important to recognise that people have multiple characteristics. The discrimination they experience may be amplified or muted by different facets of who they are, and there may be horizontal inequalities – inequalities within groups. A focus on 'who' is often expressed in crude 'binary' and zero-sum terms: that equality for one group must involve losses for another group. Such a perception is usually based on favouring the status quo and on the belief that fair allocation of 'goods' is not a principle which benefits everybody.

In many cases of legislation and policy, there are exceptions to general rules of non-discrimination. In general, non-discrimination is applied to public goods. Exceptions generally apply to 'private' behaviour, such as actions within a home, or personal services, where someone might prefer, say, to be looked after by someone of the same sex and/or a speaker of the same language or from the same religious background.

The analysis of which groups are the targets of equalities policies highlights some of the principles of how inequality can be addressed, which is discussed in the next section.

Even though there is no global consensus on which groups are the proper target of equality policies, the common features are:

- That the individual both identifies with and is identified as belonging to a group.
- They endure arbitrary differences in treatment.
- The measure of inequality is generally access to public goods and public recognition.
- Often they focus on frustrated aspirations, barriers to agency and exercising capability.

Identifying equality target groups can lead to problems in relation to the concerns raised in Chapter 2 about treating communities as internally homogeneous, externally differentiated and inert. Listing of groups may foster binary notions of 'them' and 'us' and win-lose perceptions. It may be difficult to add or remove groups as societies change. It is important to recognise that groups are socially constructed, can change and that individuals 'belong' to multiple groups.

How?

How inequality operates and how to tackle inequality have been widely written about. Neil Thompson argues that processes operate at three separate but interrelated levels: the Personal, Cultural and Social. He also talks about macro and micro levels.[58] Here, the structure of previous chapters is used. There is an established distinction between *prejudice* which is an individual attitude towards groups and their members; *stereotypes* which are attitudes that are expressed in interactions with others; and *discrimination* which is behaviour (which can be interpersonal or institutional). When prejudice and stereotyping are examined, it is apparent that they are created, communicated and reinforced through institutional and ideological structures and processes.

The individual in this context includes the aspirations of individuals, how their hopes are structured and the perceptions (including prejudices) they have of other people, including feelings of superiority or inferiority. Research on prejudice has focused on the role of:

➢ A physiological evolution element which makes people attracted to, or repelled by, others who might be a threat ('infection') or an opportunity ('mates'), based on senses such as sight, smell or sound.[59]

➢ Personality types. The early literature on this tended to categorise prejudiced people as irrational. More recent literature suggests it is a reasoned but mistaken response, say, to a threat or loss. It is also argued that personal ('I') and social identities ('we') are intertwined: 'I think or do something this way because that's what people like me think or do'.

➢ Universal processes of categorising people, including a need for 'in' and 'out' groups. These categorisations may be conscious or unconscious.

➢ Social circumstances: both material and the desire to maintain or enhance social status – motivation may also be conscious or unconscious. This is often expressed as Group Conflict.

➢ Socio-cultural processes: the mechanisms through which specific prejudices are transmitted, including the way that the objects of prejudice may absorb them or react to them.[60]

The complexity of explanations highlights why it is dangerous to treat individuals simply as bigots, dupes or victims when they display prejudice. Overcoming prejudice is more likely to be successful by recognition of common or legitimate aspirations, while not accepting their conclusions about others.

The interpersonal mechanisms of inequality may be stereotypes and lack of knowledge of different beliefs and behaviour. Physical distance or separation may reinforce (mis-)perceptions. It may be expressed in 'jokes' or 'banter' or 'blanking' (ignoring) which are micro-aggressions. Three broad kinds of micro-aggressions have been identified: micro-invalidation, micro-insults and micro-assaults.[61] It often also takes the form of 'othering': differences are exaggerated, crudely polarised into 'them' and 'us', with 'them' identified as deficient or weaker in some way.[62] Many of the processes are the same as those identified in relation to interpersonal oppression discussed below. Strategies for overcoming interpersonal inequalities often begin with the idea that contact or interaction can improve understanding and knowledge. However, this is not always the case. Contact can reinforce stereotypes, competition or feelings of insecurity. Unintentional as well as intentional disrespect can make things worse. With care, however, 'alliances across difference' can be created even between hostile groups of people in situations of long-standing violence.[63] One of the critical issues in such dialogues is that structural issues and the institutional context need to be considered. It may be fundamental issues about the relative power of two groups or asymmetry in how difficult it is for two parties to meet, which cannot be ignored.[64]

The interpersonal level is also one where social capital may be important. Networks which can help you in crisis or assist with opportunities are often unequally distributed between different social groups. Some people have argued that social capital is a way of overcoming inequality while others have noted that it may be irrelevant or part of the problem unless the structural inequality (including economic, political and human capital) are addressed. Socio-economic group, religion, gender, age and ideology all structure the social capital that people have.[65]

The institutional level is the level at which inequality is most visible and for which data is generally available. It is often the primary level on which equality is addressed. Various strategies are used:

➢ *Punishment and rewards* for eliminating discrimination and disadvantage – This might take the form of legal penalties – for example, outlawing discriminatory recruitment practices with fines for non-compliance and compensation to victims – or financial incentives – for example, grants to promote the engagement of women in sport. It may be part of a wider pressure on organisations providing goods and services, threatening boycotts or arguing that there is a business case for equality which involves not neglecting certain customers.

- *Education* – This may mean information giving or sharing, instruction in behaviour or changing 'hearts and minds'. Changing hearts and minds may be targeted at the perpetrators and/or the victims of discrimination. Education is discussed further in Chapter 6.

- *Restructuring institutions* – Organisational structures can be redesigned by, for example, reducing hierarchies or changing working arrangements or operating times to accommodate more diverse circumstances of workers, users or participants.

- *Community development* – Running through all the reasons for institutional inequality and the other strategies for addressing it is the need to engage both the people who discriminate and the people who are discriminated against (and these may be both simultaneously) in identifying the problems and the solutions.

The ideological level has some global and long-lasting ideas which are used to justify inequality but others that are more specific to a time and place. The idea that males and masculinity are superior to females and femininity – often described as patriarchy – is near universal but the specific forms it may take varies. When, where and what roles are seen as powerful, desirable or masculine may be different or change. Racialist ideas may generally privilege paler skins over darker skins or Occidentalism, a belief that West and East are opposites and the West is superior. Some ideas about 'race' are more specific to a place and religious context – for example, caste, most associated with Hinduism but influencing other religions in the Indian subcontinent and raising specific questions about how to change it.[66]

The World Values Surveys (WVS) highlight several different ideological strands influencing values. They suggest there are two broad dimensions of values:

- Traditional versus secular-rational
- Survival versus self-expression.

This may oversimplify the patterns they observed which show values varying according to whether societies are:

- Agrarian, industrial or post-industrial 'knowledge' economies or economic systems that are capitalist, communist or post-communist.

- Characterised by economic status differences between societies and within societies. The authors of the WVS argue that the former are much more important than the latter. Others give more weight to intra-society differences.
- Religious or secular, including that countries which are broadly Protestant tend to be more secular.
- Political: stemming from concerns with survival (including questions of national identities) or prioritising self-expression, and different ideas about individual liberty and participation in decision-making.[67]

All these dimensions have significant implications for inequality. They may be used to justify homogeneity and mistreatment of minorities or outsiders or the concentration of power or resources in elites, for example.

Power and emancipation

The discourse around promoting equality and human rights makes frequent references to power and often to empowerment. Some of the confused and contradictory uses of the word power and the popularity of empowerment in social and community development may be specific to the English language. In English 'power' is a noun and only rarely a verb ('to power' a boat) but you can talk about 'empower' as a verb. In other languages, such as Spanish, there is a verb (*'poder'*) which means being able to or capable of.[68]

What is power?

Peter Bachrach and Morton Baratz said:

> a power relationship exists when (a) there is a conflict over values or discourse of action between A and B; (b) B complies with A's wishes; and (c) B does so because he is fearful that A will deprive him of a value or values which he regards more highly than those which would have been achieved by non-compliance.[69]

This definition sees power as a relationship, not a property of individuals, groups or institutions. However, it implies that when *B* complies he(!) loses, though not as much as he would if he did not comply. *A* wins whether *B* complies or not. *B*'s only power is to choose the less bad of two alternatives. It is a game of winners and losers, often a zero-sum game in which any gain is someone else's loss. Even where power over someone else may be constrained by a changed relationship, it may not be a loss. Feminists have noted that stereotypical household relationships imprison men as well as women, for example.[70]

The sociologist Max Weber saw power in terms of agency, people making choices and acting on intentions. He defined power as the chance of:

> a man or a number of men to realize their own will even against the resistance of others.[71]

Subsequent social scientists and philosophers have broadened out the analysis beyond personal acts and intentions – the way that power is structured and embodied in institutions and language; and the way that people may not be conscious of the power they have or the power exercised over them. The ways in which power may be exercised invisibly have been explored by thinkers such as Michel Foucault, Pierre Bourdieu and Steven Lukes as well as the gender and development adviser Jo Rowlands.

Foucault highlighted both the ways in which power is exercised and the ways it is resisted. For example, he drew attention to surveillance which disciplines people who think they are, or may be, being watched, even if they are not, so they conform. On the other hand, he also highlighted the ways in which people resist power over them.[72] Bourdieu showed the ways that people become accustomed to the status quo, seeing it as natural and inevitable: *habitus*.[73] Lukes identified that power can be exercised in three ways: the power to decide, the power not to decide and the power to skew the agenda (including keeping things off the agenda) – where the conflict is invisible.[74] Rowlands illustrates this with the example of a woman who goes from verbalising opinions and being violently abused for them to withholding her opinions to finally believing she has no opinions.[75]

Rowlands identifies four kinds of power:

➢ *Power over* – which must be complied with, resisted or manipulated.

➢ *Power to* – which is the idea that new forms of power can be generated that do not directly confront domination or create new forms of it but create new spaces for action.

➢ *Power with* – the power from collective action which comes not simply from weight of numbers but from the strength people can give each other.

➢ *The power within* – the inner strength which comes from self-esteem but may be translated into appreciation of the power of others in similar situations.[76]

Empowerment

Thompson describes empowerment as:

> The process of supporting individuals and groups in exercising as much control over their lives as possible.[77]

There are several problems with the term empowerment:

- It is used so widely and to cover all sorts of activity that it may be too confusing to use. A soft drinks advert claimed that drinking their product would:

    > empower women and inspire them to embrace their impulsive side ... [that] being afraid to act on your impulses can sometimes lead to self-restraint and regret.[78]

- It is used to promote directly opposing points of view. It is used by right-wing libertarians to promote self-help or self-reliance, including the withdrawal of state support. It is also used to describe the aim of state benefits.[79]
- It frequently focuses on the individual making them responsible for their condition. This generally assumes that people have agency, that they are controlling their situation. It does not address the wider conditions and relationships which are forces beyond their control.[80] At the same time it undermines agency in at least two ways:
- As the abolitionist and former slave Frederick Douglass noted in 1857, movements *on behalf* of oppressed people often marginalise or treat efforts by the oppressed people themselves as *prejudicial to the cause*.[81]
- Very often it only focuses on specific forms of power external to the individual: political participation or 'economic empowerment' – purchasing power. Political and economic power are, of course, important but they don't necessarily change the agenda (in Lukes' terminology) or the sense of self-worth and entitlement to rights. Increasing the number of women ministers, MPs (including by quotas in some countries), alone does not change systems of patronage (sic) or reinforce patterns of class and ethnicity in representation. Women-owned businesses may or may not take women out of poverty but not change their, or their daughters', access to health care or education. Some interventions may simply reinforce existing forms of domination, create new ones or increase the competition between the people they are supposed to empower.[82]

> It treats power as commodity. This goes back to the idea of power as a noun not a verb. It can't simply be sold, bought or given to someone else. Russ Moxley compares empowerment to a belief in Santa Claus (Father Christmas) bringing gifts or as a currency.[83] The recipient must believe it is real. The recipient must believe (trust) in the value of the gift and the donors must really mean it. Too often the currency is devalued by the conditions put on the giving. The recipients may (too often) believe in the value of the gift but they will frequently be disappointed.

Rowlands felt that if you used the term empowerment deliberately and with clarity about what sort of power is being talked about then it could be used creatively and effectively.[84] Two decades on, it feels as though the word itself has become so devalued that it is of very limited value. It may be better to use a less widely used word. *Emancipation* has at its heart the idea of freedom or liberation. Historically, its earliest meaning was *'setting free, delivering from intellectual, moral, or spiritual fetters'*, that is, psychological chains. It was initially used in relation to freeing children from control by their fathers and later in relation to freeing slaves.[85] This etymology lends itself to the idea that liberation requires psychological freedom, and liberation from social structures such as patriarchal relationships as well as external institutions (including the law) and ideologies that do not recognise all people as free and equal. It also links to notions of poverty being about freedom denied by power, rather than simply lack of wealth.[86] Particularly if Human Rights is seen as the pursuit of capability, it fits with the Spanish verb *poder*, discussed at the beginning of this section. 'Emancipation' still potentially could mean something done to or for other people. Understanding why that is neither necessary nor sufficient must be seen in the context of oppression and how to overcome it.

Overcoming oppression

What is oppression?

More than 2,000 years ago Plato wrote his allegory of the cave in which people have been imprisoned from childhood. Because they do not know anything different, they think the shadows of puppets held by the guards and echoes in the cave are real threats. Even when a prisoner is freed, the sunlight blinds them at first but eventually they come to understand how the sun is responsible for everything that the prisoners used to see – in modern terminology they have a critical consciousness and knowledge.[87]

The African American poet and novelist Maya Angelou's image of the singing caged bird captures the essence of overcoming oppression in her work.[88] She describes the different reactions to oppression. The caged bird starts feeling safe and doesn't know anything different. Then something happens to make them aware of their restrictions. Angelou is told that they don't employ 'colored' people on the San Francisco streetcars she says:

> I would like to claim an immediate fury which was followed by the noble determination to break the restricting tradition. But the truth is, my first reaction was one of disappointment ... From disappointment, I gradually ascended the emotional ladder to haughty indignation, and finally to that state of stubbornness, where the mind is locked like the jaws of an enraged bulldog.[89]

Angelou highlights that oppressors are often oppressed too. She writes about the clerk who lies to her about whether there are jobs on the streetcars, that they are like (Shakespeare's) Laertes and Hamlet: fellow *victims of the same puppeteer*.[90]

The American gang prevention group *Teens Advocating a Global Vision* talks about the 'Four I's of Oppression' which are the same as the four levels described in this book:

- Individual/Internal
- Interpersonal/Group
- Institutional/Systemic
- Ideological/Cultural.[91]

Iris Marion Young's five faces of oppression cover all four levels:[92]

- *Exploitation* – Young refers to poor pay and bad working conditions. Slavery is an extreme form of this. Unpaid care may be a choice but it may also be imposed as part of gendered stereotypes, for example. Sexual exploitation may be another form of work but, as noted earlier, is also a weapon of violent conflict.
- *Marginalisation* – Treating people as second-class, segregation, exclusion or disenfranchising people may be applied to formal citizenship or less formally. It may be physical marginalisation: people being forced to live, work or study in peripheral areas or institutions because of market characteristics or discrimination in how housing, jobs or education places are allocated. The most extreme form of marginalisation is premature death which might be the result of poor

environments, lack of access to health care, individual deaths through murder (including execution) or mass murder such as genocide.

- (Internalised sense of) *Powerlessness and the culture of silence* – As well as the visible, external power, Young highlights the powerlessness that comes from not knowing that you are a slave. Power has been discussed above. Hegemony is discussed below.

- *Cultural imperialism* – The influence of Judeo-Christian values in the USA and Britain, which is also spread across the former British Empire. As Ashis Nandy puts it: the West is a vector in the Indian self.[93]

- *Violence* – Young is referring not to war generally but the more personal violence such as hate crimes directed against women and anyone who is seen as different.

Ideological level

Hegemony

A key insight of the twentieth century is how dominant interests in society go about getting the active consent of dominated groups to the social order, so they don't realise they are oppressed. This is usually called *hegemony*. The term was used to mean political power well before the twentieth century, as was the idea that education or religion, for instance, socialised and controlled people or made them docile.[94] Karl Marx said:

> Religion is the sigh of the oppressed creature, the heart of a heartless world, and the soul of soulless conditions. It is the opium of the people.[95]

The concept of hegemony was significantly extended by the Italian Marxist Antonio Gramsci. He moved the idea of hegemony from unconscious, passive acquiescence to the active participation of people in their own oppression. He was troubled by why not only the general population but also trade unions, progressive political parties, newspapers and so on willingly went along with policies and practices which were not in their interest. While he was well aware of coercion intimidating people (he himself was imprisoned or in a prison room in a clinic for more than ten years), he concluded that the formal institutions of the state, employers, the (Catholic) church and education institutions all reflected, reinforced and reproduced an ideology which was invisible to most people and institutions in society. It was accepted as natural and inevitable. However, he saw that parts of society, including some intellectuals and independent civil society organisations, were (potentially) counter-hegemonic forces.[96]

Gramsci's idea of hegemony has been adopted well beyond Marxist politics. As well as being used by politicians of both the right and the left, it is used to refer to any kind of cultural dominance.

'-isms'

Gramsci's analysis also increased awareness of ideologies that do legitimise unequal treatment. He broadened the Marxist analysis of class inequality to the many other ideologies used to justify discrimination on the grounds of race; caste; religion; gender; sexuality; physical, sensory, mental or emotional ability; and so on. They are generally given shorthand names such as sexism, racism, orientalism, sectarianism, heterosexism and disablism. Movements against these forms of discrimination often already existed but Gramsci's analysis laid the foundations for seeing them as elements in a new wave of emancipatory social movements. To develop Young and Nandy's analysis above, the -isms are often vectors. In Public Health a vector is the (literal or metaphorical) wind or wave which carries a disease – thus a mosquito (or its eggs) or a flea carries malaria, Zika or the plague, but is not the actual infectious agent.[97] The forms they take are discussed in the section of this chapter on equality above, and in the institutional, interpersonal and individual contexts below.

Institutional level

Ideology is translated into structures and processes. Very often the discriminatory processes of institutions are as invisible as hegemony even if the results may be clear. The domination of men in parliaments, in senior roles in business and trade unions, and in many professions is a global phenomenon (with some exceptions and variations).[98] Here, we are concerned with how an idea such as 'men and women are different' is given justification ('biological differences' or 'different aspirations') and translated into access to resources and opportunities or unequal evaluations of performance or ability. This goes beyond individual acts or events of discrimination or expressed prejudice to the 'hidden wiring' of standard operating procedures or unconscious expectations. Applied to race it is called *Institutional Racism*. The term was probably first used by Stokely Carmichael in the 1960s:

> When ... thousands more [black children] are destroyed and maimed physically, emotionally, and intellectually because of conditions of poverty and discrimination in the black community, that is a function of institutional racism ... It is institutional racism that keeps black people locked in dilapidated slum tenements.[99]

EQUALITY AND EMANCIPATION

The idea that institutions, including professions, need to address both structural and individual oppression is explicit in the case of, for example, social work where the concept of anti-oppressive practice emerged as a response to seeing 'anti-discrimination' as only focused on the personal and not the structural.[100]

Interpersonal level

Oppression at the interpersonal level is often discriminatory behaviour, whether it is conscious or not. Thompson describes eight forms it often takes, whoever it is directed against. He focuses on eight interlinked processes:[101]

- *Stereotyping* – assumptions about or perceptions of people that are negative, and which become fixed and on which action is based.
- *Marginalisation* – as discussed above.
- *Invisibilisation* – this can take the form of simply assuming that everybody is the same (e.g. heterosexual) or using exclusive language or imagery. The writer and educationalist bell hooks has written a lot about how this operates in educational settings. She refers to working-class staff who are made to feel like *'Strangers in Paradise'*,[102] and students being openly homophobic:

    Because gayness was 'out there' not 'in here'.[103]

  Adrienne Rich has also written of the experience of lesbians and dark-skinned, disabled, old and female people or people who speak with a different accent or dialect being *'invisible in academe'*: like looking in a mirror and seeing nothing, even though you know you exist as do others like you.[104]

- *Infantilisation* – treating adults like children (but also not recognising that children are capable of making choices, for instance) and without agency, which also manifests itself as …
- *Welfarism* – assuming people must have things done for them or to them. Nita Freire uses the term assistencialise: to treat people as passive objects worthy only of benevolent gestures rather than active subjects capable of transforming their world.[105]
- *Medicalisation* – this may be treating people as ill, but it is a more profound treatment of people as not having capacity, about limiting

characteristics (rather than disabling environments) and justifying 'expert' diagnosis of needs rather than felt needs or experience. This is part of a wider pattern of oppression which *pathologises* people: treating (real or imagined) difference as deficits.

- *Dehumanisation* – often reflected in language that doesn't acknowledge that individuals or groups are people: 'the immigrants', 'the elderly' or 'the disabled'.
- *Trivialisation* – when minor or irrelevant differences are judged (positively or negatively) or are given undue emphasis. Women's appearance, for example.
- Characterisation as *oversexual, asexual or undersexed* and objectified.[106]
- *Incapable or less capable,* for example of high-level cultural accomplishment.[107]

As well as this treatment of individuals and groups, there are many other areas in which oppression distorts relations between people:

- *Homogenising people* – this is more than stereotyping: assuming that all people within a social group are the same. This is closely related to ...
- *Selective appreciation* – bell hooks talks about the individual Black women or their characteristics which White women select, treating them like:

> A box of chocolates ... for their eating pleasure so that they can decide for themselves and others which pieces are most tasty.[108]

Selective appreciation may also take the form of highlighting supposed or real characteristics but either suggesting that they are less important than other characteristics or that some groups are incapable of other behaviour or attitudes – for example, women and Black people are intuitive rather than rational, spontaneous rather than deliberate, closer to nature than men or White people.[109]

- *Expropriation* – this happens on many levels. Colonialism and global trade, migration and tourism may extract natural resources, labour and cultural artefacts from whole societies, but it also happens on a personal and interpersonal level of the individuals whose labour, assets or heritage are unfairly taken. Ideologically, it may be justified claiming these are global resources ('World Heritage' may be used in this way). '*Cultural appropriation*' – taking food, fashion, music, intellectual property, religious or cultural practices is one form of it, but there are other forms too: a non-disabled person taking a parking place from a disabled driver or a group of young men invading a space where young women have congregated. It is therefore sometimes a deliberate, personal act, often based on a mistaken belief in entitlement. On other occasions it may not be deliberately or consciously done and may be simply copying others. It may be intended as appreciation or recognition but experienced as exploitation. On the one hand diversity can be enjoyed and celebrated; cultural exchange is central to ideas of learning together discussed below. Chapter 2 argued against the idea of immunity to 'outsiders' and essentialist ideas of cultures. Elsewhere in this chapter, the idea of zero-sum human rights is questioned. On the other hand there are clear instances of misappropriation or expropriation.[110]

➢ *Treating people as defined by a single characteristic* – multiple identities as, say, Black, a woman, middle class, a parent and a professional are not acknowledged. This is often linked to the idea of a *hierarchy of oppression* or *Solitarism* in which some forms of oppression are deemed (usually by others) more important than others. It is a problem because it does not recognise important differences between people. The Black archbishop who is stopped by the police for driving a nice car when his white colleagues are not is both alike and unlike most Black people whose car is stopped.[111] It is also a problem because it may divide people by stressing their differences and not what they have in common.[112] An alternative approach is to see everybody as multi-dimensional and that people may be oppressed in many ways but also the potential for liberation may be linked to their many identities. Theorising around this is called *Intersectionality*.[113] Back in 1851 Sojourner Truth summed it up:

> I think that 'twixt the negroes of the South and the women at the North, all talking about rights, the white men will be in a fix pretty soon.[114]

➢ *Holding expectations of similarity* – can be as corrosive as the feeling of being 'othered', different or not belonging. It can lead to disappointment that others do not agree with you or share the same values, and to extreme reactions. The assumption that other people are mirrors of yourself was called the *Narcissism of Minor Differences* by Sigmund Freud.[115]

➢ *At war with each other* – Audre Lorde talked about the 1960s as a time when:

> the awakened anger of the Black community was often expressed, not vertically against the corruption of power and true sources of control over our lives, but horizontally toward those closest to us who mirrored our own impotence.

...

scars of oppression which lead us to war against ourselves in each other rather than against our enemies.[116]

On the other hand 'they are always fighting with each other' is also used as a justification for oppression: outsiders justify interventions, often authoritarian and violent ones, in the name of keeping order.

Internal level

The poet Lemn Sissay has also used a reference to the scars of oppression but highlights that the damage can be repaired:

I'm not defined by my scars but by the incredible ability to heal.[117]

Sadly, not everyone can say that they are not damaged by the experience of oppression. Frantz Fanon highlighted the way that oppressed people internalise their oppression. This may take the form of low self-esteem or a belief that they have no agency, *the over-valuation of the enemy*.[118] He said:

mental pathology is the direct product of oppression.[119]

Fanon was a psychiatrist from Martinique who worked in France and Algeria. He was also a political activist and analyst, particularly in relation to colonised and decolonising countries. As a psychiatrist, he wrote of cases of reactionary psychoses and a case of a man depressed and anxious after his wife was raped by a colonist. While Fanon recognised these as extreme cases, as a political activist, he thought it explained why, for example, so many Algerians could be dominated by so few people from Metropolitan France, not only by coercion but also by collusion and passivity; *Blacks who were Whiter than White;*[120] *the aggressiveness which has been deposited in his bones turned against his own people.*[121]

Somerset Maugham was another medically trained writer, though with rather different politics (he worked for the British Secret service trying to stop Indian Independence and the Russian Revolution!). However, he also recognised the harm done by suffering:

It is not true that suffering ennobles the character; happiness does that sometimes, but suffering, for the most part, makes men petty and vindictive.[122]

Starting with Jean-Paul Sartre, many writers have used the concept of the '*Gaze*' to describe the way that dominant groups can oppress subordinated groups – women, Black people, the people of (former) colonised countries.[123]

These very pessimistic views of internalised oppression can be balanced by the very many examples of where survivors of oppression have used their awareness of their experience and their potential for autonomy or agency (critical consciousness) to change their own situation and to work with others to change theirs, including bridging differences.

Conclusions and implications for practice

1. Oppression is multi-dimensional, both in who it affects and in how they are affected ... which means we need to take an intersectional approach.

2. None of Human Rights, Justice, Equality, by themselves, is sufficient to overcome oppression.

3. Emancipation has to be at the individual, interpersonal, institutional and ideological levels.

Intervening on one level or in one dimension is like looking at one side of a three-dimensional object like a Rubik's Cube. The puzzle cannot be solved. Actually, it isn't a puzzle, with a single solution. There may be a number of 'solutions', depending on what you understand the key terms to mean and depending on which of the perspectives on social change outlined in Chapter 4 you adopt (Figure 5.1).

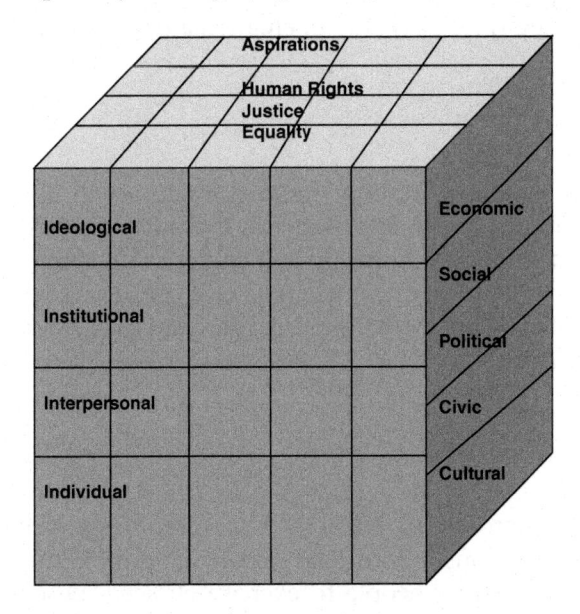

Figure 5.1 Linking domains of development to aspirations, human rights, justice and equality on four levels

A sketch of how the different strategies which each of the approaches, on the different levels could take, concludes the chapter.

Individuals

At the individual level, we need to address the ways in which people's aspirations and prejudices are structured, with some people overstating their entitlement and others claiming less than they are due. A consensus approach will tend towards action to inform people of their rights and responsibilities and to make them aware of examples of injustice and inequality. The pluralist position will see people as needing 'help' to claim what is theirs, or address voluntarily or with light incentives or deterrents the fact that they have had unfair privileges. The radical approach requires the development of critical consciousness, making people aware of their oppression and the rights that they can claim.

Interpersonal

The contrasting strategies at the interpersonal level are well set out by Lena Dominelli in relation to social work: a maintenance approach about accepting things as they are (consensus), a therapeutic approach of helping people develop (pluralist) and an emancipatory (radical) approach.[124]

Institutions

The consensus approach is about removing barriers to opportunity and exhortation through statements of (good) intentions and aspirations. The pluralist approach focuses on negotiated change with limited measures to strengthen the voice of disadvantaged groups, including some sticks and carrots to eliminate discrimination and disadvantage. The radical strategy is to redesign institutions.

Ideology

The consensus approach to ideology is to emphasise shared values or goals, rights and responsibilities. The pluralist approach stresses the value of diversity and enabling people to exercise choice. The radical perspective emphasises challenging oppressive ideologies and replacing them with an emancipatory narrative. Table 5.2 sets out the possibilities.

Table 5.2 Strategies for emancipation on four levels

	Consensus	Pluralist	Radical
Ideological	Choice and opportunity; citizenship	Diversity; Choice and control Active citizenship	Emancipation from patriarchy, racism, etc.

> **Box 5.1 Activities**
>
> 1. What Rights, Needs or Aspirations are important to you? What stops you and what enables you to achieve your aspirations and meet your needs? How does what you want and need impact on other people, now and in the future?
>
> 2. Discuss what's important to you with other people. For this (and the activity proposed below) it is important to keep the language and subjects which are to be discussed as open as possible. Different-sized groups and more or less diverse groups require different approaches. For larger, diverse groups a method such as *Open Space* could be used.
>
> 3. Choose a few issues which are a shared interest of the group. Explore the justice and equality implications. For example, people might want to talk about 'clean water'. A discussion of justice might discuss:
>
>   - Should it be allocated according to need and free at the point of use, or
>   - Is it a scarce commodity for which people should be willing to pay to encourage careful use, or
>   - Should it be allocated according to the social benefit of use?
>
>   Discuss the equality implications of the need for clean water: Who is most affected by polluted or scarcity of water? If water has to be collected, who does it and what are the costs and risks to them? Who suffers most from inadequate sewerage systems?
>
> 4. Explore how the four levels approach might clarify what you are trying to achieve. 'Clean water' might be expressed as an individual need for health and safety. A discussion might explore institutional rights and responsibilities to protect or provide clean water, or the way that water scarcity forces migration or leads to violent conflict. As well as the ideological issues of justice and equality, the ideological implications of using bottled water might be raised – 'commodification', the impact on the environment and on future generations.
>
> 5. Discuss the Consensus, Pluralist and Radical approaches that might each address the (Sustainable Development) goal of *'access to safe water sources and sanitation for all'*.
>
>   For reference see:
>   Open Space[125]
>   Water Sustainable Development Goal[126]

6

Learning Together: What and Why

Introduction

The discussion so far has been largely on the assumption that people want to make changes, if not in themselves in their situation, or to change other people and their situations. However, more often than not the starting point for social and community development is that there are at least some people who do not think change is necessary or possible. Some people will blame themselves and may feel, or be made to feel, that they have to change their mind, rather than the world. Other people will feel that somebody else is responsible for their situation and for changing it. The model of social and community development argued for here is that everybody has the capability to change their situation but there are very real constraints on doing so, the awareness that it is possible and how to do it.

Some readers' experiences of teaching and learning may have been dominated by remembering lists of events, people, mathematical rules or parts of the body. Even when we are discussing 'knowledge' that is not the kind of learning we are talking about.

There have already been many references to things that people:

➢ Know about

➢ Do

➢ Think

➢ Feel

➢ Are aware of.

These are often more formally expressed as *knowledge, skills, attitudes, beliefs, emotions* and *consciousness*. This chapter explores what these terms mean. It argues that people can learn about them, and discusses how to cultivate them to bring about change. The starting point is *why* people want to learn or teach. We then go on to *what* people can learn, addressing scepticism about whether, for example, emotions and consciousness can be learned. Specific methods of learning (*How...?*) are beyond the scope of this book. The chapter also argues that learning is not simply an individual activity, but it needs to be shared with other people; development needs to promote institutional learning and to change the way societies think about issues. Learning about what keeps us healthy and what makes us sick is referred to in the chapter as a near universal concern.

Why people learn

The starting point in development has often been someone else's perception that they need or ought to learn because they are ignorant. It is a deficit model of knowledge. This model is challenged in Plutarch's famous metaphor:

> the mind does not require filling like a bottle, but rather, like wood, it only requires kindling to create in it an impulse to think independently and an ardent desire for the truth.[1]

Plutarch (45–120 CE)

Paulo Freire referred to this as the *banking* concept in which students are only allowed to *'receive, file and store deposits'* made by the teacher.[2] The widely used term *'capacity building'* also carries this notion of students being containers or receptacles. Rejecting the deficit model of learning doesn't mean that people don't have gaps in their knowledge or consciousness, but it starts with their knowledge of what they want to know, do or be.

Jean-François Lyotard, in an essay originally written in 1979,[3] highlights two competing 'grand narratives' which have existed for centuries and which legitimate why knowledge or science is pursued. The two traditional grand narratives, which he called speculation and emancipation, have opposite views of society. One, in the language of Chapter 2 in this book, is a *Consensus* or *Pluralist* view of society: a (Functionalist) idea that everything serves a purpose of bonding society – 'progress', 'civilisation', 'discovery', 'liberty' might be examples. It is not just speculation in terms of curiosity but speculation as acquisition. The emancipation narrative is based on a *Conflict* view of society: it is fundamentally divided. Education is about the liberating of people from the state or a colonial power, for instance. Both narratives might speak of freedom, but in the latter it means self-management or autonomy. Lyotard was worried that grand narratives could mean that education was used in the service of undesirable regimes, such as Stalinism or Nazism. Whether education is for speculation or emancipation, he believed that education's primary form was *'narratives'* – *'fables, myths and legends'*, recounted by a storytelling expert.

Lyotard believed that the era of the grand narratives of society is over. He suggested that under capitalism in post-industrial society education has a distinctive, third, role to improve productivity or performance: performativity. Technology or usefulness now takes priority over truth or science. Knowledge is and will be produced to be sold and consumed.

He outlined a fourth approach to education in the post-industrial era. There are no grand narratives of integration or emancipation nor is the focus on the economic benefits of education. Instead there is a possibility of education being to develop reflexive and critical thinking.

Lyotard's ideas have been developed by others. The ideas are not completely consistent,[4] but they offer a framework for thinking about both why people learn and how the goals and methods of institutions reflect different models of education. To make the following section concise and widely applicable, little evidence has been included. It may therefore appear somewhat polemical.

Learning for speculation

Learning for the pleasure of learning or knowing or the displeasure of not knowing is familiar to most people. We want to know about..., or how to..., or why? Lyotard's point is that if we think there are right and wrong answers then it implies that there is a universally shared 'truth'. He believes that this is a myth. Learning for learning's sake might be expected to be outward- and forward-looking. Lyotard argues that it is frequently the opposite. It refers to the knowledge in the past and the great scholars of the past. Newton's comment about 'standing on the shoulders of giants' was referred to in Chapter 1. Sometimes the respect for the wisdom of ancestors or teachers is excessive. As Lyotard says, teachers (often) teach what they know. Teachers (and politicians) are often advised not to ask questions they do not know the answers to. Lyotard suggests people yearn for a narrative or a myth like the people in Plato's allegory of the cave trying to escape the darkness and get into the light. People are often looking for certainty when the world may be uncertain. Some people as learners may also be looking for consensus when there is dissensus. The history of science is full of examples of where dissent from orthodox views is unacceptable within academic institutions, between the state and scientists and to religious authorities (see later in the chapter). For people who do not share the consensus, learning for speculation can be very uncomfortable by being made invisible (discussed in the previous chapter), undervalued, censored or expelled. These reactions also happen when orthodoxy is challenged in learning for emancipation.

Learning for emancipation

Learning to improve one's own situation, or that of people you identify with, sounds, at first, very desirable. The idea that Protestants learned to read and write for religious reasons which contributed to their material well-being (and the development of capitalism) may be challenged as the sole explanation of the Industrial Revolution but it is at least a plausible motivation for learning.[5] The idea of doing a divine being's work or earning the right to a good afterlife through work in this life is a motivation for learning for some people. People may also be motivated by improving conditions in the here and now. For example, socialist, nationalist, gender, race and disability equality movements have seen education as both a necessary tool of social and political change and a reward. Emancipatory movements have often argued internally about the legitimacy and effectiveness of education as opposed to violence or electoral representation as a strategy for change. It has been argued that education for the new society (whatever it is) will not be allowed by the old society. Rather than simply reflecting divisions in society, it is argued that it creates and reinforces them to create educational institutions (only) for elites such as party members or those who have patrons or sponsors. Institutions are criticised for indoctrinating their students or not exposing them to other points of view or diverse people. As with all institutions built around a universal truth, emancipatory institutions may be authoritarian and punish deviants from the 'true' path.

Learning for practice

Learning to get better at something might be for pleasure (e.g. sport, music) or it might be to advance at work or to make a bigger contribution to a community or society. If productivity or performativity is the goal, usefulness to the individual is less important than usefulness to the institution or society. It is often defined in narrow, economic terms. People learn how to do and to be what others want (e.g. be a team worker). The benefits to society and the individual may be asserted to be complementary. Lyotard was concerned that universities were becoming too focused on this kind of learning. He saw it as a technocratic view of knowledge and knowledge is seen only in terms of competences (the ability to do). It is a *'sealed circle of facts and interpretations'*, part of the programming of a *'closed self-regulated system'*.[6] Lyotard thought that control of the programming that would determine the development and distribution of knowledge would move from administrators to computers in advanced industrial societies. Although he did not refer to algorithms (which were already in limited use), he seems to be describing precisely what they do.[7] As he said, historically, acquiring knowledge had been inseparable from training the mind but in the post-industrial society and the age of computers the two no longer go together. The acquisition of knowledge is not solely driven by usefulness in the modern era because there are still many barriers and boundaries which determine who knows what and what is considered useful. Broadly, it must be turned into something that can be bought and sold.

Learning for reflexive and critical thinking

The three previous models of why people want to learn all turn out to be less free choices than they first appear. Structure rather than agency seems to drive learning. Lyotard talks about the need to develop reflexive and critical thinking but not as an aspiration of the individual. He sees (academic) disciplinary boundaries as getting in the way of dialogue or discourse and experimentation. It is perhaps a telling reflection of such barriers that he does not reference the work of Paulo Freire on the domesticating role of education and the need to develop a pedagogy based on reflection and dialogue to liberate people from the consciousness which subordinates them.[8] At the time Lyotard wrote *The Postmodern Condition* Amartya Sen had not yet explicitly articulated the idea of 'Development as Freedom' or the fulfilment of capabilities as human rights and aspirations but Lyotard provides a rationale for learning as freedom.[9] However, Freire and Sen probably would not share Lyotard's *'incredulity towards meta-narratives'*[10] about such ideas as justice, though Sen unpicks the idea that 'justice' means the same thing to everybody in all contexts and he might agree with Lyotard that *'consensus is a horizon that is never reached'*.[11]

The motivation for learning as a synthesis

Table 6.1 shows schematically how the four models of learning are different to each other, but the reality for many learners may be that they learn for a mixture of reasons and this is presented in Figure 6.1.

Table 6.1 The characteristics of different motivations for learning

	Speculation	Emancipation	Practice	Reflexive and Critical Thinking
Legitimation	The speculative unity of all knowledge	The liberation of humanity	Maximum or optimal performance: performativity	Invention, creativity, imagination
Vision of society	Consensus Internal cohesion	Conflict, e.g. class, nation	Modern Technological	Post-modern Post-industrial Difference & dissensus
Structure of society	Machine	Binary opposites	Closed and stable system	Open and dynamic system
Goal	Truth	Liberation	Efficiency, productivity	Reflexivity
Search for ...	Certainties	Binaries	Usefulness	Paradox
Causality	Linear: mechanical	Linear: determinism	Linear and complex depending on disciplinary boundaries	Complex Contingent
Objectivity/ subjectivity	Positivism Essentialism	Partisan	Positivist and Interpretative depending on disciplinary boundaries	Interpretivist Deconstruction
Language	Fixed meaning of big ideas	Contested meanings	Expert or technical definitions	Symbols Signifiers 'Games'
Learning style	Didactic: norms Grand Narrative	Didactic: authority Grand narrative	Didactic: prescriptive Plural narratives	Dialogue Little narrative
Teacher	*The Sage on the Stage*[12]	The commissar or theologian	*The Aristocrats of Knowledge*[13]	*The Guide on the Side*[14]
Education institutions	Elite	Schools (in sense of schools of thought)	Invisible colleges	Interdisciplinary
Education results in ...	Integration	Autonomy	Competence	Reflexive and critical thinking

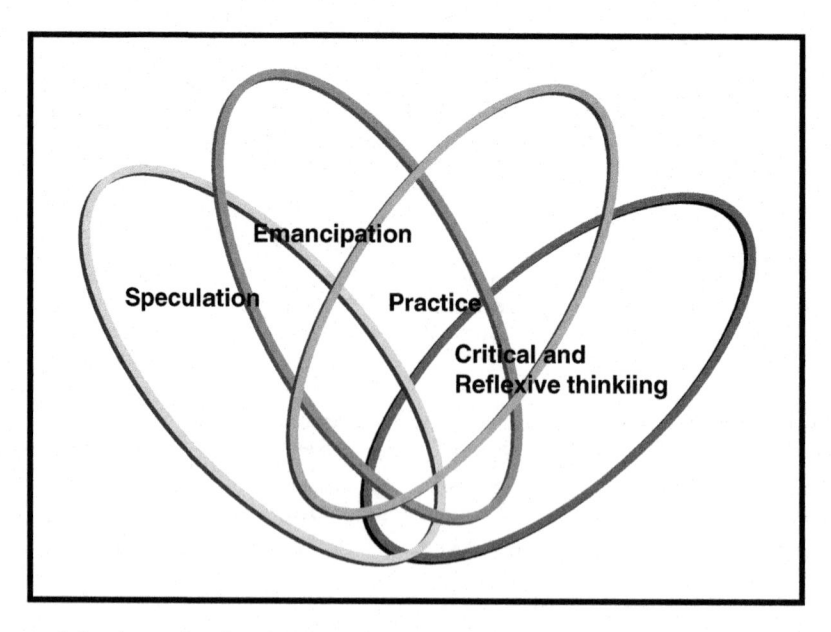

Figure 6.1 A synthesis of reasons for learning

What people learn

Most of us probably assume that we can acquire knowledge, skills or abilities but there may be disagreement about what these are. When it comes to attitudes and emotions, why we take risks and why consciousness changes, what we mean and whether they can be deliberately learned are often even less clear.

Knowledge

John Heron and Peter Reason identify four different forms of knowledge:[15]

Propositional knowledge

Propositional knowledge is also called cognitive or declarative knowledge; it is knowing *about* ... or knowledge of 'what', as opposed to other kinds of knowledge which are about knowing how ....

There are several issues with propositional knowledge:

> ➤ It is frequently associated with a *positivist* tradition about searching for and disclosing truth. Propositional knowledge is assumed to be based

on reason, objective and about 'facts' which are universal truths and theory which is true or false (see the section on scientific method later in the chapter). Very often it is associated with the idea that there is a body, canon or treasure chest of work that should be known (and admired).

➤ The implication that *some knowledge is more important than other knowledge*. If it is not about absolute truth, then it may be about the teacher or the education institution or its funders' view of what is important. In the nineteenth century, in the UK and USA, there were *Societies for the Diffusion of Useful Knowledge* that aimed to give working people the knowledge to be 'peaceful, useful citizens':

> They have given them the ability to read the factious newspaper and the seditious tract but they have not taken the trouble to provide them with the only antidote to such stimulants – a treasure of useful and pleasing knowledge.[16]

In the twenty-first century, the head of a British university asserted:

> Society doesn't need a 21-year-old who is a sixth century historian. What 'society' needs is 'a 21-year-old who really understands how to analyse things, understands the tenets of leadership and contributing to society, who is a thinker and someone who has the potential to help society drive forward.[17]

The idea that you cannot learn about leadership or how to think through history seems very strange.

➤ The distinction between 'learning about' and 'learning what' on the one hand, and 'learning to' on the other is not always clear-cut. Learning about values and principles may be both, say, learning *what* the principle of co-production is and learning *how* to elicit and appreciate other people's perspectives and experiences in order to co-produce.

➤ *Propositional knowledge is socially constructed.* It is often culturally specific though it is frequently portrayed as universal. An everyday word like 'sugar', discussed below, is not a universal, value-free object.

➤ There is a problem within institutions such as schools, colleges or universities of barriers between Subjects or Discipline. A topic such as 'Sustainable Development' may be explored by biologists, engineers, social scientists among others, in isolation from each other, missing important insights and perspectives.

There is often a bias towards quantitative propositional knowledge among public policy planners and managers. Despite the view (often misattributed to Albert Einstein) that *'Not everything that can be counted counts, and not everything that counts can be counted'*,[18] there is still a view that numerical data is more important than qualitative data. In part, that reflects the fact that qualitative data is often a reflection of experiential knowledge (see below). Quantitative and qualitative knowledge are not always not binary opposites. Quantitative knowledge can also reflect human experience. The history of qualitative research is peppered with the same claims to objectivity or neutrality as quantitative research (see below). Semi-hidden quantification such as 'some' or 'many' are (rightly) used in qualitative research.[19]

Within institutions, there is frequently a bias towards the contributions of 'Male, Pale and Stale'[20] academics. As Chapter 5 noted, it renders other people invisible, even to themselves:

> When those who have power to name and to socially construct reality choose not to see you or hear you, whether you are dark-skinned, old, disabled, female, or speak with a different accent or dialect than theirs, when someone with the authority of a teacher, say, describes the world and you are not in it, there is a moment of psychic disequilibrium.[21]

The view that Ideology and circumstances shape what is considered scientific knowledge is called constructivism. It asserts that there is systematic bias in what people choose (or are funded) to study, how they interpret results and so on. This has been highlighted by, for example, internationalist, anti-war activists, Feminists, and anti-racist and anti-colonial scholars. Critical Theory and Post-Modernism raise further questions about the role of interests in the construction of knowledge.[22] The internal, interpersonal and (intra-)institutional bias is magnified on a global (ideological) scale to be a bias towards the Global North. Whole continents and religions are written off as not having made significant contributions to contemporary knowledge. If knowledge is not assumed to be universal, it is assumed that there is a Global Northern situation (homogenising the Global North) which is the norm or inevitable. The insights of the Global South are ignored, limited to data extraction or used to add local colour. Intellectuals are co-opted on to a Northern agenda.[23]

➤ *Propositional knowledge does not necessarily lead to action*: it is not always knowledge of how to apply concepts, what to do with data or a useful interpretation. Propositional knowledge is not always necessary for action.

Two examples illustrate this:

> ➤ Categorisations of mental ill-health or well-being, diagnosis, aetiology (causes …) and care, cure or recovery have often been out of sync with each other. Knowing what is happening to oneself or someone else does not necessarily help change the situation. Unlike many other branches of (Western) medicine, mental health interventions may take place even when there is no clear diagnosis.[24]
>
> ➤ Being unemployed or getting a job, anxious or confident, can be measured externally but the experience of those conditions from the inside is very important to understanding and maintaining or changing circumstances. Part of the problem is when 'scientific' knowledge or method is narrowly defined.

➤ *No consensus on scientific method in theory or practice.*

There is a model of scientific methods which is widely repeated and which includes observation, hypotheses, prediction and experiment.[25] Sometimes replicability and explanation are also included. The orthodox account of scientific method is that it developed in a 'Scientific Revolution' in Europe between the sixteenth and eighteenth centuries. There are several problems with this account:

> ➤ *The account of the development of scientific method* – Many key ideas developed before or after the sixteenth and eighteenth centuries and outside Europe. For example, in the thirteenth century Roger Bacon identified as important: observation or experience, universal objective truths, hypothesis ('*Prediction*') and demonstration or experimentation. To experiment for Bacon is to '*confirm, refute, or challenge theoretical claims*', and independent verification is essential. Among key influences on him were Aristotle (challenging interpretations by Al Kindi and Ibn Rushd – Averroes); drawing on Al-Hyatham (Al-Hazen) and Ibn Sinha (Avicenna) all writing in the Middle East.[26] Other ideas have developed much more recently such as statistical modelling and analysis – for example, algorithms and simulations; Popper's idea of falsification; and Research Ethics.[27]
>
> ➤ *What is or is not scientific knowledge and method* – ideas that cancers could be caused by infection or that they could be inherited was dismissed as unscientific for a time but are currently seen as very important.[28] The idea that objectivity or neutrality are essential

scientific principles is a nineteenth-century invention and, even in the physical and clinical sciences, has been seen as misguided: observers select what they see or interpret based on their training, experience, values and so on. The impact of observation on what is being observed is now recognised: the *observer effect* in Physics, the *experimenter expectancy effect*; and the *Hawthorne effect* in social sciences. In some contexts, 'subjectivism' is seen as a positive advantage.[29]

Overemphasis on propositional knowledge has significant implications for social and community development but also ways in which problems can be overcome:

➤ *Knowledge Transfer* arrangements – Based on North to South or elite to popular, men to women, these will replicate and reinforce existing inequalities in power and control of resources. This can be overcome by South–South sharing and peer-to-peer sharing of knowledge.

➤ *Open source knowledge* – Much propositional knowledge is controlled by publishers and authors. Creative Commons, open source software, Massive Open Online courses (MOOCs) are making propositional knowledge much more widely available, but they also have the potential to alter where that knowledge comes from. Even traditional methods of disseminating academic knowledge, such as peer-reviewed journals, have problems with fraud, fakery and lack of verification.[30] There is considerable criticism of Wikipedia for similar problems and cultural, gender and political bias.[31] Some internet encyclopaedias and dictionaries are peer-reviewed and/or make conscious efforts to correct or acknowledge biases – for example, *The Encyclopedia of Informal Education* (*Infed*), the *Stanford Encyclopedia of Philosophy* (*SEP*), *The Internet Encyclopedia of Philosophy* (*IEP*) or the online *Oxford Reference* series.

➤ *Interdisciplinary collaboration and insights* – Overcoming the barriers of subject disciplines requires an understanding of how different disciplines may see the same concept or even word in different ways, but by collaborating new insights may be gained. There are many examples of how observations of nature have inspired scientists and engineers to make synthetic equivalents: a thistle (or similar plant) sticking to a dog leading to the invention of Velcro; or the lotus flower leading to self-cleaning surfaces.[32] Recently the potential for interdisciplinary collaboration has been formulated as the need to explore 'Superconcepts': 'System' is an example of a superconcept.[33]

Experiential knowledge

Knowledge from experience has been recognised for centuries. Some examples are:

Aristotle highlighted the connection between learning practical skills and learning 'virtues' such as justice and being a good citizen:

> For the things we have to learn before we can do them, we learn by doing them, e.g. men become builders by building and lyreplayers by playing the lyre; so too we become just by doing just acts, temperate by doing temperate acts, brave by doing brave acts.[34]
>
> Aristotle (384–322 BCE)

Chanakya and Al-Farabi made the case for practising to perfect skills:

> Learning is retained through putting into practice ... Knowledge is lost by not putting it into practice.[35]
>
> Chanakya (371–283 BCE)
>
> Whatever by its nature should be known and practiced, its perfection lies in it actually being practiced.[36]
>
> Al-Farabi (872–950 CE)

There are also similar kinds of statement attributed to the third-century BCE Confucian philosopher Xunzi, Benjamin Franklin and others, and the common observation that we learn from touching a hot stove that it will burn us and so on.

'Experiential' knowledge and learning is a twentieth-century term. At the heart of the concept of experiential learning are four ideas:

- ➢ *People have knowledge within them* – The job of the teacher is to draw it out of them. Plutarch's analysis two millennia ago has been repeated regularly since. The educationist Sylvia Ashton Warner put it thus:

    > What a dangerous activity ... teaching is. All this plastering on of foreign stuff. Why plaster on at all when there's so much inside already? So much locked in?[37]
    >
    > Sylvia Ashton Warner (1908–1984 CE)

> *People value and remember what they have discovered for* themselves more than what they are told. Blaise Pascal said:

> that People are generally better persuaded by the reasons which they have themselves discovered than by those which have come into the mind of others.[38]

Blaise Pascal (1623–1662 CE)

> *The* process of *reflection on experience is essential* to learning from experience and should be conscious.

John Dewey said that education is the *'continuing reconstruction of experience'*.[39]

The idea of reflection as the basis of learning is widely taken up in mainstream education (at least in theory) and in the training of professionals.[40]

> It is *necessary to apply the reflection in action and repeat the process.* In the 1930s Dewey described five stages of reflective thought; in the 1940s Kurt Lewin described the cycle of planning, action and evaluation which became known as Action Research. In the 1970s David Kolb outlined the Learning Cycle of experience, reflection, abstraction and testing. There are several criticisms which have been made of specific forms of reflective practice. For instance, that, often, it does not address the emotional and cultural aspects of reflection.[41] Paulo Freire highlighted that, without a catalyst, people's reflections would simply be a mirror image of the dominant values in their situation: *'The dominators live within the dominated'*.[42] This is discussed further under 'Consciousness' later in the chapter. The novelist Elif Shafak quotes the Sufi saying that:

> Knowledge that takes you not beyond yourself is far worse than ignorance.[43]

There are dangers of only reflecting on one's own experience, reinforcing narrow world views, scapegoating others or internalising negative self-images. Some writers distinguish between *reflection* – which is an individual experience (looking in a mirror or taking a 'selfie') – and *reflexivity* – which is an interpersonal experience (including others' picture of you or seeing how they see the same events as you).[44] This is why advocates of experiential learning stress the value of diverse groups of experiential learners.[45]

Experiential learning is at the heart of much community development theory, though perhaps not always practised. It may take the form of consciousness-raising groups. Such groups may take people who are stigmatised or who have a negative self-image and encourage them to reflect on where such ideas come from and why such ideas should be challenged. Or individuals with personal issues or shared problems may come together to support each other in changing their situation.

Expressive knowledge

The arts have expressed not only feelings but the state of propositional or scientific knowledge. The Renaissance was a time when artists such as Michelangelo and Leonardo da Vinci reflected and inspired developments in medicine (anatomy) and technology (human flight). More recently, the discovery of penicillin may have been inspired by painting with bacteria.[46] There is a remarkable relationship between the Islamic art of the Alhambra in Spain, the 'impossible' visual illusions of the Dutch artist M. C. Escher and the British mathematician and cosmologist Roland Penrose. Art has inspired science and science inspired art, with significant implications for theories about the universe but also practical implications for making non-stick frying pans![47]

Impossible illusions are also part of the use of magic tricks to teach professionals and business people problem-solving and creativity.[48] Magic tricks have also been used to teach about ideology.[49] Darren Way uses magic tricks to engage with disaffected and disengaged young people. He uses the tricks in the first instance to spark the young people's curiosity in him so that they listen to what he has to say, but also by showing vulnerability (looking ridiculous-the trick might go wrong) it encourages the young people to expose their vulnerability too. It is then a way of showing seemingly impossible things are possible and, finally, when the young people learn to do tricks themselves it makes them realise they have other potential skills, the importance of practising and that they can give back – giving pleasure to others.[50]

There is a long tradition of using drawing as part of public debate – for example, cartoons as satire which have frequently caused offence and have sometimes been censored;[51] and photography, film, painting and drawing, which have been used as educational tools, with graphic books, for example, leading a revival of this form with science, history and politics being popular subjects.[52] Sculpture, music with or without words, prose and poetry have often provided people with insight, inspiration and support. This is a different kind of knowledge of one's potential, through song lyrics, as with the athlete Kelly Holmes who was inspired by *Brown Girl in the Ring* and *Young, Gifted and Black* not so much because of the words themselves but because of the understanding that Black girls like her existed and could succeed.[53]

Paulo Freire was concerned about the way in which Spanish, the official language in Peru (where he was in exile), 'silenced' speakers of indigenous languages such as Quechua and Aymara. The literacy campaign that was developed taught literacy in both the first language and Spanish as well as *'the artistic [languages] such as theatre, photography, puppetry, films, journalism'*.[54] The Brazilian theatre director Augusto Boal developed a variety of theatre methods to enable people to express themselves without recourse to official or bureaucratic language.[55] All of the senses have been used in community development activities to express knowledge. Nasa Begum drew attention to the limitations of sharing 'Saris, Samosas and Reggae' for a strategy to address discrimination against Black disabled people but it captures the fact that clothing, food and music can be the starting point for people to express pride or explore what they don't know.[56]

Practical

Practical or procedural knowledge is sometimes dismissed as unimportant by enthusiasts for propositional knowledge, while 'academic' knowledge is disparaged by people who want to know how to do something. The distinction may be expressed as the difference between knowing how something works and knowing how to work it. The two kinds of knowledge may be connected in that it often helps to know how something works to work it and propositional knowledge often comes about from observations of something happening and theorising explanations of why it happens (causation or mechanism). Gilbert Ryle expressed this, albeit, a bit negatively:

> It is, however, one thing to know how to apply such concepts, quite another to know how to correlate them with one another and with concepts of other sorts. Many people can talk sense with concepts but cannot talk sense about them; they know by practice how to operate with concepts, anyhow inside familiar fields, but they cannot state the logical regulations governing their use. They are like people who know their way about their own parish, but cannot construct or read a map of it, much less a map of the region or continent in which their parish lies.[57]

Practical knowledge is often most clearly expressed in skills, abilities or competences which we consider in a later section, but before that it is worth highlighting that different kinds of knowledge all have their uses.

Combining knowledges

The interaction between Escher and Penrose, referred to above, shows how propositional and expressive knowledge can be mixed to enhance understanding. In this section, we illustrate how different kinds of knowledge are necessary to solve problems.

The first example is negotiation. It is a process critical to much development. There are many textbooks and theories about how negotiations happen and how to negotiate successfully. The authors of classic books are analysts, theorists and practitioners.[58] Their analysis and their advice have been followed in many situations. The skills and repertoire of knowledge to *train* people to negotiate are not necessarily the same as those to *be* a negotiator. It is significant that the strategy of the Harvard Programme on Negotiation relies heavily on Experiential Learning.[59] This is at odds with treatment of the programme as canon of knowledge, universally applicable, original or unique. The way the analyses become the dominant form of knowledge is reflected, for example, in *Wikipedia*. The entry for the (Harvard) Programme on Negotiation is based exclusively on material from the programme with no critique of the programme.[60] There are many alternative perspectives, including Feminist and African approaches, to negotiation.[61] Even within Harvard alternative models exist.[62]

Ideological or discipline-based views that conflict is (only) resolved by negotiation can obscure other conflict transformation strategies. For example, accounts of the Northern Ireland peace process often stress the role of elected politicians and key negotiators – very often older men.[63] Other accounts focus not only on negotiation but also on the success or failure of (state) military and paramilitary operations or material factors (external funds, improvements in housing and so on).[64] Feminist and pacifist accounts stress the role of non-state players and more grass-roots activities which are about the lived experience of violence and peacebuilding.[65] Even the institutions directly involved in both violence and the peace process understood the importance of expressive knowledge conveyed by posters, graffiti, murals and so on.[66]

A different kind of illustration of the need to combine knowledges is 'sugar'. Books have been written about sugar which simply focus on cane sugar and the food uses made of it largely in the Global North and the consequences of its production in the Global South (including the slave trade).[67] 'Science' treats white cane sugar as superior to other kinds of sugar.[68] Propositional knowledge uses a scientific definition of what sugar is based on its chemistry. Some of its chemical properties have been known for centuries. However, a scientific definition of the essential elements of the different forms of sugar and an explanation of many different reactions to sugars in its interactions with (human) bodies, heat and so on were only identified at the end of the 1940s.[69] There are still many gaps in propositional knowledge about sugar. Sugar in fruits or honey has other properties (some healthier than others), medicinal uses, use as a building material or as a fuel. In order to change the behaviour of individuals and institutions, the questions of 'what is sugar?', 'what does sugar mean to the people who use it and the institutions that promote it?' go into areas of knowledge beyond the propositional, including experiential (people's sense of agency or the consequences of their actions; people literally digesting the most harmful forms of sugar in the belief that they are better than other forms), the expressive (what people's images of sugar are affects how much they use; what does it mean to give or take a 'sweet'?) and the practical (knowing how to substitute other sweeteners, for example). To change the behaviour of individuals, groups and institutions, all the different forms of knowledge must be used.

Skills and abilities

There are many words in English which are often used interchangeably relating to what people can *do* – though they do not always have counterparts in other languages. What they have in common is that they all result in actions. They carry different connotations about whether or how much they can be taught or learned and what the barriers are to either acquiring them or using them. Among the words are:

- *'Capacities'* include the basic (possibly instinctive) actions which people are born with: grasping, sucking, swallowing. They can also be mental or emotional such as empathy. Many capacities, but perhaps not all, may be enhanced through deliberate teaching and conscious learning.
- The primary meanings of *'Capacity'* are associated with containing, absorbing or storing.[70] In relation to behaviour. Capacity is often used as container or a collection of tools necessary to perform in a situation: to lead, work in a team or deal with adversity, for instance.
- *'Abilities'* are both developed capacities and new actions which are acquired, often but not necessarily taught or learned deliberately: walking or talking, reading or writing.
- *'Aptitudes'* are often used interchangeably with abilities, but the term often carries with it a notion of quality: 'an aptitude for singing'.

- *'Attributes'* are properties, qualities or characteristics of individuals such as respect for others or being empathetic. Very often they are presented in terms of behaviour not simply attitudes – for example, 'a good listener'.
- *'Skills'* might be either the act of applying an ability or how well (effective) the application is. The literature on skills generally emphasises that it is a goal-oriented activity and it is usually taught or learned.
- *'Capability'* is the opportunity to use capacities, abilities or skills.
- *'Competence'* is effectively a theoretical ability to do something and *'performance'* is the practice of doing it.[71]

The degree to which they are simply individual characteristics, or they reflect social characteristics of age, gender, ethnicity or cultural background, is frequently asserted but often strongly contested. Such assertions have been used to justify discrimination claiming groups do or don't have particular characteristics or the capacity to acquire them. The counter-argument is that many people who have the capacity are denied the opportunity (the capability) to use them.[72]

Attitudes

We often want to learn about our own attitudes and other people's because we think it influences behaviour: 'Why don't I trust John?', 'Why doesn't he trust me?'

There is a lot of confusion about what 'attitudes' are. Loosely, they are a state of mind. In psychology, they are often divided into three components – the so-called *ABC model*.[73] Each component has different implications for what can be learned and how:

- An **A**ffective element: 'I like sugar'; 'I (don't) trust John', with whom I am negotiating. These are emotional reactions and many psychologists think they are acquired or learned through exposure and conditioning. A great deal of this happens unconsciously but is learned through observing others, with people who are important to us, we look up to or who we think are like us playing a critical part. Sociologists have been particularly interested in how social structures influence attitudes in this sense.
- A **B**ehavioural intention: 'I will put sugar in my tea', 'I will (not) reach an agreement with John'. The difficulty comes from the fact that behaviour does not necessarily follow from intention. It is not even

as simple as 'sugar has harmful properties. Although I like it, I will cut down on it' ... and then not do it. That is understandable; the three components of attitude are not in alignment.

➤ A **C**ognitive element: the belief that a thing has certain properties or a person has certain qualities – ' sugar is sweet', 'John is (not) honest'. Our beliefs may come from quite informal absorption of other people's beliefs or a conscious finding out. It may or may not be 'true' in the sense that it can or can't be verified or falsified.

There are many influences on where attitudes come from and some ways in which we can influence them deliberately.[74]

We can certainly make people aware of the harmful effects of sugar or highlight John's good or bad qualities. We may be able to influence whether people like sugar or John. However, what is more of a challenge is that even when we know something, or someone, is bad for us and we don't like it or them, we may still behave inconsistently with our beliefs and intentions. The same applies to what we think is good and what we think is good or bad about and for other people. It is very clear that attitudes and behaviour are frequently not being aligned. The implications of this, and what we can do about it, is beyond the scope of this book. Before turning to how people learn, we need to consider the part that emotions, risk and consciousness play in what people learn.

Emotions

Emotions might be an aid to people learning or a barrier, and they might be something people want to learn about or to develop.

Anger, mistrust and hopelessness or happiness, trust and hope were referred to in Chapter 4 on Collective Action. Psychologists do not completely agree on what emotions are, let alone how they are formed. They are generally understood to be feelings in reaction to outside events and often polarised as positive (appetites) or negative (aversions). They certainly have physical manifestations (such as increased heart rate, trembling or sweating), and there is evidence that they have at least some physical origins and reflect cognitive processes.[75]

Attempts to list and categorise emotions are controversial. There are linguistic and cultural obstacles to claims of universal or basic emotions. Nonetheless there are words that will be familiar to many people which give some idea of what emotions are. Paul Ekman identified six basic emotions (anger, disgust, fear, happiness, sadness and surprise) and Robert Plutchik identified eight, which he grouped into four pairs of polar opposites (joy–sadness, anger–fear, trust–distrust, surprise–anticipation).[76] Lauri Nummenmaa and colleagues use Ekman's basic emotions and also six non-basic emotions (anxiety, love, depression, contempt, pride, shame and envy) which they argue are associated with changes in different parts of the body.[77] In popular culture, DC Comics' *Green Lantern* characters display an emotional spectrum. They are also generally paired opposites.[78]

Empathy does not figure in these lists of core emotions, but other psychologists have argued both that empathy is a key ingredient in interpersonal relationships and that it can be learned. Daniel Batson defines empathy as:

> an other-oriented emotional response congruent with another's perceived welfare; if the other is oppressed or in need, empathic feelings include sympathy, compassion, tenderness, and the like.[79]

Other writers make a distinction between:

> 'cognitive empathy,' the capacity to understand the thoughts and emotions of others, and 'emotional empathy,' the capacity to feel what others feel.[80]

George Lakoff, the neurolinguist, adds another element to empathy which is that when an empathetic person sees someone else in pain, they feel pain too (and it can be seen through brain activity images). Psychopaths do not feel the pain of another.[81] However, it is not only psychopaths who may not feel the pain of others ...

Experiments (which are not the real world ...) have shown that personalising the story of someone from a stigmatised group can induce more positive feelings not only about that person but about the group more generally and that the effect lasts for a while. The effect is slightly less when the person is seen as 'responsible' for their situation. Personalising the story appears to overcome issues about whether the person is representative of a group.[82] However, Paul Bloom notes that emotional empathy tends to be stronger for people like ourselves and imagining that we are feeling what others feel can be dangerously misleading. He refers to Virtual Reality simulations of what it is like to be in a refugee camp in Lebanon, in which the sense of the physical conditions is highlighted but not:

> the fear and anxiety of having to escape your country and relocate yourself in a strange land.[83]

Arielle Michal Silverman's study of sighted people blindfolding themselves to imagine themselves blind highlights another way in which 'learning' empathy may be misleading: it may give insight (sic) into becoming blind, but not *being* blind, which people may adjust to or not have known anything else. Silverman is not arguing against learning empathy as such but against the specific method. She argues that such learning must start with the lived experiences of blind people: what they feel about the lives, not what observers feel.[84] The assumption that disabled people are (always and only) unhappy or frightened can be part of the oppression and discrimination against them.

It is generally believed by psychologists that emotions are not fixed: they can be learned or modified to some degree. They are also very influential in how we react to people and environments. A lot of the literature in the education context on emotions and learning focuses on emotions as a barrier to learning rather than a tool of learning or bringing them out as a goal of learning.[85] One study which is often used to justify arousal (which could be anger or anxiety, for instance) is Yerkes and Dodson's 1908 study of the behaviour of mice. They found that giving the mice moderate electric shocks (strong or weak didn't work) made the mice learn how to do a task better than with no electric shocks. Despite a lack of robust evidence that it works in humans, it is preached and practised as a method of enhancing performance of humans, particularly in relation to sport.[86] Stress is both a physiological and an emotional phenomenon. Some psychologists would refer to the physical effect of pain on the brain as 'sensation' or stimulation and the emotional interpretation as 'pain'. Much psychology focuses on the negative consequences of pain (of either kind) but it may have positive value in learning.[87]

The need to address both reason and emotion is captured by the words usually attributed to Antonio Gramsci:

I'm a pessimist because of intelligence, but an optimist because of will.[88]

Paulo Freire recognised the importance of emotion both as the absence of critical consciousness and as a vital part of understanding what (generative) words mean, which is essential to be critically conscious and in the process of getting to critical consciousness through dialogue. This apparent contradiction probably arises from his starting point which is that emotions are essentially irrational and critical consciousness is rational, but he modifies his view when it comes to emotions such as love and hope. Another way of looking at it is that emotions are not irrational when they are related to the underlying causes of people's situation. The raw emotion of hurting or feeling hopeless may be replaced by a reflective explanation of why...[89]

As well as risk, discussed below, emotion is linked to a sense of agency, personal norms and habits. Action may be taken to achieve agency or give effect to norms. Changing habits may require stirring up emotions, as Kurt Lewin suggested.[90]

There is a tradition which includes the psychotherapist Jacob Moreno and the theatre director Augusto Boal which sees drawing out of emotions and making sense of them as a central part of education. Boal suggests that one of the roles of *Theatre of the Oppressed* is to bring out the paradox that people can hold opposite emotions at the same time.[91]

In summary, there is not a consensus on what feelings are emotions, nor on whether all emotions can be learned, but there is a view that some emotions can be learned.

Risk and sensation seeking

The perception of risk is closely related to emotions. In some theories of behaviour change, risk and emotions are tied together. Risks are treated as feelings which, allied with cognition, form attitudes. They have been found to be increasingly important as the moment of action moves closer and may overcome intention: usually 'chickening out' but sometimes the thrill of risk overrides the intention of caution.[92]

Like emotions, there may be a physical element to perception of risk, for instance, reactions to sights, sound or smells we see as threats. Consciously or not, we assess threats. We make judgements about the relative risk of being attacked by a stranger or someone we know, getting a sexually transmitted disease, death or injury from a road traffic or plane accident, the risks of smoking or poor diet or lack of exercise. In part, we are making judgements about the likelihood (probability) and negative consequences (severity or magnitude) of risks but also whether we have any control over eliminating, reducing or dealing with the consequences of something bad happening (mitigation). All three elements raise questions about how much agency we have, or feel we have.

Statisticians distinguish between imposed risks (beyond the individual's control) such as natural disasters and ones that are voluntary choices ('exposed' risk). However, they also recognise that society makes choices about which risks to allow or prevent.[93] Sociologists and Anthropologists have argued that many of the factors in assessing risks are social: they may function as a form of social control – for example, rules against cousin marriage which may or may not carry an increased risk of genetic disorders. Risks may change with changes in the organisation of society (e.g. 'The Risk Society') and specific risks are unevenly distributed within societies, for instance.[94] Statisticians point out that we are often mistaken about the probability and severity of events and whether we can do anything about them. We often confuse relative risk with absolute risk: there may be increased risks from certain actions but the likelihood of whatever it is may still be low. People also often confuse uncertainty (we don't know if

X or Y will happen or is safe...) with risk (we can say how likely it is that it will happen but not whether it will). We also appear to worry more about *acute* risk (air travel or having surgery) than *chronic* risk to which we are permanently exposed (e.g. asteroids, comets, tsunamis) which in turn we worry about more than risks from things we do *habitually* (e.g. smoking, driving), even if the probability of adverse consequences are in the opposite order. This is also related to the fact that we tend to appraise novel situations as more risky than familiar situations. We are more concerned about immediate consequences than deferred ones. We often use shortcuts to assess risk which may be based on our interpretation of experience, what people 'like us' have experienced or think or whether we trust the source of information about risk.[95] Whether the agenda is the perceived threat of other people, 'anti-social behaviour' or people self-harming, it is necessary to understand these factors before they can be addressed. People may have strong and negative *'risk images'* of what a 'drug addict' or 'alcoholic' looks like and that they are not like them. Changing their behaviour may involve showing that people dependent on drugs or alcohol aren't necessarily more unlike us than like us.[96]

One way of looking at how to reduce or mitigate risk is to look at what instruments or tools society can use. Using the example of the risk to road users of accidents, the measures include:

- *Prevention*, avoidance – less driving; better design of roads, signs and vehicles but also locations of workplaces, homes, schools, and so on.
- *Prudence*, precautions – don't drink and drive; don't drive when tired.
- *Regulation* – vehicle and driver standards and tests; speed limits.
- *Training* – skills and knowledge.
- *Punishment* and reward – fines, licence endorsements; lower insurance costs for installing speed-limiting devices.
- *Disincentives* – speed bumps.
- *Protection* – safety belts, airbags.

All of these imply a process of learning: some behaviourist (fines, insurance premiums), some experiential (going fast over speed bumps is uncomfortable), some through didactic learning (driving instruction) and so on.

The example of road accidents, however, illustrates the problem of only looking at one specific risk. Traffic calming (speed bumps or chicanes) might reduce accidents while increasing air pollution through acceleration and deceleration. Accidents are acute events with immediate consequences. Air pollution is a chronic risk with deferred consequences. There are also likely to be significant differences in who is most vulnerable to the different risks.[97]

A different approach to risk reduction is to look at the mechanisms of mitigation – *how* measures work. Forensic psychiatry has an analysis relevant to development. Security of and for patients who might be a risk to themselves or others can be enhanced by *physical or environmental measures* such as locked doors or CCTV – used not only in secure hospitals and prisons but also in open society for crime prevention. Security may also be increased by *procedural measures* which might mean body and bag searches or rules about what items can be taken in or out of buildings (prisons, shops), carried on planes or restrictions on activities such as drinking alcohol in public places (a rule used in parts of the UK) or the use of mobile phones. However, what a government-commissioned report into secure hospital security said was that *relational security* is probably the most effective tool: a good relationship between inmates and staff in institutions. In wider society this means solidarity and positive interactions but is sometimes interpreted as confidential crime-reporting phonelines. How to increase physical, procedural and relationship security can all be learned. In institutions the three may be complementary but physical security may increase isolation among staff and inmates.[98] However, in open society measures to increase physical and procedural security may undermine relationship measures.

A major limitation to the analysis of how to mitigate risk is that people may not want to. We sometimes actively choose risky activity for its rewards. Experimental psychologists have shown in many studies that many of us are willing to engage in risky behaviour because we enjoy novel and intense stimulation. It is not risk-for-risk's sake, and not all sensation seeking activity is risky. Although we may assess novel situations as more risky, we may choose to get into them precisely because they are novel. At least in some cultures risk perception and sensation seeking patterns are significantly gendered. Risk taking has various forms – one classification used is thrill-seeking (e.g. dangerous sports, choosing a role you anticipate will be risky, for instance the military or firefighting); rebellious (breaking laws or rules on drugs and alcohol use); reckless (unprotected sex) and anti-social behaviours (bullying). The different forms attract different people for different reasons. High sensation seekers estimate the risk of harm as lower than low sensation seekers. Marvin Zuckerman and colleagues have argued that some sensation seeking has a biological basis (biochemical makeup and changes; genetics and evolutionary biology) but environments, especially peer behaviour, are also influential. Understanding the basis of sensation seeking may help explain further why information and advice, particularly about risk, have often been ineffective – putting out the message that something is risky may make it more attractive.[99]

If we want to encourage specific behaviour, understanding how people see risk is essential. Simply telling people about the probability and severity of risk ('smoking kills') will probably not change behaviour much. Making it more difficult or unattractive to take risks (restricting availability and increasing the cost of tobacco, for instance) may be more effective, but in the end, peer behaviour and relationships may be more influential ('people like me don't smoke'; 'I can be attractive without smoking').

Consciousness

It is hard to think of an academic discipline which does not use the concept of 'consciousness'. Even mathematics and physics, for example, consider consciousness in problems of measurement which are concerned with multiple perspectives, 'non-algorithmic processing', indeterminacy and the possibility of things being in two states simultaneously.[100]

A lay description of consciousness comes from Sierra Leone:

> Bringing what is in mind into the world and what is in the world into my mind.[101]

Different disciplines have had different theories of sources of consciousness.

Psychology

Psychology looks at consciousness as both an activity of the brain and a mental construction in which experiences are processed and interpreted. How much people have, or believe they have, control over their thoughts and their situation is expressed in terms such as self-efficacy, and how internal or external people feel is the locus of control: 'Can I get to sleep or stay awake?' Consciousness, in this sense, can be altered in several ways – for example, by drugs (sleeping pills, caffeine, etc.), by hypnosis or by activities such as dancing, meditation, contemplation or exercise. These methods may not in themselves change society. They might even stop people changing society as implied by the slogan *'Do not adjust your mind, there is a fault in reality'*,[102] but they may play an important role in helping groups form and stay together or maintain resilience in the face of, say, resistance to change.[103]

Philosophy and theology

Philosophers have been interested in how the interpretation of the world enters the mind. The discussion about whether people are free to interpret the world goes back to debates about free will and determinism. Determinists explain consciousness in religious, political and economic terms.

Some religions emphasise that everyday actions and thoughts are divinely inspired (alternatively, heresy or the work of the Devil or Satan in many Christian and Muslim traditions). Other religious traditions don't attribute everyday, or even any, actions directly to divine inspiration. Clearly, it matters a lot whether and which religious traditions people identify with as to how much agency they feel they have. If they feel their social and economic position, their health or their life partner are not theirs to choose, then telling them they have a choice is not likely to be an instant success. However, many people do believe they have some control. Some philosophers, social scientists and natural scientists question that from other angles.

Political economy and sociology

The idea that consciousness comes from socio-economic position certainly goes back as far as Karl Marx, but there have been important developments of the theories of consciousness in the twentieth century associated with writers such as Antonio Gramsci, Pierre Bourdieu, Frantz Fanon, Michel Foucault and Paulo Freire and movements such as Feminism, anti-racism, anti-colonialism and post-colonial studies. There are important differences between these authors and movements but here the focus is on how their analysis contributes to thinking about how people learn.

As Sandra Lee Bartky puts it, Marx started from the premise that changes of consciousness are the result of people's relationship to the means of production. Feminists have highlighted that as well as production, reproduction is relevant – for example, affordable contraception changing women's control over reproduction. But, Bartky suggests, consciousness doesn't simply reflect economic circumstances; it transforms it.[104]

Augusto Boal describes how, in the early 1960s, consciousness-raising became the new *'Divine Revelation'*.[105] The comparison with religion seems very apt: 'transformation' is treated as a moment of conversion or the 'scales falling from eyes', often brought about by prophets or clergy with sacred texts 'evangelising'. It can be oppressive. Boal describes it as the Ché (Guevara) syndrome:

> Wanting to free slaves by force. I see what they cannot see. They have to see what I see ... The best of intentions. The most authoritarian of practices.[106]

The ways in which different writers have approached the formation and change in consciousness can be expressed in terms of the four-level analysis used elsewhere in this book.

The individual level

Frantz Fanon made a psychiatric analysis of how colonised people (mainly men) internalised the negative view of them held by the colonists. Although Fanon was well aware of the external repression of the colonial powers, his point was that Black people had been deliberately injected with the idea that they were inferior to White people. This process of socialisation he called *'sociogeny'*. It is not just what White people say and do which transmits the negative message, but, for instance, Black mothers who tell their children to:

> 'stop acting like a Nigger'... The black man (sic) wants to be white.[107]

Bartky directly relates her experience as a White Feminist to Fanon's description of Algerian men's experience of 'psychic alienation'. She highlights that what makes oppression unbearable is when the individual becomes able to imagine a different state of affairs.[108]

Interpersonal

The anthropologist Mary Douglas criticised Durkheim for thinking that only in 'primitive' societies the *'individual internalises the prescriptions of the group'*. She argued that in all societies:

> The colonization of each other's minds is the price we pay for thought.[109]

Subsequently, post-colonialist writers have talked about the colonisation of the mind as legacy of the institutions of colonial rule in many contexts, including in literature, philosophy, concepts of physical, mental and spiritual health and ill-health, masculinity and femininity, and accounts of history.[110]

Institutional

The way that institutions structure consciousness is articulated by writers such as Antonio Gramsci, Pierre Bourdieu and Michel Foucault.

Gramsci explained how a process (not a System, he argued) of 'constant struggle' to assert hegemony allowed the ruling class to maintain control over subordinate classes by consent. He was trying to explain why, in interwar Italy, subordinated people did not question or challenge arrangements which were not in their interests. He argued that the state was not just the formal apparatus of government, but that the church, education, employers and trade unions were all part of the domination of the state. However, there is also space for the development of a 'counter-hegemony' to bring about change, and civil society and 'organic intellectuals' play a critical role. Gramsci's definition of 'intellectuals' is broad. As well as academics, philosophers, artists, journalists and writers, others such as managers, technicians, engineers in the 'production sphere' are included. Gramsci's definition would also include organisers such as civil servants, politicians, community workers and social workers who are active in civil society. Organic intellectuals articulate new values, pose critical questions and generate new ways of thinking to develop critical consciousness. As well as their capacity to be organisers, organic intellectuals can bridge the divide between reason and feeling, challenging what is considered normal or natural.[111] Gramsci spent more than ten years in prison so his opportunity to put these ideas into practice was limited but Paulo Freire, his followers and successors have found practical ways of doing so.[112]

Another way in which institutions structure consciousness is through symbolic violence. In the work of Pierre Bourdieu this is *'the violence which is exercised upon a social agent with his or her complicity'*. They are both the subject and the object of violence and the dominated group conspires against itself. The difference between symbolic violence and hegemony is that the former does not require active creation.[113] Bourdieu's concept of fields (*'champs'*) refers to interlocking matrices of relationships (i.e. vertical and hierarchical or horizontal) which may be intellectual, religious, educational or cultural, networks or structures. They are where people may express who they are and what they are seeking but they do so within rules specific to the different fields, which he likened to the rules of a card game in which people play by the rules (*'collude'*, he said) and may win or lose depending on what cards they hold (*'capital'*, which could be social, cultural or symbolic). A field might be, say, Journalism, and a rule 'objectivity'. Not taking sides reinforces the powerful. A rule may reproduce existing relationships, or it can transform them. People can change relationships in various ways, including bringing different fields or rules into conflict with each other or creating alliances. Citizen journalism, blogging or citizen science might be examples of changing fields and rules. Changes are not always emancipatory. Bourdieu's concept of *habitus* highlights way that everyday patterns of thought and behaviour and appearance are shaped by society, past and present, internalising external structures. He describes it as a sediment or a deposit left in individuals. It is important because it suggests that action ('practice') is not determined by a conscious, rational pursuit of interests based on intention and agency, nor is it simply a mechanical reaction to (social and economic) structures. Bourdieu himself notes that his ideas have much in common with John Dewey, discussed below.[114]

Dewey, Freire and his successors offer more practical ideas for how education can change relationships from reproducing to transforming social patterns.[115]

Ideological

The word Ideology was originally coined to suggest that ideas and actions could be verified or justified from empirical observation. Marx and Engels said that that ideology was an upside-down (*camera obscura*) image of society, used to justify class interests.[116] Gramsci shared their view that ideology is the pattern of beliefs and ideas which are generally accepted by all, but which serve to justify the interests of the dominant groups, but he took the concept further. It includes images, concepts and ideas which 'make sense' of everyday experiences – the cement that keeps society together – but, as Gramsci says, are common sense, not good sense. Gramsci had personal experience of how ideology shapes consciousness. From childhood he had a curved spine. Within his family, Sardinian society and his political life he was isolated because of his impairment: a reflection of an ideology that ridiculed and condemned deviation from the norm. His family did not understand what had caused the impairment and did not get proper treatment for it. Ideology was both a cause of his oppression but, it has been argued, may also have been formative in his developing an alternative ideology: a notion of oppression which was broader than the traditional Marxist focus on class that challenged traditional sources of authority and philanthropic models of social change.[117] Ideology is a means both of oppressing and of emancipating people. Although the term ideology is used widely both on the political right and left, there are critiques of the concept including that:

> It is simply the branding or wrapping of economic or materialist exploitation and is not very important. Social critics should concentrate on the material conditions, not the cultural artefacts.

> It perpetuates a distinction between a world which is 'real' and 'true' and one which is false and an emotional or mental construction. Claiming to be able to understand what is really going on better than the people who experience it is arrogant.

- There is no 'truth' about ideology or anything else: the important thing is the meaning people give to words and symbols – this is the core of discourse theory.
- Explaining material conditions requires a psychoanalytical approach to what people's desires are and what structures such desires.[118]

Michel Foucault analysed the interaction between the individual, institutional and ideological levels of consciousness. Surveillance by the state and other actors is internalised as self-censorship. He uses the metaphor of Jeremy Bentham's nineteenth-century design for a prison – the Panopticon – in which the layout and system of mirrors meant that a guard could observe many prisoners. Even if he (sic) wasn't observing them, the prisoners would think that he is.[119]

Graffiti from Paris in 1968 also expresses the same idea:

A cop sleeps inside each one of us. We must kill him

...

Drive the cop out of your head.[120]

Later, Augusto Boal used the same phrase to describe internalised oppression. More importantly, he described a process for 'killing' the cop in the head, which is described below.[121] Developing critical consciousness is a process of realising that we are not always being watched or even if are, we don't simply have to accept it.

These four levels provide insight into how consciousness is produced or reproduced but Freire offers a particularly coherent theory of forms or stages of consciousness and how they can be changed.

Freire: forms of consciousness

Magical consciousness, naïve consciousness', closed consciousness[a]

Freire thinks that we generally start from a state of consciousness in which we are generally submerged – a culture of silence: we are muted. When people are submerged, they merely feel their needs, not the causes of their needs.[122]

At this point, people feel their situation is the result of a superior power or natural incapacity; they feel that their condition is deserved,

---

[a] Freire also seems to refer to this state as semi-intransitive consciousness.

and that change is impossible. It is the natural order of things. Injustices are unquestioned, passively and fatalistically accepted.

People defer to their oppressors and educators. Freire describes the relationship to the oppressors as 'adhesion': they do not recognise the antagonism because the oppressor is housed within the people, making them fearful of freedom. They are victims; they feel they are powerless. They may find scapegoats. Freire stresses that this consciousness is not imposed by domination or the dominators actively but is the result of structural relations.

This form of consciousness fits into a 'Consensus' model of society.

In the state of naïve consciousness there is some understanding of the nature of individual problems, but people lack the ability to relate them to structural causes.

Rebellion

The second form of consciousness is one of anger and confrontation. The dominators are the enemy. The masses apply pressure to the elite, who they have unmasked. However, they want to be like their oppressors:

> their ideal is to become men but for them to be a man is to be an oppressor ...
>
> [They] Want to become landowners rather than share out land ... the overseer becomes tougher than the landowner.[123]

They aspire to revolution as means of domination rather than liberation.

Adrienne Rich quotes Rukeyser on the siege mentality of people in this state *having armoured and concluded minds*.[124] Freire argues that dialogue cannot take place between antagonists. A mere reversal of position is not a solution to oppression. The change process involves getting away from the binary 'them and us', 'good and bad'.

Other writers have argued against this: 'decolonising the mind' requires *'cleansing the mind'* of the *'infestation'* of the dominant power.[125]

Freire and Ledwith emphasise that this stage of consciousness is generally a very individualistic one: both success and failure are the responsibility of individuals.[126] Self-help and (only) local and concrete action initiatives are promoted. It is also often accompanied by horizontal violence against peers or people even more vulnerable than themselves. Freire references Fanon's *Wretched of the Earth*.

This form of consciousness reflects the perception of society as made up of incompatible interests which can only be resolved through winners and losers.

Reforming

The third form of consciousness corresponds to the Pluralist model. It is less confrontational than rebellion though there is recognition that interests are in conflict. It emphasises the good qualities of oppressed people and cultivates pride in themselves. However, there is a belief that oppressed people need the resources of the oppressors through welfare and a banking model of education. People ask for or make demands for sharing, power and resources.

Freire says that welfare programmes act as an anaesthetic distracting the oppressed from the causes of their problems and creating tensions between those who do and don't get welfare. Education and welfare are a *'cultural invasion'* according to him.[127]

Liberating, transforming, open consciousness

The fourth form, which is what Freire is aiming for, is Critical Consciousness: connections are made between social injustices and structural inequalities. It is a process not an end state – freedom is never achieved once and for all. He says the point of departure is that they must see their state as not fated and untenable but merely as limiting and therefore challenging. Men (*sic*) must feel they are in control. Bartky describes feminist consciousness as being about seeing things in oneself and in society which were hidden before.

> No longer do we have to practice on ourselves the mutilation of the intellect and personality. In spite of its ambiguities, confusions and trials, it is an experience of liberation.[128]

Freire says it cannot come about either through antagonistic relations between oppressors and oppressed or be individualistic. People must no longer measure themselves against their oppressors. There are new relationships between interests: oppression not oppressors are the enemy – the oppressors need liberating too.

The process through which critical consciousness is achieved is called *Conscientisation*. Bourdieu had a similar idea; he talked about *'reflexive criticism'* through which thinkers could become aware of the specificity – not to say the subjectivity – of the viewpoint of any observer of society, and of any discipline claiming to be a 'social science'.[129] In other words it rejects positivism, the idea of an objective truth, in favour of uncovering multiple perspectives.

Conclusions and implications for practice

Previous chapters have argued that communities and societies are not necessarily hospitable and inclusive, but they can become so through an emancipatory process of development. Chapter 4 analysed collective action as a means of achieving this. This chapter has looked at education as both a means to ends and as an end in itself. Insofar as education is instrumental, it could be seen either as a single tool with many functions (a Swiss Army knife or a smartphone?) or as a toolbox with different instruments for different purposes. The analysis supports the latter view: the tools needed to develop propositional knowledge for knowledge's sake are not the same as developing expressive knowledge for reflexivity or critical thinking. The tool metaphor (and Plutarch's wood metaphor) is only partially accurate, however. People are not lumps of mineral or wood, waiting for someone to ignite them or to make them useful, shape them into polished jewels or heroic statues. As well as bringing capabilities to learning, people bring emotions, consciousness and attitudes to risk. The challenge for practitioners and activists is how to bring out their own potential and that of the people they interact with.

An overview of methods is now presented, using the framework of the four levels used throughout the book. It is only an introduction to massive body of knowledge, which is sometimes contested and contradictory. It is not referenced here to keep it short.

The individual level

If social and community development only works with people who want to make changes, and want to work with each other, it will almost certainly fail and increase rather than decrease inequality. It must therefore address people who do not believe change is possible or necessary and who do not want, or feel they cannot, work with other people.

What makes an individual change their behaviour and attitudes is a preoccupation of psychologists. A crucial insight from psychology is that increased knowledge does not necessarily change attitudes, and that behaviour does not necessarily reflect attitudes. This raises the question of what does make people change. Many answers have been proposed, including:

> Drives – We have predispositions to feel certain things about ourselves and other people. If our beliefs, behaviour and situation are not aligned, we change one or more of them. That means we might not

change our behaviour; we might change our beliefs or put ourselves in a new situation.

- Reason – The costs and benefits of different courses of action. Altering the costs and benefits of behaviour (increasing excise duty on tobacco, making exercise opportunities easier) may change our behaviour.
- Fostering a sense of agency – 'I am a good parent' or 'It is really important to me to be one' so 'I can choose not to smoke round my children' or 'I am a religious person, so I can give up chocolate in Lent/ smoking in Ramadan'.

The interpersonal level

If, in principle, people are willing to learn to work with each other, there are issues about who people learn most or best from, and what processes are effective – particularly how groups work. We need to remember that people can learn both negative and positive attitudes and behaviour from each other.

Social psychology, sociology and economics, all have valuable things to say on these topics. Overall, they suggest that people are motivated to change and can learn from:

- Peers – joining a slimming group, having an exercise buddy.
- Social superiors – following doctor's orders; things my mother taught me.
- Competition – 'I don't want to be left behind'; 'If they can do it, so can we.'
- The experience of collaboration and reciprocity – 'They did something for me, I will do something for them.'

There is important evidence from the social sciences that positive relationships work better and last longer than negative ones, but that many of the ways in which people make a decision to act or not to act are unconscious and involve shortcuts rather than a fully worked out calculation.

Understanding when each of these methods is likely to work best is important, but so too is 'doing it right'. Groups can be positive and constructive experiences or they can be destructive and unproductive. A lot is known about what makes groups work well or badly. One issue, which is particularly important for social and community development, is how to work with 'asymmetric relationships' – when legitimacy, respect or status between the parties is unequal. Bringing together, say, women or young people from a divided society to discuss common issues – ending violence or increased employment opportunities – has to use processes which don't reinforce hostility and a sense that 'we' are right or good and 'they' are wrong or bad.

The institutional level

Across all the strategies for collective action, how people can change institutions, and how institutions change people, are all important. A consensus approach might seek to promote effective leadership or efficient use of resources; a pluralist approach might want to promote consultation or awareness of diverse needs; a radical approach might be seeking to abolish and replace institutions or promote accountability and inclusion. All the strategies have an interest in how institutions change the behaviour of individuals and groups.

Economists, political scientists, social psychologists, marketing and management theorists talk, for example, about 'Learning Organisations', promoting cultural change and behavioural insights. There are different views about whether at the social level:

- Behaviour is rational/instrumental or affective – why people and institutions give time or money to charities, promote equality at the workplace, or look after the environment.

- Rewards and punishments or (dis)incentives can and should be structured to bring about change in general – is it possible and desirable to encourage pro-social behaviour by fiscal measures (tax payments and deductions; fines; criminalising behaviour)?

- Specific ways of structuring behaviour work and whether they are legitimate when behaviour may be unconscious – for example, influencing decision-making by design including 'Nudge' to encourage organ donation or school attendance.

The ideological level

The ethical issues in influencing change are most apparent in relation to using ideology to justify change or how to change ideology. There are also practical issues about whether people can learn, for example, to be 'fair' or 'pro-social'.

Political philosophers, ethicists, theologians, media theorists and marketing specialists are especially interested in answering these questions. Among the factors which are important are:

- The perception of the legitimacy of change or the status quo.
- The perception of the feasibility of change or the sustainability of the present situation.
- The legitimacy and credibility of the message giver and the medium of the message.

Throughout this book, implicitly, three 'loops' of learning have been explored: the ability to decide what is right and wrong ethically; the ability to choose to do the right thing; and the ability to execute the action properly.[130]

> **Box 6.1 Activities**
>
> 1. *What* you have learned ... (Perhaps focus on thinking about something specific, e.g. your health)
>
>   Finish the sentence
>
>   - I am good at ...
>   - I know about ...
>   - I know how to ...
>
>   - When and how did you learn these things?
>
> 2. *Why*
>
>   Finish the sentence
>
>   - I want to be able to ...
>   - I want to know about ...
>   - I want to understand ...
>
>   - Why?
>
> 3. *Emotions*
>
>   - In a group, make a list of emotions

- ➢ Discuss
    - ○ What makes you (angry, happy, etc.)?
    - ○ What stops you being (anxious, trusting)?
    - ○ What do you do or say which makes other people (hopeful, feel rejected)?
- ➢ Make a list of the methods you use ...

4. *Agency*

- • What are the ...
    - ○ Things that are important to me which I can control?
    - ○ Things that are important to me that I have some control over?
    - ○ Things that are important to me which I have no control over?
- ➢ Share with other people ...
    - • What are the things you do that you think are bad for you?
    - • What are the things you don't do that are good for you?
- ➢ Why?
- ➢ Share with other people (start with people you trust or things you don't mind sharing!) your reasons

7
Conclusions and Getting Started ...

Personal reflection

Writing a book about a topic which the author has worked on as a practitioner and a teacher for decades might be expected (by both readers and the writer) to be a series of statements of what the author has learned, and case studies based on their work. To have done so, however, would have been inconsistent with the model of learning advocated:

Questioning answers: The process of writing has been an opportunity for, and has required, questioning my own practice and what I have taught. Overall, I don't think that the theory or practice has been wrong, but there are changes of emphasis. For example:

- Living or working in societies which are, or recently have been, violently divided has made me even more aware of the negative characteristics of communities.
- Reflecting on my practice, and reviewing that of others, both in writing this book and in teaching, has made me question even more than I had previously the feasibility and value of learning from case studies.
- Reflecting on what has and has not worked in learning, in education settings and practice, especially in public health, has made me even more conscious of how important understanding the individual and social psychology of behaviour is to help achieve social change.

Theory

The original intention was to write a single volume covering both theory and practice. The resulting book would have been either too sketchy, and therefore frustrating for readers or too long and expensive for readers (and publishers). The intended audience has remained practitioners and activists most likely, but not necessarily, undertaking a formal programme of study. The focus of this volume on theory and principles is purely to avoid mistakes and failures in practice. There are some ideas which may have near universal applicability. Perhaps the only universal method is critical self- and shared reflection. Others are relevant only or mainly to specific situations. There is much more to be said on social and community development in situations of violence and when practitioners must, or want to, challenge beliefs and behaviour. One of the tests of the relevance and robustness of the principles has been: Will they work in such situations?

History

This book has explored the roots of social and community development. It has argued that other accounts are incomplete in important ways:

1. *Where* – The idea that social and community development theory and practice come from Western Europe and North America is only part of the story

2. *When* – Social and community development developed as a practice. It has been argued that locating it in the nineteenth and twentieth centuries misses how deeply it is rooted in many societies and cultures, going back much further

3. *Why* – It has deep roots in many ideological and religious traditions, not just or mainly Christian practice, as is frequently suggested

4. *How* – Intellectually it draws on many disciplines, including philosophy, economics, law, sociology, anthropology and psychology.

These omissions need to be addressed to avoid several dangers. One is the assumption that the ideas are exclusively and eternally bound to particular doctrines – especially in the Judeo-Christian tradition. This can lead to a hostility to the ideas: the view that they are pure or impure varieties (as in a plant or animal being described as a 'native' or 'invasive' species). Frequently this carries the implication that outside influences are bad in themselves, that they cannot adapt or evolve, or that the 'host' cannot or should not adapt to them. Traditions are often invented and are sometimes deliberately misrepresented. The other danger is the opposite one: that social and community development have no roots. It is important to understand that theory and practice have emerged in response to specific contexts and they grew in response to those environments.

Society and community

Social science texts tend to present 'society' and 'community' as distinct and different in nature. In this book, it has been argued that they overlap and that there are differences within them as well as between them. It has been suggested here, not uniquely, that how the individual thinks of themselves and behaves and their personal relationships are structured by the institutional and ideological environment. To change society and communities, individuals must change, but there are limits as to how much individuals can do so, without society also changing. This paradox is central to the challenge of development.

In understanding individuals' relationship to 'community', 'society' or the 'world', the starting point is drawn from anthropology, psychology, political philosophy and ecology: People ...

- Are unique
- Have some things in common with all people
- Have things in common and are interdependent only on some other people and things (their environment).

Think air quality: An individual's personal experience of asthma is shared with some others but exacerbated too – for example by second-hand tobacco smoke, and also by fossil fuel use or industrial pollution – and while plants and trees may help humans, the natural environment may also be harmed. Immediately, it is obvious that there are potential allies wanting to improve air quality, but also people and places with contrary interests.

Differences between social groups are central to understanding how community or society can be bad for people as well as good. It is not only about obvious interests. They can be fortresses keeping people out or 'othering' them. Calls for 'stronger communities' can miss the dangers and drawbacks. Terms such as 'the *Open Society*' or '*Hospitable communities*', '*solidarity*' or '*empathy*', while conveying important ideas, are associated with individualism, opposition to state intervention and a limited role for rights to well-being.[1]

To reprise a theme from earlier in the book, there are, at least, four visions of how to hold societies and communities together. The first, going back to Durkheim's mechanical solidarity, is to bind people together. Authoritarian governments, who expect conformity by those who belong and reject those who do not assimilate, are characteristic of this approach. Adherence to supposed distinct national ethnic or religious values is required. A modern version was stated by the German politician Angela Merkel. She described a partnership between the richest countries and some of the poorest countries as like a reef knot used by seafarers – *'The harder you pull on it, the better it holds.'*[2] She may not have thought of all the implications of the metaphor. Knots can be a lifeline but also strangle what is inside them. What is tied together may live or die together. What is not in the bundle might float and survive or sink and die.

The second approach, derived from Durkheim's organic solidarity and the division of labour to stress the benefits of diversity, is the Velcro or thistle image whereby differences help things stick together. If people want different things, this can reduce competition for the things themselves, but it may also generate competition for the resources to achieve their goals. If the terms are unfair, one party to an exchange can be exploited.

The third idea is that 'glue', or 'forging', can achieve a benign community or society. Both involve a chemical process or a merging of materials together. Both work through dissolving differences. Frequently, in social terms, this is an asymmetric process of assimilation – *'they* have to become like *us'*. Many people have argued for processes of inclusion (or the more ambiguous term, 'integration'). For example, we are recommended to create a civic life based on altruism and mutual aid to *'forge a new sense of belonging: to neighbours, neighbourhood and society'*.[3] Altruism, mutual aid and empathy alone do not make societies and communities stick together. Too frequently they are mainly directed towards people we see as like us, people we think are deserving. Too often community involves rejection: 'immunity'.

Lastly, cohesion or solidarity can be built on the idea that opposites attract, like magnets. Obviously, this metaphor raises the possibility that repulsion occurs as well as attraction – the process of immunity described in Chapter 2.

Rather than endorse or reject any, or all, of these models, it may be necessary to mitigate their defects and dangers, where possible, and build on their strengths. This is the strategy proposed in the chapters on development (Chapter 3), collective action (Chapter 4), equality and emancipation (Chapter 5) and learning together (Chapter 6).

Development

Development is an outcome and a process. What the outcomes should be is fiercely contested, and those arguments are linked to process – because they are about who has the right or power to decide, and on what basis they should do so. Coupling the chapters on development (Chapter 3) and that on equality and emancipation (Chapter 5), we can argue that the ultimate goal is an aspiration to enhance and achieve the realisation of capabilities. It may or may not be useful to see these as needs. These aspirations are achieved through institutional 'satisficers' – home, schooling, personal relationships and so on. The ideological expression of what we may legitimately expect is encapsulated in the idea of (Human) Rights.[4] What we can expect is both constrained by the rights of others and only achievable through recognition of their rights. We must be concerned with the rights of people not only in the present but also in the future – sustainability. That means setting not only a floor below which no one should have to live, but also a ceiling above which no one is entitled to live.[5]

The processes of development which we have outlined include top-down setting of goals such as the Universal Declaration of Human Rights and the Sustainable Development Goals. Development also includes the decisions that individuals and small groups take for themselves – inside-out and bottom-up processes. The book argues that these latter processes must and can be strengthened. Capability can't simply be conferred by institutions, though they can play a powerful negative role in taking away agency. How to strengthen emancipatory collective action is the subject of the chapters on strategies for collective action (Chapter 4) and learning together (Chapter 6).

Collective action

Some writers have argued that humans are, for biological, psychological or economic reasons, 'hardwired' either to cooperate or to compete: 'human nature'. Some have argued that humans systematically pursue self-interest (even when cooperating) – *Homo economicus*. This book has taken a more agnostic view: we need to explore the different patterns of why people act individually or in groups, what they are trying to achieve and how far they succeed. Central to the analysis is that although everybody has the potential to act, individuals and groups have unequal exposure to constraints and penalties for acting and differential access to resources or enablers to act. To some extent, facilitators can remove barriers and put in place springboards, but, it is argued, it is more important to help people identify these for themselves and see how their actions impact on people both like and unalike themselves.

Not all forms and instances of collective action are the same or 'good' or 'bad'. Like strengthening communities, we need to be wary about simply endorsing collective action as a benign exercise in autonomy. It can be oppressive both for the participants and for the targets of their action. However, it can also be an unrivalled vehicle for emancipation. It is argued that for collective action to be ethical and effective it needs to:

- Maximise 'inside-out' action and minimise 'on behalfism', 'top-down' or 'outside-in' action.

- Encourage *Alliances across Difference* to avoid advancing some individuals and groups at the expense of people as badly or worse off than themselves and to create coalitions of enough strength to overcome the opposition they will face.

- Address conflict and recognise plural interests and identities. Strategies based on consensus will simply maintain the existing social order, however unjust it is. Strategies based on violence, even if they succeed in short-term goals, will fail by losing legitimacy and feeding counter-violence in a perpetual vicious circle.

Chapter 3 referred to the concept of *co-production*. This referred specifically to collaboration between public service providers and users. Biologists in the 1960s coined the term *co-evolution* to refer to the way that, in their original example, butterflies and their food sources adapt in response to their interactions.[6] Butterflies also provide the inspiration for thinking about understanding collective action as a form of transforming social relationships – *metamorphosis* – a capacity that we all have – an emergent property. There are dangers in applying the actions of insects and plants to humans, and the example is about interaction between species so the analogy is inexact in relation to collective action by humans.[7] A (mathematical) term, which conveys the idea that interaction between two entities can produce a third entity, is *convolution*.[8]

Understanding collective action as a dynamic process in a system, rather than a structure, may also require an unfamiliar word. Most (but not all) people accept that organic evolution or micro-evolution happens. Macro-evolution is when there is a leap to a new species or social form, without transitional forms.[9] To make and understand big changes in how individuals see themselves, and relate to each other and the wider world, and how 'the world' sees them, requires a new kind of instrument. The interaction between personal and interpersonal action and the operation of institutions and ideology require an ability to switch focus between microscopic detail and the telescopic big picture. The term *macroscope* has been proposed.[10] Margaret Archer's focus is on social relationships. She describes the *'macroscopic consequences'* of the different possible relationships between individuals and their context, the micro and the macro, as one of choosing whether or not to conform or to challenge their own or other people's values or the social order which change society.[11]

Equality and emancipation

Chapter 5 suggested that many of the key terms used in thinking about differences in the status of groups and individuals, and how to change them, get muddled. The framework proposed here is to distinguish ends and means, justifications, and rationales from aspirations. Equality, education and good health, often described as rights, are means to realise capability – rather than ends in themselves. Human Rights are ideological statements about different domains of capability. The right to education or a healthy life is translated into institutional arrangements for schooling or clean water. Knowledge of the what – what makes us sick, poor or lonely, for example – is not enough to change our situation; we also need the means to change it. Chapter 5 argued that calling that process 'empowerment' is unhelpful:

- It is used in so many, often contradictory, different ways.
- It does not reflect the complexity of power relationships: there are different kinds of relationships, and, crudely, empowerment can be both good and bad.
- It describes a process which is based on the idea of power as a commodity which some people have and/or can give to others. It misses the central point that power must be claimed but it is something that we all potentially have.

People are both externally repressed – by the use or threat of force – and oppressed by dominant ideologies ('hegemony') which restrict what people can be or do by framing their perception of themselves. A very important part of hegemony is the way that oppressed people are divided from each other. We are encouraged to blame other oppressed people. We are made to feel that some divisions or 'faces' of oppression are more important than others, and people are made to choose between, or suppress, multiple identities.

The strategy proposed for achieving emancipation is that a critical consciousness needs to be cultivated within individuals; that interpersonal relationships need to be based on claiming and giving recognition and respect for difference; and that discriminating and divisive institutions and ideologies need to be challenged and changed.

Learning together

'Learning' here is understood very broadly. The central idea is that it is drawing out knowledge, skills and consciousness which is within all of us to transform individuals, our relationships with others and the institutions that have a profound impact on our life chances.

The learning process is not necessarily comfortable. It may be literally an 'internal conversation' which no one else hears, but in which an individual questions who they are, what they believe and what they do. It might be triggered by an everyday event or something out of the ordinary, including once-in-a lifetime events. Other people can precipitate but not force such reflection in many ways, including through diaries, blogging, vlogging, meditating or praying. There are many methods – often drawn from psychology and social psychology – which might trigger such self-examination.

The conversation may be exchanges with other people, not necessarily in words. Although it often turns out that even the people you are closest to do not necessarily see things the same way, the book argues that transformational learning often involves people you think are unalike. The encouragement of diverse networks and the generation of 'bridging' social capital may be part of that. It is suggested that systematic facilitation of interpersonal reflection is generally necessary to be effective. There are various strategies for doing this (there is often overlap between them):

- Action Research; peer-led research and reflection in which people explore a topic together such as Cooperative/Appreciative Inquiry or Communities of Practice.

- Reflective practice such as Action Learning or telling and listening to life stories (again, not necessarily in words); Freirean Critical Literacy groups exploring what words mean and how to use them to change circumstances.

- Experiential learning: trying things out, thinking about the action, refining it, as necessary.

Changing other people should start from clarity about why it is right to do so and what methods are legitimate. Key strategies include:

- *Dialogue* which takes into account asymmetric relationships; central to this, is to start from where they are while being honest that you disagree with them.

- *Non-Violent Direct Action*: converting them by example or demonstration of the depth of your conviction: persuasion by argument; coercion by altering the balance of advantage and disadvantage or making it more difficult for them to achieve what they want so that they accommodate your point of view.

- *Negotiation*: essentially a process in which no party loses so much that they cannot live with an agreement.

➤ *Transitional justice* in which past wrongs are either put right, acknowledged or put to rest.

Changing how whole populations think and how institutions behave involves some of these methods but another suite too:

➤ *Community Organisation,* though it is important to note the limitations of organisations which may magnify hierarchies and stratification.
➤ *Inclusive policy-making* using a full range of policy development and implementation tools. Policy development strategies must prioritise the effective engagement of the least powerful, most affected stakeholders. Implementation tools include incentives and disincentives, law and regulation.
➤ *Persuasion,* exhortation and encouragement through the application of communication theory, use of social marketing and 'Nudge'.

Applied communication theory is also part of the bundle of methods for challenging ideology. Changing people's perceptions of themselves and other people is an essential part of the process of social change.

Doing it right

This book has focused on assisting the reader to decide for her- or himself *what makes something the right or wrong thing to do.* The instruments of change need to be rigorously scrutinised in order to *do the right thing.* Whatever method is used, it needs to be used in the right way. This book concludes with some suggestions for whatever you do *how to do it right.* In the 1950s the British Colonial Office prepared a booklet on community development which included *'Six ways to fail…'.*[12] Some of the original errors are still relevant. The context being imagined is that you start from the most immediate situation in which you can have conversations with other people. Global change comes later. The practice is applicable whether you are established in a community or a new arrival.

Don't

1. Make all the proposals yourself
2. Treat the community as backward …

3. Take all the credit for yourself
   A twenty-first-century list might add some other points with explanations such as:

4. Make assumptions about the situation and the people around you
   You may have been around people and places a long time or a short time, but you never know everything and everyone or nothing and no one!

5. Go out to talk to people!
   Listen don't talk. Let people talk about what they want to talk about and let them ask you questions, rather than you bombard them with questions.

6. Tackle the goals and levels of social and community development as though they are all independent of each other
   Communities without emancipation can be fortresses and prisons. Development without collective action and emancipation can simply reinforce the rich and the powerful.

7. Stick to the plan
   Not having a plan may be disastrous but sticking to your own plan, or those developed by other people, in other places and at other times, is too.[13] Fixed plans are for expected situations and where you have control or consensus, and those conditions rarely hold in social and community development. The processes needed are about starting with the here, now and us.

8. Label people as 'Mad', 'Sad' or 'Bad' and ignore them or divide the world into 'Goodies' and 'Baddies'
   'Othering' is an obstacle to changing the beliefs and behaviour of the people you don't agree with as well as an unnecessary barrier with the people you do.

Whatever people's history or circumstances, they can contribute positively or negatively to social change. Deliberately or not, 'good' people can do bad things and 'bad' people can do good things.

To end on a more positive note, there are some 'Dos' as well as 'Don'ts'. It is not suggested that these are in order of importance or in the sequence in which they should be done.

Do

1. Start with who you are and where you are
   You may not be the best person, at exactly the right time and in the optimal place, but rather than do nothing, you can reflect,

self-critically but not negatively, on why you want to intervene and what you can bring to a situation.

2. Look and listen
Take a walk, sit in a café or on a bench, read a paper, engage in social media, watch TV, listen to the radio. Who and what can you see and hear? Even in the bleakest of situations, there will be someone clearing rubbish or hazards, finding sun or shade, trying to brighten up the place with flowers or paint, growing herbs or improvising facilities for children to play and so on.

3. Start collecting pictures
Maybe literally, maybe not, gather life stories of how people got to where they are, and who and what is important to them (positive and negative).

4. Start with the willing but be aware of what they need from the relationship and think about how to go beyond the 'able and willing'
They may be the 'positive deviants' who want things to be different and may be better placed to work than you to identify other people to work with. There will be others too who may be particularly receptive to you:

   ➢ People with nothing to lose
   ➢ Risk takers
   ➢ Isolated think they are alone or unique
   ➢ People at the intersections, multiple identities
   ➢ 'Blow-ins', 'offcomers' (people who have come to a place or situation).

5. Give and take hospitality
Exchange appropriate gifts.

6. Do some 'desk' research
Collect background data:

   ➢ Numbers about people and their circumstances
   ➢ Governance structures and people
   ➢ Service providers
   ➢ History.

   What doesn't it tell you?

7. Explore the positives
   ➢ What is good about the people, the place, the group?
   ➢ What have you achieved?

- How do you …?
- Who would you go to if you need …?
- What is different about …?

8. Ask about what people want to be different
   - How could … be improved?
   - What would make … better?
   - What's stopping you …?

This is a few days' activity and a lifetime's work. Good luck.

Notes

1 Introduction

1. Quoted in Leonen, M. (2004) 'Etiquette for Activists' *Yes Magazine* http://www.yesmagazine.org/issues/a-conspiracy-of-hope/etiquette-for-activists Accessed 2 May 2018.
2. Ryle, (2009) *The Concept of Mind* (60th Anniversary edn). London: Routledge, p. lxi.
3. Schön, D. (1991) *The Reflective Practitioner*. Aldershot: Avebury.
4. Freire, P. (1972) *Pedagogy of the Oppressed*. Harmondsworth: Penguin, p. 81.
5. Marks, J. (2013) Word Roots and Routes: Route, *Macmillan Dictionary Blog* http://www.macmillandictionaryblog.com/word-roots-and-routes-route Accessed 2 May 2018; 'route, n.1.' *Oxford English Dictionary* [hereafter *OED*] *Online* Oxford University Press.
6. For instance: P. Du Sautoy (1958) *Community Development in Ghana*. Oxford: Oxford University Press; M. Dickson (1960) *The New Nigerians*. London: Dobson; M. Mayo (1975) Community Development – A Radical Alternative? In Bailey, R. & Brake M. (eds) *Radical Social Work*. London: Edward Arnold; K. Popple (2015) *Analysing Community Work: Theory and Practice* (2nd edn). Maidenhead: Open University Press.
7. Orwell, G. (2004) *1984*. London: Penguin, p. 67.
8. Dawkins, R. (1989) *The Selfish Gene* (2nd edn). Oxford: Oxford University Press.
9. Hobsbawm, E. & Ranger, T. (1992) *The Invention of Tradition*. Cambridge: Cambridge University Press.
10. Klein, R. and Marmor, T. (2008) Reflections on Policy Analysis. In: M. Moran, M. Rein & R. Goodin (2008) *The Oxford Handbook of Public Policy*. Oxford: Oxford University Press; B.G. Peter, J. Pierre & D. King (2005) 'The Politics of Path Dependency: Political Conflict in Historical Institutionalism', *Journal of Politics*, Vol. 67, No. 4 (November), pp. 1275–1300.
11. Gerth, H. & Mills, (1946) *From Max Weber: Essays in Sociology*. London: Routledge and Kegan Paul, p. 280.
12. A. Nandy (1983) *The Intimate Enemy – Loss and Recovery of Self under Colonialism*. Bombay: Oxford University Press.
13. Eliot, T.S. (1974) 'Little Gidding', in *Collected Poems 1909–1962*. London: Faber & Faber, p. 219.
14. 'theory, n.'. *OED Online*. January 2018. Oxford University Press.

15 Eliot, T.S. (1966) 'East Coker', in *Four Quartets*. London: Faber & Faber.
16 Rumsfeld, D. (2002) *Press Conference by US Secretary of Defence, Donald Rumsfeld*, 6 June, NATO Headquarters http://www.nato.int/docu/speech/2002/s020606g.htm Accessed 2 May 2018 (Rumsfeld first said it earlier in the year).
17 Erickson, P. & Murphy, L. (2013) *A History of Anthropological Theory*. Toronto: University of Toronto Press, p. 183.
18 Erickson & Murphy, *Anthropological Theory*, p. 183.
19 Holub quoted in Ledwith, M. (2011) *Community Development – A Critical Approach* (2nd edn). Bristol: Policy Press, p. 163.
20 Connell, R. (2007) *Southern Theory: The Global Dynamics of Knowledge in Social Science*. Crows Nest, NSW: Allen & Unwin, p. viii.
21 Freire began his work on literacy with the (later) famous sculptor Francisco Brennand: P. Freire (1976) *Education: The Practice of Freedom*. London: Readers and Writers Publishing Cooperative. Augusto Boal mentions, as well as Freire, himself (theatre director), Estela Linares (photography), Caetano Veloso and Gilberto Gil (music) and Roberto Freire (playwright and psychiatrist). See A. Boal (1979) *Theatre of the Oppressed*. London: Pluto, pp. 122, 158, 162; on the other hand, he is more grudging about the contribution to the development of theatre for social change of Jacob Moreno: A. Boal (1995) *The Rainbow of Desire*. Abingdon: Routledge, p. 70.
22 Hooks, b. (1994) *Teaching to Transgress: Education as the Practice of Freedom*. London: Routledge.
23 The Encyclopedia of Informal Education (INFED) is a particularly useful website: http://infed.org/mobi/welcome/ Accessed 2 May 2018.
24 Pascal, B. (1958) 'Thoughts on Mind and on Style', in *Pascal's Penseés*. New York: E.P. Dutton, sec. 22, p. 7. http://www.gutenberg.org/files/18269/18269-h/18269-h.htm Accessed 2 May 2018, quoted, for example by Scull, A. (2011) *Madness – A Very Short Introduction*. Oxford: Oxford University Press.
25 Laqueur, W. (2004) 'The Terrorism to Come', *Policy Review*, Vol. 126 (August and September), pp. 49–64.
26 Lewin, K. (1951) *Field Theory in Social Science; Selected Theoretical Papers* (edited by D. Cartwright). New York: Harper & Row quoted in Smith, M.K. (2001) 'Kurt Lewin, Groups, Experiential Learning and Action Research', The Encyclopedia of Informal Education, http://www.infed.org/thinkers/et-lewin.htm Accessed 2 May 2018.
27 Freire, *Pedagogy of the Oppressed*, pp. 53, 60.
28 Schön, D. (1991) *The Reflective Practitioner*. Aldershot: Avebury.
29 Rich, A. (1986) 'Notes Towards a Politics of Location' in *Blood, Bread and Poetry*. London: W.W. Norton, p. 123.
30 Hooks, *Teaching to Transgress*, p. 59.
31 Tawney, R. (1931) *Equality*. London: George Allen & Unwin, p. 71.
32 For critiques of 'Northern Theory' see: E. Said (1995) *Orientalism*. London: Penguin; P. Hountondji (1983) *African Philosophy: Myth and Reality*. London: Hutchinson; R. Connell (2007) *Southern Theory: The Global Dynamics of Knowledge in Social Science*. New South Wales: Crows Nest; K. Gyekye (2011)

'African Ethics' *Stanford Encyclopedia of Philosophy* http://plato.stanford.edu/archives/fall2011/entries/african-ethics/ Accessed 2 May 2018.
33 The view that they are not opposites has been put forward by writers such as Edward Said: Said, *Orientalism*.
34 Federation for Community Development Learning (2015) *Community Development National Occupational Standards*. Sheffield: FCDL https://www.cdhn.org/sites/default/files/FACTSHEETS%202.pdf Accessed 2 May 2018.
35 International Association for Community Development (2011) *IACD Strategic Plan 2011–2015*. Fife: IACD http://ylk.cdr.mybluehost.me/wp-content/uploads/2017/01/IACD_Strategic_Plan_2011-2015.pdf Accessed 2 May 2018.
36 *Community Development National Occupational Standards;* International Association for Community Development (2011) *IACD Strategic Plan 2011–2015* (the 2016–20 Strategic Plan is an operational statement).
37 CDP Information and Intelligence Unit (1973) *The National Community Development Project Inter-Project Report*. London: CDP Information and Intelligence Unit.
38 Kenny, S. (2002) 'Tensions and Dilemmas in Community Development: New Discourses, New Trojans?', *Community Development Journal*, Vol. 37, No. 4, pp. 284–299.
39 Winston Churchill used the phrase in relation to experts rather than knowledge: quoted in Churchill, R. (1965) *Twenty-One Years*. London: Weidenfeld and Nicolson, p. 127. https://todayinsci.com/C/Churchill_Winston/ChurchillWinston-Quotations.htm Accessed 2 May 2018.
40 Lakoff, G. & Johnson, M. (2003) *Metaphors We Live By*. London: University of Chicago.

2 Beyond Society and Community

1 Wagner, M. (2017) 'Blood and soil': Protesters chant Nazi slogan in Charlottesville, *CNN*, 12 August https://edition.cnn.com/2017/08/12/us/charlottesville-unite-the-right-rally/index.html Accessed 8 May 2018.
2 On display in the Documentation Centre Nazi Party Rally Grounds, Nuremberg.
3 Tönnies, F. (1887). *Gemeinschaft und Gesellschaft*. Leipzig: Fues's Verlag; Harris, J. (ed.) (2001) *Tönnies: Community and Civil Society*. Cambridge: Cambridge University Press; Plant, R. (1974) *Community and Ideology*. London: Routledge & Kegan Paul.
4 Esposito, J. (2003) *The Oxford Dictionary of Islam*. Oxford: Oxford University Press; Dallal, A.S., Sikand, Y. & Moten, A.R. (online) Ummrah *The Oxford Encyclopedia of the Islamic World* http://www.oxfordislamicstudies.com/article/opr/t236/e0818?_hi=0&_pos=2 Accessed 8 May 2018.
5 Plant, *Community and Ideology*.
6 Margaret Thatcher said: *'who is society? There is no such thing! There are individual men and women and there are families and no government*

can do anything except through people and people look to themselves first'; Thatcher, M. (1987) Interview for *Woman's Own*, 23 September http://www.margaretthatcher.org/speeches/displaydocument.asp?docid=106689 Accessed 8 May 2018.

7 'society, n.' *OED Online*. Oxford University Press http://www.oed.com/view/Entry/183776?redirectedFrom=Society Accessed 8 May 2018.

8 Simon, H. (2009) *Ibn Khaldun's Science of Human Culture* (translated by F. Baali). New Delhi: Adam; Baali, F. (1988) *Society, State and Urbanism: Ibn Khaldun's Sociological Thought*. Albany: State University of New York; Rosenthal, F. (translator) (1967*) Ibn Khaldun: The Muqaddimah: An Introduction to History* (edited by N.J. Dawood). London: Routledge & Kegan Paul.

9 Anthropology first used in 1501; Sociology in 1780 in an unpublished manuscript by Sieyès and in a published form by Comte in the 1850s: Chaabani, H. (2012)'Insights on the History of Anthropology: Its Emergence in the Wider Middle East before It Existed as a Discipline', *International Journal of Modern Anthropology*, Vol. 1, No. 5, pp. 80–87; Guilhaumou, J.-C. (2006) Sieyès et le non-dit de la sociologie: du mot à la chose, *Revue d'histoire des sciences humaines*, *No. 15*; Bourdieu, M. (2014), Auguste Comte, *The Stanford Encyclopedia of Philosophy* http://plato.stanford.edu/archives/win2014/entries/comte/ Accessed 8 May 2018.

10 Baali, F. & Wardi A. (1981). *Ibn Khaldun and Islamic Thought-Styles: A Social Perspective*. Boston: G. K. Hall.

11 Giddens, A. & Sutton, P. (2009) *Sociology* (6th edn). Cambridge: Polity Press.

12 Gourevitch, P. (1998) *We Wish to Inform You That Tomorrow We Will Be Killed with Our Families: Stories from Rwanda*. New York: Farrar, Straus and Giroux.

13 This and quotations above: 'community, n.'. *OED Online*. Oxford University Press http://www.oed.com/view/Entry/37337?redirectedFrom= Community Accessed 26 June 2015.

14 Esposito, R. (2013) 'Community, Immunity, Biopolitics' *Angelaki: Journal of the Theoretical Humanities* Vol. 18, No. 3 (September), pp. 83–89.

15 See the collection in Klein, J. (1965) *Samples from English Cultures* (Vols 1 & 2). London: Routledge & Kegan Paul; and the critical review of the work of Peter Wilmott and Michael Young in Platt, J. (1971) *Social Research in Bethnal Green*. London: Macmillan.

16 For example Audrey Richards in East Africa: Strathern, M. (2004) 'Richards, Audrey Isabel (1899–1984)' *Oxford Dictionary of National Biography*. Oxford: Oxford University Press. http://www.oxforddnb.com/view/article/31601 Accessed 8 May 2018; Edmund Leach in Burma and also a brief period studying Iraqi Kurds Laidlaw, J. (2004) 'Leach, Sir Edmund Ronald (1910–1989)' *Oxford Dictionary of National Biography*. Oxford: Oxford University Press, (online edn, May 2010) http://www.oxforddnb.com/view/article/39978 Accessed 8 May 2018; Evans-Pritchard in Sudan, Syria and Libya: Lienhardt, R.G. (2004) 'Pritchard, Sir Edward Evan Evans- (1902–1973)', rev. *Oxford Dictionary of National Biography*. Oxford: Oxford University Press, (online edn, January 2011) http://www.oxforddnb.com/

view/article/31089 Accessed 8 May 2018; Margaret Read in East Africa and at the Institute of Education in London: Whitehead, C. (2004) 'Read, Margaret Helen (1889–1991)' *Oxford Dictionary of National Biography*. Oxford: Oxford University Press (online edn, January 2008) http://www.oxforddnb.com/view/article/72739 Accessed 8 May 2018; Northcote Thomas-Blench, R. (1995) The work of N.W. Thomas as Government Anthropologist in Nigeria *The Nigerian Field* Vol. 60, pp. 20–28; Talal Asad's collection contains much material on the relationship between anthropology and empires (Including Western and Communist): Asad, T. (ed.) (1973) *Anthropology and the Colonial Encounter*. London: Ithaca Press.
17 González, R. (2007) 'Towards Mercenary Anthropology?' *Anthropology Today* Vol. 23, pp 14–19 No. 3 (June).
18 Tönnies, F. (1887) *Gemeinschaft und Gesellschaft*. Leipzig: Fues's Verlag; Harris, J. (ed.) (2001) *Tönnies: Community and Civil Society*. Cambridge: Cambridge University Press.
19 Embassy of Spain in Tel Aviv (2015) *Bill Granting Spanish Citizenship to Sephardic Jews* http://www.exteriores.gob.es/Embajadas/TELAVIV/en/Noticias/Pages/Articulos/20150617_NOT1.aspx Accessed 8 May 2018.
20 Akenson, D.H. (1992) *God's Peoples*. Ithaca, NY: Cornell.
21 Dennis, N. (1968) 'The Popularity of the Neighbourhood Community Idea' in Pahl, R. (ed.) *Readings in Urban Sociology*. Oxford: Pergamon.
22 Ardrey, R. (1969) *The Territorial Imperative*. London: Collins; Montagu, A. (1968) Man *and Aggression*. New York: Oxford University Press; Nobel Committee for Physiology or Medicine (2014) *Press Release 6 October 2014* http://www.nobelprize.org/nobel_prizes/medicine/laureates/2014/press.pdf Accessed 8 May 2018.
23 Montagu, A. 'Aggression and War' in Montagu, A. (1976) The *Nature of Human Aggression*, at http://www.panarchy.org/montagu/territorialism.html Accessed 8 May 2018.
24 Agnew, J. (2011) 'Space and Place' in Agnew, J. & Livingstone, D (eds) *The SAGE Handbook of Geographical Knowledge*. London: Sage https://www.geog.ucla.edu/sites/default/files/users/jagnew/416.pdf Accessed 8 May 2018.
25 For example, arguments about Travellers and Roma rights in Europe – see Richardson, J. and Ryder, A. (eds) (2012) *Gypsies and Travellers: Empowerment and Inclusion in British Society*. Bristol: Policy Press; nomads and pastoral farmers in the Sahel and the Horn of Africa – see UNDP (2006) *Nomads' Settlement in Sudan: Experiences, Lessons and Future Action*. Khartoum: UNDP http://www.sd.undp.org/content/dam/sudan/docs/NOMADS%20SETTLEMENT%20IN%20SUDAN.pdf Accessed 8 May 2018; Ostrom, E. (2012) *The Future of the Commons*. London: Institute of Economic Affairs http://www.iea.org.uk/sites/default/files/publications/files/IEA%20Future%20of%20the%20Commons%20web%2029-1.10.12.pdf Accessed 8 May 2018; Connell, R. (2008) *Southern Theory*. Crow's Nest, NSW: Allen & Unwin.
26 World Health Organization (Online) *Urban Population Growth* http://www.who.int/gho/urban_health/situation_trends/urban_population_growth_text/en/ Accessed 8 May 2018.

27 World Health Organization (Online) *Country Statistics* http://www.who.int/gho/countries/en/ Accessed 8 May 2018.
28 Economist (2017) 'Fewer But Still with Us' *Economist* 1 April.
29 For the philosophical debate see Janiak, A. (2009) 'Kant's Views on Space and Time' *The Stanford Encyclopedia of Philosophy* http://plato.stanford.edu/archives/win2012/entries/kant-spacetime/ Accessed 8 May 2018.
30 Winder, R. (2004) *Bloody Foreigners*. London: Abacus.
31 Jewish Virtual Library (Online) *Venice* https://www.jewishvirtuallibrary.org/jsource/vjw/Venice.html#The%20Ghetto Accessed 8 May 2018.
32 Winder, R. (2004) *Bloody Foreigners*. London: Abacus; for a Christian Zionist perspective see, for example, Ice, T. (2009) 'Lovers of Zion: A History of Christian Zionism' *Article Archives*. Paper 29 http://digitalcommons.liberty.edu/pretrib_arch/29 Accessed 8 May 2018.
33 Robinson, P. *The Plantation of Ulster: British Settlement in an Irish Landscape, 1600–1670* (1st edn, Gill and Macmillan, 1984, 2nd and 3rd edns, Ulster Historical Foundation, 1994 and 2001).
34 Pax NL (2015) *After ISIS: Perspectives of Displaced Communities from Ninewa on Return to Iraq's Disputed Territory* www.paxvoorvrede.nl/media/files/pax-iraq-report--after-isis.pdf Accessed 8 May 2018.
35 Wilkinson, R. (1996) *Unhealthy Societies: The Afflictions of Inequality*. London: Routledge; Wilkinson, R & Pickett, K. (2010) *The Spirit Level: Why More Equal Societies Almost Always Do Better*. London: Penguin.
36 See, for example, Graham, H. (ed.) (2000) *Understanding Health Inequalities*. Buckingham: Open University Press; Maguire, A. & O'Reilly, D. (2015) 'Does Conurbation Affect The Risk of Poor Mental Health? A Population Based Record Linkage Study' *Health & Place* Vol. 34, pp. 126–134.
37 Shaw, R., Atkin, K., Bécares, L., Albor, C., Stafford, M., Kiernan, K., Nazroo, J., Wilkinson, R. & Pickett, K. (2012) 'Impact of Ethnic Density on Adult Mental Disorders: Narrative Review' *British Journal Psychiatry* (July) Vol. 201, No. 1, pp. 11–19 http://www.ncbi.nlm.nih.gov/pubmed/22753852 Accessed 8 May 2018.
38 Dennis, 'The Popularity of the Neighbourhood Community Idea'; Castells, M. (2004) *The Power of Identity*. Oxford: Blackwell.
39 Quoted in Robson, T. (2000) *The State and Community Action*. London: Pluto, p. 42.
40 Castells, *The Power of Identity*.
41 Marx, K. (1973) *Surveys from Exile*. Harmondsworth: Penguin, p. 239.
42 For example, Raymond Williams, quoted in Plant, *Community and Ideology*, p. 48.
43 Oxford English Dictionary (online) 'Nimby, n.' *OED Online*. (June 2015). Oxford University Press http://www.oed.com/view/Entry/245895? From=Nimby Accessed 3 May 2018.
44 Sen, A. (2009) *The Idea of Justice*. London: Allen Lane.
45 World Commission on Dams (20 dams-and-development-a-new-framework-for-decision-making-3939 Accessed 8 May 2018; Rivers International and others (2010) *Protecting Rivers and Rights: Ten Years After the World Commission on Dams Report* https://www.internationalrivers.org/

sites/default/files/attached-files/wcdbriefingkit_0.pdf Accessed 8 May 2018; Survival International (2010) *Serious Damage: Tribal People and Large Dams* http://assets.survivalinternational.org/documents/373/Serious_Damage_final.pdf Accessed 8 May 2018.
46 Spivak, G.C. (2013) *Can There Be a Feminist World?* Amman: Speech http://www.publicbooks.org/nonfiction/can-there-be-a-feminist-world Accessed 8 May 2018; Spivak, G.C. (Unpublished) *Still Pushing for the Humanities* Speech: LSE (29 June 1015).
47 Kretzmann, J. & McKnight, J. (1993) *Building Communities from the Inside Out: A Path toward Finding and Mobilizing a Community's Assets*. Evanston, IL: Assets-Based Community Development Institute, Institute for Policy Research, Northwestern University; Gibson-Graham, J.K. (2006) *Post-Capitalist Economics*. London: University of Minnesota Press.
48 Carlson, W., Buskist, W. & Martin, G.N. (2000) *Psychology: The Science of Behaviour European Adaptation*. Harlow: Pearson.
49 Castells, *The Power of Identity* following the work of Alan Touraine.
50 Lederach, J.P. (2003) *The Little Book of Conflict Transformation*. Intercourse, PA: Good Books, p. 55.
51 Castells, *The Power of Identity*.
52 Giddens & Sutton, *Sociology*; Oliver, M. & Barnes, C. (2012) *The New Politics of Disablement*. Basingstoke: Palgrave Macmillan.
53 Castells, *The Power of Identity*.
54 Deutscher, P. (2005) *How to Read Derrida*. London: Granta.
55 Orwell, G. (1953) Notes on Nationalism in *England, Your England and Other Essays*. London: Secker and Warburg http://orwell.ru/library/essays/nationalism/english/e_nat Accessed 8 May 2018.
56 Castells, M. *The Power of Identity*.
57 See for example, Ashe, F. (2008) 'Gender and Ethno-Nationalist Politics' in Coulter, C. & Murray, M. (eds) (2008) Northern *Ireland After the Troubles*. Manchester: Manchester University Press, pp. 157–174, which addresses both the theoretical argument and its application to Northern Ireland.
58 Kidd, W. & Teagle, A. (2012) *Culture and Identity* (2nd edn). Basingstoke: Palgrave Macmillan; Castells, *The Power of Identity*.
59 Fanon, F (1967) *Black Skin White Masks*. New York: Grove Press, p. 63.
60 *Solitarism* in Sen, A. (2007) *Identity and Violence*. London: Penguin; *Intersectionality*: Crenshaw, K. (1991) Mapping the Margins: Intersectionality, Identity Politics, and Violence against Women of Color *Stanford Law Review*, Vol. 43, No. 6 (July 1991), pp. 1241–1299.
61 Solomon, A. (2013) *Far from the Tree*. London: Chatto & Windus.
62 Life in the UK Tests Limited (online) *Life in the UK Test* https://lifeintheuktests.co.uk/ Accessed 8 May 2018.
63 Natcen Social Research (2014) *British Social Attitudes 2014* http://www.bsa.natcen.ac.uk/latest-report/british-social-attitudes-31/national-identity/introduction.aspx Accessed 8 May 2018; Comres (2015) *British Values Survey* http://comres.co.uk/wp-content/uploads/2015/03/February2015_Poll_Tables.pdf Accessed 8 May 2018; European Social Survey (Online) *ESS Topline Series* http://www.europeansocialsurvey.org/findings/topline.

html Accessed 8 May 2018; World Values Survey (Online) *The World Values Survey: findings and insight* http://www.worldvaluessurvey.org/WVSContents.jsp Accessed 8 May 2018.

64 Orgad, L. (2015) How do you decide who 'qualifies' as a citizen? OUP Blog, Oxford University Press https://blog.oup.com/2015/11/citizenship-test-design/ Accessed 3 May 2018; Life in the UK Test Web (online) *A Modern Thriving Society* https://lifeintheuktestweb.co.uk/a-modern-thriving-society/ Accessed 3 May 2018.

65 Giddens & Sutton, *Sociology* summarises the social capital literature sympathetically. The original ideas of (neo) communitarianism are in writers such as Etzioni, A. (1995) *Spirit of Community: Rights, Responsibilities and the Communitarian Agenda.* London: Fontana; Putnam, R. (2000) *Bowling Alone.* New York: Touchstone; among many critiques are Navarro, V. (2002) 'A Critique of Social Capital' *International Journal of Health Services* Vol. 32, No. 3, pp. 423–432 http://www.vnavarro.org/wp-content/uploads/2002/12/a-critique-of-social-capital.pdf Accessed 8 May 2018; de Filippis, J. (2001) 'The Myth of Social Capital in Community Development' *Housing Policy Debate* Vol. 12, No. 4, pp. 781–806, http://www.urbancenter.utoronto.ca/pdfs/elibrary/DeFilippis_Myth-of-Social-C.pdf Accessed 8 May 2018; for a review on social capital data in the UK see Richards, L. (2015) *Social Capital: Are We Becoming Lonelier and Less Civic?* Oxford: Centre for Social Investigation http://csi.nuff.ox.ac.uk/wp-content/uploads/2015/03/CSI_8_Social_Capital.pdf Accessed 8 May 2018.

66 Gilchrist, A. (2009) *The Well-Connected Community: A Networking Approach to Community Development* (2nd edn). Bristol: Policy Press; Escobar, A. (2004) 'Beyond the Third World: Imperial Globality, Global Coloniality, and Anti-Globalization Social Movements' *Third World Quarterly* Vol. 25, No. 1, pp. 207–230 http://www.economia.unical.it/DES/DES_file/ARTICOLI_VITALE/Arturo%20Escobar.pdf Accessed 8 May 2018.

67 Akenson, D.H. (1992) *God's Peoples.* Ithaca, NY: Cornell.

68 Oxford English Dictionary (Online) 'culture, n.' *OED Online.* Oxford University Press http://www.oed.com/view/Entry/45746?rskey=SEI8q4&=1&isAdvanced=false#eid Accessed 8 May 2018.

69 Clifford Geertz quoted in Kuper, A. (2000) *Culture.* London: Harvard University Press.

70 See Ife, J. (2001) *Human Rights and Social Work.* Cambridge: Cambridge University Press. This is not the same use of culturalism, though it is related to the philosophical concept of culturalism which says that 'nature is not independent of culture'.

71 Trevor-Roper, H. 'The Highland Tradition' in Hobsbawm, E. & Ranger, T. (1992) *The Invention of Tradition.* Cambridge: Cambridge University Press; Costume Institute of the African Diaspora (Online) *Tartan: Its Journey through the African Diaspora* http://ciad.org.uk/2015/06/28/11326/ Accessed 8 May 2018.

72 World Values Survey (Online) *The World Values Survey: Findings and Insight* http://www.worldvaluessurvey.org/WVSContents.jsp Accessed 8 May 2018.

73 hooks, b. (1994) *Teaching to Transgress: Education as the Practice of Freedom.* London: Routledge.

NOTES

74 Wolf, E. (1982) *Europe and the People without History*. Berkeley, CA: University of California Press, p. 41 https://is.muni.cz/el/1490/podzim2013/CZS13/um/lecture1/1_4_Wolf.pdf Accessed 8 May 2018.
75 Said, E. (1993) *Culture and Imperialism*. London: Chatto & Windus; Kuper, op. cit.
76 Equal Rights Trust (Online) *Mandla (Sewa Singh) and another v Dowell Lee and others [1983] 2 AC 548* http://www.equalrightstrust.org/ertdocumentbank/Microsoft%20Word%20-%20Mandla.pdf Accessed 8 May 2018; Anderson, S. (2012) *Languages: A Very Short Introduction*. Oxford: Oxford University Press; Maher, J. (2017) *Multilingualism: A Very Short Introduction*. Oxford: Oxford University Press; Mcdonough, L. (2010) 'Linguistic Diversity in the UK and Ireland – Does the Meaning of Equality Get Lost in Translation?' In Healy, G. et al. (eds) *Equality, Inequalities and Diversity Contemporary: Challenges and Strategies. Management, Work and Organisations*. Basingstoke: Palgrave Macmillan http://eprints.lse.ac.uk/38413/1/__Libfile_repository_Content_Mcdonagh,%20Luke%20T_Linguistic%20Diversity%20in%20the%20UK%20and%20Ireland%20(publisher%20permission%20pending)_Linguistic%20diversity_Linguistic%20diversity%20(lsero).pdf Accessed 8 May 2018; Coste, D. et al. (2009) *Plurilingual and Pluricultural Competence*. Strasbourg: Council of Europe https://www.coe.int/t/dg4/linguistic/Source/SourcePublications/CompetencePlurilingue09web_en.pdf Accessed 8 May 2018; Edwards, J. (2013) *Sociolinguistics: A Very Short Introduction*. Oxford: Oxford University Press.
77 Genesis 11:1–9; *Book of Judges* Chapter 13 https://www.kingjamesbibleonline.org/ Accessed 8 May 2018.
78 Edwards, *Sociolinguistics*.
79 Deutscher, *How to Read Derrida*; Noys, B. (2003) *Politics and Friendship: A Conversation with Jacques Derrida* Centre for Modern French Thought, University of Sussex http://www.livingphilosophy.org/Derrida-politics-friendship.htm Accessed 8 May 2018.
80 See Telfer in O'Gorman, K. (2007) 'The Hospitality Phenomenon: Philosophical Enlightenment?' *International Journal of Culture, Tourism and Hospitality Research* Vol. 1, No. 3, pp. 189–202.
81 Deutscher, P. (2013) 'The Membrane and the Diaphragm: Derrida and Esposito on Immunity, Community and Birth' *Angelaki: Journal of the Theoretical Humanities* Vol. 18, No. 3, p. 49.
82 Esposito, 'Community, Immunity, Biopolitics'; Deutscher, 'The Membrane and the Diaphragm', pp. 49–68.
83 Beckett, G. (2013) 'The Politics of Emergency' *Reviews in Anthropology* Vol. 42, No. 2, pp. 85–101 https://www.academia.edu/8300433/The_Politics_of_Emergency Accessed 8 May 2018.
84 Lavender, T. (2016) 'Language of Human Rights Often Conflicts with Local Virtues, Ignatieff Tells U of T Audience' *U of T news* 4 October, University of Toronto https://www.utoronto.ca/news/human-rights-ignatieff Accessed 8 May 2018.
85 Quoted in O'Gorman 'The Hospitality Phenomenon' https://www.academia.edu/279801/

The_Hospitality_Phenomenon_Philosophical_Enlightenment Accessed 8 May 2018.

86 Young, I.M. (1986) 'The Ideal of Community and the Politics of Difference' *Social Theory and Practice* Vol. 12, No. 1 (Spring), pp. 1–26 also reprinted in Bridges, G. & Watson, S. (eds) *The Blackwell City Reader* (pp. 228–236). Chichester: Wiley-Blackwell.

87 Freud, S. (1963) *Civilization and its Discontents*. London: Hogarth Press, p. 51.

88 Walsh, C. (2011) 'Gangs are Good for Society' *Guardian* 10 November https://www.theguardian.com/society/joepublic/2011/nov/10/gangs-good-society-youth-crime Accessed 8 May 2018.

89 Berelowitz, S. et al. (2013) *'If only someone had listened' The Office of the Children's Commissioner's Inquiry into Child Sexual Exploitation in Gangs and Groups Final Report*. London: Office of the Children's Commissioner https://www.scie-socialcareonline.org.uk/if-only-someone-had-listened-office-of-the-childrens-commissioners-inquiry-into-child-sexual-exploitaiton-in-gangs-and-groups-final-report/r/a11G0000002XuSkIAK Accessed 8 May 2018.

90 Beckett, H. et al. (2013) *'It's wrong … but you get used to it' A Qualitative Study of Gang-Associated Sexual Violence Towards, and Exploitation of, Young People in England*. London: Office of the Children's Commissioner, p. 43 http://uobrep.openrepository.com/uobrep/bitstream/10547/305795/1/Gangs-Report-final.pdf Accessed 8 May 2018 Quotation.

91 Belsky, J. (1980) 'Child Maltreatment – An Ecological Integration' *American Psychologist*, April, pp. 320–335 https://www.researchgate.net/profile/Jay_Belsky/publication/15812067_Child_Maltreatment_An_Ecological_Integration/links/004635193b554a091c000000.pdf Accessed 8 May 2018; A later framework by the same author uses a different vocabulary: Belsky, J. (1993) 'Etiology of Child Maltreatment: A Developmental-Ecological Analysis' *Psychological Bulletin* Vol. 114, No. 3, pp. 413–434 https://www.researchgate.net/profile/Jay_Belsky/publication/14925757_Etiology_of_Child_Maltreatment_A_Developmental-Ecological_Analysis/links/02e7e51cc93c307a83000000.pdf Accessed 8 May 2018.

92 Child Exploitation and Online Protection Centre (2011) *Out of Mind, Out of Sight CEOP Thematic Assessment* London: CEOP http://cdn.basw.co.uk/upload/basw_101409-2.pdf Accessed 8 May 2018.

93 Gable, G. & Jackson, P. *Lonewolves: Myth or Reality?* Ilford: Searchlight www.lonewolfproject.org.uk/resources/LW-complete-final.pdf Accessed 8 May 2018.

94 Patterns of sex offending and strategies for effective assessment and intervention; Eldridge, H. (2000) 'Patterns of Sex Offending and Strategies for Effective Assessment and Intervention' in C. Itzin (ed.) *Home Truths About Child Sexual Abuse*. London: Routledge.

95 Giddens, A. (ed.) (1972) *Emile Durkheim: Selected Writings*. Cambridge: Cambridge University Press, p. 154.

96 Oxford English Dictionary (Online) 'cohesion, n.' *OED Online*. Oxford University Press http://www.oed.com/view/Entry/35943?redirected From= cohesion Accessed 8 May 2018; Giddens, *Emile Durkheim*; Baali, *Society, State and Urbanism*; Rosenthal, F. (translator) (1967) *Ibn Khaldun: The Muqaddimah: An Introduction to History* (edited by Dawood, N.J.). London: Routledge and Kegan Paul.

97 Oxford English Dictionary (Online) 'adhesion, n.' *OED Online*. Oxford University Press. June 2015. http://www.oed.com/view/Entry/2336?redirectedFrom=adhesion Accessed 8 May 2018.

98 Giddens & Sutton, *Sociology* summarised pp. 24–25.

99 Brewer, J. (2013) 'Sociology and Peacebuilding' in Mac Ginty, R. (ed.) *Routledge Handbook of Peacebuilding*. London: Taylor & Francis, pp. 159–170 https://www.qub.ac.uk/Research/GRI/mitchell-institute/FileStore/Filetoupload,756763,en.pdf Accessed 8 May 2018.

100 Fanon, *Black Skin White Masks*; Fanon, F. (1961) *The Wretched of the Earth*. London: Penguin.

101 See, for example, Ranger, T. (1992) 'The invention of tradition in Colonial Africa' in Hobsbawm & Ranger, *The Invention of Tradition*; Said, E. (1978) *Orientalism*. London: Penguin; Sardar, Z. (1999) Orientalism. Buckingham: Open University Press; Stewart, F. (2002) *Horizontal Inequalities: A Neglected Dimension of Development* QEH Working Paper 81 http://www3.qeh.ox.ac.uk/pdf/qehwp/qehwps81.pdf Accessed 8 May 2018.

102 Oxford English Dictionary (Online) 'queer, n.2.' *OED Online* Oxford University Press http://www.oed.com/view/Entry/156235?rskey=2hnELZ &result=1 Accessed 8 May 2018; 'Gay' to refer to homosexual people was first used in the 1920s largely by homosexuals: Oxford English Dictionary (Online) 'gay, adj., adv., and n.' *OED Online*. June 2015. Oxford University Press. http://www.oed.com/view/Entry/77207?rskey=2PxJh5&result=1&isAdvanced=false Accessed 8 May 2018.

103 Oxford English Dictionary (Online) 'nigger, n. and adj.' *OED Online*. Oxford University Press, June 2015 http://www.oed.com/view/Entry/126934?rskey=0Lec02&result=1 Accessed 8 May 2018.

104 Oxford English Dictionary (Online) 'black, adj. and n.' *OED Online*. Oxford University Press. http://www.oed.com/view/Entry/19670?rskey=0BGiif&result=1&isAdvanced=false Accessed 8 May 2018; Richards, N. (2014) 'Black – Political vs. Ethnic?' *Media Diversified*, 29 October http://mediadiversified.org/2014/10/29/black-political-vs-ethnic/ Accessed 8 May 2018; Ahmed, S. (2014) Black British feminism, it is collective and collaborative *Media Diversified*, 30 October http://mediadiversified.org/2014/10/30/black-british-feminism-it-is-collective-and-collaborative/ Accessed 8 May 2018; Chakrabortty, A. (2014) 'I'm Bengali and I'm black – in the same way that my parents were', 'Comment is free', 30 October *Guardian* http://www.theguardian.com/commentisfree/2014/oct/30/bengali-black-ethnic-minorities-racism Accessed 8 May 2018; Eade, J. (2013) 'Crossing Boundaries and Identification Processes' *Integrative Psychological & Behavioral Science* Vol. 47, No. 4, pp. 509–515.

105 Campbell, B. (2008) *Agreement! The State, Conflict and Change in Northern Ireland.* London: Lawrence & Wishart; Ward, M. (2005) Gender, Citizenship and the Future of the Northern Ireland Peace Process Éire-Ireland Vol. 40, Nos. 3 & 4, Fall/Winter http://www.cain.ulst.ac.uk/issues/women/docs/ward05peaceprocess.pdf Accessed 8 May 2018; Cockburn, C. (2004) *The Line: Women, Partition and the Gender Order in Cyprus.* London: Zed; Gardner, J. & el Bushra, J. (eds) (2004) *Somalia the Untold Story: The War Through the Eyes of Somali Women.* London: Pluto Press.

106 Hopkins, P. (2016) 'Three decades on from his tragic death, the debt rock world still owes Thin Lizzy's iconic frontman' *Belfast Telegraph* 2 January http://www.belfasttelegraph.co.uk/life/three-decades-on-from-his-tragic-death-the-debt-rock-world-still-owes-thin-lizzys-iconic-frontman-34329345.html Accessed 8 May 2018.

107 Streets of Growth (2010) *6 Principles of Gang Involvement* from mail@streetsofgrowth.org Correct at 8 May 2018.

108 Nicholson, J. (ed.) (2014) *Concise Oxford Dictionary of Mathematics* (5th edn). Oxford: Oxford University Press.

109 For example, Parsons, W. (1995) *Public Policy: An Introduction to the Theory and Practice of Policy Analysis.* Cheltenham: Edward Elgar; Bronfenbrenner, U., Friedman S. & Wachs T. (1999) (eds) *Measuring Environment Across the Life Span: Emerging Methods and Concepts.* Washington, DC: American Psychological Association Press; Westoby, P. & Dowling, G. (2013) *Theory and Practice of Dialogical Community Development: International Perspectives.* Abingdon: Routledge.

110 For example, Thompson, N. (2003) *Promoting Equality-Challenging Discrimination and Oppression* (2nd edn). London: Palgrave; Lederach, J *The Little Book of Conflict Transformation.*

111 Pawson, R., Greenhalgh, T., Harvey, G. & Walshe, K. (2005) 'Realist Review: A New Method of Systematic Review Designed for Complex Policy Interventions' *Journal of Health Services Research & Policy* Vol. 10, Suppl 1.

112 Private Troubles, Public Issues from: Mills, C.W. (1959) *The Sociological Imagination.* Oxford: Oxford University Press.

113 Lakoff, G. (2014) *The All New Don't Think of an Elephant.* White River Junction, VT: Chelsea Green.

114 Lakoff, *The All New Don't Think of an Elephant.*

3 Development

1 Rose or skunk: Scott, J.C. (2014) 'In Conversation' *After 2015: Development and Its Alternatives* (Conference) British Academy.

2 OED Online 'development, n.' Oxford University Press. http://www.oed com/view/Entry/51434?redirectedFrom=Development Accessed 15 May 2018; Rist, G. (2002) *The History of Development: From Western Origins to Global Faith.* London: Zed.

3   Sen, A. (2001) *Development as Freedom*. Oxford: Oxford Paperbacks; Sen, A. (2009) *The Idea of Justice*. London: Allen Lane; Nussbaum, M. (2000) *Women and Human Development: The Capabilities Approach*. Cambridge: Cambridge University Press; Doyal, L. & Gough, I. (1992) *A Theory of Human Need*. Basingstoke: Macmillan; Sachs, J. (2012) 'Introduction' in Helliwell, J., Layard, R. & Sachs, J. (eds) *World Happiness Report*. Columbia: Earth Institute http://worldhappiness.report/wp-content/uploads/sites/2/2012/04/World_Happiness_Report_2012.pdf Accessed 15 May 2018.

4   Inglehart, R., Foa, R., Peterson, C. & Welzel, C. (2008) 'Development, Freedom, and Rising Happiness A Global Perspective (1981–2007)' *Perspectives on Psychological Science* Vol. 3, No. 4, pp. 264–285.

5   United Nations (1948) *Declaration of Human Rights* http://www.un.org/en/documents/udhr/ Accessed 15 May 2018; Ishay, M. (2004) *The History of Human Rights*. London: University of California Press; United Nations (1976) *International Covenant on Economic, Social and Cultural Rights* http://www.ohchr.org/EN/ProfessionalInterest/Pages/CESCR.aspx Accessed 15 May 2018.

6   United Nations (1976) *International Covenant on Economic, Social and Cultural Rights* http://www.ohchr.org/EN/ProfessionalInterest/Pages/CESCR.aspx Accessed 15 May 2018.

7   This chapter draws extensively on Rist, *The History of Development*; Lewis, D. (2005) 'Anthropology and Development: The Uneasy Relationship' in Carrier, J.G. (ed.) *A Handbook of Economic Anthropology* (pp. 472–486). Cheltenham: Edward Elgar. LSE http://eprints.lse.ac.uk/253/ Accessed 15 May 2018; Ferguson, J. (2009). 'Development' in Barnard, A. & Spencer, J. (eds) *Encyclopedia of Social and Cultural Anthropology*. London: Routledge; Sachs, W. (ed.) (2010) *The Development Dictionary*. London: Zed. For the background and detail of the Point Four Program see Bilger, D. & Sowell, R. (1999) *Point Four Program of Technical Assistance to Developing Nations – Archival Materials at the Library*. Harry S. Truman Library and Museum https://www.trumanlibrary.org/hstpaper/point4.htm Accessed 15 May 2018.

8   Thane, P. (1996) *The Foundations of the Welfare State*. Abingdon: Routledge; Stedman Jones, G. (2013) *Outcast*. London: Verso.

9   In Popple, K. (2015) *Analysing Community Work*. Maidenhead: Open University Press.

10 Bulmer, M., Bales, K. & Kish Sklar, K. (1991) *The Social Survey in Historical Perspective 1880–1940*. Cambridge: Cambridge University Press.

11 Meacham, S. (1987) *Toynbee Hall and Social Reform 1880–1914*. London: Yale University Press.

12 Newsome, D. (2009) 'Manning, Henry Edward (1808–1892)', *Oxford Dictionary of National Biography*. Oxford University Press http://www.oxforddnb.com/view/article/17970 Accessed 15 May 2018.

13 Lipman, V. (1959) *A Century of Social Service, 1859–1959: The Jewish Board of Guardians*. London: Routledge and Kegan Paul.

14 Smiles, S. (1867) *The Huguenots*. London: John Murray, p. 317; Smiles, S. (1859) *Self-Help*. London: John Murray.
15 Kropotkin, P. (1970) *Mutual Aid*. Boston, MA: Porter Sargent; Thompson, E. (1968) *The Making of the English Working Class*. Harmondsworth: Penguin.
16 Lugard, F. (1926) *The Dual Mandate in British Tropical Africa*, p. 17 http://www.fafich.ufmg.br/~luarnaut/Lugard-dual%20mandate.pdf Accessed 15 May 2018.
17 Frederick Lugard quoted in Hill, R. (1992) 'Zion on the Zambesi: Dr J. Albert Thorne, "a descendant of Africa of Barbados", and the African colonial enterprise: The "preliminary stage", 1894–7' in Gundara, J. & Duffield, I. (eds) *Essays on the History of Blacks in Britain*. Aldershot: Avebury, p. 110.
18 Holford, J. (1988) 'Mass Education and Community Development in the British Colonies, 1940–1960: A Study in the Politics of Community Education' *Journal of Lifelong Education* Vol. 7, No. 3, pp. 163–183 https://www.academia.edu/1548782/Mass_education_and_community_development_in_the_British_colonies_1940-1960_A_study_in_the_politics_of_community_education Accessed 15 May 2018.
19 Colonial Office, 1944, p. 4 quoted in Brokensha, D. & Hodge, P. (1969) *Community Development: An Interpretation*. San Francisco, CA: Chandler; Midgley, J. (1995) *Social Development: The Developmental Perspective in Social Welfare*. London: Sage; Colonial Office (1944) *Mass Education in African Society no. 186*. London: HMSO; Colonial Office (1955) *Social Development in the British Colonial Territories: Report of the Ashridge Conference on Social Development 3rd to 12th August, 1954*. London: Colonial Office; Du Sautoy, P. (1958) *Community Development in Ghana*. London: Oxford University Press.
20 Alec Dickson (A. G. Dickson) was an army officer in World War II in Africa initially working for the Mobile Propaganda Unit (where he employed Barack Obama's grandfather as a cook!). Later he became a Social Development Officer in West Africa. He was involved in setting up an innovative training course in the Cameroons in the 1950s. He also set up both Voluntary Service Overseas and Community Service Volunteers Dickson, A. (1976) *A Chance to Serve*. London: Dennis Dobson; Obama, B. (2004) *Dreams from My Father*. New York: Three Rivers Press.
21 Bhattacharyya, S.N. (1972) *Community Development in Developing Countries*. Calcutta: Academic Publisher; Fitch and Oppenheimer quoted in Mayo, M. 'Community Development' in Bailey, R. & Brake, M. (1975) *Radical Social Work*. London: Edward Arnold.
22 Quoted in Dickson, A. (1950) 'Mass Education in Togoland' *African Affairs* Vol. 49, No. 195 (April), pp. 136–150 (London: Royal African Society).
23 Lovell, G. (2007) 'T. R.(Reg) Batten and Madge Batten: Their Worldwide Contributions to the Non-directive Approach to Community Development', The Encyclopaedia of Informal Education http://infed.org/mobi/t-r-reg-batten-and-madge-batten-non-directivity-and-community-development/ Accessed 15 May 2018; Whitehead, C. (2004) 'Read,

Margaret Helen (1889–1991)', Oxford Dictionary of National Biography, Oxford University Press; online edn, January 2008 http://www.oxforddnb.com/view/article/72739 Accessed 15 May 2018.
24 Brokensha & Hodge, *Community Development*; Midgley, J. (1995) *Social Development: The Developmental Perspective in Social Welfare*. London: Sage Colonial Office (1955) *Social Development in the British Colonial Territories: Report of the Ashridge Conference on Social Development 3rd to 12th August, 1954*. London: Colonial Office; Du Sautoy, P. (1958) *Community Development in Ghana*. London: Oxford University Press; Colonial Office (1958) *A Handbook Prepared by a Study Conference on Community Development Held at Hartwell House, Aylesbury, Buckinghamshire, September, 1957*. London: HMSO.
25 Holford, J. (1988) 'Mass Education and Community Development in the British Colonies, 1940–1960: A Study in the Politics of Community Education' *Journal of Lifelong Education*, Vol. 7, No. 3, pp. 163–183 https://www.academia.edu/1548782/Mass_education_and_community_development_in_the_British_colonies_1940-1960_A_study_in_the_politics_of_community_education Accessed 15 May 2018; Benson, T. (1936) 'The Jeanes School and the Education of the East African Native', *African Affairs* Vol. 35, No. 141, pp. 418–431 (London: Royal African Society); Nitocris (2014) *History of Jamaica Welfare* http://www.eachoneteachone.org.uk/history-of-jamaica-welfare/ Accessed 15 May 2018.
26 Brokensha & Hodge, *Community Development*.
27 Betts, R. (1991) *France and Decolonisation 1900–1960*. Houndmills: MacMillan Minister, quoted on p. 31.
28 Robert Charlick quoted in Machethe, C. (1995) *Approaches to Rural Development in the Third World: Lessons for South Africa*. Department of Agricultural Economics, Michigan State University http://ageconsearch.umn.edu/bitstream/11213/1/pb95ma02.pdf Accessed 15 May 2018; Hapgood, D. (1962) *Rural Animation in Senegal*. Dakar: Institute of Current World Affairs.
29 Sharp, G. (1973) *The Politics of Nonviolent Action* (Vol. 1). Boston, MA: Porter Sargent.
30 Gandhi, M. (1910) *Hind Swaraj or Indian Home Rule*, p. 66 http://soilandhealth.org/wp-content/uploads/0303critic/hind%20swaraj.pdf Accessed 15 May 2018.
31 Gangrade, K.D. (1986) *Social Work and Development: Role of Religion and Caste in Three Delhi Villages*. New Delhi: Northern Book Centre; Burke, B. (2000) 'Mahatma Gandhi on Education', *the Encyclopaedia of Informal Education* http://infed.org/mobi/mahatma-gandhi-on-education/ Accessed 15 May 2018; Bombay Sarvodaya Mandal/Gandhi Book Centre (Online) *What Is Satyagraha?* http://www.mkgandhi.org/faq/q17.htm Accessed 15 May 2018.
32 Midgley, J. (2003) 'Social Development: The Intellectual Heritage' *Journal of International Development* Vol. 15, No. 7, pp. 831–844.
33 Clapson, M. (2004) *A Social History of Milton Keynes: Middle England/Edge City*. London: Frank Cass; Department for Communities, Northern Ireland (Online)

Our Responsibilities https://www.communities-ni.gov.uk/ Accessed 15 May 2018.

34 Midgley, J. (2014) *Social Development: Theory and Practice*. London: Sage Publications, p. 13.
35 Midgley, *Social Development*.
36 The linear view is critiqued from a 'path dependency perspective in, for instance: Yeates, N. (2014) *Understanding Global Social Policy*. Bristol: Policy Press; Deacon, B. (2007) *Global Social Policy and Governance*. London: Sage.
37 Brundtland, G.H. (1987) *Report of the World Commission on Environment and Development: Our Common Future*. New York: United Nations http://www.un-documents.net/our-common-future.pdf Accessed 15 May 2018; Nyerere, J. (1990) *The Challenge to the South*. Oxford: Oxford University Press; UNDP (Online) *Human Development Reports* http://hdr.undp.org/en/data Accessed 15 May 2018.
38 Aristotle in 'The Nicomachean Ethics' in UNDP (1990) *Human Development Report 1990* (p. 9) http://hdr.undp.org/sites/default/files/reports/219/hdr_1990_en_complete_nostats.pdf Accessed 15 May 2018.
39 Sen, *Development as Freedom*; Nussbaum, *Women and Human Development*; Sen, *The Idea of Justice*.
40 Midgley, *Social Development*, p. 65.
41 UNESCO (2015) *EFA Global Monitoring Report 2015*. Paris: UNESCO http://unesdoc.unesco.org/images/0023/002322/232205e.pdf Accessed 15 May 2018.
42 World Health Organization (2015) *World Health Statistics 2015 Part I Health-Related Millennium Development Goals* http://www.who.int/gho/publications/world_health_statistics/EN_WHS2015_Part1.pdf?ua=1 Accessed 15 May 2018.
43 United Nations (2015) The *Millennium Development Goals Report 2015* http://www.un.org/millenniumgoals/2015_MDG_Report/pdf/MDG%202015%20rev%20%28July%201%29.pdf Accessed 15 May 2018; United Nations (Online) *The Sustainable Development Goals* https://sustainabledevelopment.un.org/?menu=1300 Accessed 15 May 2018.
44 World Bank (2005) *Empowering People by Transforming Institutions: Social Development in World Bank Operations*. Washington, DC: World Bank http://documents.worldbank.org/curated/en/2005/01/5583580/empowering-people-transforming-institutions-social-development-world-bank-operations Accessed 15 May 2018.
45 Midgley, *Social Development*.
46 Truman, H. (1949) *Inaugural Address* 20 January independence MO Harry S. Truman Presidential Library https://www.trumanlibrary.org/whistlestop/50yr_archive/inagural20jan1949.htm Accessed 28 July 2018.
47 United Nations (1976) *International Covenant on Economic, Social and Cultural Rights* http://www.ohchr.org/EN/ProfessionalInterest/Pages/CESCR.aspx Accessed 15 May 2018.
48 Sen, *Development as Freedom*.

49 De Vogli, R. and Owusu, J. (2015) 'The Causes and Health Effects of the Great Recession: From Neoliberalism to "Healthy de-growth"' *Critical Public Health* Vol. 25, No. 1, pp. 15–31.

50 USAid (2014) *The Future of Food Assistance: U.S. Food Aid Reform* https://www.usaid.gov/sites/default/files/documents/1869/TheFutureofFoodAssistance-USFoodAidReform.pdf Accessed 15 May 2018; Barrett, C. (2006) *Food Aid's Intended and Unintended Consequences* Rome: Food and Agricultural Organization http://www.fao.org/3/a-ag301t.pdf Accessed 15 May 2018.

51 Mason, N., Jayne, S. & Shiferaw, B. (2015) 'Wheat Consumption in Sub-Saharan Africa: Trends, Drivers, and Policy Implications' *Development Policy Review* Vol. 33, No. 5 (September), pp. 581–613 (London: Wiley).

52 In 2009 it was estimated that 70% of global food consumption was derived from peasant production of crops, livestock, fish and other aquatic foods, hunting and gathering, and urban food growing. Much of this is consumed or exchanged within and between households not using money and is therefore not counted: ETC Group (2009) *Who Will Feed Us?* http://www.etcgroup.org/files/030913_ETC_WhoWillFeed_AnnotatedPoster.pdf Accessed 15 May 2018; Haldane, A. (2014) *In Giving, How Much Do We Receive? The Social Value of Volunteering.* London: Bank of England https://www.bankofengland.co.uk/-/media/boe/files/speech/2014/in-giving-how-much-do-we-receive-the-social-value-of-volunteering.pdf Accessed 15 May 2018.

53 Organised crime and prostitution, for example, are both included in official economic statistics United Nations Office on Drugs and Crime (Online) *Transnational Organized Crime: The Globalized Illegal Economy* http://www.unodc.org/toc/en/crimes/organized-crime.html Accessed 15 May 2018. O'Connor, S. (2014) 'Drugs and Prostitution Add £10bn to UK Economy' *Financial Times* 29 May http://www.ft.com/cms/s/2/65704ba0-e730-11e3-88be-00144feabdc0.html#axzz3kn8bKykc Accessed 15 May 2018; Abramsky, J & Drew, S. (2014) *Changes to National Accounts: Inclusion of Illegal Drugs and Prostitution in the UK National Accounts.* Office for National Statistics http://www.ons.gov.uk/ons/guide-method/method-quality/specific/economy/national-accounts/articles/2011-present/inclusion-of-illegal-drugs-and-prostitution-in-the-uk-national-accounts.pdf Accessed 15 May 2018.

54 Ferreira H. et al (2015) *A Global Count of the Extreme Poor in 2012: Data Issues, Methodology and Initial Results.* Washington D.C.: World bank Group http://www-wds.worldbank.org/external/default/WDSContentServer/WDSP/IB/2015/10/03/090224b08311e963/1_0/Rendered/PDF/A0global0count00and0initial0results.pdf Accessed 15 May 2018; Economist (Online) *The Big Mac Index* http://www.economist.com/content/big-mac-index; Accessed 15 May 2018 Economist (2016) *Patty Purchasing Parity* 23 July, p. 59; Economist (2017) *Meat Reversion* https://www.economist.com/news/finance-and-economics/21725034-dollar-has-slipped-over-past-six-months-still-looks-dear-big-mac Accessed 15 May 2018.

55 Midgley, *Social Development*, p. 23.
56 Brand, U. & Sekler, N. (2009) 'Post Neoliberalism – A Beginning Debate Development' *Dialogue 51*, January Uppsala (Sweden: Dag Hammarskjöld Centre) http://www.daghammarskjold.se/wp-content/uploads/2009/01/Development_Dialogue_51.pdf Accessed 15 May 2018; Yeates, *Understanding Global Social Policy*; Deacon, *Global Social Policy and Governance*.
57 Galbraith, J.K. (1984) 'The Heartless Society', *New York Times* 2 September https://www.nytimes.com/1984/09/02/magazine/the-heartless-society.html Accessed 28 July 2018.
58 Kennedy, J.F. (1963) *Remarks in Heber Springs, Arkansas, at the Dedication of Greers Ferry Dam* October 3, The American Presidency Project http://www.presidency.ucsb.edu/ws/?pid=9455 Accessed 15 May 2018; Jackson, J. (1984) 1984 *Democratic National Convention Address*, delivered 18 July, San Francisco http://www.americanrhetoric.com/speeches/jessejackson1984dnc.htm Accessed 15 May 2018.
59 Midgley, *Social Development*.
60 Dalton, G. (1974) *Economic Systems and Society*. Harmondsworth: Penguin.
61 Ostrom, E. (2012) *The Future of the Commons*. London: Institute of Economic Affairs http://www.iea.org.uk/sites/default/files/publications/files/IEA%20Future%20of%20the%20Commons%20web%2029-1.10.12.pdf Accessed 15 May 2018; Godbout, J. & Caillé, A. (1998) *The World of the Gift*. London: McGill- Queen's University Press.
62 Degrowth (Online) *Research and Actions to Consume Less and Share More* https://degrowth.viper.ecobytes.net/ Accessed 15 May 2018; Co-munity (online) Science https://degrowth.community/conference2014/science log in as user to access https://co-munity.net/user Accessed 15 May 2018.
63 Raworth, K. (0nline) *What on Earth is the Doughnut?...* https://www.kateraworth.com/doughnut/ Accessed 15 May 2018.
64 Community Economies (Online) About Community Economies http://www.communityeconomies.org/about Accessed 15 May 2018; Botsman, R. & Rogers, R. (2010) *What's Mine is Yours* HarperCollins e-books.
65 Lipset, S.M. (1959) 'Some Social Requisites of Democracy: Economic Development and Political Legitimacy' *The American Political Science Review* Vol. 53, No. 1 (March), pp. 69–105 http://media.aucegypt.edu/Pols/final%20cairo%20files/lipset.pdf Accessed 15 May 2018.
66 Shaw, M. (2008) 'Civil Society' in Kurtz, L. (ed.) *Encyclopaedia of Violence, Peace and Conflict*, pp. 269–78. San Diego, CA: Academic Press; Open Society Foundations (Online) *About Us – Mission and Values*.
67 Foley, M. & Edwards, B. (1996) 'The Paradox of Civil Society' *Journal of Democracy* Vol. 7, No. 3, pp. 38–52. Johns Hopkins University Press; Portes, A. & Landolt, P. (2000) 'Social Capital: Promise and Pitfalls of its Role in Development' *Journal of Latin American Studies* Vol. 32, pp. 529–547.
68 UN Commission on Human Rights (2000) *The Role of Good Governance in the Promotion of Human Rights Resolution 2000/64* Office of the High Commissioner for Human Rights http://ap.ohchr.org/documents/S/CHR/

resolutions/E-CN_4-RES-2000-63.doc Accessed 15 May 2018; Transparency International (Online) 2014 Corruption Perceptions Index http://www.transparency.org/cpi2014 Accessed 15 May 2018; Sustainable Governance Indicators (Online) *SGI 2015 Survey* http://www.sgi-network.org/2015/ Accessed 15 May 2018.

69 Newman, M. (2009) *Humanitarian Interventions.* London: Hurst.
70 UNESCO (2010) *UNESCO at a Glance* http://unesdoc.unesco.org/images/0018/001887/188700e.pdf Accessed 15 May 2018.
71 Good country Index (Online) *Culture* http://www.goodcountry.org/overall Accessed 15 May 2018.
72 Welzel, C. et al (2003) 'The Theory of Human Development: A Cross-Cultural Analysis' *European Journal of Political Research* Vol. 42, pp. 341–379 https://onlinelibrary.wiley.com/doi/epdf/10.1111/1475-6765.00086 Accessed 15 May 2018.
73 UNESCO (2001) *Universal Declaration on Cultural Diversity* http://unesdoc.unesco.org/images/0012/001271/127162e.pdf Accessed 15 May 2018.
74 Brundtland, G.H. (1987) *Report of the World Commission on Environment and Development: Our Common Future* United Nations http://www.un-documents.net/our-common-future.pdf Accessed 15 May 2018; United Nations Conference on Environment and Development (1992) *Rio Declaration on Environment and Development* http://information-habitat.net/agenda21/rio-dec.htm Accessed 15 May 2018.
75 Brennan, A. & Lo, Y.-S. (2015) 'Environmental Ethics' *The Stanford Encyclopedia of Philosophy* (Winter 2015 edn), Edward N. Zalta (ed.) https://plato.stanford.edu/entries/ethics-environmental/ Accessed 15 May 2018.
76 Clugston, R. & Holt, S. (2012) *Exploring Synergies between Faith Values and Education for Sustainable Development.* Costa Rica: University for Peace http://www.earthcharterinaction.org/invent/images/uploads/Febr_2_2012.pdf Accessed 15 May 2018.
77 Brennan, & Lo, 'Environmental Ethics'.
78 Gudynas, E. (2011) 'Buen Vivir: Today's Tomorrow' *Development* Vol. 54, No. 4, pp. 441–447. Society for International Development http://www.palgrave-journals.com/development/journal/v54/n4/pdf/dev201186a.pdf Accessed 15 May 2018.
79 Fabricant, N. (2013) 'Good Living for Whom? Bolivia' Climate Justice Movement and the Limitations of Indigenous Cosmovisions' *Latin American and Caribbean Ethnic Studies* Vol. 8, No. 2, pp. 159–178 http://climateandcapitalism.com/wp-content/uploads/sites/2/2014/06/Fabricant-Good-Living-for-Whom.pdf Accessed 15 May 2018; Kothari, A. et al. (2014) 'Buen Vivir, Degrowth and Ecological Swaraj: Alternatives to Sustainable Development and the Green Economy' *Development* Vol. 57, No. 3–4, pp. 362–375 http://www.kalpavriksh.org/images/alternatives/Articles/BuenVivirDegrowthandEcologicalSwarajDevelopment2015.pdf Accessed 15 May 2018.
80 Gapminder (Online) *Gapminder World* http://www.gapminder.org/ Accessed 15 May 2018.

81 OECD (Online) *High-Level Expert Group on the Measurement of Economic Performance and Social Progress* http://www.oecd.org/statistics/measuring-economic-social-progress/ Accessed 15 May 2018.
82 Escobar, A. (2010) 'Planning' in Sachs, *The Development Dictionary*.
83 *Global Youth Well-being Index* http://www.youthindex.org/ Accessed 15 May 2018; *Gender Inequality Index* http://hdr.undp.org/en/data Accessed 15 May 2018; *Global Agewatch Index* http://www.helpage.org/global-agewatch/ Accessed 15 May 2018.
84 Hickey, D. & Doherty, J. (eds) (2003) A *New Dictionary of Irish History from 1800*. Dublin: Gill & Macmillan; Land Warfare Centre (2010) Army Field Manual Countering Insurgency Volume I part 10 Warminster: British Army http://news.bbc.co.uk/1/shared/bsp/hi/pdfs/16_11_09_army_manual.pdf Accessed 2 September 2018.
85 UK Data Service (Online) *Deprivation Data* https://census.ukdataservice.ac.uk/get-data/related/deprivation Accessed 15 May 2018.
86 Hickey, D. & Doherty, J. (2003) 'Congested Districts Board' in Hickey & Doherty, *A New Dictionary of Irish History from 1800*.
87 Escobar, A. (2010) 'Planning' in Sachs, *The Development Dictionary*.
88 Piketty, T. (2014) *Capital in the Twenty First Century*. Boston, MA: Harvard University Press uses data from Europe and the USA to make this argument: Wilkinson, R. & Pickett, K. (2010) *The Spirit Level: Why More Equal Societies Almost Always Do Better*. London: Penguin.
89 Illich, I. (2010) 'Needs' in Sachs, *The Development Dictionary*; Doyal & Gough, *A Theory of Human Need*; Bradshaw, J. (2013) 'The Taxonomy of Social Need' in Cookson, R., Sainsbury, R. & Glendinning, C. (eds) *Jonathan Bradshaw on Social Policy Selected Writings 1972–2011*. York: University of York http://www.york.ac.uk/inst/spru/pubs/pdf/JRB.pdf Accessed 15 May 2018.
90 Talbott, T. (2014) 'Heaven and Hell in Christian Thought' *The Stanford Encyclopedia of Philosophy* Edward N. Zalta (ed.) http://plato.stanford.edu/archives/spr2014/entries/heaven-hell/ Accessed 15 May 2018; Baker-Smith, D. (2014) 'Thomas More', *The Stanford Encyclopedia of Philosophy*, Edward N. Zalta (ed.) http://plato.stanford.edu/archives/spr2014/entries/thomas-more/ Accessed 15 May 2018; Held, D. et al. (eds) (1983) *States and Society*. Oxford: Martin Robertson; see also 'Heaven', 'Hell' and 'Afterlife' in Esposito, J. (2003) *The Oxford Dictionary of Islam*. Oxford: Oxford University Press and 'Afterlife' and 'Olam Ha-Zeh and Olam Ha-Ba' in Berlin, A. & Grossman, M. (2011) *The Oxford Dictionary of the Jewish Religion* (2nd edn). Oxford: Oxford University Press.
91 Binwanger-Mkhize, H., de Regt, J. & Spector, S. (2009) *Scaling Up Local & Community Driven Development (LCDD)*. Washington, DC: World Bank http://siteresources.worldbank.org/EXTSOCIALDEVELOPMENT/Resources/244362-1237844546330/5949218-1237844567860/Scaling_Up_LCDD_Book_rfillesize.pdf Accessed 15 May 2018.
92 Morgan, G. (1997) *Images of Organisation*. London: Sage; his metaphors have been critiqued and they have been revisited by him in Örtenblad, A., Putnam, L. & Trehan, K. (2016) 'Beyond Morgan's eight metaphors ...'

Human Relations Vol. 69, No. 4 (April), pp. 875–889 (London: Tavistock Institute).

93 'Metaphors that Kill' in Lakoff, G. (2014) *The All New Don't Think of an Elephant*. White River Junction, VT: Chelsea Green.

94 Rosenthal, F. (Trans) (1967) *Ibn Khaldun: The Muqaddimah: An Introduction to History* (edited by Dawood, N.J.). London: Routledge and Kegan Paul.

95 Bernard of Chartres (d. AD 1130) quoted in Merton, R. (1965) *On the Shoulders of Giants: A Shandean Postscript*. Glencoe, IL: Free Press.

96 OED, op. cit.: J. H. Newman *Ess. Devel. Christian Doctr.*

97 Engels, F. (1883) *Speech at the Grave of Karl Marx, Highgate Cemetery*. https://www.marxists.org/archive/marx/works/1883/death/burial.htm Accessed 15 May 2018.

98 Rostow, W. (1960) *The Stages of Economic Growth: A Non-Communist Manifesto*. London: Cambridge University Press.

99 OED Online 'Regeneration, n.' March 2018. Oxford University Press http://www.oed.com/view/Entry/161223?redirectedFrom=Regeneration Accessed 16 May 2018.

100 OED Online 'Revolution, n.' March 2018. Oxford University Press http://www.oed.com/view/Entry/164970?rskey=EwqdoQ&result=1&isAdvanced=false Accessed 16 May 2018.

101 Pingali, P. (2012) 'Green Revolution: Impacts, Limits, and the Path Ahead' *Proceedings of the National Academy of Science* Vol. 109, No. 31 (July 31) http://www.pnas.org/content/109/31/12302 Accessed 15 May 2018; Dowie, M. (2001) *American Foundations: An Investigative History*. Boston, MA: MIT Press.

102 Eliot, T.S. (1974) 'The Dry Salvages' in *Collected Poems 1909–1962*. London: Faber & Faber, p. 208.

103 Kretzmann, J. & McKnight, J. (1993) *Building Communities from the Inside Out: A Path Toward Finding and Mobilizing a Community's Assets*. Evanston, IL: Assets-Based Community Development Institute, Institute for Policy Research, Northwestern University.

104 Gandhi, M. (1910) *Hind Swaraj or Indian Home Rule* http://soilandhealth.org/wp-content/uploads/0303critic/hind%20swaraj.pdf Accessed 15 May 2018. Rostow described Communism which his manifesto was designed to combat as a disease: Rostow, *The Stages of Economic Growth*.

105 Escobar, A. (2010) 'Planning' in Sachs, *The Development Dictionary*.

106 Westoby, P. & Dowling, G. (2013) *Theory and Practice of Dialogical Community Development: International Perspectives*. Abingdon: Routledge.

107 Burke, B. (2000) 'Mahatma Gandhi on education', *The Encyclopaedia of Informal Education* http://infed.org/mobi/mahatma-gandhi-on-education/ Accessed 15 May 2018; Smith, M.K. (1998) 'Julius Nyerere, Lifelong Learning and Education' *The Encyclopaedia of Informal Education* http://infed.org/mobi/julius-nyerere-lifelong-learning-and-education/ Accessed 15 May 2018.

108 In Frank's original formulation of this theory he uses the metaphors of satellites (machines) and 'sucking capital' (like a vampire – an organism). Later his ideas were associated more with the idea of 'core' and 'periphery' – more of

a cultural metaphor: Frank, A.G. (1966) *The Development of Underdevelopment*. London: Monthly Review Press https://archive.monthlyreview.org/index.php/mr/article/view/MR-018-04-1966-08_3/1604 Accessed 15 May 2018.
109 Nyerere, *The Challenge to the South*.
110 Femia, J. (1981) *Gramsci's Political Thought: Hegemony, Consciousness and the Revolutionary Process*. Oxford: Clarendon.
111 Fanon, F. (1961) *The Wretched of the Earth*. London: Penguin and (2008) *Black Skin White Masks*. London: Pluto; Faubion, J. (2002) *Michel Foucault Power – Essential Works of Foucault 1954–84* (Vol. 3). London: Penguin.
112 Freire, P. (1972) *Pedagogy of the Oppressed*. Harmondsworth: Penguin; Ledwith, M. (2011) *Community Development – A Critical Approach*. Bristol: Policy Press.
113 Said, E. (1978) *Orientalism*. London: Penguin; Bilger & Sowell, *Point Four Program of Technical Assistance to Developing Nations – Archival Materials at the Library*; Rostow, W. (1960) *The Stages of Economic Growth – A Non-Communist Manifesto*. London: Cambridge University Press.
114 The term was coined by Alfred Sauvy, who made the comparison with the French Third Estate at the time of the French Revolution: The First and Second estates were the clergy and aristocracy. He said that it was a joke to compare the Communists to the Clergy and the Capitalist world as the nobility. Sauvy, A. (1952) 'Trois Mondes, Une planete', *L'Observateur*, No. 118 (14 August) http://www.homme-moderne.org/societe/demo/sauvy/3mondes.html Accessed 15 May 2018.
115 Huntingdon, S. (1993) 'The Clash of Civilizations?' *Foreign Affairs* (Summer edn) http://www.jstor.org/stable/20045621?seq=1#page_scan_tab_contents Accessed 15 May 2018.
116 Fukuyama, F. (1992) *The End of History and the Last Man*. New York: Free Press.
117 Dickinson, E. (2009) 'New Order: How "The Multipolar World" Came To Be'. *Foreign Policy* (15 October) http://foreignpolicy.com/2009/10/15/new-order/# Accessed 15 May 2018.
118 Brundtland, G.H. (1987) *Report of the World Commission on Environment and Development: Our Common Future* United Nations http://www.un-documents.net/our-common-future.pdf Accessed 16 May 2018.
119 Alinsky, S. (1972) *Rules for Radicals: A Pragmatic Primer for Realistic Radicals*. New York: Vintage; O'Malley, J. (1977) *The Politics of Community Action*. Nottingham: Spokesman.
120 Kitson, F. (1971) *Low Intensity Operations*. London: Faber & Faber; de Baroid, C. (1990) *Ballymurphy and the Irish War*. London: Pluto.
121 US Government (2009) *Counterinsurgency Guide* (p. 15) http://www.state.gov/documents/organization/119629.pdf Accessed 16 May 2018.
122 US Army (2014) *Insurgencies and Countering Insurgencies* http://fas.org/irp/doddir/army/fm3-24.pdf Paragraph 7–8.
123 Land Warfare Centre (2009) *Army Field Manual Countering Insurgency* (*Vol. I part 10* Section 3–16). Warminster: British Army http://news.bbc.co.uk/1/shared/bsp/hi/pdfs/16_11_09_army_manual.pdf Accessed 16 May 2018.

124 Weizman, E. (2012) *The Least of All Possible Evils: Humanitarian Violence from Arendt to Gaza*. London: Verso.
125 Cameron, D. (2015) *PM's Speech to the UN Sustainable Development Goals Summit 2015*, 27 September https://www.gov.uk/government/speeches/pms-speech-to-the-un-sustainable-development-goals-summit-2015 Accessed 16 May 2018; Selous, A. (2015) *Corruption: Written Question – 9735 Answer 28 September Hansard* http://www.parliament.uk/business/publications/written-questions-answers-statements/written-question/Commons/2015-09-09/9735 Accessed 16 May 2018.
126 Not entering the same river twice is Plato's version of what Heraclitus said: Graham, D. (2015) *'Heraclitus' The Stanford Encyclopedia of Philosophy* (Fall 2015 edn), Edward, N. Zalta (ed.) http://plato.stanford.edu/archives/fall2015/entries/heraclitus/ Accessed 16 May 2018.
127 Hope, A. (online) *The TfT Story* http://www.grailprogrammes.org.za/docs/tft_story.pdf Accessed 16 May 2018; Hope, A. & Timmel, S. (1984–8) *Training for Transformation Books 1–4*. Harare: Mambo Press.
128 Gilchrist, A. (2009) *The Well-Connected Community: A Networking Approach to Community Development* (2nd edn). Bristol: Policy Press; Escobar, A. (2004) 'Beyond the Third World: Imperial Globality, Global Coloniality, and Anti-Globalization Social Movements' *Third World Quarterly* Vol. 25, No. 1, pp. 207–230; Escobar, A. (2010) 'Planning' in Sachs, *The Development Dictionary*.
129 Sanyal, B. (1998) *The Myth of Development From Below* Association of Collegiate Schools of Planning, Annual Conference, Pasadena, CA http://web.mit.edu/sanyal/www/articles/Myth%20of%20Dev.pdf Accessed 16 May 2018.
130 African Economic Outlook (2015) *External Financial Flows and Tax Revenues for Africa 2015* http://www.africaneconomicoutlook.org/fileadmin/uploads/aeo/2015/PDF_Chapters/02_Chapter2_AEO2015_EN.pdf Accessed 16 May 2018; Fdi Intelligence (2015) *The Africa Investment Report 2015* https://www.fdiintelligence.com/Landing-Pages/Africa-Investment-Report-2015/The-Africa-Investment-Report-2015 Accessed 16 May 2018.
131 World Bank (2015) *Community-Driven Development – Overview* http://www.worldbank.org/en/topic/communitydrivendevelopment Accessed 16 May 2018; Binswanger-Mkhize, H., de Regt, J. & Spector, S. (2009) *Scaling Up Local and Community Driven Development (LCDD)* Washington, DC: World Bank http://siteresources.worldbank.org/EXTSOCIALDEVELOPMENT/Resources/244362-1237844546330/5949218-1237844567860/Scaling_Up_LCDD_Book_rfillesize.pdf Accessed 16 May 2018.
132 Prebble, J. (1963) *The Highland Clearances*. London: Secker & Warburg; Davies, R.W. (1980) *The Industrialization of Soviet Russia, The Soviet Collective Farm, 1929–1930* (Industrialization of Soviet Russia, Vol. 2). Boston, MA: Harvard University Press; Macfarquhar, R. (1983) *Origins of the Cultural Revolution* (Vol. 2). Oxford: Oxford University Press.
133 Carter, I. (2011) 'Throffers' in Dowding, K. (ed.) *Encyclopedia of Power*. Thousand Oaks, CA: Sage.

134 Specht, H. (1969) 'Disruptive Tactics' in Kramer, R. & Specht, H. (eds) *Readings in Community Organization Practice* (p. 375). Englewood Cliffs, NJ: Prentice Hall.
135 CDP Information and Intelligence Unit (1974) *The National Community Development Project Inter-Project Report*. London: CDP Information and Intelligence Unit.
136 Westoby & Dowling, *Theory and Practice of Dialogical Community Development*; Lederach, J.P. (2003) *The Little Book of Conflict Transformation*. Intercourse, PA: Good Books.
137 Lederach, J.P. (1996) *Preparing for Peace*. Syracuse, NY: Syracuse University Press.
138 One Nation UK Charity (Online) https://www.onenationuk.org/ Accessed 16 May 2018; One Nation Australian Political Party (Online) http://www.onenation.org.au/ Accessed 16 May 2018.
139 Held, D. (1996) *Models of Democracy* (2nd edn). Cambridge: Polity.
140 Nicholls, D. (1974) *Three Varieties of Pluralism*. London: MacMillan.
141 Furnivall in Nicholls, *Three Varieties of Pluralism*; McEvoy, J. & O'Leary, B. (eds) (2013) *Power Sharing in Deeply Divided Places*. Philadelphia, PA: University of Pennsylvania Press; Marks, S. (2004) 'Smuts, Jan Christiaan' *Dictionary of National Biography*. Oxford: Oxford University Press: MacMillan. Smuts didn't like the term pluralism.
142 M.G. Smith in Nicholls, *Three Varieties of Pluralism*; Marks, 'Smuts'.
143 DeRienzo, H. (2007) 'Rebuilding Community' *National Civic Review* Vol. 96, No. 3 (Fall), pp. 16–26.
144 Fisher, S., Abdi, D.A. & Ludin, J. et al (2000) *Working with Conflict – Skills & Strategies for Action*. London: Zed/Responding to Conflict; Lederach, *The Little Book of Conflict Transformation*; Berghof [online] *The Berghof Handbook for Conflict* Transformation http://www.berghof-handbook.net/.
145 Femia, J. (1981) *Gramsci's Political Thought: Hegemony, Consciousness and the Revolutionary Process*. Oxford: Clarendon.
146 Roy, A. (2010) 'Arundhati Roy: Maoists being Forced into Violence' *CNN-IBN* https://www.youtube.com/watch?v=808dmR90C6Y Accessed 16 May 2018.
147 Lewis, G. (2015) 'Fanon, Frantz' in LaFollette, H. (ed.) *International Encyclopedia of Ethics*. Chichester: Wiley-Blackwell; Fanon, *The Wretched of the Earth*.
148 Kellner, D. (2005) 'Radical Politics, Marcuse, and the New Left' in Kellner, D. (ed.) *The New Left and the 1960s: Collected Papers of Herbert Marcuse* (Vol. 3, Herbert Marcuse: Collected Papers) Abingdon: Routledge.
149 Galtung, J. (1969) 'Violence, Peace, and Peace Research' *Journal of Peace Research*, Vol. 6, No. 3, pp. 167–191 http://www2.kobe-u.ac.jp/~alexroni/IPD%202015%20readings/IPD%202015_7/Galtung_Violence,%20Peace,%20and%20Peace%20Research.pdf Accessed 19 May 2018.
150 The University of Uppsala has a sobering database of armed conflicts since the 1970s, which reflect how few violent conflicts are resolved through victory or defeat Uppsala Conflict Data Program (Online) *UCDP Conflict Encyclopedia (UCDP database)* http://ucdp.uu.se/?id=1 Accessed 19 May 2018.

151 'Colonialism and Mental Disorders' in Fanon, *The Wretched of the Earth*.
152 Taylor, A.J.P. (1985) *How Wars End*. London: Hamish Hamilton.
153 Healey, J. (2001) 'African Proverb of the Month November 2001' *Afripoverb.org* http://www.afriprov.org/african-proverb-of-the-month/27-2001proverbs/172-nov2001.html Accessed 19 May 2018.
154 The Children's Rights Information Network has many resources on the impact of wars on children: https://www.crin.org/en Accessed 19 May 2018; even Andrew Roberts who is generally 'pro-war' and is sceptical of the claim that 90% of casualties of war are civilians, acknowledges that there are many: Roberts, A. (2010) 'Lives and Statistics: Are 90% of War Victims Civilians?' *Survival: Global Politics and Strategy* Vol. 52, No. 3, pp. 115–136 (London: Routledge) https://weblearn.ox.ac.uk/access/content/user/1044/Survival_Jun-Jul_2010_-_AR_on_lives___statistics_-_non-printable.pdf Accessed 19 May 2018.
155 Rist, *The History of Development*, p. 27.

4 Collective Action

1 The subheading 'Of cabbages and kings' is taken from L. Carroll (1872) 'The Walrus and The Carpenter' in *Through the Looking-Glass and What Alice Found There* http://www.jabberwocky.com/carroll/walrus.html Accessed 17 May 2018. The poem starts with the Walrus and the Carpenter asking what can collective action achieve – and shedding a bitter tear.
2 Royal Collection Trust (Online) *Buckingham Palace* https://www.royalcollection.org.uk/sites/default/files/Buckingham_Palace_Fact_Sheet.pdf Accessed 17 May 2018; Crouch, D. & Ward, C. (1994) *The Allotment: Its Landscape and Culture*. Nottingham: Mushroom; Boyce, F.C. (2007) *Grow Your Own* (Screenplay) https://www.imdb.com/title/tt0847830/ Accessed 17 May 2018; Trussell Trust (Online) *What We Do* https://www.trusselltrust.org/ Accessed 17 May 2018; Lemon Tree Trust (Online) *Stories* http://lemontreetrust.org/film-and-interactive/ Accessed 21 May 2018.
3 Morgan, G. (1997) *Images of Organization*. London: Sage; Morgan, G. (1997) *Imaginization: New Mindsets for Seeing, Organizing and Managing*. Newbury Park, CA: Sage.
4 O'Connor, T. (2014) 'Free Will' in Edward N. Zalta (ed.) *The Stanford Encyclopedia of Philosophy* http://plato.stanford.edu/archives/fall2014/entries/freewill/ Accessed 18 May 2018.
5 Kvanvig, J.& Vander Laan, D. (2014) 'Creation and Conservation' in Edward N. Zalta (ed.) *The Stanford Encyclopedia of Philosophy* http://plato.stanford.edu/archives/win2014/entries/creation-conservation/ Accessed 18 May 2018; Hussaini, S.H. (2016) 'Islamic Philosophy between Theism and Deism' *Revista Portuguesa de Filosofia*, T. 72, Fasc. 1, Teísmos: Aportações Filosóficas do Leste e Oeste/Theisms: Philosophical Contributions from the East to the West (pp. 65-83). Braga: Revista Portuguesa de Filosofia; Esposito, J. (2003) *The Oxford Dictionary of Islam*. Oxford: Oxford University Press.

6   Akenson, D.H. (1992) *God's Peoples*. Ithaca, NY: Cornell; 'Pillars of Islam, 'Qismah' and 'Jihad' in Esposito, *The Oxford Dictionary of Islam* and 'Commandments, Reasons for' and 'Duty' in Berlin, A. & Grossman, M. (eds) (2011) '"Charity", "Social justice", "Partnership"' in *The Oxford Dictionary of the Jewish Religion* (2nd edn). Oxford: Oxford University Press.
7   Jenkins, K. (1991) *Re-thinking History*. London: Routledge; Tosh, J. (2010) *The Pursuit of History: Aims, Methods, and New Directions in the Study of Modern History* (5th edn). London: Longman, p. 221. Abrams quotes Tosh.
8   Gerth, H. & Mills, C.W. (eds) (1946) *From Max Weber: Essays in Sociology*. London: Routledge and Kegan Paul.
9   Giddens, A. (1993) 'Problems of Action and Structure' in Cassell, P. (ed.) *The Giddens Reader*. Houndmills: Macmillan; Giddens, A. & Sutton, P. (2009) *Sociology* (6th edn). Cambridge: Polity; Archer, *Structure, Agency and the Internal Conversation*; Bourdieu, P. (1977) *Outline of a Theory of Practice*. Cambridge: Cambridge University Press.
10 Bourne, L. & Ekstrand, B. (1985) *Psychology: Its Principles and Meanings*. London: Holt, Rinehart, Winston.
11 Kahneman, D. (2011) *Thinking Fast and Slow*. London: Penguin; Thaler, R. & Sunstein, C. (2009) *Nudge*. London: Penguin; Goldstein, N., Martin, S. & Cialdini, R. *Yes: 50 Secrets from the Science of Persuasion*. London: Profile.
12 Orford, J. (2008) *Community Psychology*. Chichester: John Wiley, p. 6.
13 Archer, *Structure, Agency and the Internal Conversation*; Archer, M. (2012) *The Reflexive Imperative in Late Modernity*. Cambridge: Cambridge University Press.
14 Quoted in Roberts, A. (2014) *Napoleon the Great*. London: Penguin.
15 Ziff, T. (2006) Che Guevara: Revolutionary & Icon Abrams Image.
16 Marx, K. (1973) *Surveys from Exile*. Harmondsworth: Penguin, p. 146.
17 BBC (2014) 'Behavioural Ecology' *In Our Time* 11 December http://www.bbc.co.uk/programmes/b04tljk0 Accessed 18 May 2018.
18 Dawkins, R. (1976) *The Selfish Gene*. Oxford: Oxford University Press.
19 Kropotkin, P. (1970) *Mutual Aid*. Boston, MA: Porter Sargent.
20 Maxmen, A. (2012) 'E. O. Wilson and Poet Laureate on Altruism and Mystery' *New Scientist Culture Lab* 10 December https://www.newscientist.com/blogs/culturelab/2012/12/wilson-hass-conversation.html Accessed 18 May 2018.
21 Dunbar, R (2010) *How Many Friends Does One Person Need? Dunbar's Number and Other Evolutionary Quirks*. London: Faber.
22 Harari, Y.N. (2014) *Sapiens*. London: Harvill Secker.
23 Dalton, G. (1974) *Economic Systems and Society*. Harmondsworth: Penguin; Robert, J. (2010) 'Production' in Sachs, W. (ed.) *The Development Dictionary*. London: Zed.
24 Weber, M. (2002) *The Protestant Ethic and the Spirit of Capitalism: and Other Writings*. Harmondsworth: Penguin (twentieth-century classics); Tawney, R. (1929) *Religion and the Rise of Capitalism*. London: John Murray.
25 Gibson-Graham, J.K. & Roelvink, G. (2011) 'The Nitty Gritty of Creating Alternative Economies' *Social Alternatives* Vol. 30, No. 1, p. 29;

Gibson-Graham, K. (2006) *Post-capitalist Economics*. London: University of Minnesota Press.

26. Smith, A. (1776) *An Inquiry into the Nature and Causes of the Wealth of Nations* (Vol. 1, Ch. 2, para 2) http://www.econlib.org/library/Smith/smWN1.html#B.I,%20Ch.2,%20Of%20the%20Principle%20which%20gives%20Occasion%20to%20the%20Division%20of%20Labour Accessed 18 May 2018.
27. IMDb (Online) *Wall Street quotes* http://www.imdb.com/title/tt0094291/quotes Accessed 18 May 2018.
28. Balaram, B. (2016) *Fair Share: Reclaiming Power in the Sharing Economy*. London: Royal Society of Arts; Huws, U. & Joyce, S. (2016) *Size of the UK's 'Gig Economy' Revealed for the First Time*. Hertfordshire: University of Hertfordshire http://www.feps-europe.eu/en/publications/details/363 Accessed 18 May 2018.
29. Berthoud, G. (2010) 'Market' in Sachs, *The Development Dictionary*.
30. Berthoud, G. (2010) 'Market' in Sachs, *The Development Dictionary*, p. 80.
31. Becker, G. (1976) *The Economic Approach to Human Behavior*. Chicago: University of Chicago Press, p. 5.
32. Becker, G. (1992) *Prize Lecture: The Economic Way of Looking at Life*. Stockholm: Nobel Foundation.
33. Lugard, F. (1970) *Political Memoranda, Revision of Instructions to Political Officers on Subjects Chiefly Political and Administrative*. London: Frank Cass.
34. Tarn, J. (1974) *Five Per Cent Philanthropy: An Account of Housing in Urban Areas between 1840 and 1914*. Cambridge: Cambridge University Press; Horesh, R. (2000) 'Injecting Incentives into the Solution of Social Problems: Social Policy Bonds'. *Economic Affairs*, September pp. 39–42 http://socialgoals.com/ieaspbs.pdf Accessed 18 May 2018; Social Finance (2010) *Towards a New Social Economy – Blended Value Creation through Social Impact Bonds* http://www.socialfinance.org.uk/sites/default/files/publications/towards-a-new-social-economy-web.pdf Accessed 18 May 2018; Ellen MacArthur Foundation (Online) *What is a Circular Economy?* https://www.ellenmacarthurfoundation.org/circular-economy Accessed 18 May 2018.
35. Berthoud, G. (2010) 'Market' in Sachs, *The Development Dictionary*; Piketty, T. (2014) *Capital in the Twenty First Century*. Boston, MA: Harvard University Press.
36. Thaler & Sunstein, *Nudge*; Goldstein, Martin & Cialdini, *Yes: 50 Secrets from the Science of Persuasion*; Kahneman, *Thinking Fast and Slow*.
37. Darnton, A. (2008a) *GSR Behaviour Change Knowledge Review Reference Report: An Overview of Behaviour Change Models and their Uses*, Government Social Research https://www.gov.uk/government/uploads/system/uploads/attachment_data/file/498065/Behaviour_change_reference_report_tcm6-9697.pdf Accessed 18 May 2018.
38. Foweraker, J. (1995) *Theorizing Social Movements*. London: Pluto.

39 Smith, A. (1776) *An Inquiry into the Nature and Causes of the Wealth of Nations* (Vol. 1, Ch. 8 para 12) http://www.econlib.org/library/Smith/smWN3.html Accessed 18 May 2018.

40 Olson, M. (1971) *The Logic of Collective Action*. London: Harvard University Press.

41 In 2016, the Supreme Court in the USA upheld the right of trade unions to collect a 'fair share' or agency fee from non-union members who gain from improvements in salaries and benefits: Economist (2016) 'Handed a Victory' *Economist* April 2 (p. 41). In 2018, this decision was reversed: BBC News (2018) US Supreme Court rules public sector union fees violate first amendment BBC 27 June https://www.bbc.co.uk/news/business-44633482.

42 Ostrom, E. (2009) *Prize Lecture: Beyond Markets and States: Polycentric Governance of Complex Economic Systems*. Stockholm: Nobel Foundation http://www.nobelprize.org/nobel_prizes/economic-sciences/laureates/2009/ostrom_lecture.pdf Accessed 18 May 2018; New Economics Foundation (2008) *Co-production: A Manifesto for Growing the Core Economy* http://www.i-r-e.org/docs/a008_co-production-manifesto.pdf Accessed 18 May 2018; Ostrom, E. (2012) *The Future of the Commons*. London: Institute of Economic Affairs http://www.iea.org.uk/sites/default/files/publications/files/IEA%20Future%20of%20the%20Commons%20web%2029-1.10.12.pdf Accessed 18 May 2018.

43 Turocy, T. & von Stengel, B. (2002) 'Game Theory' in Bidgoli, H. (ed.) *Encyclopedia of Information Systems* (Vol. 2, pp. 403–420). Cambridge, MA: Academic Press http://www.cdam.lse.ac.uk/Reports/Files/cdam-2001-09.pdf Accessed 18 May 2018; Winter, E. (2015) 'Game Theory: How to Put Oneself in Someone Else's Shoes' *Independent* 1 June http://www.independent.co.uk/life-style/health-and-families/features/john-nashs-game-theory-how-to-put-oneself-in-someone-elses-shoes-10290371.html Accessed 18 May 2018.

44 Galton, F. (1907) 'Vox Populi' *Nature* March 7 (pp. 450–451) http://galton.org/essays/1900-1911/galton-1907-vox-populi.pdf?page=7 Accessed 18 May 2018; Surowiecki, J. (2004) *The Wisdom of Crowds*. New York: Random House.

45 Mitchell, D. (2004) *Cloud Atlas*. London: Hodder & Stoughton, p. 140.

46 Gibson-Graham & Roelvink, 'The Nitty Gritty of Creating Alternative Economies', p. 29.

47 ETC Group (2009) *Who will feed us?* ETC Group http://www.etcgroup.org/sites/www.etcgroup.org/files/web_who_will_feed_us_with_notes_0.pdf Accessed 18 May 2018.

48 Acton, L. (2015) *Growing Space: A History of the Allotment Movement*. Nottingham: Five Leaves.

49 Barrett, C. (2006) *Food Aid's Intended and Unintended Consequences*. Ithaca, NY: Cornell http://barrett.dyson.cornell.edu/files/papers/MixedEffectsv2Mar2006.pdf Accessed 18 May 2018.

50 UN Habitat (Online) *Housing & Slum Upgrading* http://unhabitat.org/urban-themes/housing-slum-upgrading/ Accessed 18 May 2018.

51 Bredenoord, J., Van Lindert, P. & Smets, P. (2014) *Affordable Housing in the Urban Global South: Seeking Sustainable Solutions*. Abingdon: Routledge.

NOTES

52 Cahn, E. in New Economics Foundation (2008) *Co-production: A Manifesto for Growing the Core Economy*. London: New Economics Foundation http://www.i-r-e.org/docs/a008_co-production-manifesto.pdf Accessed 18 May 2018.

53 Illich, I. (2001) *Tools for Conviviality*. London: Marion Boyars http://www.davidtinapple.com/illich/1973_tools_for_convivality.html. Accessed 18 May 2018.

54 Godbout, J. & Caillé, A. (1998) *The World of the Gift*. London: McGill-Queen's University Press.

55 This section is largely based on Duncan, L. (2012) 'The Psychology of Collective Action' in Deaux, K. & Snyder, M. (eds) *The Oxford Handbook of Personality and Social Psychology*. New York: Oxford University Press; Gamson, W. (1992) 'The Social Psychology of Collective Action' in Morris, A. & Mclurg Miller, C. (eds) *Frontiers in Social Movement Theory* (pp. 53–76). London: Yale University Press.

56 Bruininks, P. & Malle, B. (2005) 'Distinguishing Hope from Optimism and Related Affective States' *Motivation and Emotion* Vol. 29, No. 4, pp. 324–352; Snyder, C. (2002) 'Hope Theory: Rainbows in the Mind' *Psychological Inquiry* Vol. 13, No. 4, pp. 249–275.

57 Mosley, M. (2013) 'Can Science Explain Why I'm a Pessimist?' *BBC Magazine* 10 July http://www.bbc.co.uk/news/magazine-23229014 Accessed 18 May 2018.

58 It is not in any of his published works, so the original source is unknown.

59 Archer, L. et al. (2013) *ASPIRES: Young People's Science and Career Aspirations, Age 10–14*. London: Kings College http://www.kcl.ac.uk/sspp/departments/education/research/aspires/ASPIRES-final-report-December-2013.pdf Accessed 18 May 2018.

60 Gandhi, M. (1910) *Hind Swaraj or Indian Home Rule* http://soilandhealth.org/wp-content/uploads/0303critic/hind%20swaraj.pdf Accessed 18 May 2018.

61 Alinsky, S. (1972) *Rules for Radicals: A Pragmatic Primer for Realistic Radicals*. New York: Vintage, pp. 113–116.

62 Kennedy J.F. Library (online) *John F. Kennedy's Favorite Quotations: Dante's Inferno* http://www.jfklibrary.org/Research/Research-Aids/Ready-Reference/JFK-Fast-Facts/Dante.aspx Accessed 18 May 2018; Franklin Roosevelt and Martin Luther King also misquoted Dante.

63 Gramsci, A. (1975) 'Indifferents' letter 11 February 1917 in Cavalcanti, P. & Piccone, P. (eds) Trans *History, Philosophy and Culture in the Young Gramsci* (pp. 64–66). St Louis: Telos Press.

64 Wiesel, E. (1999) *The Perils of Indifference* http://www.historyplace.com/speeches/wiesel.htm Accessed 18 May 2018.

65 van Stekelenburg, J. & Klandermans, B. (2010) 'The Social Psychology of Protest' *Sociopedia* https://www.researchgate.net/publication/258131447_The_Social_Psychology_of_Protest Accessed 18 May 2018.

66 Gandhi, M. (1961) *Non-Violent Resistance* (p. 18). New York: Schocken Books.

67 Cialdini, R. & Goldstein, N. (2004) 'Social Influence: Compliance and Conformity' *Annual Review of Psychology* Vol. 55, pp. 591–621 http://www2.psych.ubc.ca/~schaller/Psyc591Readings/CialdiniGoldstein2004.pdf Accessed 18 May 2018.

68 Carlson, W., Buskist, W. & Martin, G.N. (2000) *Psychology – The Science of Behaviour European Adaptation*. Harlow: Pearson.

69 Parkin, S. (2010) *Positive Deviants* (p. 2). London: Earthscan.

70 Marsh, D., Sternin, M., Khadduri, R. et al (2002) 'Identification of Model Newborn Care Practices through a Positive Deviance Inquiry to Guide Behavior-Change Interventions in Haripur, Pakistan' *Food and Nutrition Bulletin*, Vol. 23, No. 4, pp. 107–116. https://www.researchgate.net/publication/10972790_Identification_of_Model_Newborn_Care_Practices_through_a_Positive_Deviance_Inquiry_to_Guide_Behavior-Change_Interventions_in_Haripur_Pakistan Accessed 18 May 2018; Tufts University (2010) 'Positive Deviance Initiative' in *Basic Field Guide to the Positive Deviance Approach*. Boston, MA: Tufts University https://stepsandleaps.files.wordpress.com/2010/08/pd-basic-field-guide.pdf Accessed 18 May 2018.

71 Eliot, T.S. (1974) 'Choruses from "The Rock"' in *Collected Poems 1909–1962* (p. 169). London: Faber and Faber.

72 Freire, P. (1972) *Pedagogy of the Oppressed* (p. 41). Harmondsworth: Penguin.

73 Johnston, R. (1993) 'Praxis for the Powerless and Punch-Drunk' *Adults Learning* (England), Vol. 4, No. 6 (February), pp. 146–148 (Leicester: NIACE).

74 Bookchin, M. (1975) *On Spontaneity and Organisation*. London: Solidarity https://theanarchistlibrary.org/library/murray-bookchin-on-spontaneity-and-organisation.pdf Accessed 18 May 2018.

75 Kellner, D. (2005) 'Radical Politics, Marcuse, and the New Left' in Kellner, D. (ed.) *The New Left and the 1960s: Collected Papers of Herbert Marcuse* (Vol. 3, p. 17) (Herbert Marcuse: Collected Papers). Abingdon: Routledge.

76 Economist (2016) *The Signal and The Noise-Technology and Politics*. Special Report March 26. London: Economist.

77 Sharma, S.K. (2008) 'Edward Said Humanism and Democratic Criticism' Review *Journal of Literary Criticism* Vol. XII, Nos 1 & 2 (June/December).

78 Duncan, 'The Psychology of Collective Action'.

79 Gamson, W. (1992) 'The Social Psychology of Collective Action', pp. 53–76.

80 van Stekelenburg & Klandermans, 'The Social Psychology of Protest'.

81 Hogg, M., Hohman, Z. & Rivera, J. (2008) 'Why Do People Join Groups? Three Motivational Accounts from Social Psychology' *Social and Personality Psychology Compass* Vol. 2, No. 3, pp. 1269–1280.

82 Cairns, E. (1994) *A Welling Up of Deep Unconscious Forces: Psychology and the Northern Ireland Conflict*. Coleraine, NI: University of Ulster http://cain.ulst.ac.uk/csc/reports/forces.htm#apply Accessed 18 May 2018.

83 Thaler & Sunstein, *Nudge*; Cialdini, R. (2001) *Influence Science and Practice* (4th edn). London: Allyn & Bacon; Dolan, P. et al (2010) *MINDSPACE: Influencing Behaviour through Public Policy*. London: Cabinet Office and

Institute for Government http://www.instituteforgovernment.org.uk/images/files/MINDSPACE-full.pdf Accessed 18 May 2018.

84. This section draws on sources and concepts, but not necessarily arguments in Held, D. (1996) *Models of Democracy* (2nd edn). Cambridge: Polity; Held, D. et al (eds) (1983) *States and Society*. Oxford: Martin Robertson.

85. Thompson, E. (1968) *The Making of the English Working Class*. Harmondsworth: Penguin.

86. Berlin, A. & Grossman, M. (eds) (2011) '"Charity", "Social justice ", "Partnership"' in *The Oxford Dictionary of the Jewish Religion* (2nd edn). Oxford: Oxford University Press; Esposito, *The Oxford Dictionary of Islam*.

87. OED Online (2015) 'charity, n'. Oxford University Press.

88. Krausen, H. (2013) 'Religion – A Private Matter?' *Friday Thoughts 142* 20 September https://www.facebook.com/FaithandKhidmah/posts/248339815314370?stream_ref=5 Accessed 18 May 2018.

89. Koran Surah 13; Verse 11 http://quran.com/13/11 Accessed 18 May 2018.

90. Zank, M. & Braiterman, Z. (2014) 'Martin Buber' in Edward N. Zalta (ed.) *The Stanford Encyclopedia of Philosophy* (Winter 2014 Edition) http://plato.stanford.edu/archives/win2014/entries/buber/ Accessed 18 May 2018; Smith, M.K. (2009) 'Martin Buber on Education', *The Encyclopaedia of Informal Education* http://infed.org/mobi/martin-buber-on-education/ Accessed 18 May 2018; Westoby, P. & Dowling, G. (2013) *Theory and Practice of Dialogical Community Development: International Perspectives*. Abingdon: Routledge.

91. Meszler, J. (2015) *Gifts to the Poor: Moses Maimonides' Treatise on Tzedakah 10:7*. North Charleston, SC: CreateSpace Independent Publishing Platform.

92. Burke, B. (2000). 'Mahatma Gandhi on Education', *The Encyclopaedia of Informal Education* http://infed.org/mobi/mahatma-gandhi-on-education Accessed 18 May 2018.

93. Singer, P. (1972) 'Famine, Affluence, and Morality' *Philosophy and Public Affairs* Vol. 1, No. 1 (Spring), pp. 229–243 [revised edition]. http://www.utilitarian.net/singer/by/1972----.htm

94. Singer, P. (1972) 'Famine, Affluence, and Morality' *Philosophy and Public Affairs* Vol. 1, No. 1 (Spring), pp. 229–243 [revised edition]. http://www.utilitarian.net/singer/by/1972----.htm. Accessed 18 May 2018.

95. British Library (Online) *English translation of Magna Carta* http://www.bl.uk/magna-carta/articles/magna-carta-english-translation#sthash.YvlSaUfz.dpuf Accessed 18 May 2018.

96. Lerski, G. (1996) 'Nihil Novi' *Historical Dictionary of Poland, 966–1945*. London: Greenwood Press;

97. It is not clear when disabled people first used the phrase but the sentiment was evident in debates in the late 1960s and early 1970s in the UK in disabled people's relationship both with care providers and academic allies in lobbying: Finkelstein, V. (2001) *A Personal Journey into Disability Politics* http://www.independentliving.org/docs3/finkelstein01a.pdf Accessed 18 May 2018; UPIAS & Disability Alliance (1975) *Fundamental Principles of Disability* https://disability-studies.leeds.ac.uk/wp-content/uploads/sites/40/library/UPIAS-fundamental-principles.pdf Accessed 18 May 2018.

98 Held, *Models of Democracy*, p. 37.
99 Woodcock, G. (1962) *Anarchism: A History of Libertarian Ideas and Movements*. New York: Meridian Books http://rebels-library.org/files/woodcock_anarchism.pdf Accessed 18 May 2018.
100 Bookchin, M. (1982) *The Ecology of Freedom*. Palo Alto, CA. Cheshire https://libcom.org/files/Murray_Bookchin_The_Ecology_of_Freedom_1982.pdf Accessed 18 May 2018. Best, S. (1998) 'Murray Bookchin's social Ecology – An Appraisal of the Ecology of Freedom' *Organization & Environment* (September) (London: Sage); For Bookchin's influence on the Kurdish leader Abdullah Ocalan see Enzinnanov, W. (2015) 'A Dream of Secular Utopia in ISIS' Backyard' *New York Times* New York http://www.nytimes.com/2015/11/29/magazine/a-dream-of-utopia-in-hell.html?_r=1 Accessed 18 May 2018.
101 Mayo, M. (2005) *Global Citizens*. London: Zed.
102 Plant R. (1974) *Community and Ideology*. London: Routledge and Kegan Paul, pp. 60–61.
103 Fromm, E. (2001) *The Fear of Freedom*. London: Routledge; Smith, M.K. (2001) 'Kurt Lewin, Groups, Experiential Learning and Action Research', *The Encyclopedia of Informal Education* http://www.infed.org/thinkers/et-lewin.htm Accessed 18 May 2018; Moreno, J.D. (2014) *Impromptu Man – J.L. Moreno and the Origins of Psychodrama, Encounter Culture and the Social Network*. New York: Bellevue Press.
104 Held, *Models of Democracy*, pp. 60–61.
105 Plant, *Community and Ideology*.
106 Crosland, C.A.R. (1974), 'Socialists in a Dangerous World' in *Socialism Now*. London: Jonathan Cape, pp. 65–66.
107 Crosland, C.A.R. (1974) 'A Social-Democratic Britain' in Crosland, *Socialism Now*, p. 89.
108 Clegg, H. (1960) *A New Approach to Industrial Democracy*. Oxford: Blackwell. Although said in the context of workplaces it follows the lines from Crosland quoted above.
109 Anon (1968) *Je participe*. http://gallica.bnf.fr/ark:/12148/btv1b90183285.r=%22mai+1968%22.langFR Accessed 18 May 2018.
110 Popular Participation comes from debates about development in Latin America in the 1960s. The term 'Popular Planning' was used by proponents of prefigurative politics later: Economic Commission for Latin America (1973) 'Popular Participation in Development' *Community Development Journal* Vol. 8, No. 2 (1 April 1973), pp. 77–92; Perrault, C. (2017) 'Interview with Hilary Wainwright' *The GLC Story Oral History Project*. http://glcstory.co.uk/wp-content/uploads/2017/03/HilaryWainwrightTranscript.pdf Accessed 18 May 2018.
111 Boggs, C. (1977) 'Marxism, Prefigurative Communism, and the Problem of Workers' Control' *Radical America* 11 (November) https://libcom.org/library/marxism-prefigurative-communism-problem-workers-control-carl-boggs Accessed 18 May 2018; Rowbotham, S. et al (1979) *Beyond the Fragments: Feminism and the Making of Socialism*. London: Merlin Press; Yates, L. (2015)

'Rethinking Prefiguration: Alternatives, Micropolitics and Goals in Social Movements', *Social Movement Studies* Vol. 14, No. 1, pp. 1–21.
112. Cooke, B and Kothari, U. (eds) (2002) *Participation: The New Tyranny?* London: Zed; Hickey, S. & Mohan, G. (eds) (2004) *Participation: From Tyranny to Transformation? Exploring New Approaches to Participation in Development.* London: Zed.
113. Ideas drawing on Stephen Lukes and Pierre Bourdieu: Lukes, S. (2004) *Power: A Radical View* (2nd edn). Basingstoke: Palgrave Macmillan; *habitus* in Bourdieu, *Outline of a Theory of Practice*.
114. Rowlands and Friedmann referred to in Cornwall, A. (2004) 'Spaces for Transformation? ...' in Hickey & Mohan, *Participation: From Tyranny to Transformation?*, p. 77.
115. Lister, R. (1997) 'Citizenship: Towards a Feminist Synthesis' *Feminist Review*, No. 57, pp. 28–48 (Basingstoke: Palgrave Macmillan); hooks, b. (1994) *Teaching to Transgress: Education as the Practice of Freedom.* London: Routledge.
116. Kelly, U. (2004) 'Confrontations with power...' in Hickey & Mohan, *Participation: From Tyranny to Transformation?*.
117. Cornwall, A. (2004) 'Spaces for Transformation?...' in Hickey & Mohan, *Participation: From Tyranny to Transformation?*. Problems with deliberative spaces referencing Kohn and problems with the state referring to Habermas. The 'weak' subverting states and the powerful from James C. Scott; Cornwall, A. et al (2008) 'Introduction: Reclaiming Feminism: Gender and Neoliberalism' *IDS Bulletin* Vol. 39, No. 6 (December) http://www.ids.ac.uk/files/dmfile/bull39.6intro3.pdf Accessed 18 May 2018.
118. Miraftab, F. (2004) 'Invited and Invented Spaces of Participation: Neoliberal Citizenship and Feminists' Expanded Notion of Politics' *Wagadu* Vol. 1 (Spring) http://www.rrojasdatabank.info/neolibstate/miraftab.pdf Accessed 18 May 2018.
119. Powercube.net (2011) 'Power Pack: Understanding Power for Social Change' https://www.powercube.net/wp-content/uploads/2011/04/powerpack-web-version-2011.pdf Accessed 18 May 2018; Gaventa, J. (2005) *Reflections on the Uses of the 'Power Cube' Approach for Analyzing the Spaces, Places and Dynamics of Civil Society Participation and Engagement.* Randwijk, NL: Learning by Design https://www.powercube.net/wp-content/uploads/2009/11/reflections_on_uses_powercube.pdf Accessed 18 May 2018.
120. Gaventa, J. (2006) 'Finding the Spaces for Change: A Power Analysis', *IDS Bulletin* Vol. 37, No. 6, p. 25 https://www.researchgate.net/publication/228040214_Finding_the_Spaces_for_Change_A_Power_Analysis Accessed 18 May 2018.
121. Kersting, N. (2013) 'Online Participation: From "Invited" to "Invented" Spaces' *International Journal of Electronic Governance* Vol. 6, No. 4, pp. 270–280 https://www.researchgate.net/publication/264814417_Online_participation_From_'invited'_to_'invented'_spaces Accessed 18 May 2018.
122. Kersting, 'Online Participation', diagram p. 272.

123 Clark, H. (2001/2014) 'Be Realistic, Demand the Impossible' *Open Democracy* https://www.opendemocracy.net/civilresistance/howard-clark/be-realistic-demand-impossible Accessed 18 May 2018.
124 Ife, J. (2001) *Human Rights and Social Work*. Cambridge: Cambridge University Press (present author's commentary).
125 Arnstein, S. (1969) 'A Ladder of Citizen Participation' *Journal of the American Planning Association* (June) http://www.participatorymethods.org/sites/participatorymethods.org/files/Arnstein%20ladder%201969.pdf Accessed 18 May 2018; Stonorov, O. & Kahn, L. (1944) *You and Your Neighborhood . . . A Primer for Neighborhood Planning*. New York: Revere Copper and Brass, Inc.
126 Finkelstein, *A Personal Journey into Disability Politics* http://www.independentliving.org/docs3/finkelstein01a.pdf Accessed 18 May 2018; UPIAS & Disability Alliance, *Fundamental Principles of Disability*.
127 Hobbes, T. (1962) *Leviathan* (p. 143). Fontana: Glasgow.
128 Rosenthal, F. (Translator) (1967) *Ibn Khaldun: The Muqaddimah: An Introduction to History* (edited by NJ Dawood). London: Routledge and Kegan Paul.
129 Locke, J (1924) *Two Treatises of Government* (p. 164). London: Dent.
130 Shaw, M. (2008) 'Civil Society' in Kurtz, L. (ed.) *Encyclopaedia of Violence, Peace and Conflict* (pp. 269–278). San Diego, CA: Academic Press.
131 London Edinburgh Weekend Return Group (1979) *In and Against the State*. London: Pluto, p. 42.
132 Robson, T. (2000) *The State and Community Action*. London: Pluto; de Baroid, C. (1990) *Ballymurphy and the Irish War*. London: Pluto; Frazer, H. (Compiler) (1981) *Community Work in a Divided Society*. Belfast: Farset; McAlister, R. (2011) 'The Struggle to Belong When Feeling Disconnected: The Experience of Loyalist East Belfast' *RC21 Conference 2011* http://www.rc21.org/conferences/amsterdam2011/edocs/Session%2015/RT15-1-McAlister.pdf Accessed 18 May 2018.
133 Stamatopoulos, D. (2006) 'From Millets to Minorities in the 19th-Century Ottoman Empire: An Ambiguous Modernization' in Ellis, S., Halfdanarson, G. & Isaacs, A. (eds) *Citizenship in Historical Perspective*. Pisa: Pisa University Press https://www.researchgate.net/publication/234169305_From_Millets_to_Minorities_in_the_19th_-_Century_Ottoman_Empire_an_Ambiguous_Modernization_in_S_G_Ellis_G_Halfadanarson_AK_Isaacs_epim_Citizenship_in_Historical_Perspective_Pisa_Edizioni_Plus_-_Pisa_U Accessed 18 May 2018; Berlin, A. & Grossman, M. (eds) (2011) 'Autonomy' in *The Oxford Dictionary of the Jewish Religion* (2nd edn). Oxford: Oxford University Press; Lijphart, A. (1969) 'Consociational Democracy' *World Politics* Vol. 21, No. 2, pp. 207–225.
134 International Assessment of Agricultural Knowledge, Science and Technology for Development (2008) *Summary for Decision Makers of the Global Report* Johannesburg, SA, IAASTD https://www.globalagriculture.org/fileadmin/files/weltagrarbericht/IAASTDBerichte/SDMLatinAmericaCaribbean.pdf Accessed 18 May 2018.
135 It is not likely to have been said by Benjamin Franklin, partly because it was not his view and partly because the word lunch was not

widely used in the eighteenth century: OED (Online) 'lunch' n.2. *OED Online.* Oxford University Press http://www.oed.com/view/Entry/111184?rske =EkAJUY&result=2#eid Accessed 18 May 2018.
136 Kesselman, D. (2011) 'Direct Democracy on Election Day: Ballot Measures as Measures of American Democracy', *Transatlantica* [online] https://transatlantica.revues.org/5279#text Accessed 18 May 2018; Economist (2016) 'Referendumania' *The Economist* May 21st, p. 32 http://www.economist.com/news/europe/21699146-direct-democracy-spreading-across-europe-not-always-good-thing-referendumania Accessed 18 May 2018.
137 Quoted in Held, *Models of Democracy*, pp. 162–163.
138 Yiftachel, O. (2006) *Ethnocracy: Land and Identity Politics in Israel/Palestine*. Philadelphia: University of Pennsylvania Press.
139 O'Leary, B. (2012) 'The Federalization of Iraq and the Break-Up of Sudan' *Government & Opposition* Vol. 47 No. 4 (October), pp. 481–516; McGarry, J. & O'Leary, B. (2006) 'Consociational Theory, Northern Ireland's Conflict, and its Agreement' Parts 1 & 2 *Government and Opposition* Vol. 41, Nos 1 & 2 http://www.polisci.upenn.edu/ppec/PPEC%20People/Brendan%20O'Leary/publications/Journal%20Articles/Consociational_Theory_NIreland_conflict_part_1.pdf Accessed 18 May 2018; Taylor, R. (ed.) (2009) *Consociational Theory: McGarry and O'Leary and the Northern Ireland Conflict*. Abingdon: Routledge.
140 Heller, P. (2013) *Challenges and Opportunities: Civil Society in a Globalizing World*. New York: UNDP http://hdr.undp.org/sites/default/files/hdro_1306_heller.pdf Accessed 18 May 2018; Heller, P. (2009) 'Democratic Deepening in Brazil, India and South Africa: Towards a Comparative Framework' http://web.fflch.usp.br/centrodametropole/antigo/static/uploads/seminario/Patrick_Heller.pdf Accessed 18 May 2018.
141 Lenin, for example, very critical of spontaneity, Rosa Luxemburg and Antonio Gramsci much more sympathetic. For a libertarian perspective, see Bookchin, M. (1975) 'On Spontaneity and Organisation' in *Solidarity*. London https://theanarchistlibrary.org/library/murray-bookchin-on-spontaneity-and-organisation.pdf Accessed 18 May 2018.
142 Bennett, A. (2004) *The History Boys*. London: Faber & Faber.
143 Tosh, *The Pursuit of History*.
144 Bulwer-Lytton, E. (1866) *Speech* http://hansard.millbanksystems.com/commons/1866/apr/13/second-reading-adjourned-debate Accessed 18 May 2018.
145 Gandhi, M.K. (1960) 'Non Violent Technique and Parallel Government' *My Non-Violence* Harijan, p. 234, 17 February 1946 http://www.mkgandhi.org/ebks/my_nonviolence.pdf Accessed 18 May 2018.
146 Goldstone, J. (2014) *Revolutions: A Very Short Introduction*. Oxford: Oxford University Press.
147 Mudde, C. & Kaltwasser, C.R. (2017) *Populism: A Very Short Introduction*. Oxford: Oxford University Press.
148 Mudde & Kaltwasser, *Populism*; Conservative Party (2005) *Conservative Election Manifesto 2005*. London: Party http://news.bbc.co.uk/1/shared/bsp/hi/pdfs/11_04_05_conservative_manifesto.pdf Accessed 17 May 2018.

149 Caiani, M. (2013) 'Populism/Populist Movements' *The Wiley-Blackwell Encyclopedia of Social and Political Movements* http://onlinelibrary.wiley.com/doi/10.1002/9780470674871.wbespm370/pdf Accessed 18 May 2018; Free exchange (2017) 'Take Back Control: When Elites Appear Ineffective, Voters Give Radicals a Chance' *Economist* (22 July) https://www.economist.com/news/finance-and-economics/21725298-when-elites-appear-ineffective-voters-give-radicals-chance-power Accessed 18 May 2018.

150 Goldstone, J. (2017) *Jack Goldstone - A World in Revolution: The Inevitable Backlash against Global Elites.* Lecture 6 March Brown University https://brown.hosted.panopto.com/Panopto/Pages/Viewer.aspx?id=05e9d4f3-7b17-43a6-b844-fb48844a8ef4 Accessed 18 May 2018; Arditi, B. (2007) *Politics on the Edges of Liberalism.* Edinburgh: University of Edinburgh Press https://1arditi.files.wordpress.com/2012/10/arditi_politics_edges_2007_fullversion.pdf Accessed 18 May 2018; Caiani, M. (2013) 'Populism/Populist Movements' *The Wiley-Blackwell Encyclopedia of Social and Political Movements* http://onlinelibrary.wiley.com/doi/10.1002/9780470674871.wbespm370/pdf Accessed 18 May 201.

151 Mudde & Kaltwasser, *Populism*.

152 Tosh, *The Pursuit of History*, pp. 153, 155, 215–217.

153 Brinton, C. (1973) *Anatomy of Revolution*. New York: Vintage.

154 Knutsen, T. & Bailey, J. (1989) 'Over the Hill? The Anatomy of Revolution at Fifty' *Journal of Peace Research* Vol. 26, pp. 421–431.

155 Goldstone, *Revolutions* (though this summary is the present author's not Goldstone's).

156 Scott, J.C. (1985) *Weapons of the Weak: Everyday Forms of Peasant Resistance.* New Haven, CT: Yale University Press.

157 Tosh, *The Pursuit of History*; Jenkins, *Re-thinking History*.

158 Mudde & Kaltwasser, *Populism*.

159 Allison G. and Zelikow, P. (1999) *Essence of Decision*. Harlow: Longman; Moran, M., Rein, M. & Goodin, R. (eds) (2006) *The Oxford Handbook of Public Policy*. Oxford: Oxford University Press; John, P. (1998) *Analysing Public Policy*. London: Continuum.

160 Westoby & Dowling, *Theory and Practice of Dialogical Community Development*, p. 61.

161 Brehaut, J. & Juzwishin, D. (2005) *Bridging the Gap: The Use of Research Evidence in Policy Development* http://wayback.archive-it.org/2063/20151216034512/http://www.ewc-popcomm.org/pdf/2_Selected_Readings/Use%20of%20Research%20in%20Policy.pdf Accessed 18 May 2018.

5 Equality and Emancipation

1 International Association for Community Development (2011) *IACD Strategic Plan 2011–2015*. Fife: IACD http://ylk.cdr.mybluehost.me/wp-content/uploads/2017/01/IACD_Strategic_Plan_2011-2015.pdf Accessed 19 May 2018.

NOTES

2 Federation for Community Development Learning (2015) *Community Development National Occupational Standards*. Sheffield: FCDL http://www.esbendorsement.org.uk/index.php/nos-2015-guidance-from-esb Accessed 19 May 2018.

3 Galtung, J. (1984) *How Universal are Human Rights?* Berlin: Berghof https://www.transcend.org/galtung/papers/How%20Universal%20Are%20the%20Human%20Rights.pdf Accessed 19 May 2018.

4 The historical part of this section follows Ishay, M.(2004) *The History of Human Rights*. London: University of California Press though not necessarily all her specific arguments.

5 Harvey, D. (2009) *Social Justice and The City* (revised edn). Athens: University of Georgia Press; Boyle, A. (2006) 'Human Rights or Environmental Rights? A *Reassessment*' *Fordham Environmental Law Review* Vol. 18, No. 3, Article 5 https://ir.lawnet.fordham.edu/cgi/viewcontent.cgi?referer=http://scholar.google.co.uk/&httpsredir=1&article=1634&context=elr.

6 Locke, J. (1924, reprinted 1975) *Two Treatises of Government* (pp. 129–130). London: Dent.

7 Sweet, W. (Online) 'Jeremy Bentham (1748–1832)' *Internet Encyclopedia of Philosophy* http://www.iep.utm.edu/bentham/#SH5b Accessed 19 May 2018.

8 Ife, J. (2001) *Human Rights and Social Work*. Cambridge: Cambridge University Press, p. 6.

9 Gibbons, H. & Skinner, N. (2003) 'Biological Basis of Human Rights' *Public Interest Law Journal* Vol. 13, No. 1, pp. 52–76 http://www.bu.edu/law/journals-archive/pilj/vol13no1/documents/13-1gibbonsandskinnerarticle.pdf Accessed 19 May 2018, presents a particularly simplistic model; the argument that animals do not have duties was cited in a court case involving Tommy the Chimpanzee in an American court: McKinley, J. (2014) 'Chimps Don't Have Same Rights as Humans, Court Says' *New York Times* 4 December, http://www.nytimes.com/2014/12/05/nyregion/chimps-dont-have-same-rights-as-humans-court-says.html?_r=0 Accessed 19 May 2018.

10 Ignatieff, M. (2003) *Human Rights as Politics and Idolatry*. Princeton, NJ: Princeton University Press, pp. 3–100 http://pgil.pk/wp-content/uploads/2014/11/Human-Rights-politics1.pdf Accessed 19 May 2018.

11 Nussbaum, M. (2000) *Women and Human Development: The Capabilities Approach*. Cambridge: Cambridge University Press; Sen, A. (1980) 'Equality of What?' in McMurrin, S. (ed.) *The Tanner Lectures on Human Values*. Cambridge: Cambridge University Press; Vizard, P. (2006) *Poverty and Human Rights: Sen's 'Capability Perspective' Explored*. Oxford: Oxford University Press.

12 Ignatieff, *Human Rights as Politics and Idolatry*, pp. 3–100.

13 Maslow, A. (1943) 'A Theory of Human Motivation' *Psychological Review* Vol. 50, No. 4, pp. 370–396 http://psychclassics.yorku.ca/Maslow/motivation.htm Accessed 19 May 2018.

14 Harvey, D. (2009) *Social Justice and the City* (revised edn). Athens: University of Georgia Press.
15 Doyal, L. & Gough, I. (1992) *A Theory of Human Need*. Basingstoke: Macmillan.
16 Burchardt, T. & Vizard, P (2016) *Developing an Equality Measurement Framework: A List of Substantive Freedoms for Adults and Children*. Research Report 18 http://webarchive.nationalarchives.gov.uk/20170207010302/ https://www.equalityhumanrights.com/sites/default/files/research_report_18_developing_equality_measurement_framework_substantive-freedoms-for-adults-and-children.pdf Accessed 19 May 2018.
17 Illich, I. (2010) 'Needs' in Sachs, W. (ed.) *The Development Dictionary*. London: Zed, p. 97.
18 Bertaut, J. (1916) *Napoleon in His Own Words* (translated by Law, H. & Rhodes C). Chicago: A.C.Mclurg https://ia801403.us.archive.org/11/items/napoleoninhisown00naporich/napoleoninhisown00naporich_bw.pdf Accessed 19 May 2018.
19 An inconvenience or dissatisfaction, experienced by people who are in a global context enjoy privileges, not available to most of the world: OED 'First World, n. and adj.'. *OED Online*. June 2015. Oxford University Press. http://www.oed.com/view/Entry/249401?redirectedFrom= First+world+problem Accessed 19 May 2018; Abdelmoneim, J. (2014) 'Dispatches from the Ebola Zone: The Traumas and Successes of Working in a Sierra Leone Treatment Centre' *Independent*. 16 November http://www.independent.co.uk/news/world/africa/dispatches-from-the-ebola-zone-the-traumas-and-successes-of-working-in-a-sierra-leone-treatment-centre-9864120.html Accessed 19 May 2018.
20 Bradshaw, J. (2013) 'The Taxonomy of Social Need' in Cookson, R., Sainsbury, R. & Glendinning, C. (eds) *Jonathan Bradshaw on Social Policy Selected Writings 1972–2011*. York: University of York http://www.york.ac.uk/inst/spru/pubs/pdf/JRB.pdf Accessed 19 May 2018.
21 Cahill, M. (1994) *The New Social Policy*. Oxford: Blackwell.
22 Knox, J. (2008) 'Horizontal Human Rights Law' *The American Journal of International Law* Vol. 102, No. 1 (January), pp. 1–47 http://papers.ssrn.com/sol3/papers.cfm?abstract_id=1014381 Accessed 19 May 2018.
23 Doyal & Gough, A *Theory of Human Need*.
24 Sands, P. (2016) *East West Street*. London: Weidenfeld & Nicholson.
25 United Nations (1948) *UN Declaration of Human Rights* http://www.un.org/en/documents/udhr/ Accessed 19 May 2018; African National Council (1955) *The Freedom Charter* https://web.archive.org/web/20110629074215/http://www.anc.org.za/show.php?id=72 Accessed 19 May 2018.
26 Speciesism coined by Richard Ryder in 1970: Singer, P. (1976) *Animal Liberation: A New Ethics for Our Treatment of Animals*. London: Cape; Buddhism and Hinduism as examples of where the lives of animals are protected.
27 Knox, 'Horizontal Human Rights Law'.

NOTES

28 Hobbes, T. (1962) *Leviathan*. Glasgow: Fontana. Chapter 17.
29 Sen, A. (2009) *The Idea of Justice*. London: Allen Lane.
30 Aristotle (1999) *Politics* (translated by Jowett, B. Kitchener). Ontario: Batoche Books https://socialsciences.mcmaster.ca/econ/ugcm/3ll3/aristotle/Politics.pdf Accessed 19 May 2018; Sen, *The Idea of Justice*, pp. 12–15.
31 Fraser, N. (1996) 'Social Justice in the Age of Identity Politics: Redistribution, Recognition, and Participation' *Tanner Lecture* http://tannerlectures.utah.edu/_documents/a-to-z/f/Fraser98.pdf Accessed 19 May 2018.
32 Fischer, M. (online) 'Transitional Justice and Reconciliation: Theory and Practice' in *Berghof Handbook for Conflict Transformation* (pp. 406–430) http://www.berghof-foundation.org/fileadmin/redaktion/Publications/Handbook/Articles/fischer_tj_and_rec_handbook.pdf Accessed 19 May 2018.
33 Native American Rights Fund (Online) *Trust Fund Matters* http://www.narf.org/our-work/accountability-governments/ Accessed 19 May 2018.
34 Quoted in Office of the High Commissioner for Human Rights (2014) *Transitional Justice and Economic, Social and Cultural Rights* (p. 5) http://www.ohchr.org/Documents/Publications/HR-PUB-13-05.pdf Accessed 19 May 2018.
35 All this section follows and elaborates on Mantle, G., Fox, D. & Dhami, M. (2005) 'Restorative Justice and Three Individual Theories of Crime' *Internet Journal of Criminology* https://pdfs.semanticscholar.org/f2ff/2248c22f975b80a502cabbb0566b51cb3dcc.pdf Accessed 19 May 2018.
36 Restorative Justice Council (Online) *What is Restorative Justice?* https://www.restorativejustice.org.uk/what-restorative-justice Accessed 19 May 2018.
37 Torney, K. (2015) 'Above The Law: Paramilitary "Punishment" Attacks in Northern Ireland' *The Detail* 22 March http://www.thedetail.tv/articles/above-the-law-paramilitary-punishment-attacks-in-northern-ireland Accessed 19 May 2018; Kennedy, L. (2014) '*They Shoot Children, Don't They?*' http://www.michaelnugent.com/2014/11/10/they-shoot-children-dont-they-part-1/ Accessed 19 May 2018.
38 Sachs, W. (ed) (2010) 'Preface' in Sachs, *The Development Dictionary*, p. ix.
39 This section draws on but does not always follow: Thompson, N. (2003) *Promoting Equality: Challenging Discrimination and Oppression*. Basingstoke: Palgrave Macmillan; Baker, J. et al (2004) *Equality: From Theory to Action*. Basingstoke: Palgrave.
40 Kipling, R. (1902) 'The Elephant's Child' *Just So Stories*. London: MacMillan http://www.telelib.com/authors/K/KiplingRudyard/prose/JustSoStories/chap5_elephantchild.html Accessed 19 May 2018.
41 See Doré, G. (1984) *Fables of La Fontaine*. Ware: Orion, p. 31.
42 Michael Young's fear of a Meritocracy: Young, M. (1967) *The Rise of the Meritocracy*. Harmondsworth: Pelican.
43 Tawney, R. (1931) *Equality*. London: George Allen & Unwin, p. 112.
44 Tawney, *Equality*, p. 112.
45 Sen, 'Equality of What?'; Vizard, *Poverty and Human Rights*.

46 Attributed, location not found.
47 Lister, R. (1997) *Citizenship: Feminist Perspectives*. Basingstoke: MacMillan.
48 See Alvesson, M. & Billing, Y. (2010) 'Understanding Gender and Organizations' in Grint, K. (ed.) *Leadership: A Very Short Introduction*. Oxford: Oxford University Press, p. 74.
49 Wilkinson, R. & Pickett, K. (2010) *The Spirit Level: Why More Equal Societies Almost Always Do Better*. London: Penguin; Wilkinson, R. (1996) *Unhealthy Societies: The Afflictions of Inequality*. London: Routledge; Wilkinson, R. & Pickett, K. (Online) *Professors Richard Wilkinson and Kate Pickett, Authors of The Spirit Level, Reply to Critics*. London: Equality Trust https://www.equalitytrust.org.uk/sites/default/files/responses-to-all-critics.pdf Accessed 19 May 2018.
50 Dabla-Norris, E. et al (2015) *Causes and Consequences of Income Inequality: A Global Perspective*. Washington, DC: International Monetary Fund http://www.imf.org/external/pubs/cat/longres.aspx?sk=42986.0 Accessed 19 May 2018.
51 Freire, P. (1972) *Pedagogy of the Oppressed*. Harmondsworth: Penguin.
52 Tawney, *Equality*, p. 42.
53 United Nations (1948) *UN Declaration of Human Rights* http://www.un.org/en/documents/udhr/ Accessed 19 May 2018.
54 Republic of South Africa (1996) 'Equality' Chapter 2, Bill of Rights *Constitution of the Republic of South Africa* http://www.justice.gov.za/legislation/constitution/SAConstitution-web-eng.pdf Accessed 19 May 2018.
55 H.M. Government (2010) *The Equality Act 2010*. London: The Stationery Office http://www.legislation.gov.uk/ukpga/2010/15/pdfs/ukpga_20100015_en.pdf Accessed 19 May 2018.
56 Equality Commission for Northern Ireland (2011) *Goods, Facilities, Services and Premises: A Short Guide to Discrimination Law* http://www.equalityni.org/ECNI/media/ECNI/Publications/Employers%20and%20Service%20Providers/GoodsFacilitiesServicesDiscriminationLawShortGuide2011.pdf Accessed 19 May 2018.
57 The title of a book and so on which asserts that there are significant psychological differences between men and women. It has been vigorously challenged on both the grounds that it is not generally true, and, where it is, it the result of social pressures to conform with gender stereotypes. Gray, J. (2015) *Men are from Mars, Women are from Venus*. London: Harper Thorsons.
58 Thompson, *Promoting Equality*.
59 For an example of research based on smells' relationship to political views, see Liuzza, M. et al (2018) 'Body Odour Disgust Sensitivity Predicts Authoritarian Attitudes' *Royal Society Open Science* Vol. 5, p. 71091 (London: Royal Society) http://rsos.royalsocietypublishing.org/content/royopensci/5/2/171091.full.pdf Accessed 19 May 2018.
60 Dovidio, J. et al (eds) (2005) *On the Nature of Prejudice: Fifty Years After Allport*. Oxford: Blackwell; Dovidio, J. et al (eds) (2010) *The Sage Handbook of Prejudice, Stereotyping and Discrimination*. London: Sage.

61 A taxonomy proposed by Sue in 2010. The original concept of micro aggressions was articulated by Pierce in 1970: see Huber, L.P. & Solorzano, D. (2015) 'Racial Microaggressions as a Tool for Critical Race Research' *Race Ethnicity and Education* Vol. 18, No. 3, pp. 297–320.
62 Said, E. (1978) *Orientalism*. London: Penguin.
63 Ledwith, M. & Asgill, P. (2000) 'Critical Alliance: Black and White Women Working Together for Social Justice' *Community Development Journal* Vol. 35, No. 3, pp. 290–299.
64 Cockburn, C. (2004) *The Line: Women, Partition and the Gender Order in Cyprus*. London: Zed; Darweish, M. & Rigby, A. (2015) *Popular Protest in Palestine*. London: Pluto; Hassouna, S. (2015) 'An Assessment of Dialogue-Based Initiatives in Light of the Anti-Normalization Criticisms and Mobility Restrictions' *Palestine-Israel Journal* Vol. 21, No. 2 http://www.pij.org/details.php?id=1669 Accessed 19 May 2018.
65 Campbell, A. & Hughes, J. et al (2010) 'Social Capital as a Mechanism for Building a Sustainable Society in Northern Ireland' *Community Development Journal* Vol. 45, No. 1 (January), pp. 22–38; Leonard, M. (2004) 'Bonding and Bridging Social Capital: Reflections from Belfast' *Sociology* Vol. 38, No. 5, pp. 927–944; Gray, A.M. & Neill, G. (2011) 'Creating a Shared Society in Northern Ireland: Why We Need to Focus on Gender Equality' *Youth and Society* Vol. 43, No. 2, pp. 468–487.
66 Ambedkar, B.R. (2014) *Annihilation of Caste: The Annotated Critical Edition* (edited by S. Anand; Introduction by Arundhati Roy). London: Verso.
67 World Values Survey (Online) *The World Values Survey: Findings and Insight* http://www.worldvaluessurvey.org/WVSContents.jsp Accessed 19 May 2018.
68 Chambers, E. & Cowan, M. (2004) *Roots for Radicals*. London: Continuum, p. 28 highlights this.
69 Bachrach, P. & Baratz, M. (1970) *Power and Poverty: Theory and Practice*. New York: Oxford University Press, p. 24.
70 Batliwala in Rowlands, J. (1997) *Questioning Empowerment: Working with Women in Honduras*. Oxford: Oxfam, pp. 23–24.
71 Gerth, H. & Mills, C.W. (1946) *From Max Weber: Essays in Sociology* (p. 180). London: Routledge and Kegan Paul.
72 Faubion, J. (2002) *Michel Foucault Power: Essential Works of Foucault 1954–84* (Vol. 3). London: Penguin.
73 Bourdieu, P. (1977) *Outline of a Theory of Practice*. Cambridge: Cambridge University Press.
74 Lukes, S. (2004) *Power: A Radical View* (2nd edn). Basingstoke: Palgrave Macmillan.
75 Rowlands, *Questioning Empowerment*.
76 The classification is from Rowlands. The explanations are the present author's: Rowlands, *Questioning Empowerment*.
77 Thompson, *Promoting Equality*, p. 42.
78 Coca Cola GB (2015) *'Regret Nothing' with Diet Coke's New Campaign* 29 Jan http://www.coca-cola.co.uk/stories/regret-nothing-with-diet-coke-s-new-campaign Accessed 19 May 2018.

79 Citizens Advice (2015) *Personal Independence Payments: Supporting Participation in Society and the Labour Market* https://www.citizensadvice.org.uk/Global/CitizensAdvice/welfare%20publications/PIP.pdf Accessed 19 May 2018.
80 Johnston, R. (1993) 'Praxis for the Powerless and Punch-Drunk' *Adults Learning* (England) Vol. 4, No. 6 (February), pp. 146–48 (Leicester: NIACE).
81 Douglass, F. (18587) '(1857) Frederick Douglass, "If There Is No Struggle, There Is No Progress"' Black Past.Org http://www.blackpast.org/1857-frederick-douglass-if-there-no-struggle-there-no-progress#sthash.QUHbPkuX.dpuf Accessed 19 May 2018. He was talking about the slave uprisings in the Caribbean and the Anti-slavery movement which William Wilberforce had led but earlier in the year in which he spoke, the Indian Uprising by soldiers had taken place.
82 Rowlands, *Questioning Empowerment*.
83 Moxley, R. (2015) *Becoming a Leader Is Becoming Yourself*. Jefferson. NC: McFarland.
84 Rowlands, J. (1996) 'Empowerment Examined' in Eade, D. (ed.) *Development and Social Diversity*. Oxford: Oxfam, pp. 86–92.
85 OED Online (2018) 'Emancipation, n.'. March 2018. Oxford University Press. http://www.oed.com/view/Entry/60721?redirected From=Emancipation Accessed 19 May 2018.
86 Rahnema, M. (2010) 'Poverty' in Sachs, *The Development Dictionary*, p. 175.
87 Plato (1974) 'The Simile of the Cave' in *The Republic* (translated by Lee, H). London: Penguin.
88 Angelou, M. (Online) *Still I Rise* http://www.poemhunter.com/poem/still-i-rise/ Accessed 19 May 2018; *Caged Bird* http://www.poemhunter.com/poem/caged-bird-21/ Accessed 19 May 2018.
89 Angelou, M. (1984) *I Know Why the Caged Bird Sings*. London: Virago, p. 258.
90 Angelou, *I Know Why the Caged Bird Sings*, p. 260.
91 TAGV (Teens Advocating a Global Vision). (2010) *TAGV Program Manual*, pp. 27–28 https://anyfile.255bits.com/wix/download?id=1252f166af6fcd0bcc9e0bb0edb08f71 Accessed 19 May 2018.
92 Young, I. (2004) 'Five Faces of Oppression' in Heldke, L. & O'Connor, P. *Oppression, Privilege, & Resistance*. Boston: McGraw Hill.
93 Nandy, A. (1983) *The Intimate Enemy: Loss and Recovery of Self under Colonialism*. Bombay: Oxford University Press, p. 13.
94 OED (online) 'hegemony, n.' OED Online. Oxford University Press.
95 Marx, K. (1975) 'A Contribution to the Critique of Hegel's Philosophy of Right. Introduction' in *Early Writings* (translated by Nairn, T.). Harmondsworth: Penguin, p. 244.
96 Gramsci, A. (1971) *Selections from the Prison Notebooks of Antonio Gramsci* (edited and translated by Hoare, Q. & Nowell Smith, G). London: Lawrence & Wishart; Sassoon, A.S. (1987) *Gramsci's Politics*. London: Hutchinson.
97 Last, J. (2007) *A Dictionary of Public Health*. Oxford: Oxford University Press.

98 UNDP (Online) *Gender Inequality Index* http://hdr.undp.org/en/content/gender-inequality-index-gii Accessed 19 May 2018.
99 Ture, Kwame (1967). *Black Power: Politics of Liberation* (November 1992 edn, p. 4) New York: Vintage; Carmichael, S. & Hamilton, C. (1968) *Black Power: The Politics of Liberation*. Harmondsworth: Penguin.
100 Dominelli, L. (1998) 'Anti-Oppressive Practice in Context' in Adams, R., Campling, J., Dominelli, L., & Payne, M. (eds) *Social Work Themes, Issues and Critical Debates*. Basingstoke: Palgrave Macmillan; Thompson, *Promoting Equality*.
101 Thompson, *Promoting Equality*, pp. 81–92. The classification is Thompson's; the descriptions are the present author's.
102 For example, hooks, b (1994) *Teaching to Transgress: Education as the Practice of Freedom*. London: Routledge; hooks, b. (2003) *Teaching Community: A Pedagogy of Hope*. Abingdon: Routledge.
103 hooks, *Teaching Community*, p. 135.
104 Rich, A. (1986) 'Invisibility in Academe' in *Blood, Bread, and Poetry*. London: WW Norton, pp. 198–201.
105 Freire, N. (2016) 'Foreword' in Ledwith, M. (ed.) *Community Development in Action*. Bristol: Policy Press, pp. vii–viii.
106 Bartky, S.L. (1990) *Femininity and Domination*. London: Routledge, p. 23.
107 Bartky, *Femininity and Domination*, p. 23.
108 hooks, *Teaching to Transgress*, p. 80.
109 Bartky, *Femininity and Domination*, p. 23.
110 Ziff, B. & Rao, P. (eds) (1997) *Borrowed Power: Essays on Cultural Appropriation*. New Brunswick, NJ: Rutgers University Press.
111 Daily Telegraph (2010) 'Archbishop "Stopped and Searched Eight Times"' *Daily Telegraph* 28 July http://www.telegraph.co.uk/news/uknews/law-and-order/7913745/Archbishop-stopped-and-searched-eight-times.html Accessed 19 May 2018.
112 Sen, A. (2007) *Identity and Violence*. London: Penguin.
113 Crenshaw, K. (1991) 'Mapping the Margins: Intersectionality, Identity Politics, and Violence Against Women of Color' *Stanford Law Review* Vol. 43, No. 6 (July 1991), pp. 1241–1299; Anthias, F. & Yuval-Davies, N. (1993) *Racialized Boundaries: Race, Nation, Colour and Class and the Anti-Racist Struggle*. London: Routledge.
114 Truth, S. (Online) 'Ain't I A Woman?' *Modern History Sourcebook* http://legacy.fordham.edu/halsall/mod/sojtruth-woman.asp Accessed 19 May 2018.
115 Freud, S. (1963) *Civilisation and Its Discontents*. London: Hogarth, p. 51.
116 Lorde, A. (2007) 'Learning from the 60s' in *Sister Outsider: Essays & Speeches by Audre Lorde*. Berkeley, CA: Crossing Press, pp. 134–144 http://www.blackpast.org/1982-audre-lorde-learning-60s#sthash.Zpl6nyX0.dpuf Accessed 19 May 2018.
117 Sissay, L. (2012) *A Rebel with Applause* 7 May http://destinationhackney.co.uk/news/2F61F85A48824B3CA5069BCC4AABE58E#.VlIuyL895yo Accessed 19 May 2018; (2013) *Post* 15 June Facebook https://www.facebook.com/Lemnsissay/posts/210265835788315 Accessed 19 May 2018.

118 Fanon, F. (1961) *The Wretched of the Earth*. London: Penguin, p. 116.
119 Fanon, *The Wretched of the Earth*, p. 201.
120 Fanon, *The Wretched of the Earth*, p. 115.
121 Fanon, *The Wretched of the Earth*, p. 40.
122 Maugham, W.S. (1919) *The Moon and Sixpence*. London: Heinemann, ch. 19. http://www.gutenberg.org/files/222/222-h/222-h.htm#Chapter_XIX Accessed 19 May 2018.
123 Sartre, J.-P. (2003) *Being and Nothingness: An Essay on Phenomenological Ontology*. London: Routledge Classic. Later Michel Foucault, Edward Said and Judith Butler, for example.
124 Dominelli, 'Anti-Oppressive Practice in Context'.
125 For Open Space and many other methods, see Zera, A. & Murray, S. *Getting on Brilliantly: Getting on Brilliantly Recipes for Managing Successful Meetings* https://facilitationanywheredotnet.files.wordpress.com/2016/01/c7e9d-getting_on_brilliantly.pdf Accessed 19 May 2018.
126 United Nations (Online) *Sustainable Development Goals: Goal 6: Ensure Access to Water and Sanitation for All* https://www.un.org/sustainabledevelopment/water-and-sanitation/ Accessed 19 May 2018.

6 Learning Together: What and Why

1 Plutarch (1968) *Moralia* (translated by deLacy, P. & Einarson, B.). Cambridge, MA: Harvard University Press, p. 259.
2 Freire, P. (1972) *Pedagogy of the Oppressed*. Harmondsworth: Penguin, pp. 45–46.
3 Lyotard, J.-F. (1984) *The Postmodern Condition: A Report on Knowledge*. Manchester: Manchester University Press.
4 Butler, A. & Ford, B. (2003) *Postmodernism*. Harpenden: Pocket Essentials; Scott, J. (ed.) (2014) *'Postmodernism' A Dictionary of Sociology* (4th edn). Oxford: Oxford University Press.
5 Weber, M. (2002) *The Protestant Ethic and the Spirit of Capitalism: And Other Writings*. Harmondsworth: Penguin (twentieth-century classics); Tawney, R. (1929) *Religion and the Rise of Capitalism*. London: John Murray.
6 Lyotard, *The Postmodern Condition*, p. 12.
7 The word algorithm is derived from the Latin form of the ninth century mathematician al-Khwarizmi whose work also gave rise to the name and concept of algebra: Elwes, R. (2012) 'The Algorithm that Runs the World' *New Scientist* 8 August https://www.newscientist.com/article/mg21528771.100-the-algorithm-that-runs-the-world/ Accessed 21 May 2018; Ewes (2012) 'The World Maker' *New Scientist* 11 August; http://www.stat.ncsu.edu/people/reiland/courses/st504/new_scientist_simplex_article.pdf Accessed 21 May 2018; Al-Khalili, J. (2012) *Pathfinders: The Golden Age of Arabic Science*. London: Penguin.
8 Lyotard, *The Postmodern Condition*.

9 Sen, A. (2001) *Development as Freedom*. Oxford: Oxford Paperbacks; Sen, A. (1980) 'Equality of What?' in McMurrin, S. (ed.) *The Tanner Lectures on Human Values*. Cambridge: Cambridge University Press.
10 Lyotard, *The Postmodern Condition*, p. xxi.
11 Sen, A. (2009) *The Idea of Justice*. London: Allen Lane; Lyotard, *The Postmodern Condition*, p. 61.
12 King, A. (1993) 'From Sage on the Stage to Guide on the Side' *College Teaching* Winter 93, Vol. 41, No. 1, pp. 30–35; Freire, P. (1976) Education: *The Practice of Freedom*. London: Readers and Writers Publishing Cooperative.
13 Lyotard, *The Postmodern Condition, p. 99, n. 185*.
14 King, 'From Sage on the Stage to Guide on the Side'.
15 Heron, J. (1996) *Co-operative Inquiry: Research into the Human Condition*. London: Sage.
16 SDUK 1833 quoted in Goldstrom, J.M. (1972) *The Social Content of Education 1808–1870*. Shannon: Irish University Press, p. 83.
17 Patrick Johnston in Black, R. (2016) 'The Big Interview' *Belfast Telegraph* 30 May http://www.belfasttelegraph.co.uk/news/northern-ireland/more-than-a-third-of-students-leave-northern-ireland-at-18-we-cannot-afford-to-lose-such-talent-but-theyll-only-return-if-there-are-opportunities-34756003.html Accessed 21 May 2018.
18 Although often attributed to Einstein, its first recorded use seems to be Cameron, W.B. (1963) *Informal Sociology: A Casual Introduction to Sociological Thinking*. New York: Random House, p. 13.
19 Denzin, N. (2008) 'Evolution of Qualitative Research' (pp. 311–317) and Donmoyer, R. (2008) 'Quantitative Research' (pp. 713–718) in Given, L. (ed.) *The Sage Encyclopedia of Qualitative Research Methods*. London: Sage.
20 Attributed to NASA administrator, Daniel Goldin, in 1992 in Douglas, D.G. (2004) *American Women and Flight since 1940*. Lexington: The University Press of Kentucky, p. 251.
21 Rich, Adrienne. (1986) 'Invisibility in Academe' in *Blood, Bread, and Poetry*. London: WW Norton.
22 Longino, H. (2016) 'The Social Dimensions of Scientific Knowledge' *The Stanford Encyclopedia of Philosophy* (Spring 2016 edn), Edward N. Zalta (ed.) http://plato.stanford.edu/archives/spr2016/entries/scientific-knowledge-social/ Accessed 21 May 2018; Gorton, W. (Online) 'The Philosophy of Social Science' *The Internet Encyclopedia of Philosophy* http://www.iep.utm.edu/soc-sci/#SH2b Accessed 21 May 2018.
23 Said, E. (1978) *Orientalism*. London: Penguin; Hountondji, P. (1983) *African Philosophy: Myth and Reality*. London: Hutchinson; Connell, R. (2008) *Southern Theory*. Crow's Nest, NSW: Allen & Unwin; Al-Khalili, *Pathfinders*. Al-Khalili argues that modern science owes much to a historical period but that contemporary science in Arab-speaking regions is in less healthy state.
24 Scull, A. (2011) *Madness – A Very Short Introduction*. Oxford: Oxford University Press.
25 Garland, T. (2015) *The Scientific Method as an Ongoing Process* http://idea.ucr.edu/documents/flash/scientific_method/story.htm Accessed

21 May 2018; Wikipedia 'Scientific Method' https://en.wikipedia.org/wiki/Scientific_method#cite_note-Garland2015-1 Accessed 21 May 2018.

26 Molland, G. (2004) 'Bacon, Roger (c.1214–1292?)', *Oxford Dictionary of National Biography*. Oxford: Oxford University Press http://www.oxforddnb.com/view/article/1008 Accessed 21 May 2018; Al-Khalili, *Pathfinders*; Hackett, J. (2015) 'Roger Bacon' *The Stanford Encyclopedia of Philosophy* (Spring 2015 edn), Edward N. Zalta (ed.) http://plato.stanford.edu/archives/spr2015/entries/roger-bacon/ Accessed 21 May 2018.

27 Andersen, H. & Hepburn, B. (2016) 'Scientific Method', *The Stanford Encyclopedia of Philosophy* (Summer 2016 edn), Edward N. Zalta (ed.) https://plato.stanford.edu/entries/scientific-method/ Accessed 21 May 2018; Elwes 'The Algorithm that Runs the World'; Resnik, D. (Online) 'Research Ethics Timeline (1932–Present)' *National Institute of Environmental Health Sciences* http://www.niehs.nih.gov/research/resources/bioethics/timeline/ Accessed 21 May 2018.

28 American Cancer Society (Online) *The History of Cancer* http://www.cancer.org/cancer/cancerbasics/thehistoryofcancer/ Accessed 21 May 2018.

29 Colman, A. (2009) 'Experimenter Expectancy Effect' in *A Dictionary of Psychology*. Oxford: Oxford University Press; Elliot, M. & Fairweather, I. et al. (2016) 'Interpretivism', 'Constructionism', 'Subjectivism' in *A Dictionary of Social Research Methods*. Oxford: Oxford University Press.

30 Smith, R. (2006) 'Peer Review: A Flawed Process at the Heart of Science and Journals', *Journal of the Royal Society of Medicine,* Vol. 99, pp. 178–171; Fanelli, D. (2009) 'How Many Scientists Fabricate and Falsify Research? A Systematic Review and Meta-Analysis of Survey Data' *PLoS One*. 29 May http://journals.plos.org/plosone/article/file?id=10.1371/journal.pone.0005738&type=printable Accessed 21 May 2018 ; Ferguson, C. (2014) 'Publishing: The Peer-Review Scam' *Nature* Vol. 515, pp. 480–482, 27 November http://www.nature.com/news/publishing-the-peer-review-scam-1.16400 Accessed 21 May 2018.

31 Hube, C. (2017) 'Bias in Wikipedia' *WWW'17 Companion* https://pdfs.semanticscholar.org/c5c5/f3a4f177af2de8ec61039ebc6e43bb377041.pdf Accessed 21 May 2018; Wikipedia (Online) 'Criticism of Wikipedia' Wikipedia https://en.wikipedia.org/wiki/Criticism_of_Wikipedia#References Accessed 21 May 2018.

32 Forbes, P. (2006) *The Gecko's Foot*. London: Harper Perennial.

33 Wilson, A. (2010) *Knowledge Power: Interdisciplinary Education for a Complex World*. London: Routledge.

34 Aristotle (1908) *Nicomachean Ethics* (translated by Ross, W.D., Book 2:1). Oxford: Clarendon http://classics.mit.edu/Aristotle/nicomachaen.html Accessed 21 May 2018.

35 Bhatia, V.P. (2016) *A Panoramic View of Ethical Values; from Chanakya's Niti Sastra* (Sections 5.7 & 5.8). Chennai: Notion Press.

36 al-Talbi, A. (1993) 'Al-Farabi' *Prospects: The Quarterly Review of Comparative Education* Vol. 23, No. 1/2, pp. 353–372. www.ibe.unesco.org/sites/default/files/farabie.pdf Accessed 21 May 2018.

37 Ashton Warner, S. (1980) (From earlier book) 'Spinster' in *Teacher*. London: Virago.
38 Pascal, B. (1958) 'Thoughts on Mind and on Style' 10 *Pascal's Penseés*. New York E.P. Dutton http://www.gutenberg.org/files/18269/18269-h/18269-h.htm Accessed 21 May 2018 p. 6.
39 Dewey, J. (1897) 'My Pedagogic Creed', *The School Journal* Vol. LIV, No. 3 (16 January), pp. 77–80 http://infed.org/mobi/john-dewey-my-pedagogical-creed/ Accessed 21 May 2018.
40 Schön, D. (1991) *The Reflective Practitioner*. Aldershot: Avebury.
41 Dewey, J. (1998) *How We Think: A Restatement of the Relation of Reflective Thinking to the Educative Process*. Boston: Houghton Mifflin, p. 107; Smith, M. (1999) 'Reflection, Learning and Education' *The Encyclopedia of Informal Education* http://infed.org/mobi/reflection-learning-and-education/ Accessed 21 May 2018; Smith, M. (2001) 'Kurt Lewin, Groups, Experiential Learning and Action Research' *The Encyclopedia of Informal Education* http://www.infed.org/thinkers/et-lewin.htm Accessed 21 May 2018; Smith, M. (2010) 'David A. Kolb on Experiential Learning', *The Encyclopedia of Informal Education*.
42 Freire, P. (1972) *Cultural Action for Freedom*. London: Penguin, p. 35.
43 Shafak, E. (2010) 'The Politics of Fiction' *TED Talk* https://www.ted.com/talks/elif_shafak_the_politics_of_fiction/transcript?language=en Accessed 21 May 2018.
44 Archer, M. (20003) *Structure, Agency and the Internal Conversation*. Cambridge: Cambridge University Press.
45 Freire, *Pedagogy of the Oppressed*; Ledwith, M. (2011) *Community Development: A Critical* Approach (2nd edn). Bristol: Policy Press.
46 Dunn, R. (2010) 'Painting With Penicillin: Alexander Fleming's Germ Art' *Smithsonian Magazine* 11 July http://www.smithsonianmag.com/science-nature/painting-with-penicillin-alexander-flemings-germ-art-1761496/#6gxu4MxsQKTYJTZE.99 Accessed 21 May 2018.
47 Hitchcock, C. (2015) *The Art of the Impossible: MC Escher and Me*. BBC Scotland https://www.youtube.com/watch?v=f7kW8xd8p4s Accessed 21 May 2018; World of Escher (2012) *Recreational Mathematics?* http://www.worldofescher.com/misc/penrose.html Accessed 21 May 2018.
48 Howell, C. (2014) *Project Illusions – What is Your Reality?* http://www.projectillusions.com/index.htm Accessed 21 May 2018.
49 Saville, I. (Online) *Ian Saville – Magic for Socialism* http://www.redmagic.co.uk/ Accessed 21 May 2018.
50 Way, D. (2017) 'The Magic Interventionist' *Magicseen Magazine* Vol. 12, No. 6, pp. 28–31; personal communication www.streetsofgrowth.org Accessed 21 May 2018.
51 Navasky, V. (2013) '15 Cartoons that Changed the World' *Buzzfeed* https://www.buzzfeed.com/victornavasky/15-historic-cartoons-that-changed-the-world?utm_term=.lkra8ZoJD#.opOYnXQdr Accessed 21 May 2018.
52 A search of any bookseller's website or bookshop for graphic book non-fiction confirms this.

53 Holmes, K. (2008) *Kelly Holmes: Black, White & Gold: My Autobiography.* London: Virgin.
54 Boal, A. (2008) *Theatre of the Oppressed.* London: Pluto, pp. 96–97; the World Bank acknowledges that this is still a problem: World Bank (2014) 'Discriminated Against for Speaking Their Own Language' *News* 16 April http://www.worldbank.org/en/news/feature/2014/04/16/discriminados-por-hablar-su-idioma-natal-peru-quechua Accessed 21 May 2018.
55 Boal, A. (1994) *Rainbow of Desire.* London: Routledge; Boal, A. (2005) *Games for Actors and Non-Actors* (2nd edn). London: Routledge; Boal, A. (2008) *Theatre of the Oppressed.* London: Pluto.
56 Begum, N. (1995) *Beyond Samosas and Reggae: A Guide to Developing Services for Black Disabled People.* London: Kings Fund.
57 Ryle, G. (2009) *The Concept of Mind* (60th Anniversary edn, p. lx). London: Routledge.
58 Allison, G. & Zelikow, P. (1999) *Essence of Decision.* Harlow: Longman; Fisher, R., Ury, W. & Patton, B. (1997) *Getting to Yes: Negotiating an Agreement Without Giving In.* London: Random House.
59 Susskind, L. et al (2014) Teaching *Negotiation: Understanding the Impact of Role-Play Simulations.* Cambridge, MA: Harvard University http://www.pon.harvard.edu/wp-content/uploads/images/posts/Teaching_Negotiation_Free_Report_thumbnail_lrg.png Accessed 21 May 2018.
60 Wikipedia (2016) *The Programme on Negotiation* (Updated 28 September) https://en.wikipedia.org/wiki/Program_on_Negotiation Accessed 21 May 2018.
61 Brock-Utne, B. (2001) *Indigenous Conflict Resolution in Africa.* Paper presented to a seminar on indigenous solutions to conflicts, Oslo http://www.africavenir.org/fileadmin/_migrated/content_uploads/BrockUtneTradConflictResolution_06.pdf Accessed 21 May 2018.
62 Grace, R. (2015) *Understanding Humanitarian Negotiation: Five Analytical Approaches.* Cambridge, MA: Harvard Advanced Training Program on Humanitarian Action http://www.atha.se/sites/default/files/understanding_humanitarian_negotiation-_five_analytical_approaches_0.pdf Accessed 21 May 2018.
63 Curran, D. & Sebenius, J. (2011) *The Mediator as Coalition Builder: George Mitchell in Northern Ireland* Vol. 3.4 https://people.rit.edu/wlrgsh/Mitchell.pdf Accessed 21 May 2018; Powell, J. (2008) *Great Hatred, Little Room – Making Peace in Northern Ireland.* London: The Bodley Head.
64 Ministry of Defence (2006) *Operation Banner – An Analysis of Military Operations in Northern Ireland* http://www.vilaweb.cat/media/attach/vwedts/docs/op_banner_analysis_released.pdf Accessed 21 May 2018; Archick, K. (2015) *Northern Ireland: The Peace Process.* Congressional Research Service https://www.fas.org/sgp/crs/row/RS21333.pdf Accessed 21 May 2018.
65 McCartney, F. & Le Mare, A. (2011) *Coming from the Silence: Quaker Peacebuilding Initiatives in Northern Ireland 1969–2007* (2nd edn). Belfast: Quaker Service Belfast; Campbell, B. (2008) *Agreement: The State, Conflict and Change in Northern Ireland.* London: Lawrence & Wishart.

NOTES

66 Murphy, Y. (2001) *Troubled Images: Posters and Images of the Northern Ireland Conflict from the Linen Hall Library, Belfast* (CD ROM). Belfast: Linen Hall Library; Linen Hall Library (2018) *Divided Society Northern Ireland 1990–98* https://www.dividedsociety.org/ Accessed 21 May 2018; Rolston, B. (2013) *Drawing Support 4: Murals and Conflict Transformation in Northern Ireland.* Belfast: Beyond the Pale Publication; Rolston, B. (Online) *Bill Rolston* http://billrolston.weebly.com/ Accessed 21 May 2018; Ministry of Defence (2006) *Operation Banner – An Analysis of Military Operations in Northern Ireland* http://www.vilaweb.cat/media/attach/vwedts/docs/op_banner_analysis_released.pdf Accessed 21 May 2018.

67 Abbott, E. (2009) *Sugar: A Bittersweet History.* London: Duckworth; Mintz, S. (1986) *Sweetness and Power – The Place of Sugar in Modern History.* London: Penguin.

68 Alvares, C. (2010) 'Science' in Sachs, W. (ed.) *The Development Dictionary.* London: Zed.

69 Myrbäck, K. (1970) 'Award Ceremony Speech' Nobel Prize for Chemistry awarded to Luis Leloir https://www.nobelprize.org/nobel_prizes/chemistry/laureates/1970/press.html Accessed 21 May 2018.

70 OED (2016) 'capacity, n.' *OED Online* Oxford University Press http://www.oed.com/view/Entry/27368?redirectedFrom=Capacity Accessed 21 May 2018.

71 For an attempt to distinguish the concepts in practical terms see: Winterton, J. et al (2006) *Typology of Knowledge, Skills and Competences: Clarification of the Concept and Prototype.* Luxembourg: Cedefop http://www.cedefop.europa.eu/files/3048_en.pdf Accessed 21 May 2018.

72 Sen, 'Equality of What?'; for a summary of Sen and Martha Nussbaum's contributions and criticism of them see: Wells, T. (Online) 'Sen's Capability Approach' *Internet Encyclopedia of Philosophy* http://www.iep.utm.edu/sen-cap/ Accessed 21 May 2018.

73 Carlson, W., Buskist, W. & Martin, G.N. (2000) *Psychology: The Science of Behaviour European Adaptation.* Harlow: Pearson.

74 Reddy, N.K. & Ajmera, S. (2015) *Ethics, Integrity and Aptitude.* New Delhi: McGraw Hill India.

75 Carlson, Buskist & Martin, *Psychology*, pp. 456–474.

76 Carlson, Buskist & Martin, *Psychology*, p. 456.

77 Nummenmaa, L. et al. (2014) 'Bodily Maps of Emotions' *PNAS* Vol. 111, No. 2 (January), http://www.pnas.org/content/111/2/646.full.pdf Accessed 21 May 2018.

78 Green Lantern (Online) *Emotional Spectrum* http://greenlantern.wikia.com/wiki/Emotional_Spectrum Accessed 21 May 2018.

79 Batson in Batson, C.D. et al (1997) 'Empathy and Attitudes: Can Feeling for a Member of a Stigmatized Group Improve Feelings Toward the Group?' *Journal of Personality and Social Psychology* Vol. 72, No. 1, p. 105; American Psychological Association http://www.socialemotiveneuroscience.org/pubs/batson_etal97.pdf Accessed 21 May 2018.

80   Bloom, P. (2014) 'Against Empathy' *Boston Review* 10 September http://bostonreview.net/forum/paul-bloom-against-empathy Accessed 21 May 2018; see also the responses to Bloom's article.
81   Lakoff, G. (2014) *The All New Don't Think of an Elephant*. White River Junction, VT: Chelsea Green, pp. 42–43.
82   Batson et al. 'Empathy and Attitudes: Can Feeling for a Member of a Stigmatized Group Improve Feelings Toward the Group?'.
83   Bloom, P. (2017) 'It's Ridiculous to Use Virtual Reality to Empathize With Refugees' *The Atlantic* 3 February https://www.theatlantic.com/technology/archive/2017/02/virtual-reality-wont-make-you-more-empathetic/515511/ Accessed 21 May 2018.
84   Silverman, A.M. (2015) 'The Perils of Playing Blind: Problems with Blindness Simulation and a Better Way to Teach About Blindness' *The Journal of Blindness Innovation and Research* Vol. 5, No. 2 https://nfb.org/images/nfb/publications/jbir/jbir15/jbir050201.html Accessed 21 May 2018.
85   Sylwester, R. (1994) 'How Emotions Affect Learning' *Educational Leadership* Vol. 52 (October), No. 2, pp. 60–65 http://www.ascd.org/publications/educational-leadership/oct94/vol52/num02/How-Emotions-Affect-Learning.aspx Accessed 21 May 2018.
86   Tomlinson, A. (2010) 'Arousal' in *A Dictionary of Sports Studies*. Oxford: Oxford University Press.
87   Carlson, Buskist & Martin, *Psychology*, pp. 565–583, 174; Grodsky, D. (2013) 'Stress as a Positive: Recent Research that Suggests it Has Benefits' *Ted Blog* 4 September http://blog.ted.com/could-stress-be-good-for-you-recent-research-that-suggests-it-has-benefits/ Accessed 21 May 2018.
88   Gramsci, A. (1971) *Selections from the Prison Notebooks of Antonio Gramsci* (edited and translated by Hoare, Q. & Nowell, S.G.), p. 175, but originally said by Romain Rolland.
89   Sherman, A. (1980). 'Two Views of Emotion in the Writings of Paulo Freire' *Educational Theory* Vol. 30, No. 1, pp. 35–38.
90   Darnton, A. (2008a) *GSR Behaviour Change Knowledge Review Reference Report: An Overview of Behaviour Change Models and Their Uses*. Government Social Research https://www.gov.uk/government/uploads/system/uploads/attachment_data/file/498065/Behaviour_change_reference_report_tcm6-9697.pdf Accessed 21 May 2018.
91   Boal, A. (2005) *Games for Actors and Non-Actors* (2nd edn). London: Routledge.
92   Loewenstein et al. in Darnton, A. (2008a) *GSR Behaviour Change Knowledge Review Reference Report: An Overview of Behaviour Change Models and their Uses*. Government Social Research, pp. 24–25 https://www.gov.uk/government/uploads/system/uploads/attachment_data/file/498065/Behaviour_change_reference_report_tcm6-9697.pdf Accessed 21 May 2018.
93   Duckworth, F. (2015) 'A One-Dimensional Scale to Compare Risks from Exposure to Various Hazards' *Safety and Reliability* Vol. 35, No. 1, pp. 5–18.
94   Caplan, P. (ed.) (2000) *Risk Revisited*. London: Pluto.

95 gmp26 (2009) '2845 Ways to Spin the Risk' *Understanding Uncertainty* https://understandinguncertainty.org/node/233 Accessed 21 May 2018; Brown, V. (2014) 'Risk Perception – it's Personal' *Environmental Health Perspectives*, Vol. 122, No. 10 (October), pp. 278–279 https://www.ncbi.nlm.nih.gov/pmc/articles/PMC4181910/pdf/ehp.122-A276.pdf Accessed 21 May 2018.

96 FRANK campaign in Darnton, A. (2008a) *GSR Behaviour Change Knowledge Review Reference Report: An Overview of Behaviour Change Models and their Uses.* Government Social Research https://www.gov.uk/government/uploads/system/uploads/attachment_data/file/498065/Behaviour_change_reference_report_tcm6-9697.pdf Accessed 21 May 2018.

97 Duckworth, 'A One-Dimensional Scale to Compare Risks from Exposure to Various Hazards'; National Institute for Health and Care Excellence (2017) *Guideline: Air Pollution: Outdoor Air Quality and Health* https://www.nice.org.uk/guidance/ng70# Accessed 21 May 2018.

98 Exworthy, T. & Gunn, J. (2003) 'Taking Another Tilt at High Secure Hospitals: The Tilt Report and Its Consequences for Secure Psychiatric Services. *The British Journal of Psychiatry* Vol. 182, No. 6 (June), pp. 469–471 http://bjp.rcpsych.org/content/182/6/469.full-text.pdf+html Accessed 21 May 2018; Doyle, M. (2013) 'High Secure Hospitals' in Towl, G. et al (eds) *Dictionary of Forensic Psychology.* Abingdon: Routledge.

99 Zuckerman, M. (2007) *Sensation Seeking and Risky Behavior.* London: American Psychological Association.

100 Gregory, R. (ed.) (2004) 'Consciousness' in *Oxford Companion to the Mind* (2nd edn). Oxford: Oxford University Press, see the entry by Roger Penrose and Carlson, Buskist & Martin, *Psychology*, p. 284.

101 Hickey, S. & Mohan, G (2004) *Participation: From Tyranny to Transformation? Exploring New Approaches to Participation in Development.* London: Zed, p. 230.

102 Popular in the 1960s and associated with the psychiatrists R.D Laing and David Cooper.

103 Buskist, W. & Martin, G. (2000) *Psychology: The Science of Behaviour European Adaptation.* Harlow: Pearson, pp. 278–310.

104 Bartky, S.L. (1990) *Femininity and Domination.* London: Routledge, p. 15. Confusingly, when Bourdieu uses the terms 'reproduction' and 'transformation' it is in a different way.

105 Boal, A. (2001) *Hamlet and the Baker's Son: My Life in Theatre and Politics.* London: Routledge, p. 185.

106 Boal, *Hamlet and the Baker's Son*, pp. 186–187.

107 Fanon, F. (2008) *Black Skin White Masks.* London: Penguin, pp. 3, 149.

108 Bartky, *Femininity and Domination.*

109 Douglas, M. (1978) *Implicit Meanings.* London: Routledge, pp. xiii and xviii.

110 Thiong'o, N. (1986) *Decolonising the Mind: The Politics of Language in African Literature.* London: Heinemann Educational; Hountondji, *African*

Philosophy; Nandy, A. (1983) *The Intimate Enemy: Loss and Recovery of Self under Colonialism*. Bombay: Oxford University Press.
111 Gramsci, *Selections from the Prison Notebooks of Antonio Gramsci*; Sassoon, A.S. (1987) *Gramsci's Politics*. London: Hutchinson; Femia, J. (1981) *Gramsci's Political Thought: Hegemony, Consciousness and the Revolutionary Process*. Oxford: Clarendon.
112 Freire, *Pedagogy of the Oppressed*; Freire, *Education*; Ledwith, *Community Development: A Critical Approach*; Ledwith, M. (2016) *Community Development in Action*. Bristol: Policy Press; hooks, b. (1994) *Teaching to Transgress: Education as the Practice of Freedom*. London: Routledge; hooks, b. (2003) *Teaching Community: A Pedagogy of Hope*. Abingdon: Routledge.
113 Bourdieu, P. & Wacquant, L. (1992) *An Invitation to Reflexive Sociology*. Cambridge: Polity Press, pp. 165–168.
114 Bourdieu, P. (1986) 'The Forms of Capital', in Richardson, J.G. (ed.) *Handbook of Theory and Research for the Sociology of Education*. New York: Greenwood Press; Bourdieu & Wacquant, *An Invitation to Reflexive Sociology*.
115 Hope, A. & Timmel, S. (1984–8) *Training for Transformation Books 1–4*. Harare: Mambo Press; Sheehy, M. (2001) *Partners Companion to Training for Transformation*. Dublin: Partners.
116 Freeden, M. (2003) *Ideology: A Very Short Introduction*. Oxford: Oxford University Press.
117 Gramsci, *Selections from the Prison Notebooks of Antonio Gramsci*; Sassoon, A.S. (1987) *Gramsci's Politics*. London: Hutchinson; Femia, *Gramsci's Political Thought*; Coogan, T. (2014) 'The "Hunchback" Across Time' in Bolt, D. (ed.) *Changing Social Attitudes Toward Disability: Perspectives from Historical, Cultural and Educational Studies*. Abingdon: Routledge, pp. 77–79.
118 Freeden, *Ideology: A Very Short Introduction*; Morejón, G. (2017) *Ideology Critique After Deleuze and Guattari* https://www.academia.edu/33491243/Ideology_Critique_after_Deleuze_and_Guattari?auto=download&campaign =weekly_digest Accessed 21 May 2018.
119 Foucault, M. (1985). *Discipline and Punish: The Birth of the Prison*. Harmondsworth: Penguin.
120 Bureau of Public Secrets (Online) *May 1968 Graffiti* http://www.bopsecrets.org/CF/graffiti.htm Accessed 21 May 2018.
121 Boal, A. & Epstein, S. (1990) 'The Cop in the Head: Three Hypotheses' The *Drama Review*, Vol. 34, No. 3 (Autumn), pp. 35–42 http://www.populareducation.co.za/sites/default/files/Boal%20cop%20in%20the%20head.pdf Accessed 21 May 2018.
122 Freire, *Cultural Action for Freedom*.
123 Freire, *Pedagogy of the Oppressed*, pp. 22–23.
124 Rich, A. (1986) *Blood, Bread and Poetry*. London: W.W. Norton, p. 205.
125 Hotep and Wiredu quoted in Dascal, M. (2009) 'Colonizing and decolonizing minds' in I. Kuçuradi (ed.) *Papers of the 2007 World Philosophy Day*. Ankara: Philosophical Society of Turkey, pp. 308–332 http://www.tau.ac.il/humanities/philos/dascal/papers/Colonizing%20and%20decolonizing%20minds.doc Accessed 21 May 2018.

126 Ledwith, *Community Development in Action*.
127 Freire, *Pedagogy of the Oppressed*, p. 121.
128 Bartky, *Femininity and Domination*, p. 21.
129 Paraphrased by Eric Hobsbawm in Hobsbawm, E. (2016) 'Pierre Bourdieu: Critical Sociology and Social History' *New Left Review* September–October, p. 40.
130 Flood, R.L. & Romm, N. (1996) *Diversity Management: Triple Loop Learning* Chichester: Wiley.

7 Conclusions and Getting Started …

1 Popper, K. (2013) *The Open Society and Its Enemies*. Oxford: Princeton University Press; Ignatieff, M. (ed.) (2003) *Human Rights as Politics and Idolatry*. Princeton, NJ: Princeton University Press http://pgil.pk/wp-content/uploads/2014/11/Human-Rights-politics1.pdf Accessed 22 May 2018.
2 Merkel, A. (2107) *Speech by Federal Chancellor Angela Merkel at the 'G20 Africa Partnership – Investing in a Common Future' Conference on 12 June 2017 in Berlin* https://www.bundeskanzlerin.de/Content/EN/Reden/2017/2017-06-12-bk-merkel-g20-africa-conference_en.html Accessed 22 May 2018.
3 Monbiot, G. (2017) 'It's Time to Tell a New Story' *Guardian Review* September 9 https://www.theguardian.com/books/2017/sep/09/george-monbiot-how-de-we-get-out-of-this-mess Accessed 22 May 2018.
4 Heller, P. (2013) *Challenges and Opportunities: Civil Society in a Globalizing World*. New York: UNDP http://hdr.undp.org/sites/default/files/hdro_1306_heller.pdf Accessed 22 May 2018; Doyal, L. & Gough, I. (1992) *A Theory of Human Need*. Basingstoke: Macmillan; Nussbaum, M. (2000) *Women and Human Development: The Capabilities Approach*. Cambridge: Cambridge University Press; Sen, A. (2001) *Development as Freedom*. Oxford: Oxford Paperbacks.
5 Raworth, K. (2017) *What on Earth is the Doughnut? …* https://www.kateraworth.com/doughnut/ Accessed 22 May 2018.
6 Ehrlich, P. & Raven, P. (1964) 'Butterflies and Plants: A Study in Coevolution' *Evolution* Vol. 18, No. 4, pp. 586–608 http://www.esf.edu/efb/parry/Insect%20Ecology%20Reading/Ehrlich_Raven_1964.pdf Accessed 22 May 2018.
7 Friedrich Engels wrote '*The essential difference between human and animal society is that animals are at most gatherers whilst men are producers. This single but cardinal distinction alone makes it impossible simply to transfer the laws of animal societies to human societies*': Letter from Engels to *Lavrov* 12 November 1875 https://www.marxists.org/archive/marx/works/1875/letters/75_11_12.htm Accessed 22 May 2018.
8 OED (Online) 'convolution, n.'. Oxford University Press. March 2018. http://www.oed.com/view/Entry/40879?redirectedFrom=convolution Accessed 22 May 2018.

9   Odum, E.P. (1997) *Ecology: A Bridge Between Science and Society.* Sunderland, MA: Sinauer Associates.
10 Odum, H.T. (1971) *Environment, Power, and Society.* Hoboken, NJ: Wiley & Sons; Rosnay de, J. (2004) *The Macroscope* https://www.appreciatingsystems.com/wp-content/uploads/2011/05/The-Macroscope.pdf Accessed 22 May 2018. The term was used earlier by the systems ecologist Howard T. Odum in 1971.
11 Archer, M. (2003) *Structure, Agency and the Internal Conversation* (p. 358). Cambridge: Cambridge University Press.
12 Colonial Office (1958) *A Handbook Prepared by a Study Conference on Community Development Held at Hartwell House, Aylesbury, Buckinghamshire, September 1957.* London: HMSO.
13 '*By failing to prepare, you are preparing to fail*' is often attributed to Benjamin Franklin but there is no evidence that he ever said this: http://franklinpapers.org/franklin//framedVolumes.jsp Accessed 22 May 2018; Dwight Eisenhower did not claim that his mantra that '*Plans are worthless, but planning is everything*' was original: Eisenhower, D. (1957) *Remarks at the National Defense Executive Reserve Conference.* 14 November http://www.presidency.ucsb.edu/ws/?pid=10951 Accessed 22 May 2018.

Index

Note: Page numbers with *f* indicate figures and those with *t* indicate tables.

ABCD (asset-based community development), 77
ABC model, 183–84
   Affective element, 183
   Behavioural intention, 183–84
   Cognitive element, 184
abilities, learning, 182–83
Aboriginal Australians, 19, 39
Abrahamic religions, 20, 61, 85, 105–6
Abrahamic traditions, 106
Accident and Emergency Department in London, 134
accommodation, 113
Action Research, 178, 210
action rule, 97
activism, 7, 100, 102
activists, 1–2
   armed [sic] chair, 100
   challenge for, 198
   on difference between hope and optimism, 97
   Fanon, 162
   Freire, 6
   implications for practice, 45
   justice and, 140
   nimbies as, 92–93
   non-conformity and, 99
   Parkin, 99
   populist movements and, 120
   power of negative and positive feelings identified by, 98
   religion and collective action and, 104
   revolutions and, 119, 120, 123
   roots and routes twisted by, 3–4
   social marginalisation experienced by, 113
   spontaneity and, 99–100
   state opposed by, 115
   strategies for collective development and, 126
   theory and, 204
   violence used by, 81
activities, in collective action, 127
actors, in collective action, 86–87
adhesion, 37, 196
Affective element in ABC model, 183
affective measures, 101
African Americans, 38–39, 156
African National Congress Freedom Charter, 136
Africa Strategy, 63
age
   discrimination based on, 146–47
   equality and, 128, 144, 150
   human rights and, 146–47
   identity and, 68
   skills and ability and, 183
   values and, 26
agency, 43, 85, 86–87
Al-Hazen, 175
Al-Hyatham, 175
alienation, 122
Alinsky, Saul, 72, 98
Allah, 106
almsgiving. *See* charity
American Women's movement, 102
ancestry, 18
Angelou, Maya, 156
Anglicans, 48
Animation Rurale, 51
anthropology
   to analyse institutions, 43
   culture and, 28, 30

anthropology (*continued*)
    functionalist explanations of beliefs and behaviour, 123
    identity and, 24–25, 26
    Khaldun and, 15, 16
Apartheid South Africa, 18
aptitudes, 182
Arabisation, 20
Archer, Margaret, 86–87
Aristotle, 31, 53–54, 108, 139, 175, 177
artificial intelligence, 74
as a word, meanings of, 46
Asaybiyyah, 15
asexual, 160
aspirations, 97
asset-based community development (ABCD), 68–69, 77
assimilationist, 120
assistencialise, 159
attitudes, learning, 183–84
attributes, 183
at war with each other, 161–62
autonomy
    autonomous action, 99–100
    citizenship and, 145
    collective action and, 128, 207
    development strategies and, 75
    Gandhi's idea of *Swaraj* and, 52, 70, 106
    learning for, 168, 171*t*
    needs and, 133, 137*t*
    oppression and, 163
    participation in political philosophy and, 108
    pursuit of, 47
    rights and, 138
    sovereignty and, 116
    spontaneity and, 100

Bachrach, Peter, 152
Bangladesh, 19, 39, 75
banking concept, 167
Barnett, Samuel and Henrietta, 49
Barrett, Christopher, 55–56
Bartky, Lee, 191, 192, 197
Batson, Daniel, 185
Batten, T. R. (Reg), 51
Becker, Gary, 90–91, 93
behavioural economics, 43, 86, 91

Behavioural intention in ABC model, 183–84
Belgium, 76
Belsky, Jay, 34–35
Bennett, Alan, 119
Bentham, Jeremy, 130, 195
Berlin Wall, 71, 114
Berthoud, Gérald, 90
Beveridge, William, 57
big data, 74
Big Mac Index, 56
biological evolution, 66–67, 88
Black, use of term, 39
blood and soil, 13, 20
Bloom, Paul, 185
Boal, Augusto, 191
Boggs, Carl, 110
Bookchin, Murray, 100, 108
Booth, Charles, 49
bottom-up strategy, 10, 62, 68, 74, 75, 83, 207
Bourdieu, Pierre, 153, 191–93, 194, 197
BRAC, 75
Bradshaw, Jonathan, 134
Brayne, F. L., 52
BRICS, 76
Brinton, Crane, 122
British
    Army, 64, 72
    colonialism, 50–51, 52, 60
    Colonial Office, 50, 51, 211
    Colonial Office booklet, 211
    community development and, 48, 50–51
    Empire, 63, 157
    equality legislation, 133–34
    human rights and, 136
    identity, 39
    rule in India, 52
    social development and, 51
    values, 26–27
British Community Development Projects (CDPs), 78
Brown Girl in the Ring, 180
Brundtland Commission, 53, 61, 71
Buber, Martin, 106
Buddhism, 61, 105, 131
buen vivir concept, 61–62
Bulwer-Lytton, Edward, 119

Cahill, Michael, 134
Cahn, Edgar, 96
Cantor's Theorem, 41
capability, 183
capacities, 182
capacity building, 77, 167
capitalism, 68
casework, 3, 48, 49
Castells, M., 24
Catholics, 48, 49, 157
causation, 124
Causes of the English Revolution (Stone), 121
CDPs (British Community Development Projects), 78
charity, 105
  assessment of individual needs for, 48
  in economies without money, 95
  history of, 3
  Maimonides's levels of, 106
  religious justification for giving, 105
  self-help and, encouraging, 49
  Singer's supererogatory and, 107
Charity Organisation Society, 48, 49
Chartists movement, 104
Ché (Guevara) syndrome, 191
child abuse, 34–35
Child Sexual Exploitation in Gangs and Groups (report), 34
China, 57, 70, 76, 77
Christians
  collective action and, 85, 104, 105, 107, 108
  cultural and sustainable development and, 60, 61
  difference and, 34
  human rights and, 131
  identity and, 25
  interaction of different social groups and, 49
  language and, 14
  learning and, 191
  metaphors of development and, 66, 67
  territory and, 20
Christian Socialism, 49
chronic risk, 188
circular economy, 91

citizen. *See also* citizenship
  in community-led local development, 76
  concept of, 145
  experiential knowledge and, 177
  participation in political philosophy, 108, 109
  propositional knowledge and, 173
  propositions initiated by, 117
citizen journalism, 58, 109, 193
citizen science, 193
citizenship, 39. *See also* citizen
  ancestry and, 18
  collective action and, 117
  concept of citizen and, 145
  emancipation and, 165t
  equality and, 145
  marginalisation and, 156
  participation in social and community development and, 110
  social groups and, 39
  values and, 26–27
Citizens' Juries, 109
civil society
  organisations, 39, 43, 59, 63, 70, 110, 116, 117–18, 157
  participation in, 113–15
  strengthening, 59
Clark, Howard, 113
coercion, 113
co-evolution, 208
Cognitive element in ABC model, 184
cognitive knowledge. *See* propositional knowledge
cognitive measures, 101
cohesion, 36–37
collective action, 84–127
  activities, 127
  actors and, 86–87
  agency and, 86–87
  conclusions, 207–8
  control and, 104–5
  economics and, 89–96
    commons, 93
    cooperation and self-interest, 92–93
    crowds, wisdom of, 94
    economies without money, 94–96

collective action (*continued*)
    game theory, 93–94
    markets, 89–91
    qualified reasoning, 91–92
  forms of, 105–7
  implication for practice, 126
  introduction, 84
  levels of
    ideological, 85, 104, 110
    individual, 86–87, 111
    institutional, 88–125, 111–12, 112*f*
    interpersonal, 88–125, 111
  multi-disciplinary perspectives on, 85–86
  nature and, 88–89
  participation
    emancipatory, agenda for, 117–18
    in political philosophy, 108–10
    professionals and, 113
    in social and community development, 110–13
  policy studies, 124–25
  political and social processes in, relationship between, 116–17
  political movements, 118–24
    economic and social conditions, 123–24
    populist movements, 119–21
    revolutions, 119–23
    triggers, catalysts, inertia, 118–19
  political philosophy and, 107–17
    participation in, 108–10
    prefigurative politics, 110
    representation, 107–8
    state and civil society, 113–15
  psychology and, 97–100
  reasons for, 86–87
  religion and, 104
  social psychology and, 100–104
  sovereignty, right to self-determination and, 115–16
  summary and conclusion, 125
  theology and, 104–7
Colonial Development Officers, 3
Colonial Office, 50, 51, 211
common fate, sense of, 101
commons, in collective action, 93
Communist bloc, 71
community. *See also* community development
  activities, 45
  association leading to, types of, 17
  conclusions, 205–6
  dimensions of, 17–21
    ancestry, 18
    place or territory, 18–21
  ethical, overlapping domains of, 41*f*
  implications for practice, 45
  interests, 21–36
    culture, 28–30
    diversity, 35–36
    harmful or unethical communities, 34–35
    hospitality and exchange, 31–33
    identity, 23–26
    language, 30–31
    networks and meshworks, 28
    social capital, 27
    values, 26–27
  introduction, 13
  language and, 14–15
  society differentiated from, 13–14
  study of, 16–17
Community Action model, 72
community development
  conclusions, 203–14
    collective action, 207–8
    development, 206–7
    doing it right, 211–14
    emancipation, 209
    equality, 209
    history, 204
    holding societies and communities together, 205–6
    learning together, 209–11
    personal reflection, 203
    society and community, 205–6
    theory, 203–4
  geography and culture in, 9
  history of, 3–5
  levels of, 42–45
    ideological, 43
    illustrated, 44*f*
    individual, 42–43
    institutional, 43
    interpersonal, 43
    issues at different levels, 44–45, 44*f*
  participation in, 110–13
  theory of, 5–8

INDEX

Community Development Projects (CDPs), 78, 78*t*
Community Driven Development (CDD), 76
community education, 77
Community instead of Society (slogan), 14
Community Led Local Development, 76
Community Organising model, 72
comparative need, 134
competence, 183
Comte, Auguste, 16
conflict, 37–38, 41–42, 80
conflict/dissensus model, 78*t*, 79–80
conflict transformation, 80
Confucian teaching, 131
Congested Districts policy, 64
conscientisation, 197
consciousness, 190–97
  anger and confrontation, 196
  Freire's forms of, 195–96
  learning, 190–97
  levels of
    ideological, 194–95
    individual, 192
    institutional, 192–94
    interpersonal, 192
  liberating, 197
  open, 197
  philosophy of, 191
  political economy and, 191–92
  psychology of, 190
  rebellion and, 196
  reforming, 197
  reforming and, 197
  sociology and, 191–92
  theology of, 191
  transforming, 197
consensus model, 78, 78*t*, 79
consociational political structures, 117
consociational structures, 39, 79, 116, 117
constructivism, 174
consultation, 106
consumer-managed cooperatives, 58
converse rights, 136, 138
conversion, 113
conviviality, 96
convolution, 208

cooperation, in collective action, 92–93
co-production, 58, 93, 96, 118, 173, 208
Cornwall, Andrea, 111
correlative duties, 136, 138
counterhegemonic movements, 114
counter-hegemony, 137*t*
Creative Commons licensing, 93
critical thinking
  characteristics of, 171*t*
  learning for, 170
Crosland, Anthony, 109
crowdfunding, 58, 74, 90
crowds in collective action, wisdom of, 94
cultural appropriation, 160–61
cultural imperialism, 157
culturalism, 29
cultural level. *See* ideological level
culture
  anthropology and, 28, 30
  in community development, 9
  community interests and, 28–30
  cultural and sustainable development, 60–62
    Brundtland Commission, 61
    buen vivir concept, 61–62
    Summit declaration, 61
    UNESCO and, 60–61
  in ethical communities, 28–30
  geography and, 9
  identity and, 29, 30, 61
  interests and, 28–30
  introduction, 9
  metaphor of development, 69–70
  population and, 70
  religion and, 69–70, 160
  of silence, powerlessness and, 157

Dante, 98
Darwin, Charles, 66–67, 88
declarative knowledge. *See* propositional knowledge
decolonisation, 51, 59
deficits, 23, 69, 133, 160
degrowth, 55, 58, 62
dehumanisation, 160
Deism, 85
demand-responsiveness, 76

dematerialization of economies, 62
democracy, protective argument for, 116
denial of rights, 135
Department for Communities, 53
Department for Social Development, 53
deprivation, sense of, 101
deprivation indexes, 64
DeRienzo, Harold, 79
Derrida, Jacques, 24–25, 31–32, 33, 34, 35
development, 46–83
  activities, 83
  for autonomy, 47
  community, 48–52
    assessment of individual needs, 48, 49
    in British colonies, 50–51
    encouraging self-help, 49
    French Empire, 51
    Indian subcontinent, 51–52
    interaction of different social groups, 49
    mutual aid, 49
    North American influences, 51
    social investigation tradition, 49
    solidarity, 49
    Swaraj and *Swadeshi*, 52
  conclusions, 82–83, 206–7
  cultural and sustainable, 60–62
    Brundtland Commission, 61
    buen vivir concept, 61–62
    Summit declaration, 61
    UNESCO and, 60–61
  differences, 79
  economic, 54–58
    measuring, 55–56
    models, 56–58
  for freedom, 47
  for happiness, 47
  historical overview of, 46
  of humans, 47–48
  implications for practice, 83
  introduction, 46
  issues, overarching, 62–66
    equality, 64–65
    hybrid and new measures, 63–64
    infrastructural and institutional focus, 65–66
    objectivity and subjectivity, 65
    organisation of development, 62–63
    population groups or areas, focus on specific, 64
  levels of, 42–45, 48, 48*f*
    illustrated, 44*f*
    individual, 42–43
    institutional, 43
    interpersonal, 43
    issues at different levels, 44–45, 44*f*
  metaphors of, 66–74
    brain, flux and transformation, 73–74
    culture, 69–70
    machine, 68–69
    organism, 66–68
    political system, 71–73
    prison, 70–71
  political and civic, 59
    good governance, 59
    humanitarian interventions, 59
    measuring, 59
    strengthening civil society, 59
  social, 52–54
    goals of, 54
    measuring, 53–54
  Specht's tactics for social change, 77–78, 78*t*
    conflict/dissensus model, 79–80
    consensus model, 78, 79
    pluralist/difference model, 79
    violence/insurrection model, 80–82
  strategies, 75–77
    asset-based community development, 77
    capacity building, 77
    community-driven development, 76
    community-led local development, 76
    incentives, 77
    vertical and horizontal, 75–76
development bonds, 91
'Development from Below,' 75
Dewey, John, 6, 178, 194
dimensions of community, 17–21

ancestry, 18
  place or territory, 18–21
disability
  collective action and, 107
  equality and, 146
  human rights and, 136
  identity and, 24, 25, 38
  learning for emancipation and, 169
  levels of, 44
  values and, 26
discontent, 98
disincentives, to reduce risk, 188
disintegration, 113
Disraeli, Benjamin, 48
diversity, community interests and, 35–36
Divine Revelation, 191
division of labor, 36
doing it right, 211–14
Doise, Willem, 86
domains of development, 48, 48f
  issues relevant to, 62–66
    equality, 64–65
    focus on specific population groups or areas, 64
    hybrid and new measures, 63–64
    infrastructural and institutional focus, 65–66
    objectivity and subjectivity, 65
    organisation of development, 62–63
  linked to equality and emancipation, 163–64, 164, 165t
Dominelli, Lena, 164
Dominions, 59
Doughnut Economics, 58
Douglass, Frederick, 154
Douglass, Mary, 154
Dowling, Gerard, 126
Doyal, Len, 133
Dual Mandate, 50
Dunbar, Robin, 89
Duncan, Lauren, 101–3, 102f
Duncan's model, 101–3, 102f
Durkheim, Emile, 35–36, 37, 192, 205–6
Duty to Protect, 59

East Africa, 50
economic conditions
  economies without money, 94–96
  political movements and, 123–24
economic development, 54–58
  inequalities in, 56, 57
  measuring, 55–56
  models, 56–58
economics
  activism and, 102
  behavioural, 43, 86, 91
  collective action and, 89–96
    commons, 93
    cooperation and self-interest, 92–93
    crowds, wisdom of, 94
    economies without money, 94–96
    game theory, 93–94
    markets, 89–91
    political movements, 123–24
    psychologists' perspectives on, 86
    qualified reasoning, 91–92
  consciousness and, 191–92
  free markets, 53
  interpersonal level of relationships and, 43, 199
  Khaldun and, 15, 16
  market-based economies, 57–58
  non-monetised transactions, 57–58
  Ostrom and, 19, 95
  Raworth's Doughnut Economics, 58
education, 3, 50–51
Education for All (UNESCO), 54
Education for All programme (UNESCO), 54
efficacy, 101
Egypt, 76
Einstein, Albert, 174
Ekman, Paul, 184
Eliot, T. S., 5, 68
elite rule, 38
emancipation, 9, 11
  activities, 165
  characteristics of, 171t
  conclusions, 209
  democracy and, 116–17
  introduction, 128–29
  learning for, 169, 171t
  levels of, 137t, 165t
  power and, 155

emancipatory participation, agenda for, 117–18
emergent property, 87
emotions, learning, 184–87
　basic, Ekman's, 184–85
　drawing out of/making sense of, 187
　empathy and, 185–86
　non-basic, 185
　reason and, 186
empathy, 185–86
empowerment
　collective action and, 128
　described, 154
　emancipation and, 152, 154–55
　engagement by, 72
　problems with, 154–55, 209
enablements, 86
Engels, Friedrich, 67
English Magna Carta of 1215, 107–8
environmental sustainability, 54, 115, 130
equality, 142–52
　arguments for, 144–45
　conclusions, 163–64, 209
　defined, 142–44
　distinctions of, 146–49
　implications for practice, 163–64
　introduction, 128–29
　justice and, 138–41
　levels of
　　ideological, 136, 137t, 138, 151–52, 164
　　individual, 132–34, 137t, 149–50, 164
　　institutional, 135, 137t, 150–51, 164
　　interpersonal, 134, 137t, 150, 164
　needs and, 132–34
　place and time in relation to, 145–46
Equality Act, 146
equality of consideration, 143
equality of process, 143
equilibria, in game theory, 94
Esposito, Roberto, 17, 31–32
espoused theory, 8
essentialising 'us,' 45
essentialism, 29, 40, 147, 171t
ethical communities, domains of, 41f

ancestry, 18
culture, 28–30
identity, 23–26
interests, 21–23
language, 30–31
place, 18–21
values, 26–27
ethnic density, 21
ethnicity. *See* race
ethnocracies, 117
eugenics, 32
exchange, 31–33
excluding 'them,' 45
exo, 42
exosystem in family, 35
experiential knowledge, 174, 177–79
experimenter expectancy effect, 176
exploitation, 156
expressed need, 134
expressive knowledge, 179–80
expropriation, 160–61

face-to-face relationships, 13–14, 33
faith organisations, 89, 114
fake news, 100
Fanon, Frantz, 25, 38, 71, 81, 82, 162, 191, 192, 196
felt need, 134
feudalism, 68
First World, 71
flux and transformation, 73, 74
focus groups, 74
food sovereignty, 116
foreign direct investment (FDI), 76
Foucault, Michel, 71, 153, 191–92, 195
Four I's of Oppression, 156
　ideological, 156, 157–58, 164, 165t
　individual, 162–63, 164
　institutional, 158–59, 164
　interpersonal, 159–62, 164
four-level models, 42–45, 55–56, 86.
　　See also multi-level approach
framing, 91, 125, 209
Frank, Andre Gunder, 70
Franklin, Benjamin, 117, 177
Fraser, Nancy, 139
freecycling, 58
freedom
　to act at individual level, 85

of choice, 55, 87
emancipation and, 155
of expression *versus* freedom from fear, 80
Freire's forms of consciousness and, 196, 197
learning for, 168, 170
participation as threat to, 109
pursuit of, 47
religions that promote, 131
Sen's concept of development as, 54, 170
top-down approaches and, 138
UN Declaration of Human Rights and, 47
free market, 53
free will and determinism, 85
Freire, Nita, 159
Freire, Paulo, 6–7, 71, 100, 170, 180, 186, 194–97
French Empire, 51
Freud, Sigmund, 24, 33–34, 35, 161
Fromm, Erich, 100
functionalism, 85

Galbraith, John Kenneth, 57
game theory, in collective action, 93–94
Gamson, William, 102
Gandhi, 4–5, 52
gangs, 34
Gapminder World, 63
Gaventa, J., 111–12, 112*f*
Gaventa's power cube, 111–12, 112*f*
Gemeinde, 15
Gemeinschaft, 14
gender
 collective action and, 98, 99, 101, 111
 conflict and, 41, 42
 differences, 99
 discrimination based on, 101, 142, 144, 146, 147, 158
 empowerment and, 154
 equality, 54, 128, 142, 143, 146
 Equality Act and, 146
 equality and, 150
 human rights and, 132, 136, 146
 identity and, 25, 115
 justice and, 139
 knowledge and, 176
 learning for emancipation and, 169
 oppression and, 54
 power and, 153
 reassignment, 146
 skills and abilities and, 183
 South African Constitution and, 146
 UNDHR distinctions and, 146, 147
 values and, 26
geography, culture and, 9
German Conservative nationalists, 13, 20
Gesellschaft, 14
Gibson-Graham, J. K., 95
gig economy, 90
Global North, 8, 9, 28, 68, 71, 76, 174, 181
Global South, 28, 70, 71, 73, 141, 174, 181
goal-based development, 63
Goldstone, Jack, 119, 120, 122
good governance, 59
Gough, Ian, 133
Grameen Bank, 75
Gramsci, Antonio, 6, 70, 71, 80, 98, 114, 157–58, 186, 191, 192–93, 194
Greece, 76
Green Revolution, 68
gross domestic product (GDP), 55–56
group consciousness, 101–2, 102*f*
Gudynas, Eduardo, 61–62
Guevara, Che, 87
Guevara (Ché) syndrome, 191
Guiding Principles (International Association for Community Development), 115

habitual risk, 188
habitus, 85, 153, 193
Hailey, Lord, 50
Hammurabi Code, 130–31
happiness
 human rights and, 131
 learning for, 184
 pursuit of, 47
 suffering and, 162
Harari, Yuval Noah, 89

Harvard Programme on Negotiation, 181
Harvey, David, 132–33
Hatch, Spencer, 52
Hawthorne effect, 176
healthy degrowth, 55
Hegel, Georg, 114
hegemony, 70, 104, 157–58, 192–93, 209
Held, David, 108, 109, 116–17
Heller, Patrick, 117–18
Heraclitus, 73, 74
Heron, John, 172
Hicks, Ursula, 75
hierarchy of needs, 132
hierarchy of oppression, 161
Hinduism, 30, 61, 106, 131, 151
historical institutionalism, 4
history of social and community development
  conclusions, 204
  introduction, 3–5
Hobbes, Thomas, 14, 113–14, 138
Hobhouse, Leonard, 52, 53
Hogg, M., 103
holding expectations of similarity, 161
Holmes, Kelly, 179–80
homogenising, 30, 40–41, 45, 160, 174
hooks, bell, 8
hope, 97
horizontal development strategy, 75–76
horizontal expression, 161
horizontal human rights, 136–37, 138
horizontal identities, 25–26
horizontal inequalities, 118, 148
horizontal/lateral conflicts, 80
horizontal networks, 28
horse and sparrow theory, 57
hospitality and exchange, 31–33
Human Development Index (HDI), 53
Human Development Reports, 53
humanitarian interventions, 59
human rights, 129–41
  activities, 165
  arguments for, 130–32
  causes of crime and, theories about, 141
  divided into generations, 129–30
  history of, 129
  as ideology, 136, 138
  as individual aspirations, 132
  justice and, 138–41
  levels of
    ideological, 136, 137t, 138
    individual, 132–34, 137t
    institutional, 135, 137t
    interpersonal, 134, 137t
  to private property, 130
Hussein, Saddam, 20
hybridity, 37
hybrid measures, 63–64
hyperbolic discounting, 91

identity
  claim to territory and, 19, 20
  collective action and, 91–92, 100–102
  communities based on, 23–26
  conflict and, 38
  culture and, 29, 30, 61
  in dimensions of communities, 17
  in Duncan's model of the relationship, 101, 102f
  in history, 4
  humanitarian interventions and, 59
  imposed and self-identified, 38–39
  individual and group, linking, 24–25
  issue-based programs of development and, 63
  language and, 30
  multiple and contradictory, 25
  narcissism of minorities and, 25
  nationalism and, 25
  personal and social, distinguishing between, 23
  resource mobilisation theory and, 91–92
  revolution and, 68
  self-identification, 23–24, 39
  social capital and, 27
  social psychology and, 100–101
  Solomon's concepts of vertical and horizontal, 25–26
  in study of communities, 16
  values and, 26
  violence and, 81
ideological level, 9–10, 43

collective rights, 85, 93, 104, 110, 119, 124, 125, 126
consciousness, 194–95
cultural rights, 60
development goals, 65–66
equality, 136, 137t, 138, 151–52, 164
in Four I's of Oppression, 156
human rights, 47, 48f, 136, 137t, 138
inequalities, 151–52, 164, 165t
issues, 44f
learning, 174, 181, 194–95, 200, 200–201
oppression, 156, 157–58, 164, 165t
idle chatter, 7
Ife, Jim, 113, 130
Ignatieff, Michael, 32, 131–132
Illich, Ivan, 96, 133
immigration policies, 32
incapable, 160
Indian subcontinent, 51–52
indifference, 98
indirect rule, 3, 51
Indirect Rule, 51
individual level, 9, 42–43
　collective action, 88, 126
　consciousness, 192
　cultural rights, 60
　equality, 132–34, 137t, 149–50, 164
　in Four I's of Oppression, 156
　freedom to act, 85
　human rights, 47, 48f, 132–34, 137t
　inequalities, 149, 164, 198
　issues, 42–43, 44f
　learning, 198–99
　oppression, 162–63, 164
　revolutions, 68
individual needs, 48–49
industrialisation, 52, 56–57
Industrial Revolution, 67
inequalities. *See also* equality
　arguments for, 144–45
　buen vivir concept and, 62
　collective action and, 11, 91, 111, 118
　conceptions of, as applied to social groups, 147–48
　to create incentives to generate wealth, 142

　in economic development, 56, 57
　horizontal, 118, 148
　ideologies used to justify, 158
　of interest within communities, 22
　intersectionality and, 25
　justice and, 141
　knowledge transfer and, 176
　levels of
　　ideological, 151–52, 164, 165t
　　individual, 149, 164, 198
　　institutional, 150–51, 164
　　interpersonal, 150–51, 164
　markets and, 91
　of outcomes, 143, 144
　place and time in relation to, 145–46
　in social groups, 111, 143, 150, 160
　structural, social injustices and, 197
　views of morality used to justify, 147
inequality of outcome, 143
inertia, 68, 91, 98, 118–19
inertia, indifference leading to, 98
infantilisation, 159
inferiority, 69, 147, 149
Inferno (Dante), 98
informal education, 77
information sharing, 58
infrastructural level. *See* ideological level
inside-out strategy, 10, 74, 208
institutional development, 63
institutional level, 9, 43
　consciousness, 192–94
　development goals, 65–66
　emancipation, 158–59, 164
　equality, 135, 137t, 150–51, 158–59, 164
　in Four I's of Oppression, 156
　freedom to act, 88
　human rights, 47, 48f, 135, 137t
　inequalities, 150–51, 164
　issues, 44f
　learning, 200
　oppression, 158–59, 164
institutional racism, 158
integration, 168, 171t, 206
intellectuals, 6, 157, 174, 193
interdisciplinary collaboration and insights, 176–77

interests, 21–36
  culture, 28–30
  diversity, 35–36
  hospitality and exchange, 31–33
  identity, 23–26
  language, 30–31
  networks and meshworks, 28
  social capital, 27
  values, 26–27
internal conversation, 86
internalised oppression, 71, 137t, 148, 163, 195
International Association for Community Development, 9, 115, 128
International Covenant on Economic, Social and Cultural Rights, 47–48, 55
International Monetary Fund, 59, 70, 145
interpersonal level, 9, 43
  collective action, 111
  consciousness, 192
  equality, 134, 137t, 150, 164
  in Four I's of Oppression, 156
  freedom to act, 88
  human rights, 47, 48f, 134, 137t
  inequalities, 150–51, 164
  issues, 44f
  learning, 199–200
  oppression, 159–62, 164
  revolutions, 68
intersectionality, 25, 39, 137t, 161
intervention-based development, 63
introduction, 1–12
  activities, 12
  argument of book, 11
  geography and culture, 9
  history, 3–5
  structure of book, 11
  style of book, 10–11
  themes of book, 9–10
  theory, 5–8
invisibilisation, 159
Ireland, 64
Islam
  art in expressive knowledge and, 179
  collective action and, 105–6
  human rights and, 131
  One Nation and, 79
  territory and, 20
'-isms,' 158
issue-based development, 63

Jainists, 106
Jeanes Fund, 51
Jewish Board of Guardians, 49
Jews
  collective action and, 85, 105, 106, 108
  community development and, 48
  human rights and, 131
  language and, 14
  sustainable development and, 61
  territory and, 20
Johnston, Rennie, 100
Judaism, 20, 105–6, 131
Judeo-Christian tradition, 9, 157, 204
justice, 138–41
  activities, 165
  causes of crime, theories of, 141
  crime and law associated with, 139
  defined, 138–39
  levels of, 137t
  outcomes, 139
  religious, 105–6
  theories of, 139–41
    reconciliation or rapprochement, 140
    reductivism, 140
    restorative justice, 137t, 140–41
    retribution, 137t, 139
    transitional justice, 137t, 140, 211
    vigilante action, 141
  views on, 139

Kaltwasser, Cristobal Rovira, 124
Kennedy, John F., 57
Kersting, Norbert, 112, 112f
Kersting's model, 112, 112f
Keynes, John Maynard, 57
Khaldun, Ibn, 15–16, 66, 113–14
knowledge, 172–82
  combining, 181–82
  experiential, 174, 177–79
  expressive, 179–80

interdisciplinary collaboration and insights, 176–77
literacy campaign, 180
open source, 176
practical or procedural, 180
propositional, 172–77, 180, 181–82, 198
qualitative, 174
quantitative, 174
re-presenting, 7
scientific method, 175–76
transfer, 176
known unknowns, 5–6
Kropotkin, Peter, 49, 88, 108

Labour Party movement, 104
Lakoff, George, 42–43, 185
language, 14–15, 30–31
Laqueur, Walter, 7
Laubach, Frank, 51
learning, 166–202
  activities, 201–2
  conclusions, 198–201, 209–11
  implications for practice, 198–201
  introduction, 166–67
  levels of
    ideological, 200
    individual, 198–99
    institutional, 200
    interpersonal, 199–200
  models of, 167–70
    characteristics of, 171t
    emancipation, 169
    practice, 169–70
    reflexive or critical thinking, 170
    speculation, 168–69
  motivation for, as synthesis, 170, 172f
  what people learn, 172–97
    attitudes, 183–84
    consciousness, 190–97
    emotions, 184–87
    knowledge, 172–82
    risk and sensation seeking, 187–90
    skills and abilities, 182–83
Lederach, John Paul, 23, 78
Lenin, Vladimir, 99–100
less capable, 160
Lewin, Kurt, 7, 178, 186

Lewis, Arthur, 56–57
liberating consciousness, 197
liberation
  animation rurale and, 51
  consciousness and, 196, 197
  emancipation and, 137t, 155, 171t
  intersectionality and, 161
  learning for, 171t
  revolution and, 196
Liberté Sans Frontières, 73
life experiences, 101
Life in the UK test, 26, 27
linear progress, 68
Linguistics, 15, 17
Lister, Ruth, 111
literacy campaign, 180
local action groups, 76
Local and Community Driven Development (LCDD), 65, 76
Local Exchange Trading Systems (LETS), 58
Locke, John, 21, 114
Luddites movement, 104
Lugard, Frederick, 50
Lukes, Steven, 153

machine metaphor, 68–69
Macpherson, C. B., 109
macro, 42. *See also* institutional level
macroscope, 208
macroscopic consequences, 208
macrosystem in family, 35
Maimonides, 106
Mandates, 59
Manley, Norman, 51
Manning, Henry, 49
Marcuse, Herbert, 24, 81, 100
marginalisation, 113, 137t, 156–57, 159
marital status, discrimination based on, 146
market-based economies, 57–58
markets, in collective action, 89–91
Marx, Karl, 22, 67, 68, 87, 108, 114, 115, 117, 123, 157, 158, 191, 194
Maslow, Abraham, 132
mass education, 3, 50–51
material well-being, 55, 57, 62, 169

maternal mortality, 54
mechanical solidarity, 37, 205–6
Médecins Sans Frontières, 73
medicalisation, 159–60
memes, 4
meshworks, 28
meso, 42. *See also* institutional level
meta, 42. *See also* ideological level
metamorphosis, 208
metaphors of development, 66–74
  brain, flux and transformation, 73–74
  culture, 69–70
  machine, 68–69
  organism, 66–68
  political system, 71–73
  prison, 70–71
Metropolitan France, 51
mezzo, 42
micro, 42. *See also* interpersonal level
microeconomics, 43
micro mobilisation, 102
microsociology, 43
microsystem in family, 35
Midgley, James, 53
Mill, John Stuart, 91, 130
Millennium Development Goals, 54
millet system, 116
Ministry of Development, 53
misappropriation, 161
Missions, 69
Mitchell, David, 95
mitzvah, 105
Mobile Propaganda Unit, 50
mobilisation, 113
modernisation, 56–57, 61
monolingualism, 31
Montagu, Ashley, 18–19
moralistic rule, 97
Morgan, Gareth, 66, 73, 85
motivation, 31
Moxley, Russ, 155
Mudde, Cas, 124
Mugabe Complex, 23
multi-level approach, 42–45, 48, 48*f*
  to equality
    ideological, 136, 137*t*, 138, 151–52, 164
    individual, 132–34, 137*t*, 149–50, 164
    institutional, 135, 137*t*, 150–51, 164
    interpersonal, 134, 137*t*, 150, 164
  to human rights
    ideological, 136, 137*t*, 138
    individual, 132–34, 137*t*
    institutional, 135, 137*t*
    interpersonal, 134, 137*t*
  illustrated, 44*f*
  individual, 42–43
  to inequalities
    ideological, 151–52, 164, 165*t*
    individual, 149, 164, 198
    institutional, 150–51, 164
    interpersonal, 150–51, 164
  infrastructural or ideological, 43
  institutional, 43
  interpersonal, 43
  issues at different levels, 44–45, 44*f*
  to learning
    ideological, 200
    individual, 198–99
    institutional, 200
    interpersonal, 199–200
  to oppression
    in Four I's of Oppression, 156
    ideological, 156, 157–58, 164, 165*t*
    individual, 162–63, 164
    institutional, 158–59, 164
    interpersonal, 159–62, 164
  to society, 42–45
    ideological, 43
    illustrated, 44*f*
    individual, 42–43
    institutional, 43
    interpersonal, 43
    issues at different levels, 44–45, 44*f*
munus, 17
Musa Ibn Maimun, 106
Muslims
  collective action and, 85, 106
  culture and geography, 9
  human rights and, 131
  identity and, 25, 39, 40
  language and, 14
  learning and, 191
  One Nation and, 79

sustainable development and, 61
  territory and, 20
mutual aid, 49, 88, 106

Nandy, Ashis, 4–5, 157, 158
nano, 42. *See also* individual level
Napoleon, 133–34
narcissism of minor differences, 161
narcissism of minorities, 24–25
Nash, John, 93
nationalism, 25
nationalists, 115, 119, 120
  consensus model and, 79
  domination or control legitimised by, 24
  education and, 169
  Manley, 51
  populist movements and, 120
  revolutions and, 119
  state opposition and, 115
  territory and, 20
National Occupational Standards, 129
National Occupational Standards (NOS) for Community Development, 9
Native Americans, 19, 140
natural selection, 66, 88
natural selection, Darwin's theory of, 66, 88
nature and nurture, 88
Nazism, 13, 14, 18, 20, 37, 106, 116, 168
need, in motivation, 31
needs-based development, 63
negative emotions, 101
Nehru, Jawaharlal, 52, 75
neoliberalism, 56–57, 90
neoliberal model, 56–57
networks, 28
Newton, Isaac, 6, 168
NGOs (non-governmental organisations), 75
Nigeria, 76
Nimby (Not In My Back Yard), 22, 92–93
1984 (Orwell), 4
Nkrumah, Kwame, 50
nonconformists, 104
non-conformity, 99

non-governmental organisations (NGOs), 75, 110, 114
non-monetary/non-market economics, 95–96
non-monetised exchanges, 58, 95, 96
non-monetised transactions, 57–58
Non-Violent Direct Action, 113
normative need, 134
North America, 51, 53, 143, 204
Northern Ireland, 53, 103, 146–47
NOS (National Occupational Standards) for Community Development, 9
not-for-profit. organisations, 58, 114
Nozick, Robert, 115
Nummenmaa, Lauri, 185
Nussbaum, Martha, 47, 87, 131, 133
Nyerere, Julius, 70

objectified, 160
obligation, in motivation, 31
observer effect, 176
Occupations, 59
Occupy movement, 108, 120
OECD (Organisation for Economic Cooperation and Development), 63
Official Development Aid, 76
O'Keefe, John, 18
Olson, Mancur, 92, 93
One Nation, 48, 79
one-offs, 94
ontogenic development, 35
open consciousness, 197
open science, 58
open source knowledge, 176
open source software, 58
open source technology, 93
Open Space, 165
opinion polls, 74
oppression, 155–63
  activities, 165
  autonomy and, 163
  conclusions and implications for practice, 163–64
  hierarchy of, 161
  internalised, 71, 137*t*, 148, 163, 195
  levels of
    in Four I's of Oppression, 156

oppression (*continued*)
    ideological, 156, 157–58, 164, 165*t*
    individual, 162–63, 164
    institutional, 158–59, 164
    interpersonal, 159–62, 164
    Young's five faces of, 156–57
        cultural imperialism, 157
        exploitation, 156
        marginalisation, 156–57
        violence, 157
optimism, 97
Orford, Jim, 86
organic intellectuals, 193
organic solidarity, 37, 206
Organisation for Economic Cooperation and Development (OECD), 63
organism metaphor, 66–68
Orwell, George, 4, 25
Ostrom, Elinor, 19, 93, 95, 96, 118
othering, 30, 45, 150, 205, 212
otherness, 33, 39
oversexual, 160

Pakistan, 99
parasitic relationships, 37
Parkin, Sara, 99
participation, collective action and
    arguments against, 109–10
    emancipatory, agenda for, 117–18
    Gaventa's power cube, 111–12, 112*f*
    Kersting's model, 112, 112*f*
    in political philosophy, 108–10
    in prefigurative politics, 110
    professionals and, 113
    in social and community development, 110–13
    sovereignty, 115–17
    in state and civil society, 113–15
partnership, 106
Pascal, Blaise, 7
passion, 97
Pateman, Carole, 109
path dependency analysis, 4
patriotism, 25
Pawson, R., 42
peer-to-peer development, 75–76
peer-to-peer lending, 90

peer-to-peer sharing, 27, 176
Penrose, Roger, 181
performance, 183
personality variables, 101
personal level. *See* individual level
pessimism, 97
philanthropy, 3, 84, 91, 96, 126, 194
philosophy. *See also* political philosophy
    of consciousness, 191
    territory and, 20
Pickett, Kate, 145
place or territory, 18–21
planned social change, 53, 77–78, 78*t*, 118
Plant, Raymond, 14, 15, 108
platform economy, 90
pleasure, in motivation, 31
PLoS (Public Library of Science), 93
pluralist/difference model, 78*t*, 79
plurilingualism, 30
Plutchik, Robert, 184
Point Four programme, 54–55, 71
policy studies, 124–25
Polish Constitution of 1505, 107–8
politically Black, 39
political movements, 118–24
    economic and social conditions, 123–24
    populist movements, 119–21
    revolutions, 119–23
    triggers, catalysts, inertia, 118–19
political philosophy
    collective action and, 107–17
    participation in, 108–10
    prefigurative politics, 110
    representation, 107–8
    state and civil society, 113–15
political representation for social groups, 117
political system metaphor, 71–73
politics of location, 8
polycentric systems, 93
population
    culture and, 70
    development and
        as an organism, 66
        community development, 49
        cooperation and, 89

cultural and sustainable
    development, 61
  domains of, issues relevant to, 64
  economic development, 55, 57
  equality and, 64–65, 145
  focus on specific groups or areas, 64
  social development and, 53
global, 19
housing and, 96
learning and, 211
movements, 20
needs and, 134
participation and, 109, 111
urban, 19
population-focused development, 63
populist movements, 119–21
positive deviance, 99
positivists, 29
poverty
  economic models and, 57
  measurement of material well-being and, 55–56
  responses to, 3
  in rural areas, 19
  UNESCO and, 60
power, 152–55
  defined, 152–53
  emancipation and, 155
  empowerment and, 154–55
  kinds of, 153
powerlessness and the culture of silence, 157
power over, 153
power to, 153
power with, 153
power within, 153
Practicable Socialism, 49
practical knowledge, 180
practice
  characteristics of, 171*t*
  for learning, 169–70
prefigurative politics, 110
pregnancy, discrimination based on, 146
prejudice, 149–50
prevention, to reduce risk, 188
priority rule, 97
Prisoners' Dilemma, 94
prison metaphor, 70–71
procedural knowledge, 180

propositional knowledge, 172–77, 180, 181–82, 198
Proshika initiative, 75
protection, to reduce risk, 188
protective argument for democracy, 116
Protectorates, 59
prudence, to reduce risk, 188
prudential rule, 97
psychic alienation, 192
psychology
  collective action and, 97–100
  of consciousness, 190
Public Library of Science (PLoS), 93
punishment, to reduce risk, 188
Purchasing Power Parity, 56
pursuit of freedom, autonomy or happiness, 47
Putnam, Robert, 115

qualified reasoning, in collective action, 91–92
qualitative knowledge, 174
quantitative knowledge, 174
quotas, 39, 154

race
  collective action, 98, 101
  conflict and, 41, 42
  culture and, 29
  discrimination based on, 101, 142, 146, 158
  economics and, 89
  empowerment and, 154
  Equality Act and, 146
  equality and, 128, 142, 143, 144, 146, 147, 151
  ethnic groups, 18, 30, 63, 103, 117, 144, 146
  human rights and, 136, 146
  identity and, 23, 25, 38, 39, 68, 115
  inequality and, 146
  institutional racism, 158
  learning for emancipation and, 169
  oppression based on, 39, 71
  skills and ability and, 183
  South African Constitution and, 146
  UNDHR distinctions and, 146, 147
  values and, 26

rapprochement, 140
Raworth, Kate, 58
Read, Margaret, 51
realisation argument, 108
rebellion, 196
reconciliation, 140
reductivism, 140
reflection, personal, 203
reflective action, 99–100
reflexive criticism, 197
reflexive thinking
  characteristics of, 171t
  learning for, 170
reforming, 197
refugees, 32
regulation, to reduce risk, 188
rejecting Western dualism, 62
relational security, 189
religion
  beliefs in, 44, 61, 63, 65, 66, 67, 81, 89, 95
  collective action and, 104, 105, 111, 122
  conflict and, 41, 42
  consciousness in, 191, 193
  culture and, 69–70, 160
  equality in, 132, 144, 146, 148, 151
  groups, 14, 16, 18, 20, 28, 48, 61, 63
  human rights and, 135, 136
  identity in, 26, 34, 39, 59, 103
  justice, 105–6
  learning and, 169
  movements and, 67–68
  oppression in, 70
  teaching in, 144
  UNDHR distinctions and, 146
  values, 152
representation, in collective action, 107–8
resizing the value of capital, 62
Restorationist belief or heresy, 20
restorative justice, 137t, 140–41
retribution, 137t, 139
revolutions, 119–23
  circumstances of, 121–23
  populist movements, 119–21
Rich, Adrienne, 8, 159, 196
rights-based development, 63

rising tide metaphor, 57
risk
  imposed distinguished from voluntary, 187–88
  learning, 187–90
  mechanisms of mitigation, 189
  reduction, 188–90
  understanding how people see, 190
risk images, 188
Roelvink, Gerda, 95
roots, 3–4
Rosello, Mireille, 32
Rostow, Walter, 56–57, 68, 71
Rousseau, Jean-Jacques, 114
rout, 4
routes, 3–4
Rowntree, Seebohm, 49
Rumsfeld, Donald, 5–6
rupture, 4
Ryle, Gilbert, 180

Sachs, Wolfgang, 141
Said, Edward, 73
same-sex relationships, 132, 135–36
satisficers, 135
scapegoating, 23, 34, 178
Schön, Donald, 8
scientific method, 175–76
Scott, James C., 123
Second World, 71
security
  core capabilities and, 133
  identity and, 23
  mechanisms of mitigation and, 189
  revolutionary movements and, 120, 122
selective appreciation, 160
self-actualisation, 132
self-conscious action, 99–100
self-definition, 38–39
self-determination, right to
  collective action and, 128, 130
  cultural and sustainable rights, 61
  identity and, 25
  sovereignty and, 115–16
  top-down approaches and, 138
  UN Declaration of Human Rights and, 48

Self-Employed Women's Association (SEWA), 75
self-esteem, 100, 103
self-government, 50–51
self-help, encouraging, 49, 106
self-identification, 23–24, 38–39
self-interest, 92–93
selfish gene, 88
self-reliance, 106
self-sufficiency, 106
Sen, Amartya, 47, 54, 87, 131, 133, 143
sensation seeking, 189–90
sensation seeking, learning, 187–90
service/social action, 106
SEWA (Self-Employed Women's Association), 75
sex. *See* gender
sexual revolution, 68
sexual violence, 34
Shafak, Elif, 178
Shanti Niketan, 52
sharing, 106
sharing economy, 58, 90
Sharp, Gene, 113
shibboleth, 30
SIMCA (Social Identity Model of Collective Action), 100–101
similarity, holding expectations of, 161
Singer, Peter, 106–7
skills, learning, 182–83
Smiles, Samuel, 49
Smith, Adam, 89–90, 92, 97
social capital
  bridging, 210
  civil society and, 59, 115
  concept of, 27
  at interpersonal level, 43, 150
  theorists, 28
social change
  action and, 7
  activists and, 99, 123
  bottom-up or inside-out, 10
  CDPs' strategies for, 78, 78*t*
  communication theory and, 211
  deliberate social action in, 119
  economic and social conditions and, 123
  ideology and, 194, 211
  implications for practice, 126, 163
  individual contributions to, 2, 73, 212
  multi-level approach to, 42–45
  planned, 53, 77–78, 78*t*, 118
  policy analysis and, 124–25
  political movements and, 123–24
  premeditated, 118
  reflection and, 203
  revolution and, 68, 123
  social mobilisation and, 113
  Specht's tactics for, 77–78, 78*t*
  spontaneity in, 118
  violence and, 81–82
social development
  conclusions, 203–14
    collective action, 207–8
    development, 206–7
    doing it right, 211–14
    emancipation, 209
    equality, 209
    history, 204
    holding societies and communities together, 205–6
    learning together, 209–11
    personal reflection, 203
    theory, 203–4
  geography and culture in, 9
  history and use of term, 52–53
  history of, 3–5
  multi-level approach to, 42–45
  participation in, 110–13
  theory of, 5–8
Social Development Strategy, 54
social enterprises, 58
social evolution, 66
social groups
  beliefs and behaviours structured by, 98
  capacities and capabilities in, 143
  citizenship and, 39
  collective action and, 98, 103, 116, 117
  combinations, change and location, 39–40
  conflict, 37–38, 80
  differences between, to understand community or society, 205

gangs, 34
  homogenising people in, 160
  ideological context of, 43
  inequalities in, 111, 143, 147–48, 150, 160
  interaction of different, 49
  issues in analysing, 40–42
  joining, theories of, 103
  multi-level approach to, 42–45
  nature of, 36–40
  political representation for, 117
  self-definition, 38–39
  self-identification in, 38–39
  solidarity and cohesion, 36–37
  sovereignty in, 116
Social Identity Model of Collective Action (SIMCA), 100–101
social identity theory, 103
social impact, 91
social investigation, 3, 49
socialism, 68
socialists, 33, 49, 106, 108, 119, 169
social mobilisation, 113
social networks, 93
social psychology, 43
  collective action and, 100–104
  identity and, 100–101
social research, 3
social researchers, 50
social workers, 48–49, 50, 193
Societies for the Diffusion of Useful Knowledge, 173
society. *See also* social development
  activities, 45
  community differentiated from, 13–14
  conclusions, 205–6
  implications for practice, 45
  introduction, 13
  language and, 14–15
  levels of, 42–45
    ideological, 43
    illustrated, 44*f*
    individual, 42–43
    institutional, 43
    interpersonal, 43
    issues at different levels, 44–45, 44*f*
  study of, 15–16

socio-economic groups, 21–22, 76, 139, 150, 191
sociogeny, 192
sociology
  conflict and, 37–38
  interpersonal level of relationships and, 43, 199
  Khaldun and, 15, 16
  microsociology and, 43
  opposites attracting and, 37
  political economy and, 191
sociometer theory, 103
solidarity, 36–37, 49
solitarism, 25, 137*t*, 161
Solomon, Andrew, 25–26
South Africa, 18, 28, 76, 79, 81, 146
South African Constitution, 146
South Commission, 53, 70, 75
sovereignty, 115–16
Specht, Harry, 77–78, 78*t*
Specht's tactics for social change, 77–78, 78*t*
  conflict/dissensus model, 79–80
  consensus model, 78, 79
  pluralist/difference model, 79
  violence/insurrection model, 80–82
speciesism, 136
speculation, 167–68
  characteristics of, 171*t*
  learning for, 168–69
Spirit Level: Why Equality Is Better for Everyone? (Wilkinson and Pickett), 145
spiritual well-being, 62
Spivak, Gayatri Chakravorty, 22–23
Stages of Economic Growth: A Non-Communist Manifesto, The (Rostow), 71
stakeholders, 124–25
standard model, 56–57
state, participation in, 113–15
stereotyping, 137*t*, 149, 159, 160
Stone, Laurence, 121
stratum consciousness, 101
structural adjustment, 90–91
structural level. *See* institutional level
structuration, 85, 87
structure, 85

subjectivism, 176
subjunctive history, 119
sub-Saharan Africa, 56
subtractability of use, 93
sugar, propositional knowledge about, 181–82
Summit declaration, 61
superconcepts, 176–77
supererogatory, 107
superiority, 28, 69–70, 81, 147, 149
survival of the fittest, 88
Sustainable Development Goals for 2030, 54
Swadeshi, 52, 70, 106
Swaraj, 52, 70, 106
symbiotic relationships, 37

Tagore, Rabindranath, 52
Tajfel, Henri, 100, 103
taking sides, 98
target-based development, 63
Tawney, R. H., 8, 143, 146
taxonomy of need, 134
Taylor, A. J. P., 119
Teens Advocating a Global Vision, 156
territorial-based development, 63
territory, 18–21
Terrorism Studies, 7
terror management theory, 103
Thatcher, Margaret, 15
Theatre of the Oppressed, 187
Theism, 85
Them and Us model, 72
theocracies, 104
theology
  collective action and, 104–7
  control and, 104–5
  forms of collective action, 105–7
  religion, 104
  territory and, 20
theorists, 6–7
theory
  action and, 7
  conclusions, 203–4
  dangers in presenting and using, 6
  espoused theory, 8
  in everyday experiences, 8
  introduction, 5–8
  pace of, 8

theory in use, 7
theory in use, 8
third sector organisations, 114
Third World, 71, 73
Thompson, Neil, 149, 154, 159
Thorne, J. Albert, 50
throffers, 77
time banks, 58
tithes, 105
Tolstoy, Leo, 108
Tönnies, Ferdinand, 14, 17, 32
Tosh, John, 119, 121
totalitarianism, 110
Toynbee, Arnold, 16, 49
Toynbee Hall, 49
trade union movements, 104
trade unions, 15, 28, 49, 89, 92, 104, 114, 157, 158, 198
training, to reduce risk, 188
Training for Transformation, 74
transforming consciousness, 197
transitional justice, 137t, 140, 211
trapeze method, 6
treating people as defined by a single characteristic, 161
Treaty of Berlin, 59
trickle down strategy, 57, 75
trivialisation, 160
Truman, Harry, 54–55, 71
Trusteeships, 59
tuberculosis, 54

UK Citizenship Test, 27
Ummah, 14
uncertainty–identity theory, 103
UN Declaration of Human Rights (UNDHR), 136, 146, 147
undersexed, 160
UNDHR (UN Declaration of Human Rights), 136, 146, 147
UNESCO (UN Education, Scientific and Cultural Organization), 54, 60–61
United Nations (UN)
  Brundtland Commission, 53, 61, 71
  Declaration of Human Rights (UNDHR), 136, 146
  Earth Summit, 61

United Nations (UN) (*continued*)
  Education, Scientific and Cultural Organization (UNESCO), 54, 60–61
  funding, 59
  Human Development Index, 53
  Human Development Reports, 53
United Nations (UN)International Covenant on Economic, Social and Cultural Rights, 47–48
universalism, 132
unknown unknowns, 5–6
urbanisation, 56–57, 96
urban populations, 19
Utopian Socialists, 49

values, 26–27, 151–52
verbalism, 7
vertical conflicts, 80
vertical development strategy, 64, 75–76
vertical expression, 161
vertical human rights, 136–37
vertical identities, 25–26
vertical networks, 28
vertical (state-society) relations, 118
vigilante action, 141
violence, in Young's five faces of oppression, 157
violence/insurrection model, 78t, 80–82
voluntary organisations, 76, 114
von Hayek, Friedrich, 115

Wardi, Ali, 16
Washington, Booker T., 51
Watson, Lilla, 2
weavers' revolts, 104
Weber, Max, 4, 85, 89, 117
welfarism, 159
Westoby, Peter, 76, 78, 126

Who Wants To Be A Millionaire (TV programme), 94
Wiesel, Elie, 99
Wikipedia, 58, 93, 176, 181
Wilkinson, Richard, 145
Wilson, Edward O., 88–89
Win-Lose dynamic of violence, 82
wisdom of crowds, 94
Wollstonecraft, Mary, 115
words, origin of, 17
worker-managed cooperatives, 58
World Bank, 59, 70
  Africa Strategy, 63
  food sovereignty defined by, 116
  Local and Community Driven Development, 65
  Social Development Strategy, 54
World Health Organization, 19, 54
World Heritage sites, 60, 160
World Values Surveys (WVS), 29, 151–52
World Wide Web, 93
Wretched of the Earth (Fanon), 196
WVS (World Values Surveys), 29, 151–52

Young, Gifted and Black, 180
Young, Iris Marion, 33–34, 35, 156–57, 158
Younghusband report, 49
Young's five faces of oppression, 156–57
  cultural imperialism, 157
  exploitation, 156
  marginalisation, 156–57
  violence, 157

zebra-striping of the mind, 25
zero-sum games, 94
Zionism, 106

Printed by Printforce, the Netherlands